CONFESSIONS OF THE SHTETL

STANFORD STUDIES IN JEWISH HISTORY AND CULTURE
Edited by David Biale and Sarah Abrevaya Stein

CONFESSIONS OF THE SHTETL

Converts from Judaism in Imperial Russia,
1817–1906

ELLIE R. SCHAINKER

Stanford University Press
Stanford, California

Stanford University Press
Stanford, California

Printed in the United States of America on acid-free, archival-quality paper

Library of Congress Cataloging-in-Publication Data

Names: Schainker, Ellie R., 1978- author.
Title: Confessions of the shtetl : converts from Judaism in imperial Russia, 1817-1906 / Ellie R. Schainker.
Other titles: Stanford studies in Jewish history and culture.
Description: Stanford, California : Stanford University Press, 2016. |
   Series: Stanford studies in Jewish history and culture | Includes
   bibliographical references and index.
Identifiers: LCCN 2016030140 (print) | LCCN 2016031643 (ebook) |
   ISBN 9780804798280 (cloth : alk. paper) | ISBN 9781503600249
Subjects: LCSH: Christian converts from Judaism--Russia--History--19th
   century. | Jews--Conversion to Christianity--Russia--History--19th
   century. | Jewish Christians--Russia--History--19th century. |
   Jews--Russia--Identity--History--19th century. | Religious
   tolerance--Russia--History--19th century.
Classification: LCC BV2620 .S24 2016 (print) | LCC BV2620 (ebook) |
   DDC 248.2/46600947--dc23
LC record available at https://lccn.loc.gov/2016030140

Cover design: Rob Ehle
Cover illustrations: (painting) *My Village*, Issachar Ryback; (background) Wikimedia
Typeset by Bruce Lundquist in 10.25/15 Adobe Caslon Pro

To my family and inspiration—
Hillel, Mollie, Noam, and Alex

CONTENTS

ACKNOWLEDGMENTS

I was privileged to find wonderful mentors at the University of Pennsylvania in Benjamin Nathans, David Ruderman, Jonathan Steinberg, and Peter Holquist. My graduate years were perhaps the only time I resisted the encouragement to spread my wings and fly, when I decided to pursue my graduate degree at my undergraduate institution so that I could study with Ben Nathans—a brilliant, humble, kind, and down-to-earth scholar. I thank Ben for training me in the art of research, writing, and teaching, and for his constant support and encouragement. I also thank David Ruderman for encouraging me since my undergraduate years to study Jewish history and pursue a doctorate, and for continuing to be a mentor to me.

I have benefited over the years from conversations and feedback from many generous scholars. I am indebted to Anne Oravetz Albert, Eugene Avrutin, Theodor Dunkelgrün, Glenn Dynner, Todd Endelman, David Engel, ChaeRan Freeze, Viktoria Gerasimova, Agnieszka Jagodzińska, Josh Karlip, Viktor Kel'ner, Nadieszda Kizenko, Yvonne Kleinmann, Rebecca Kobrin, Chaviva Levin, Vladimir Levin, Raymond Lillevik, Olga Litvak, Paweł Maciejko, Natan Meir, Efim Melamed, Olga Minkina, Ken Moss, Ekaterina Norkina, Alyssa Quint, Shaul Stampfer, and Paul Werth. I thank the librarians and archivists in St. Petersburg, Kiev, Jerusalem, and New York for assisting my research. In particular, I want to thank Benyamin Lukin at the Central Archives for the History of the Jewish People for helping guide and support my research. This book has benefited from the close feedback of Paola Tartakoff and Sarah Gracombe—wonderful scholars and friends. I also want to thank the scholars of conversion from the Center for Advanced Judaic Studies cohort from AY 2010–2011, where I was privileged to spend a year learning with a diverse group of academics from around the world. The weekly seminars and shadow seminars enriched my teaching and research on conversion and forged great friendships.

I was fortunate to join Emory University after graduate school, where I have been further mentored and trained in my postdoctoral years by generous faculty in both history and Jewish studies. This book would not have been possible without the mentoring and feedback from my colleagues, including Elena Conis, Astrid Eckert, Eric Goldstein, Jeff Lesser, Jamie Melton, Matt Payne, Don Seeman, Miriam Udel, Brian Vick, and Yanna Yannakakis. A special thank you goes to Nick Block and Dawn Peterson, my writing colleagues extraordinaire, who not only shared their time and constructive feedback, but also gave me the camaraderie and accountability I needed to complete this book.

My research has been supported over the years from a number of fellowships and institutions. I thank the Center for Jewish History, YIVO Institute, Hadassah-Brandeis Institute, Memorial Foundation for Jewish Culture, Katz Center for Advanced Judaic Studies, Yad Hanadiv-Beracha Foundation, Emory University Research Council, Tam Institute for Jewish Studies, and Emory History Department for supporting my research and scholarship over the years. I thank Emory College of Arts and Sciences, Laney Graduate School, and Tam Institute of Jewish Studies for supporting the publication of this book.

At Stanford University Press, I have had the opportunity to work with talented editors. A heartfelt thank you to Kate Wahl, Mariana Raykov, Nora Spiegel, Margo Irvin, Eric Brandt, and Friederike Sundaram. Thank you to David Biale and Sarah Stein for accepting this book into their series Stanford Studies in Jewish History and Culture and for their constructive feedback. Thank you as well to the anonymous manuscript readers whose comments and suggestions were invaluable to me in the revision process.

Finally, a debt of gratitude to my family. I thank my parents, Bruce and Sheryl Schainker, for providing me with wonderful educational opportunities and always grounding the pursuit of knowledge in a foundation of loving kindness and generosity. Thank you for allowing me to follow my passions and quest for adventure as I traveled the globe in search of culture, language, and history. I am also blessed with wonderful in-laws, Jeff and June Glazer, and loving siblings who are unwavering in their support, interest, and love.

Lastly, I thank my husband, Hillel, and children, Mollie, Noam, and Alex, who have created for me a loving and lively home and uncritical space which anchors me and my work. I love your humor, and I thank you for helping me to stay grounded yet committed to my work. This book is for you.

NOTE ON TRANSLITERATION

This book follows the Library of Congress transliteration system for Russian, the YIVO system for Yiddish, and the *Encyclopedia Judaica* system for Hebrew, with several exceptions. Most places and names are transliterated from the Russian source original, with exceptions for commonly accepted English spellings such as Bialystok and Yakov. The soft sign is transliterated, but not the hard sign and diacritical marks for vowels. Several Hebrew words are transliterated according to commonly accepted usage, such as Hasid, tsadik, and Chabad; omitted is the doubling of a letter to denote a *dagesh ḥazak*. Throughout this book, Russian Orthodoxy, an autocephalous Eastern Orthodox Church, is referred to as Russian Orthodoxy or simply as Orthodoxy. All dates are according to the prerevolutionary Julian calendar, which was twelve days behind the Gregorian calendar for the majority of time covered by this book.

CONFESSIONS OF THE SHTETL

INTRODUCTION

Converts and Confessions

ONE DAY early in December 1874, on the outskirts of Vilna a sixteen-year-old Jewish wife knocked on her parents' door, just months after disappearing from home to convert to Russian Orthodoxy. Pera Girsenovich, or Ita Pera according to her father's deposition to the police, came home to pick up some of her belongings, but she wanted to avoid conversation with her mother, who had tried for months to visit her at the Mariinskii Convent and had even petitioned Tsar Alexander II for permission to speak with her daughter. Church and state authorities had given Pera's Jewish husband, Ovsei Rubinson, the option to stay married to his baptized wife as long as he promised not to lure her back to Judaism or thwart the baptism of their future children. But when the police tracked him down a month or so after his wife's baptism, he chose to opt out of the mixed marriage.

Aside from Pera's Jewish parents and husband, who interacted with state and ecclesiastic personnel over her conversion, the Vilna kahal, or local governing body of the Jewish community, was required to verify Pera's identity, as it was the confession, or religious corporation, legally empowered to maintain her vital statistics. In a short note to the Vilna police, Jewish communal leaders Isaac and Dovid testified that there was no record in their community of Pera. This was a common tactic to forestall conversions, but in this case, it failed since Pera's parents unwittingly confirmed her parentage and Vilna domicile in their attempt to reclaim her from the hands of the church.

In addition to the web of Jewish family and community brought into Pera's conversion, a variety of local Christians figured prominently in her religious journey as well. A Catholic woman, the wife of a senior clerk in the Vilna provincial administration, guided Pera to the Vilna Convent. The clerk's wife, together with some other women, repeatedly attempted to visit Pera, but the convent's personnel, wary of "Latin" influences on the Russian Orthodox neophyte, rebuffed them. Pera's Catholic mentor was also concerned since she witnessed several Jews entering the convent whom she feared were attempting to derail Pera's conversion. The mother superior of the convent allayed the Lithuanian Consistory's concerns over this report when she explained that the Jews were simply domestic workers arriving for their daily job.[1]

The story of Pera's conversion is an illustrative case for the multiple ways converts from Judaism in imperial Russia functioned both in Jewish life and in the confessionally, or religiously, diverse life of the imperial Russian western provinces, which included Catholics, Lutherans, Old Believers, and Uniates. The term "confession" (*ispovedanie*) employed throughout this book conveys how contemporary Russians understood religion since all non-Russian-Orthodox groups were dubbed "foreign confessions" (*inostrannyia ispovedaniia*). Confession constituted a key body of law that the state could use to govern and discipline its subjects. The terminology of confession emphasizes the communal rules and formal doctrines of religious groups, thus conceiving of religion as a set of laws or practices rather than individual belief.[2] Rather than just an act that excised an individual from Jewish society, conversion from Judaism in the imperial Russian provinces was—by virtue of place and process—a family and communal affair. While it may have spiritually marked the "death" of the apostate in the Jewish collective, as symbolically enacted in the traditional Jewish mourning ritual for apostates—think *Fiddler on the Roof* and Tevye's bereavement over his daughter Chava—conversion by no means ended the convert's engagement with family and community members. The story of Pera and the complex negotiation of her individual will versus family and communal expectations compels us to broaden the historical narrative of where and how Jews in the famed shtetls of imperial Russia crossed religious borders while subject to the disciplining gaze of Jewish society.

Confessions of the Shtetl analyzes Jewish conversions, like that of Pera, to a variety of Christian confessions in imperial Russia, the heartland of nineteenth-century East European Jewry. According to published and archival data, every year nearly every province in the Pale of Jewish Settlement on the empire's western borderlands produced Jewish converts to Russian Orthodoxy, Catholicism, and Lutheranism. Over the course of the nineteenth century, an estimated 69,400 Jews were baptized in the Russian Orthodox Church, and at least 15,000 converted to the tolerated, foreign confessions in the empire.[3] Three quarters were civilian, "voluntary" conversions, as opposed to coerced baptisms of young military conscripts, with women constituting a majority of converts in the second half of the nineteenth century. In the pages that follow, we will examine the religious climate and the social and institutional means that enabled Jews in tsarist Russia to cross religious borders. What made conversion possible within communities long thought of as culturally isolated and politically alienated? How did Jewish communities view converts, and how do the dynamics of conversion change our understanding of these communities? The setting of the book—alternatively configured as the multiconfessional western borderlands of the Russian Empire and the mythic shtetls of Eastern Europe—presents a rich area for exploring how Jews, and Jewish women in particular, found the contacts, daring, and space to move between cultures and communal allegiances. By considering the question of conversion, we can shed new light on several aspects of the Russian Jewish experience: the profound religious and ethnic diversity of the shtetl—both internally among Jews and externally among other ethno-religious groups in the western borderlands; the fluidity and permeability of boundaries between Jewish and non-Jewish worlds; and the relationship between ethno-religious groups and the state, which tolerated and even sponsored religious diversity.

We will examine several interrelated themes. First, the role of the Russian government in managing religious diversity and toleration, and thus the relationship between mission and empire with regard to the Jews. Second, the day-to-day world of converts from Judaism in imperial Russia, including the social, geographic, religious, and economic links among converts, Christians, and Jews. And finally, the challenges of constructing, transgressing, and maintaining ethno-confessional boundaries, since the convert violated the seemingly clear borders of community and national identity.[4] Through the lens of conversion, the Jewish encounter with imperial Russia emerges as a profoundly religious drama in which a diverse, alluring, and at times aggressive Christianity—as spiritual confession and social order—attracted many Jews, threatened Jewish communal cohesion, and shaped the defensive behavior and thus identity of Russian Jewry as a whole.

᭡

Scholarship on conversions from Judaism and relapsed converts in the Russian Empire has evolved from early twentieth-century biographical sketches of famous converts to recent archive-driven articles on aspects of conversion and monographs on the army, with a focus on conversions among Jewish cantonists, or underage recruits.[5] In synthesizing and adding to this growing body of scholarship, I reframe the narrative of Russian Jewish conversion beyond the chronological markers of 1827 and 1881—the former, the date of the beginning of Jewish conscription into the Russian army and young Jewish boys into cantonist units; the latter, the year of Tsar Alexander II's assassination by revolutionaries, a wave of pogroms in the Pale of Jewish Settlement, and discriminatory legislation, including academic quotas, against Jews.[6] Although restrictive tsarist legislation undeniably affected conversion rates, it does not illuminate the sociocultural factors promoting apostasy or how converts continued to function in Jewish society even after baptism.[7] The decision to convert was tied not only to economic and political factors but also to subjective factors such as love, desperation, loneliness, and spirituality, which are often overlooked in the metanarratives of minority integration in the modern era. Here, I will present conversions from Judaism in imperial Russia as part of a larger story of religious diversity, toleration, and empire. Thus, the book begins in 1817 with the legal introduction of confessional choice for converts from Judaism and ends in 1906 with the legalization of relapse among converts to the tolerated confessions, part of the liberal concessions granted by the tsar after the failed 1905 revolution. This chronology sheds light on how Russian Jews, though politically unemancipated, experienced religious choice and the modern exploration of Jewish identity, not just through army conscription and the pursuit of higher education and mass politics, but through religious encounters in the context of empire. Drawing on previously untapped or seldom-used archives, newspapers and journals, memoirs, and novels, *Confessions of the Shtetl* shows that baptism did not constitute a total break with Jewishness or the Jewish community and that conversion marked the start of a complicated experiment with new forms of identity and belonging.

Religious Diversity and Toleration in the Russian Empire

The image and reality of the East European shtetl has received enormous attention in recent years, leading many scholars to avoid altogether the term "shtetl," which they argue serves more as a cultural construction than a historical reality.[8] For many, we live in a post-shtetl age, when the unchanging, unfailingly traditional, insular Jewish everytown no longer serves as "the foundation myth of Ashkenazi culture."[9] This study of social and cultural encounters between Jews and Christians in the imperial Russian provinces highlights the multiconfessional backdrop of Russian Jewish life and the ways that small market towns and villages of Eastern Europe must be read as interreligious zones, not just zones of economic encounter.[10] In this light, while there has been much recent scholarly attention to the diverse religious landscape of Christianity within the empire and the diversity of ethno-confessional groups in the empire's east, there has been less attention to the diverse landscape of Jewish life in the western provinces—both within Judaism and among Jews and the plethora of other religious and ethnic minorities in this borderland region.[11]

The Russian Empire in the nineteenth century operated as a "confessional state," committed to supporting multiple confessional orthodoxies and their respective clerics as a means of governing a diverse and large empire.[12] As such, tsarist confessional policies were less repressive than one might assume of an exclusively Russian Orthodox state; instead, the state tried to create a harmonious relationship between the preeminent church and the tolerated confessions.[13] Evidence of this can be seen in Jewish society through the institutions of the crown rabbinate, the Rabbinic Commission, and the informal alliance between the state and maskilim (followers of the Jewish enlightenment) that formed under the reign of Tsar Nicholas I and served to integrate Jews linguistically, educationally, and professionally into Russian society.[14] While scholars of Russian history have emphasized the bureaucratic view of the confessional state—focused on state cooptation of indigenous elites and clerics for metrical record keeping and centralized religious and communal management—I wish to highlight the impact of the confessional state on converts from Judaism in the form of confessional choice and communal empowerment.[15] In line with recent studies of conversion that move beyond religious conflict to explore cultural contact and constructions of difference, I investigate, on the one hand, how church and state managed confessional difference, and, on the other, how individuals lived and functioned within these differences.[16]

Recent scholarly interest in lived religion and the politics of confessional diversity in imperial Russia has produced new reflections on the nature and development of tsarist religious tolerance (*veroterpimost'*).[17] Though toleration in the autocratic tsarist regime continued to function more as political expediency than as a rights-based principle, it is significant for understanding the primacy ascribed to religious law and to the functioning of religious communities until the end of the old regime. Rather than a dead letter to be ignored out of hand, imperial Russian religious toleration not only helps to explain the longevity of tsarist rule, but it also helps to frame the currency of religion as an essential marker of difference in the nineteenth century and the ways conversion was bound up in a multiplicity of legal regimes.[18] By understanding the confessionalization of Judaism in the Russian Empire and imperial support for Jewish life, we can better frame official and lay missionary interest in Jews. In addition, state patronage of Judaism for administrative control ironically created avenues for Jewish contestation of out-conversions through the community's power to identify and conscript its members.

Everyday Converts

In modern European history, Jewish conversion has traditionally been cast as a phenomenon of upwardly mobile, urban, middle-class Jews striving for political and civic emancipation. Increased educational and professional prospects, paired with an increasingly open social encounter with non-Jews in cities, have been seen as conditions that made Jews amenable and receptive to baptism.[19] Considering that the majority of conversions from Judaism in nineteenth-century Russia were voluntary and that converts were increasingly female (the percentage of women started to surpass men in the

1860s), thus outside the orbit of military coercion and considerations of career advancement, it is worth evaluating what conversions can teach us about Jewish-Christian sociability, accessibility, and intimacy in regions that depart from the teleology of modern conversions in the West.[20] The dominant narrative of modern Jewish conversions as urban, bourgeois, strategic ancestral abandonment overlooks the many provincial Jews who converted under the gaze of their community, for whom the social aspects of conversion were perhaps more important than issues of civic inclusion or profession.

We know much about the aspirations and cultural explorations of a certain cohort of upwardly mobile, city-bound converts in the modern period, but much less about their provincial city, small town, and rural contemporaries for whom Christianity was less a model of civilization and inclusion and more a face-to-face encounter with the people and institutions of other religions. While contemporary Russian Jews humorously referred to careerist converts from Judaism as having "baptized passports" rather than having undergone a true, individually transformative baptism, this emphasis on motivation and sincerity in the scholarly literature has led analyses of conversion far from the people or practices of religion. In contrast to the radical assimilation model of conversion—as an instrumental and insincere flight from Jewishness—*Confessions of the Shtetl* analyzes conversion as a form of cultural mobility fostered by personal encounters. Beyond analyzing motivation, we will scrutinize the social and cultural contacts that enabled converts to move between confessional communities. Drawing lessons from scholarship on conversion petitions and autobiographies as crafted texts, often in a missionary or anti-missionary vein, I treat the published and unpublished conversion records presented here as narratives of self-fashioning subject to generic constraints and employing particular rhetoric to effect desired outcomes.[21] Thus, I use these sources to draw contextual information on people and place and the contestations surrounding conversions rather than to elicit individual motivation.

In asking questions about motivation and sincerity, conversion studies have unwittingly adopted Enlightenment discourses separating toleration and religious choice from political subjecthood, such that the less one stood to gain from conversion the more "sincere" the conversion.[22] Yet, for all of the modern investment in the separation of private and public spheres, and the

Protestant-inflected view of the interiority of faith and religious conscience, faith historically incorporated the social and political concerns of believers whereby conversion often entailed turning to God and king.[23] In the imperial Russian ancien régime, faith was by no means a private commitment in the eyes of the empire. Religion along with social estate (*soslovie*) defined the duties and privileges of group standing in the era before individual rights, and thus conversion cannot be plotted as a private act divorced from community.[24] A modern, rarefied notion of religion as interior faith commitment independent of ethnicity or community does little to convey how confession in imperial Russia continued to be conceived of as a marker of community and religious law. In this way, the social context and communal dynamics of conversion become more significant for understanding Jewish conversion than the quest for individual motivation.

Complementing recent scholarship on the *concept* of empire and the supraethnic space it afforded Jewish civic engagement in Russia, we will explore social diversity and its effects on interfaith sociability and conversion, considering a broader range of sites of Jewish imperial encounters beyond big cities and imperial institutions.[25] We will treat the actual encounters between Jews and Christians in small towns and villages. What did conversion look like in places where the parish church, village clerk, and tavern patron were the faces of Christianity, where a Jewish father and Christian godfather lived close by each other, and where any Jew could enter a police station or church and apply for conversion?[26] This exploration of daily life focuses on everyday relations of trust and attraction between Jews and their neighbors in the imperial Russian borderlands.

Thinking with Converts:
Constructing and Challenging Jewish Borders

Conversion and intermarriage in the Russian Empire fascinated and alarmed the contemporary Jewish community. The number of Jewish conversions in the east exceeded those in the west, but the numbers relative to population size in the east were still low.[27] Nonetheless, conversions—real and threatened— left an outsized cultural imprint on the self-understanding and experience of Russian Jews of various religious ideologies, political persuasions, socio-economic origins, and regional backgrounds. Jews in imperial Russia used converts and the fear of apostasy to think about the margins of Jewish community and construct the boundaries of modern Jewish nationhood.

Aside from actual baptisms, the very threat of conversion functioned as a historical force in Russian Jewish society.[28] As in other times and places in Jewish history, individuals or marginalized groups used the ever-present possibility of baptism (or not fulfilling Jewish law—especially the laws of ritual purity for women) to force rabbis to act in their favor, to coerce recalcitrant husbands into issuing a *get* (Jewish bill of divorce), or to effect some communal reform.[29] In his autobiography, *Kniga zhizni* (Book of Life, 1934–1940), the Russian Jewish historian Simon Dubnov recalls the story of a Jew from his hometown of Mstislavl' who had converted to Russian Orthodoxy and entered a nearby monastery in the village of Pustynki. This conversion became a paradigm for the local Jews, who were known to threaten hostile family members or employers with the ever-present option to run away to "Pustynki to be baptized."[30] In her memoirs, the Zionist feminist activist Puah Rakovsky (1865–1955) extracted a Jewish divorce from her traditionalist first husband after sending him a letter saying, "if you won't release me and send me a divorce immediately, I will convert with both of the children."[31]

Conversions also functioned discursively to vilify threatening behavior and practices. When Puah Rakovsky had previously informed her first husband that she was moving to St. Petersburg to study midwifery and gain economic independence to assist the family's finances, the husband retorted, "'What! You'll study to be a midwife? Well then, go and convert instead—as far as I'm concerned, it's the same thing!'"[32] In Eastern Europe, books (especially in the vernacular) and secular education were often represented as conduits or even fronts for heresy. Jewish communities in Eastern Europe were among the least interested in non-Jewish learning from the early modern period, and the spread of Hasidism in the late eighteenth century only strengthened this.[33] The extreme boundary crossing of conversion was evoked to stigmatize undesirable, threatening behavior that crossed other kinds of boundaries, including those of gender and education.

Though the exaggerated conversion language in East European Jewish society implied that actual apostasy was unconscionable and inconceivable, this hopeful naïveté should not blind scholars to the phenomenon of conversions nor to the variety of ways families and communities responded to the shock and trauma of religious abandonment. Reactions to converts were sometimes extreme, as, for example, in the ritual mourning, depicted by Sholem Aleichem, of Tevye and his wife over the "loss" of their daughter through conversion, but in reality conversion did not necessarily cut converts off from Jewish society nor preclude the family from attempting to bring back the apostate. Even rabbinic law was conflicted on the negative Jewish theological stance on conversions versus the legal concept of an eternal Jewishness that marked converts as Jews in family law, business relations, and as repentant apostates.[34] By asking how converts functioned in Jewish society, I hope to sidestep the emotional, literary rendering of apostates as dead to their Jewish kin, and account for the overwhelming archival evidence of ongoing social, religious, and economic ties between converts and Jews in imperial Russia. In this vein, my work on converts is as much about a minority of radical boundary crossers as it is about the majority of their former, traditionalist coreligionists who tried to defend cultural and communal boundaries in the face of conversion.

By Jews invoking conversions—both real and imagined—to construct communal boundaries, we see a society trying to manage the rise of religious choice. Religious choice was not just a product of nineteenth-century Central European religious reforms, nor of the exceptional case of American Jewry, whose religious life was entirely voluntary by political design. Making religion an individual choice rather than a birthright, including detaching Orthodoxy from Russianness, took place in Russia as well as in the West.[35]

To fully understand converts and the confessional world they traveled, we will explore the structure of their world from above and below. Part I charts the institutionalization of confessional difference in the Russian Empire as it related to Jews, from Tsar Alexander I and the genesis of confessional choice for the empire's Jews in 1817, to freedom of conscience measures instituted by Tsar Nicholas II in the wake of the revolution of 1905, which allowed Jewish converts to all tolerated confessions to legally reclaim their ancestral faith. The Russian Jewish experience unfolded within an empire that, despite attempts to alternatively encourage and forcibly integrate its various minority groups, ruled with a policy of religious tolerance and relied on confessional communities to help govern and unify a diverse imperial polity. In this section, Chapters 1 and 2 look at institutional missions and individual missionaries to Jews alongside imperial support for the confession of Judaism.

Part II explores the social dynamics of religious tolerance and the confessional state from below by examining the spaces of Jewish conversion. It analyzes daily social interactions among Jewish and neighboring Polish, Lithuanian, Belorussian, and Ukrainian communities, and how these encounters nurtured intimate knowledge of other confessional lifestyles, facilitated interfaith relationships, and provided access to the personnel and institutions of other faiths. In this section, Chapter 3 presents a range of conversion cases that locate interfaith encounters at the local tavern as the springboard for migrating to a different confessional community. Chapter 4 analyzes narratives of Jewish violence against converts as another aspect of the social threads of conversion. Here, the local spaces of conversion are important not just for cultural encounters with non-Jews, but for proximity of baptisms to the controlling gaze of family and community. By taking a geographical approach, I present the western provincial towns and villages of imperial Russia as interreligious zones where conversion was predicated on interconfessional networks, sociability, and a personal familiarity with Christianity via its adherents.

Part III analyzes the intricate connections between physical and cultural mobility and confessional migration. Chapter 5 explores narratives of relapsed converts and their multiple cultural fluencies using legal cases of converts suspected of relapsing to Judaism. Chapter 6 charts the proliferation of Jewish Christian sects in southern Russia in the 1880s and the confessional journeys of their leaders and adherents, which reflected the porousness of confessional boundaries and the possibilities of crossing cultural borders. These sects provided a forum for a cross-cultural conversation in the public press on Jewish and Russian fears of cultural hybridity, religious reforms and unorthodox religion, and the impossibility of absolute confessional separation. In the Epilogue, I summarize how the phenomenon of Russian Jewish conversion, though marginal in the sense that the number of converts was never large, left an outsized imprint on the cultural map of East European Jews, who grappled with questions of Jewish identity and the role of religion in the increasingly powerful Jewish secular nationalist ideologies of the late nineteenth and early twentieth centuries. Finally, the Epilogue looks ahead to the inter-revolutionary period (1906–1917) and the Soviet era when conversions from Judaism accelerated, accompanied by a growing ethnic conception of Jewish identity whereby national Jewishness found harmony with Christianity.

(PART I)

THE CONFESSIONAL STATE AND THE JEWS

CHAPTER 1

THE GENESIS OF CONFESSIONAL CHOICE

PERHAPS the most sensational Jewish conversion to Christianity in nineteenth-century imperial Russia—aside from Lenin's great-grandfather Moshko Blank—was that of Moshe Schneerson, scion to the Chabad Hasidic dynasty.[1] The Schneerson family hailed from Liubavichi (Mogilev Province), and after marriage, Moshe settled near his in-laws in the small town of Ula (Vitebsk Province), where he became communal rabbi. Together with his brothers, Dov Ber and Chaim Avraham, Moshe wrote *haskamot* (rabbinic approbations) for two of his father's most revered works, the *Tanya* and the *Shulḥan aruḥ harav*.[2] In his early career, Moshe received the honorary title of member of the Liozno *ḥevra kadisha* (Jewish burial society), and he alone among his brothers was known to recapitulate and help clarify his father's teachings.[3] Moshe's brothers petitioned provincial authorities in 1820 to annul the conversion due to the documented mental instability of their brother. According to them, Moshe's conversion to Catholicism was provoked by a disgruntled Lieutenant-Colonel Puzanov, who was billeted in Ula and was denied superior housing by Moshe's in-laws. In retaliation, Puzanov lured Moshe to his quarters, where he gave the rabbi alcohol, non-kosher food, and shaved his beard and sidelocks. Puzanov coaxed Moshe to sign a letter of intent to convert, after which he was given shelter by a local Catholic priest and baptized on July 4, 1820.[4]

The enigmatic story of a Russian officer luring Moshe to the Catholic Church over a billeting debacle is highly suspect, but it is possible that Puzanov, like the other witnesses to Moshe's declaration of conversion intent (three local nobles, a parish priest, and local civil and military officials), served more as mediating rather than vengeful forces. The provinces of Mogilev and Vitebsk, partitioned from the Polish-Lithuanian Commonwealth in 1772, were part of the northwestern imperial periphery with a large and ethnically varied Catholic population; as late as 1863, the Ministry of the Interior estimated that about a quarter of the population in the western provinces was Catholic.[5]

Moshe's shocking conversion was succeeded by an unsuccessful attempt to convert a second time to Russian Orthodoxy in October 1820, just months after his Catholic baptism.[6] Though his bid for multiple baptisms aroused some intrigue among clerics, Moshe's serial conversions were enabled by imperial Russian religious toleration and state sponsorship of religious diversity in the western borderlands of the empire, which permitted Jews to convert to the tolerated, "foreign" faiths of the empire. Empowered by Moshe's documented history of mental illness and the confusion engendered by his second conversion petition, the Schneersons temporarily succeeded in wresting Moshe from a Catholic monastery in Mogilev and taking him into custody. The family reunion was short-lived; Moshe's conversion caught the attention of the metropolitan of the Catholic Church in Russia, Sistrensevich Bogush, who convinced officials in St. Petersburg that Moshe's Catholic conversion was legitimate despite his poor mental health, and that the metropolitan himself—rather than local Jewish deputies—should care for Moshe in the capital and keep him in the Christian fold.[7]

Tsar Alexander I took an interest in Moshe's conversion case, and acquiesced to the metropolitan's desire to care for Moshe as a Catholic. Even so, there were lingering suspicions in the capital that Moshe's illness unsettled the efficacy of his baptism and that he would be better served medically and financially by the state-sponsored Jewish deputies, or communal representatives, in the capital.[8] The issue of money highlights a practical side of confessional belonging—in the case of conversion, which family member or acquaintance could claim responsibility for a neophyte? In this moment of confessional confusion, Jewish claims of filial responsibility struck a chord with tsarist officials. In this high-profile case, though, the interest of the Catholic Church in conversion and the ecumenical zeal of the tsar momentarily converged to trump any financial or legal objections to Moshe changing his community. Moshe was famous enough to warrant Christian charity and the assistance of the metropolitan himself. In the end, Moshe's medical condition proved too troublesome for Metropolitan Bogush, and Moshe was transferred to a St. Petersburg hospital that specialized in nerve treatment.[9]

In the extended bureaucratic wrangling over the legitimacy of Moshe's conversion and which confessional community should care for him, a Catholic cleric cited the tsar's 1817 manifesto of the Society of Israelite Christians as a prooftext for the imperial promotion of Jewish conversion to any of the tolerated faiths in the empire—an initiative that will be discussed shortly.[10] Thus, Moshe's case illuminates the multiconfessional backdrop of the earliest imperial discussions of Jewish conversion—when the tsar himself supported the Catholic Church's control of a high-profile Jewish convert in the imperial capital, and when there were Jewish deputies in St. Petersburg who disputed Moshe's conversion in their capacity as representatives of the Jewish community to the imperial government. Though exemplary in some ways due to Moshe's documented mental illness, the Schneerson affair has much to recommend it as a pendant case of conversion from Judaism in imperial Russia—it was civilian, voluntary, and conditioned by the multiconfessional politics of Jewish life in the empire's western borderlands.

The Schneerson story is exemplary of circumstances in pre-reform imperial Russia (1817–1855) that shaped the conversion landscape for Jews. The state was interested and involved in proselytizing Jews and yet its missionary impulse was tempered by religious toleration and the empire's increasing patronage and sponsorship of a variety of Christian and non-Christian religions. In other words, a tension lay at the heart of the Russian imperial enterprise; religious toleration and recognition of ethno-religious difference existed alongside state-sponsored programs for the assimilation of minorities. Thus, the state encouraged and rewarded Jewish conversion to a variety of Christian confessions, all while attempting to create an indigenous Jewish elite and buoy up the confession of Judaism. Such a story would in many ways be an impossibility by the late imperial period, when the state exited the Jewish conversion business and state officials increasingly started to conflate minority integration with conversion to Russian Orthodoxy, alongside a growing political conservatism suspicious of baptism as a means to upend Jewishness.

Overall, religious toleration, extending to confessional choice, set the terms for how the state and its Russian Orthodox Church engaged Jewish conversion. Thus, an overview on state policy and interactions between the state and the tolerated confessions will lay the groundwork for the book as a whole, which explores the influence of toleration and multiconfessionalism on everyday encounters and interactions between imperial subjects. In addition to illuminating the social geography of conversion in the imperial Russian provinces, the Schneerson case highlights the responses of Jewish families to conversion. Contemporary Jews grappled with the problem of Jewish conversion and leveraged their confessional status to vie with the state for control over apostasy and communal belonging.

Religious Toleration and Empire

One of the striking aspects of the Schneerson case, and one that confounded post-Soviet scholars searching for archival documentation of Moshe's baptism, was that Moshe initially sought out the Catholic Church rather than the state religion of Russian Orthodoxy. The Russian Empire legally promoted Russian Orthodoxy as the "preeminent and predominant" imperial faith, and it was led by an Orthodox autocrat who was hailed as the "supreme defender and keeper of dogmas of the ruling faith."[11] The state nonetheless recognized and granted religious toleration to a host of non-Orthodox confessions and non-Christian groups in the empire and even sought to bolster a variety of confessional orthodoxies and their clerics as key instruments in imperial management. Imperial Russia's strategy of religious toleration was not just a nominal acceptance of religious diversity but a structure for integrating non-Orthodox subjects based on the Enlightenment principle of the essential similarities of organized religions as elaborate systems of discipline.[12]

The Russian Empire by the nineteenth century controlled and supported the faithful of four world religions—Christianity, Islam, Judaism, and Buddhism—in addition to followers of "nature religions" or animists.[13] The diversity of imperial confessional life was especially pronounced in the conquered western provinces of the empire and New Russia, an area of imperial expansion north of the Black Sea, where the majority of Russian Jews lived alongside sizeable indigenous populations of Catholics, Uniates, and Lutherans. By 1827, imperial law extended permission to Jews to convert to all of the tolerated Christian confessions, not just Orthodoxy.[14] As late as 1863, the Ministry of the Interior (MVD) created a color-coded map of the western provinces (excluding New Russia) to document this confessional diversity at the level of province and town as it responded to a recent Polish uprising and tried to reassess the strength of Russian Orthodoxy in the region. While Jews by virtue of their diffusion throughout the provinces did not merit a distinguishing color on the atlas according to the cartography notes, the MVD mapped the populations of Orthodox, Catholic, Protestant, and Muslim faithful in the area with an accompanying statistical table of all ethno-confessional groups in the region (see Map 1.1).[15] According to published statistics, around 15,000 Jews in total are estimated to have converted to Catholicism (about 12,000) and Protestantism (about 3,136) over the course of the nineteenth century, and roughly 69,400 are reported to have converted to Russian Orthodoxy.[16]

Published statistics on conversions from Judaism in imperial Russia were collected by the tsarist bureaucracy, which documented each religious conversion for the corporate status change that it initiated. A subject's civil status (place of residence, community, tax obligation, liability to conscription) was determined by confession and social estate, and, therefore, one's documented religious ascription largely determined his or her legal and social standing in the empire. Since the empire had neither civil marriage nor the legal category of *konfessionslos* (without a religion), one's confession also determined permitted marriage partners. Official data on conversions to Russian Orthodoxy were culled by both the Russian Orthodox Church's Holy Governing Synod (for the years 1836–1914) and the MVD from annual reports from governors-general in the western provinces. Not always with precision, the Synod maintained data on the conversions of non-Orthodox Christians, Orthodox sectarians, and non-Christians, including Jews. In addition, as of 1842 the MVD mandated that governors-general reports from the western provinces include conversion information on *inovertsy* (non-Orthodox subjects). Inconsistent reporting from the provincial governors over the years makes it difficult to analyze the regional data, but still there are a few statistical novelties to note (see Table 1.1). There appears to have been a higher proportion

Within the map image, the following labels appear:

KURLAND
LIFLAND
PSKOV
Tel'shi · Shavli
KOVNO
Liutsin
LATVIANS
SAMOGITIANS
Rossieny
VITEBSK
Polotsk
Vitebsk
SMOLENSK
Sventsiany
Lepel'
PRUSSIA Kovno
VILNA
Orsha
SAMOGITIANS
Vilna
Oshmiany
AVGUSTOV
Lida
Mstislavl'
Minsk
Mogilev
MASURIANS · Grodno
Goniondz
MOGILEV
Bialystok
Slonim
Slutsk
Bobruisk
Bel'sk GRODNO
MINSK
Brest-Litovsk
Pinsk
LUBLIN
Kovel'
CHERNIGOV
Lutsk
VOLYNIA
AUSTRIA
Zhitomir
Kiev
KIEV
Berdichev
POLTAVA
Percentage of Population in Western Region
Vinnitsa · Lipovets
Confession
Kamenets-Podol'skii · Bratslav · Uman
Russian Orthodox and Old Belief   63.54%
PODOLIA
Roman Catholic   24.7
Protestant   0.62
Iampol'
KHERSON
Jewish   11.07
Muslim   0.06

Ethnic Group
BESSARABIA OBLAST'
Russian (little, great, and white Russian)   64.73%
Polish   8.86
Lithuanian   12.82 (with Samogitian*)
Samogitian   *
Latvian   1.75
Russian Orthodox
German   0.32
Roman Catholic
Moldovan   0.39
0   50   100 mi
Protestant
Jewish   11.07
0   50   100   150 km
Muslim
Tatar   0.06

Map 1.1 The confessions in the Russian western provinces, printed by the Ministry of the Interior, 1863. RGIA f. 821, op. 145, f. 24, l. 2, "Atlas—narodonaseleniia zapadno-russkago kraia, po ispovedaniiam (1863)."

Table 1.1 Conversions from Judaism by province, 1842–1869

Province	Jewish population, 1842	Jewish population, 1869	Number of converts from Judaism, 1842–1869
Bessarabia	45,833	99,124	203[a]
Chernigov	20,622	36,120	760[b]
Ekaterinoslav	6,950	35,118	380[c]
Grodno	75,578	119,549	237[d]
Kherson	32,948	97,915	298[e]
Kiev	-	-	-
Kovno	96,923 (in 1843)	146,460	171[f]
Minsk	103,403	102,122	323[g]
Mogilev	91,076	117,237	354[h]
Podolia	167,833	232,768	1,080[i]
Poltava	16,826	51,460	423[j]
Tavrich	3,185	13,621	198[k]
Vilna	128,650	108,191	257[l]
Vitebsk	-	-	-
Volynia	184,346	207,427	397[m]
Total	974,173	1,367,112	5,081

SOURCE: Annual reports of the governors-general of the fifteen western provinces to the Ministry of the Interior. Data from Genrich M. Deych, *Putevoditel': Arkhivnye dokumenty po istorii evreev v Rossii v XIX–nachale XX vv.*, ed. Benjamin Nathans (Moscow: Blagovest, 1994), 40–86.

a Missing annual reports for 3 years.
b Missing 5 years.
c Missing 2 years.
d Missing 2 years.
e Missing 15 years.
f Missing 10 years of conversion data.
g Missing 4 years.
h Missing 5 years.

i Missing 3 years. The large total reflects the large number of converts (605) listed for 1854.
j Missing 1 year.
k Missing 2 years.
l Missing 4 years.
m Missing 3 years.

of converts from Judaism in the southern provinces of the Pale of Jewish Settlement. This can be connected to the prevalence of agricultural colonies in the south that attracted some Jews, especially those looking for economic opportunity and tax abatements. There is evidence from the first quarter of the nineteenth century of Jewish male members of agricultural colonies in the south who converted to escape debt.[17] Beyond that, the provinces of New Russia were a Jewish frontier, with newly formed Jewish communities that tended to attract more enlightened, or non-traditionalist, Jewish migrants. The regional statistics also reveal a spike in conversions in Podolia in 1854, surely connected to coerced cantonist conversions around that time.

Published data on Jewish conversions to all Christian confessions in imperial Russia combine published Synod data for the period 1836–1914 with a modest estimate of Jewish conversions to Russian Orthodoxy for 1800–1835, based on the lowest yearly number (322, in 1836), from which a scaled-back average of three hundred conversions per year is derived for the undocumented thirty-five-year period. Statistics on non-Orthodox conversions are based on piecemeal data, mostly from the late imperial period, from Evangelical, Reformed, and Lutheran Consistories in imperial Russia (including statistics for Congress Poland). From these data, a minimum number of converts for the long, undocumented periods has been extrapolated. In statistics on conversions to Catholicism, Jewish conversions via evangelical missions (approximately 1,716) were multiplied by a factor of seven, based on the greater proportion of Catholics to evangelicals in the former Polish territories.

Fluctuations in the statistics on Jewish conversion in various tsarist reigns suggest there was a connection between political repression and conversion. Modest rates of conversion under Alexander I (r. 1801–1825) sharply increased under Nicholas I (r. 1825–1855) and the induction of Jews, especially underage boys or cantonists, into the Russian military beginning in 1827. The period from 1827 to 1855 witnessed the largest proportion of conversions in the century, with the highest yearly average of 4,439 converts in 1854, during a period of coerced cantonist conversions. During the Great Reform era of the more liberal reign of Alexander II (r. 1855–1881), conversion rates dropped considerably. Rates rose again in the last decades of the century, when the more reactionary and conservative reign of Alexander III (r. 1881–1894) initiated admissions quotas for Jews in institutions of higher education and restrictions on Jews in the liberal professions. The years following the liberal concessions of Nicholas II (r. 1894–1917) in the wake of the failed 1905 revolution witnessed a drop in conversion numbers and the legal relapse of over 600 apostates to Judaism. Between 1907 and 1917, statistics reveal a new wave of conversion among Russian Jews.[18]

After the revolution of 1905, the tsar liberalized some restrictions, allowing converts to officially relapse to their ancestral faith.[19] The St. Petersburg Jewish communal registry of relapsed converts from 1917 to 1923 shows 157 conversion relapses, the majority from Reformed and Lutheran churches, following the Bolshevik revolution and the end of official Jewish disabilities.[20] Thus, as Moshe Schneerson's Catholic conversion attests, a religious marketplace existed for converts from Judaism whereby confessional choice was mediated by local contacts and diverse forms of Christian rites and culture. While restrictive legislation affected conversion rates, it does not fully illuminate the sociocultural factors conditioning conversion nor the relationship between conversion and confessional choice.

To the extent that the Russian Orthodox Church never experienced a reform movement and Russian Orthodoxy retained a monopoly on proselytizing and criminalizing apostasy in the Russian Empire, historians long ignored the ways imperial Russian religious tolerance empowered minority groups and undermined the hold of Eastern Orthodoxy on imperial identity and local confessional politics. Only recently has the confessional state model (or more aptly, the multiconfessional state model) of early modern Central Europe been applied and modified to nineteenth-century Russia to better frame the triangular power relations between the state, religious minorities, and the Orthodox Church, and how state centralization was accompanied by the "clericalization, centralization and social regulation of religious life."[21]

In this light, Alexander I's support of a Jewish convert to Catholicism in 1820 is understandable. From the reign of Catherine the Great (1762–1796) during the partitions of Poland through to the reform era under Alexander II, the state made the non-Orthodox, or "foreign," confessions of the empire into state religions, thus institutionally and administratively bringing these religions into the imperial order.[22] Before this, Peter the Great (r. 1682–1725) brought the Russian Orthodox Church into the structure of imperial governance by abolishing the patriarchate, or independent spiritual leadership over the Eastern Orthodox Church, in 1721. Peter established synodal oversight of the Russian Orthodox Church and it thus became an arm of the state in its overarching goal of creating loyal imperial subjects.[23] For most of the nineteenth century, confession was the "salient feature" of imperial policy, thus effecting a tsarist politics that transcended ethnicity and embraced religion as a means of undergirding autocracy.[24]

State regulation and institutionalization of the foreign faiths continued under Alexander I and Nicholas I, by which point Russia's "multiconfessional establishment" was firmly in place.[25] Although Nicholas I famously articulated an Orthodox imperial identity and deeply invested the state in Jewish missionary work through the institution of the military, his reign must be analyzed alongside his continued support and patronage of the tolerated confessions.[26] In this context, the banner of Nicholas I's reign, "Orthodoxy, Autocracy, and Nationality," designed by his minister of education Sergei Uvarov, takes on greater nuance. In a key proposal, Uvarov referred to religion in general rather than "Orthodoxy" in particular as embodying one of the core tenets of the empire.[27] In this revised reading of the motto of Nicholas I's reign, "Nationality" should be understood in an imperial sense, connoting imperial loyalty as opposed to Russian nationalism, such that the autocracy self-consciously transcended ethnicity.[28]

As a result, when Moshe Schneerson converted to Catholicism in 1820, he joined many other Jews who converted to non-Orthodox faiths over the course of the nineteenth century according to imperial laws that recognized and regulated non-Orthodox conversions. There is evidence throughout the nineteenth century of Jewish conversions, or attempted ones, in a variety of non-Orthodox churches, and even in Orthodox sectarian ones, including Uniate (Greek Catholicism), Old Belief (sect of Orthodoxy), Armenian, Lutheran, Reformed, Evangelical, and Catholic.[29] Nonetheless, Jews were prohibited from converting to non-Christian faiths, including that of the Karaites, a Jewish sect formally recognized by the state, which in 1795 forbid rabbinic Jews from joining its ranks.[30] Thus, from the perspective of converts, the confessional state did not just entail administrative advantage, but it promoted religious diversity and imperial sociability.

Alongside missionary work in the service of empire and imperial expansion, especially in the middle of the sixteenth and beginning of the eighteenth centuries, religious toleration and the integration of the tolerated confessions into imperial statecraft undergirded Russia's empire-building in the nineteenth century.[31] The Russian state for the most part looked to adherents of the foreign faiths as agents of empire rather than foreigners in need of proselytizing. There was a fundamental tension, however, in confessional politics between the imperial logic of disciplining and discrediting the tolerated faiths, whereby the state at times questioned the loyalty and legitimacy of non-Russian-Orthodox faiths.[32] Thus, even studies of confessional integration and state patronage of the foreign faiths need to consider that toleration and confessional support could harbor both emancipatory and repressive aims, to strengthen the tolerated confessions and to force them to do the bidding of the state.[33] Minorities' distrust of state legislation and regulation of religious communal life ran high. It was widely believed among Jews that the unifying element of tsarist Jewish policy was an explicit and coordinated commitment to baptize all of the empire's Jews. For example, the policy of state-sponsored Jewish education promulgated in the 1840s was interpreted as a pretext for dismantling Jewish institutional autonomy and forcibly assimilating Jewish youth through religious indoctrination in state-run schools.[34] Distrust among Muslim Tatar communities in the Volga-Kama region surfaced with the cessation of military exemptions in 1859 and a new fire ordinance for mosques in 1866, which were interpreted as veneers for conversion campaigns in the empire's southeast.[35] In this way, minorities often perceived toleration and the institutionalization of foreign faiths as furtive missionary campaigns.

Confession and Statecraft

The Moshe Schneerson case illustrates how state investment in conversion existed alongside state sponsorship of Judaism and the incorporation of Jewish elites into imperial governance—in Moshe's case, the Jewish deputies in St. Petersburg who were jockeying for control of the prominent Chabad Hasid. From the time of Alexander I, the state sought to bring Jews into the project of governance, provided it could discern or engineer an indigenous elite or ruling class. Alexander I created the institution of Jewish deputies—

which lasted from 1812 to 1825—as official state representatives of the Jewish population to bring a clear and recognizable structure of governance to the Jewish community and include it in the system of imperial rule.[36]

The institutionalization of Judaism into imperial statecraft reached its apogee under Nicholas I, even as this tsar was notorious for officially dissolving the kahal, or Jewish corporate government, in 1844. Despite the dissolution of Jewish corporatist autonomy in favor of state centralization and direct governance, the Nikolaevan regime still sought to create a transparent Jewish leadership hierarchy whereby Jews and the systematic rule of Jewish law could be brought into statecraft.[37] First, the Russian Empire engineered a state rabbinate, such that the Russian rabbinate became bifurcated between traditional, homegrown rabbis and state-educated and, for a few decades, ordained crown rabbis. This meant that each Jewish community needed one official rabbi as the communal liaison to the state. Beginning in 1847, the state created two rabbinical seminaries—in Vilna and Zhitomir—to offer rabbinical degrees, but due to the unpopularity of the program and the resistance of communities to its graduates, the government closed the rabbinical program at both seminaries in 1873. State rabbis' official correspondence bore the imprint of the MVD, and although state rabbis were elected by the Jewish community and financed by Jewish communal taxes, they had to be approved by the provincial governor and take an official oath of office. In their oath, state rabbis promised to inculcate in Jews "obedience to civil authorities and the preservation of social order and peace" and to disclose to the authorities "anything harmful or contrary to the laws of the empire."[38]

Just as the crown rabbinate was an imperial attempt to streamline Jewish leadership and make it responsible to the state, so too was the Rabbinic Commission. It was formed by the MVD's Jewish Committee in 1845 to be a supra-communal institution to advise and oversee local rabbis, serve as a court of appeals in Jewish divorce cases, and fulfill other jobs the MVD deemed necessary.[39] Like state rabbis, the elected officials to the Rabbinic Commission had to be approved by the state and take an oath of office. Together with the crown rabbinate, the Rabbinic Commission was intended to give some coherence to Jewish governance that traditionally operated on a decentralized, local level, without a strict clerical hierarchy as existed in the

Russian Orthodox and Catholic churches.[40] The Rabbinic Commission met six times between 1848 and 1910, though it was never made into a formal institution of Jewish governance. In deference to the mandates of religious tolerance and the rule of Jewish law in internal Jewish matters, civil courts deferred to the MVD and its Department for the Religious Affairs of Foreign Confessions (DDDII) to rule on Jewish law.[41] In these circumstances, the MVD turned to its in-house Jewish advisory committee or court of appeals, the Rabbinic Commission, which mainly dealt with issues of family law and personal status, including those that resulted from conversions.

The state's cooptation of indigenous elites to strengthen confessional orthodoxies and achieve greater imperial discipline also led to educated Jews being appointed as censors, advisors to district school superintendents, crown rabbis, and *uchenye evrei* (expert Jews) who advised provincial governors-general.[42] Metrical records, or parish registers, maintained by clerics became a key element of the confessional state and its institutional support of the foreign confessions.[43] Although an 1826 decree obligated rabbis to record vital statistics, an 1835 statute on the Jews formalized the role state rabbis would play in this practice. At this time, rabbis were required to record in metrical books the vital statistics—births, deaths, marriages, and divorces—for the entire Jewish population, male and female.[44] This was a remarkable turning point in imperial administration, considering that only Russian Orthodox parish priests had, since 1724, maintained vital individual statistics for the government.[45] In 1857, after the government grumbled for years over the inaccuracies in record keeping, an imperial decree stipulated that only crown rabbis could perform life cycle rites like marriage and circumcision, so as to provide more centralized oversight over the recording of vital data. These steps show that state centralization proceeded through the confessions and the strengthening of religious institutions.

Thus, a tension between toleration and political centralization sits at the heart of the story of Jewish conversions in imperial Russia, where state missions or incentive programs existed in tandem with state support of Jewish confessional autonomy. As we will see, this tension in toleration and empire-building would open up a space for Jewish families and communal officials to contest baptisms in the Jewish community and try to use toleration as a means of regulating and preventing Jewish apostasy from below.

The Confessionalization of Conversion

Until the partitions of Poland, no Jews were allowed to permanently settle in the empire unless they converted to Eastern Orthodoxy, or *pravosla-vie* (the true belief). With the partitions and Russia's inheritance of some three-quarters of a million Jews, though the old laws remained on the books, there were now Jewish subjects of the empire who did not need to convert to maintain Russian subjecthood. Alexander I's Passover Manifesto of March 25, 1817, or the edict on the Society of Israelite Christians, gave voice to the multiconfessional character of the empire and the tsar's affirmation of the realm of confessional choices for Jewish proselytes. In this decree, which Catholic officials referenced in 1820 to support Moshe Schneerson's conversion to Catholicism, the tsar announced the founding of a state initiative to provide land for convert agricultural colonies in the western provinces. These colonies would function as both family and community for converts estranged from their "brothers in flesh" (*sobrat'ia po ploti*) and not yet accepted by their "brothers in spirit" (*sobrat'ia po vere*). The tsar's openness to all Christian confessions found expression in the lack of an Orthodox bias in the edict; Jewish converts to any tolerated Christian confession were eligible to receive benefits and join these colonies.[46] However, Jews who sought out sects like Old Belief, a group considered schismatic by the Russian Orthodox Church, were denied the benefits of Christian status (residential freedom beyond the Pale of Jewish Settlement) since the state did not legally recognize sectarian groups as churches with legitimate clergy who could perform baptisms.[47]

According to Alexander I's Israelite Christian manifesto, Jewish converts were in limbo. Those who desired baptism needed to weigh the advantages of spiritual salvation against the twin losses of family and community that were the backbone of material sustenance in imperial Russian society. A juridical change in confession did not grant one immediate entrée into another confessional community and its closed network of communal welfare. Considering Moshe Schneerson's case and state concern over who would finance his doctor bills in the capital after his contested Catholic baptism, the tsar's concerns were realistic. In the March 25, 1817, decree, the tsar thus lamented: "Jews, who have separated themselves from their brethren in flesh for the Christian religion, deprive themselves of any community with them, leave all ties, and not only alienate themselves from all rights of assistance from them, but subject themselves to persecutions from them and oppression of all kinds. From the other side, among Christians, who are their new brethren in faith, to whom they are still unknown, they do not immediately find themselves ready-made shelter, or such a secure establishment, which would provide each of them, in case of need, a safe stay and a means of honestly gaining sustenance from their labor."[48] Rather than trying to effect an artificial union of Jewish converts and native Christians, the state found it expedient to bypass the established estates and create an entirely new communal prototype for an imperial hybrid that defied conventional legal and personal belonging.

The innovative coupling here of convert colonies and confessional choice reflects Alexander I's Jewish policies as well as his domestic policies in the wake of the Napoleonic wars, a watershed in the European and Atlantic worlds. In 1801, Alexander I ascended the throne with aspirations for reforms that included issuing a Russian constitution and emancipating the serfs, neither of which happened. The overarching influence on Alexander I's Jewish policies was a Western reform tradition that empowered the state to enlighten and transform Jewish society.[49] Following Russia's war with Napoleon in 1812, Alexander I underwent a profound spiritual transformation that made him receptive to Christian mysticism and a vigorous promoter of religious toleration.[50] In 1813, he welcomed the British and Foreign Bible Society to Russia and pledged a yearly contribution of 10,000 rubles for its dissemination of the New Testament in a variety of indigenous languages (though not Yiddish, an oversight that native Jewish missionaries tried to rectify).[51] In March 1817, Alexander I established the Society of Israelite Christians to provide shelter and sustenance for Jews who desired to convert to any of the tolerated Christian confessions in the empire. Converts were promised farmland from the state, the right to reside anywhere in the empire, and the right to enter state service. And, in October 1817, the tsar created the "Dual Ministry," which affirmed Christian morality as the ideological cornerstone of the empire and housed all religious confessions under one ministry, ostensibly denying Russian Orthodoxy primacy over other imperial faiths.[52]

In this context, the various components of the tsar's Society of Israelite Christians initiative seem ideologically coherent. In an attempt to undo the Napoleonic order and subdue liberal revolutions in Europe and the Atlantic world, Alexander I as leader of the Holy Alliance promoted religion as a counterweight to popular rebellion. Following Napoleon's defeat and the attempted restoration of the prerevolutionary political order, British missionary Lewis Way was very influential with Alexander I at the 1818 Congress of Aix-la-Chapelle (a follow-up to the more famous 1814–1815 Congress of Vienna), where he advocated Jewish conversion and the improvement of Jewish status as part of the post-Napoleonic order.[53] These ideas combined with Alexander I's Christian ecumenicism moved him to come to the aid of Jewish converts irrespective of their chosen Christian denomination. For a Jewish family of seven that converted to Russian Orthodoxy in 1816, the tsar ordered a one-time handout of 1,000 rubles to the male head of the house.[54] The tsar's openness to all Christian confessions found expression in the lack of an Orthodox bias of the ukase and in his support of the evangelical Russian Bible Society (RBS). Though the latter was short-lived, it ultimately helped to support several native missionaries to Jews over the course of the century. Following his reform-minded efforts to enlighten his Jewish subjects and push them into productive labor, the tsar encouraged converts seeking refuge and sustenance to form agricultural colonies. Although Alexander hired a large staff and provided a generous budget, the Society of Israelite Christians was minimally successful by the time it was abolished by Nicholas I in 1833.[55]

Despite the failure of the initiative, the language and genesis of the 1817 Passover decree is instructive in that it reveals a central problem in the convert experience in nineteenth-century imperial Russia, namely that of belonging. Just as Jewish emancipation in Western Europe was incomplete due to the state's inability to legislate social integration, Jewish conversion in Russia as a means of integration into Christian estates was often stymied by social barriers that were beyond the reach of state regulation. Although the state attempted to legislatively enforce acceptance of Jewish converts by Christian estates, this was insufficient to deal with the core problem of communal and filial belonging, not to mention persistent native fears of Jewish economic competition and "exploitation."[56]

The precedent for Jewish confessional choice remained in imperial law codes through to the end of the old regime, despite the eventual dissolution of the Society of Israelite Christians due to its overall failings and a succession of tsars who were less ecumenically inclined than Alexander I.[57]

Alexander I's legacy of bringing Jews into imperial statecraft also remained, shifting from the institution of Jewish deputies, who were involved in Moshe Schneerson's conversion, to state rabbis and "expert Jews." In 1827, during the reign of Nicholas I, who in many ways undid the ecumenical reforms of his brother, the possibility of Jewish conversion to the tolerated confessions was officially ensconced in imperial law, thus solidifying confessional choice and religious diversity as the defining features of Jewish conversion in the Russian Empire.

As mentioned earlier, in an effort to control Jewish conversions to non-Orthodox confessions, the government in 1827 officially permitted Jewish conversions to any of the tolerated Christian confessions (*vsiakago terpimago ispovedaniia*), provided that local clergy petition the MVD for permission on a case by case basis.[58] One of the main government players in the 1827 legislation was Alexander Semionovich Shishkov, minister of public enlightenment and head of the DDDII.[59] Shishkov, a conservative romantic nationalist, replaced the more ecumenical Prince A. N. Golitsyn after the latter's dismissal in 1824 amid a crackdown by Alexander I on "revolutionary" activity in imperial Russia. Despite the presence of a new minister serving Nicholas I, who ascended the throne in 1825 following his brother's death, the favoring of all expressions of Christian values continued to guide state policy at least at the level of conversions. Responding to many requests of Jews, especially those temporarily residing in St. Petersburg, to convert to Catholicism and Lutheranism, Shishkov asked the Committee of Ministers to agree to the requests even though past cases revealed that "some Jews have converted more for acquiring civil rights" (*delali sie bolee dlia priobreteniia grazhdanskikh prav*) than for becoming Christians. Shishkov argued that despite these concerns, laws permitting Jews to convert to Orthodoxy should be applied to other confessions as well, assuming the conversions were willful and grounded in a course of conversion study.[60]

Thus, under Nicholas I, confessional choice as an outgrowth of religious toleration was inscribed into imperial law for Jews within the religious freedoms granted to the foreign faiths in the empire.[61] In this light, 1827 stands as a significant turning point in Russian Jewish history, when imperial policy acknowledged the local faces Christianity could take for Jews living in a large and diverse empire—like Moshe Schneerson in the heavily Catholic northwest region—and opened up a confessional choice regime for Jews seeking conversion. While this confessional freedom immediately created the problem of multiple baptisms (e.g., Moshe Schneerson and his attempted second conversion to Russian Orthodoxy) and exacerbated imperial concerns over insincere Jewish conversions, the legitimacy of a confessional marketplace democratized the need for all churches—including the Russian Orthodox—to be vigilant against instrumental baptisms and to systematize conversion procedures.[62] Denominational choice as developed under Nicholas I had nothing to do with the ecumenicism of his brother—as seen in Nicholas I's abolition of the Russian Bible Society and its investment in multilingual translations of scripture in partnership with the evangelical movement. Rather, denominational choice further evolved from the conceptual and structural nexus of toleration and imperial stability. While confessional choice remained, state support of Jewish converts under Nicholas I shifted from funding a neophyte assistance program to engaging in direct Jewish proselytism, and from responding to the problem of convert isolation to using baptism as an instrument of imperial *sliianie*, or "merging."

From Convert Colonies to Conscription

In pre-reform Russia there were two governmental initiatives that can be typed as state-sponsored missions to Jews. Alexander I's Society of Israelite Christians was the first, but even with its generous benefits for baptism, few Jews converted through this mission. It is interesting to note that despite the initiative's failure—only one Jew had converted through the society as of 1827—Nicholas I continued to underwrite the program and insisted on continued state support of the colony and the salary of its director, Mizko (4,000 rubles annually for salary plus 2,000 rubles for expenses).[63] Finally, in 1833, Nicholas I abolished the program, perhaps realizing that he had found a much more efficient institution of imperial integration in the army.

Nicholas I's Conscription Edict of 1827 was the second state-sponsored conversion initiative in the pre-reform period. The law drafted Jews into the Russian army for the first time and made allowances for underage Jewish conscripts to join cantonist training units. This initiative has received the bulk of scholarly attention regarding imperial conversion policies toward Jews. And yet, the revised historiographical consensus is that Nicholas I and his reforming ministers used the army to forcibly integrate, not necessarily convert, Jews into imperial Russian society.[64] The cloistered and disciplined life of soldiers was thought to be ideal for making Jews into productive and patriotic subjects. At the top echelons of imperial statecraft, there was never a directive to forcibly convert Jews in the army, though the army did prove to be a popular site for Jewish baptisms. Already in 1827, Nicholas I realized the potential for converting Jewish recruits, especially cantonists. He therefore instructed the military settlements administration to let it be known that the army should not impede cantonists who desired conversion. Rather, military personnel should instill in underage Jewish recruits Christian law, and welcome to the faith those who voluntarily desired to convert. Monthly reports to the tsar on cantonist recruits and their conversions were then instituted.[65] In 1843, after seeing the growing incidence of baptism among young Jewish recruits, Nicholas I encouraged the military to promote—not necessarily coerce—the conversion of Jewish cantonists to Russian Orthodoxy.[66] In February 1842 a "secret and confidential" circular was sent to all military districts and police announcing that Jewish conversion in the military could avoid formal channels involving provincial and local administrators and instead concern only the church and police. The Synod relayed the tsar's decision to begin converting Jewish cantonists to Christianity "with all possible circumspection, meekness, and without the least bit of oppression."[67] In that year, the Synod published a manual for military priests to guide their proselytizing to Jewish cantonists (see Figure 1.1).[68] The tsar ordered all cantonist regiments to report annually on their conversion successes.[69] Indeed, the statistics on Jewish conversion kept by the Synod record a spike in Jewish conversions between 1843 and 1856, the years between Nicholas I's endorsement of cantonist conversions and Alexander II's dismantling of the cantonist units (though they lasted through 1859).[70]

The official policy of voluntary military conversions and the tsar's interest in cantonist conversions does not tell the whole story of this conversion mission. Likewise, official religious tolerance in the military and special rights granted to Jewish conscripts did not mean that Jews were free to ignore invitations to convert. Memoirs of cantonists and popular Jewish literature offer another perspective on the missionary project of the army and reveal that zealous officers often terrorized and forced young Jewish recruits

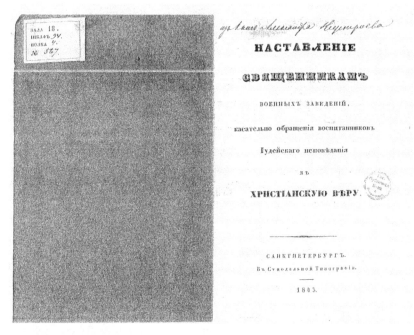

Figure 1.1 Title page of cantonist conversion training manual for military priests, *Nastavlenie sviashchennikam voennykh zavedenii, kasatel'no obrashcheniia vospitannikov iudeiskogo ispovedaniia v khristianskuiu veru* (St. Petersburg, 1843). Central Archives for the History of the Jewish People, Jerusalem.

to the baptismal font.[71] As such, it is hard to assess where imperial policy ended and religious politics began. Irrespective of direct or indirect state involvement in the approximately thirty thousand conversions among Jewish soldiers between 1827 and 1856, and irrespective of the missionary goals of conscripting Jews, the Russian military proved to be the most successful imperial "mission" to Russian Jews.

Rather than focusing on state-sponsored missions to Jews over the long nineteenth century, it is more fruitful to look at state sponsorship of Jewish conversion through the benefits of conversion inscribed into law. An awards system for the conversion of non-Orthodox subjects was well suited to the twin commitments of imperial religious policy—the supremacy of Orthodoxy and the freedom of faith of the tolerated confessions. That most Orthodox proselytizing of Jews in the empire occurred passively through legal incentives is a remarkable counterpoint to the lachrymose narrative of

Russian Jewish history that portrays imperial Jewish policy as based on a concerted mission to convert the Jews. The passive nineteenth-century imperial Russian approach to Jewish missionizing is also notable in comparison to the long and sustained missions to other non-Orthodox populations such as the Volga-Kama Muslims and animists, though the main goal in this case was to strengthen the religiosity of subjects who had already converted.[72]

Under imperial law, Jewish civilian converts received tax breaks, monetary grants and clothing, exemption from military service, reduction of criminal sentences, freedom of movement, and the choice of a new *rod zhizni* (way of life) or tax-paying community and legal estate. Until 1837, all converts to Orthodoxy were entitled to a three-year tax holiday and a grant of money and goods. In 1837, imperial law ended one-time monetary and clothing stipends for Muslim and pagan converts, but retained them for Jewish converts.[73] Jewish converts were entitled to 30 rubles; children received half of that.[74] Following the conscription edict of 1827, military law codes did not immediately replicate the benefits to converts from Judaism inscribed into civil law. There were no specific material enticements for Jewish soldiers to embrace Orthodoxy until 1829, when, in response to exaggerated statistics of Jewish cantonists converting in the army, Nicholas I ordered that 25 rubles be given to every Jewish recruit who converted.[75] According to sources in the navy, the head of the Black Sea Fleet, Admiral Greig, also military governor of Nikolaev and Sevastopol, gave every Jewish convert in his fleet 40 rubles upon conversion. In response, the Nikolaev archpriest Stefan Zhaushkevich, a naval adviser, inquired whether there was a precedent in the navy for paying Jews to convert. Apparently, in the Baltic Fleet, Nicholas I set a precedent for conversion awards during his visit to Kronstadt in 1828. Pleased by the number of converted Jews at Kronstadt, the tsar promised each of them five rubles, two pounds of meat, and two cups of wine.[76] In 1831, Zhaushkevich received the Synod's approval of the Black Sea Fleet's incentive program for Jewish converts.[77]

In addition to permitting material rewards, imperial law allowed the authorities to commute certain criminal sentences of Jewish converts and exempt them from Jewish communal conscription quotas. In the first case, depending on the severity of the crime, criminals who converted could receive a reduction in the years of sentence or exemption from corporal punishment.[78] For example, in 1826 a Grodno court found the Jewess Dvorka Esterka Yoseleva guilty of four times setting fire to the home of the Jew Berkovich and sentenced her to lashes and exile to hard labor. She consequently converted to Orthodoxy, and the tsar overruled the State Senate's cautious approach to the case and ordered that she not be subject to the whipping portion of her sentence.[79] In terms of recruitment exemption, Jewish converts by virtue of juridically leaving the Jewish community enjoyed the attendant freedom from serving as a communal recruit.[80] Since this conversion incentive inspired many conversions of Jews already conscripted, lawmakers were forced to stipulate that only conversion before conscription would be accepted as grounds for receiving an exemption.[81] Thus, Jews who converted while in the military continued their tour of duty.

Whereas conversion incentives were not particular to Jews, there was one benefit that was addressed to Jews alone—freedom of residency.[82] Legally, Jewish settlement was limited to the Pale of Jewish Settlement, an area of the western borderlands roughly coterminous with the Polish-Lithuanian lands partitioned by the Russian Empire in the last decades of the eighteenth century. Before the era of the Great Reforms (1855–1881), a period of political and social reform under Tsar Alexander II, and the legal exemptions of various Jewish groups from residential restrictions, the only way for Jews to obtain access to the Russian interior was through conversion. Baptism initiated a complete socioeconomic reorientation of the neophyte, requiring the convert to choose a new Christian estate and allowing freedom of residence and business travel throughout the empire.[83] In a case where one spouse converted to Christianity and did not divorce the Jewish partner, an 1835 imperial law withheld from the convert the freedom to live outside of the Pale of Settlement for the duration of the interfaith marriage.[84]

These incentives laid a legal basis for the preeminence and predominance of Russian Orthodoxy, but they also legally linked conversion to material advantage. For example, only converts to Russian Orthodoxy received a three-year tax holiday following baptism as per a Senate ruling in February 1823.[85] Hence, bureaucrats and clerics often expressed concern that Jews converted for mercenary or instrumental reasons. Anxieties over insincere Jewish baptisms were widely voiced throughout the nineteenth century. In the case of the Bermans who asked the Vilna archbishop in 1838 to baptize their youngest son, Movshe, in exchange for state support of his education, the cleric rejected the petition out of hand and lamented that it was solely motivated by material considerations, thus rendering the son "like any criminal or Jewish fugitive who in the last resort gives up his faith."[86] The priest's accusation highlights how the conversion perk of commuting sentences helped forge an association between insincere converts and criminality, even in the absence of criminal activity. Throughout the nineteenth century, conversion benefits both ensured a continuous stream of Jewish converts to Christianity and provided rhetoric for state, church, and lay actors to question the motives and intentions of converts who violated no law. These discursive attempts to criminalize motivation reflect widespread anxiety about the desirability or possibility of crossing ethno-confessional communal lines.

Perpetual anxieties over insincere conversions raised by this system of rewards never succeeded in actually overturning legal benefits to Jewish converts. Conversion incentives continued to guide the state's approach to the Christianization of the Jews until the dissolution of the empire in 1917, in contrast to conversion policies in the empire's east, which moved away from material benefits in the reform era.[87] The link between converts from Judaism and material need continued to guide state and church support of neophytes even in the reform and post-reform era when the state officially ceased to proselytize Jews and parish clergy, philanthropists, and native missionaries tried to promote convert assistance programs, as we will see in the next chapter.

The Jewish Family and the Confessional State

The Moshe Schneerson case is helpful in framing how religious toleration, confessional choice, and state patronage of the tolerated confessions conditioned the terms of Jewish conversion in pre-reform imperial Russia. Besides the political backdrop of the Schneerson story, which explains the role of the tolerated faiths such as Catholicism and multiple baptisms in Moshe's story, this case of the conversion of a Hasid also sheds light on the social geography of conversion from Judaism in the western provinces. This view of Jewish conversion from below, explored in depth in Part II, illuminates the proactive response of Moshe's family to his conversion and the provincial social threads among Jews, Christians, and converts that structured Moshe's confessional journey and his Jewish family's contestation of his religious and communal status.

Moshe appears to have had the unflagging support of his family throughout his life, despite his illness and the stress it placed on family finances. While his father, Shneur Zalman, was alive, Moshe was taken to doctors in Vitebsk, St. Petersburg, and Smolensk. After his father's death in 1812, his two brothers continued to seek medical care for him in Starobykhov, Vilna, and Königsberg (Prussia).[88] Even after conversion, the Schneerson family together with the Vitebsk Jewish community repeatedly petitioned the state to grant them the right to tend to Moshe's illness. The Jewish deputies in St. Petersburg petitioned for Moshe's release to his relatives or to them after he was transferred to the capital. The last petition by Jews recorded in the archives was from Moshe's wife, Shifra, in the summer of 1821. While the contemporary family of Moshe the convert sought to maintain ties with him, descendants and later Hasidim quietly excised him from their collective memory.[89]

The staying power of family and community as social anchors of belonging in imperial Russia despite the emotional strain caused by conversion is a story yet to be told in its entirety and one that warrants exploration from a variety of vantage points. The story of convert-family relations intersects with state policy on conversion and religious toleration. Toleration created an ambivalence about the state's relationship to converting its ethno-confessional minorities, and this ambivalence opened up avenues for Jewish families to contest the conversion of their kin and assert local communal control. Besides the Schneerson family, many other Jewish families used the legal argument of a convert's incompetence to petition for the release of their loved ones from the embrace of the church. Aside from mental instability, status as a minor could also legally invalidate a conversion. According to imperial law, fourteen constituted the age of majority in matters of conversion.[90] While at first glance age would seem to be a fact and hence not legally contestable, there were no official state birth records in imperial Russia. Vital statistics were recorded by clerics, and the state only became involved by mandating uniform and regular metrical records in the 1830s and 1840s.[91] Although Jewish families and the kahal could contest a convert's age based on local censuses and communal metrical records, a convert's own testimony was often accorded greater weight than written evidence. In many cases, it is unclear whether a convert and clergy purposely inflated a convert's age, or the kahal fudged identification records in the hope of stymie-ing the conversion of one of their flock.

In 1821 a Jewish mother from the western provinces petitioned Alexander I to return her daughter Feygele to her after the girl entered a Benedictine convent to convert to Catholicism. Feygele's age was disputed. According to her mother, she was seven years old; according to the church, she was ten. While the mother claimed that her underage daughter had been "seduced" by a peasant woman to join an alien religion, local provincial authorities discovered that the Catholic woman had been Feygele's caretaker. Feygele's conversion was voluntary—according to the witness testimony of her uncle and three governing members of her Jewish community— and it stemmed not from official missionizing but from her own involvement with Catholics in her community. Minister of Public Enlightenment and Religious Affairs Golitsyn ordered the convent to halt conversion until Feygele reached legal age, even though he concluded that the mother was partially to blame for her daughter's wish to convert. When, in 1825, according to the church's calcula-tions, Feygele reached majority, the tsar granted permission to the Catholic Church to convert her.[92]

Although there is no available outside information to corroborate Feygele's exact age, two facts emerge from this case. Conversion was halted by state au-thorities until the prospective convert reached majority; and age was disputed, used by both parties to further their own interests in the case. In the reign of Nicholas I, when Jews were conscripted into the army, the state clearly al-lowed young Jewish recruits to be baptized in cantonist units, irrespective of whether their parents consented, or even knew. The army, though, "adopted" cantonist recruits and assumed the parental role of educating young Jewish boys to serve the tsar and state, and cantonist baptisms were allowed to cir-cumvent civil legal channels.

In addition to bringing arguments about insanity and age, Jewish families often claimed that their children, especially daughters, were "seduced" into conversion due to their naïveté, a subjective status irrespective of the legal age of maturity.[93] In 1815, for example, a Jewish father from Lida petitioned the Vilna military governor for the return of his sixteen-year-old daughter, Tsepa Shliomova, who was in a convent and could not, he claimed, willingly choose to convert. The father and community members repeatedly tried to meet with Tsepa to find out her intentions, but according to the police, she remained steadfast in her desire to convert and was soon baptized a Catholic with the new name of Elizaveta.[94] In line with gendered analyses of parental petitions to return child converts, the father, Shliom Notkovich, exploited the cultural notion of his daughter's female naïveté to try to reassert his legal right as a parent to determine her religious affiliation.

Using a different tactic of parental concern for a vulnerable child convert, a Jewish mother petitioned for the return of her baptized son in the army arguing that his conversion left him bereft of real family and proper care (*bez prizreniia*).[95] Playing to the state's belief that sound families were the bedrock of the empire, Rivka Varnovitskaia hoped to convince the Kiev governor-general that conversion and the attendant severing of filial and communal ties were not in the best interests of her son or the state. In response to the mother's petition, the governor-general's office asked the Kiev chief of police to investigate. The police found that the seventeen-year-old son, Semen, had been living with his godfather and had been cared for by his godmother, who taught him grammar, registered him in the Kiev *meshchanstvo* (townsperson estate), and found him a position as an apprentice with a local tailor to learn a trade. The boy spent holidays with his godfather, who also kept an eye on the new convert's observance. The mother's petition was thrown out.

In all of these cases, Jewish families petitioned for the return of their wayward kin by stressing their responsibility for juvenile or incompetent children unable to make important decisions for themselves, let alone to care for themselves as new Christians bereft of family and community. Although families rarely won these legal battles since the criteria of sanity and age were contestable, it is noteworthy that their petitions were read and taken seriously and always initiated an investigation or reconsideration of the facts of the case. With state oversight, conversions were accountable to legal standards, and the state had an interest in assuring that its converts were prepared to meet the challenges of a changed corporate status and the loss of parental/communal care. On the Jewish side, these cases highlight the continuation of family and communal interest in converts and the willingness of families to reaccept their heretical kin.

The picture painted thus far by family and communal responses to conversion suggests an ongoing dialogue between converts and family, and an active, engaged Jewish response to apostasy that challenges the simplistic narrative of families passively accepting conversion as a death knell and severing all connections with their spiritually deceased kin. Active engagement, though, does not necessarily imply acceptance of conversion. Two tales from the Vilna archives reveal Jewish families—contemporaries of the Schneersons—who actually sought to promote the conversion of their children.[96]

In Vilna in the 1820s–1830s two Jewish families promoted the conversion of their children while the parents remained Jewish. Despite the different socioeconomic positions of the families and the different confessions chosen for conversion, both families were united in viewing conversion as a means of furthering the educational and social integration of their children into imperial Russian life. In both cases, permission for conversion was granted by the highest state authorities even though the parents' warm regard for Christianity did not extend to desiring baptism for themselves. In both cases, state officials acknowledged the great weight of community and family bearing down on the parents, and hence the state still honored the sincerity of the parents' petitions and the legitimacy of their children's conversions. Together, the cases illustrate how confessional choice mediated conversions in the civilian realm throughout the reign of Nicholas I and the pre-reform era, and how the state supported both converts and Jews within the same family.

In the summer of 1826, first-guild Vilna merchant Solomon Geiman petitioned clerical authorities in Vilna for permission to convert his five children to Lutheranism.[97] Because of the unusual nature of the request—the petitioner himself did not seek baptism—the Vilna governor, Rimskii Korsakov, ventured a guess as to why Geiman would promote the conversion of his children but not seek to convert himself. "Judging by the enlightened ideas of merchant Geiman and his wife," the governor suggested, "it can be proposed that they themselves sincerely desire to convert, but part of the obstacle lies in the old age of their mothers, who are extremely attached to Jewish law, and part of it, probably, is that merchant Geiman, being in commercial and financial contact with the premier European commercial houses, among which there are many wealthy Jewish houses, fears losing their trust and with that their business."[98] Considering Geiman's high socioeconomic standing and, more importantly, the value to the empire of his lucrative international business, the governor provided a rationale for why Geiman's conversion would be a detriment to himself and to the state. In the midst of the case, Geiman was awarded a gold medal for his stellar and long service to the imperial treasury complemented by his peaceful and noble behavior.[99] His 1834 induction into the ranks of "honorary citizens" as a commercial councilor strengthened the case of Geiman's valuable service to the treasury and the government's interest in maintaining his Jewish identity and access to Jewish lending houses.[100] The Ministry of Public Enlightenment approved the children's conversion without their parents due to the sincerity of Geiman's determination to rear his children in the laws of Lutheranism and the Protestant ethics of the Jewish parents, who would continue to raise their baptized children.

It is noteworthy that there is no Orthodox polemic in this case. At no time was Geiman's inclination toward Lutheranism a detriment to his sincere Christian leanings, and the successful earlier conversions of his eldest two children (a daughter married a captain in the tsar's suite and a son matriculated into the University of Vilna to study medicine) proved that Protestantism was not a roadblock to social and educational integration into the upper echelons of Russian society. By 1826 the state's attitude favoring all expressions of Christian values continued to guide policy under Nicholas I at least at the level of conversions, even though the ecumenical culture of Alexander I's court had died out.

According to the formulation of the Vilna military governor in the Geiman case, the ultimate value of conversion lay in the adoption of "European Christian Law," not in the confession chosen or in some innate transformative power of baptismal waters. The Geiman parents in all but name had created a productive, civic-minded Christian home such that their official Jewish faith did not detract from the success of their children's official Christian conversions.[101] The language used in the case reaffirms currents of Enlightenment thought linking civic duty with Christian values that often informed Alexander I's and Nicholas I's Jewish policies, and highlights the confessional stance of the empire that tolerated religious orthodoxies as agents of imperial management and incubators of morality, obedience, and discipline. Though clearly Christianity was preferred, both provincial and state bureaucrats in this case acknowledged that a Jew could also be useful, moral, and obedient, and trusted to rear like-minded children. Of course, the parental Bible in such a case was "European Christian Law."

A decade after Geiman's petition to convert his children, another Jewish family in Vilna asked both the Orthodox Church and the state to allow their youngest child to convert without the conversion of the parents. Eliash and Malka Berman unabashedly promoted the conversion of their fourteen-year-old son Movshe provided the state cover his educational expenses post-baptism. The Bermans embraced the conversion of their fourth child after the three others had already converted and proven the educational and financial value of baptism.[102] Though the Vilna archbishop had already rejected Malka Berman's request as solely motivated by material considerations, Eliash persisted in bringing his son's case to the head of the tsar's Third Section of the Imperial Chancellery, Count Benckendorff.[103]

Eliash continued to tie his endorsement of the conversion to Movshe being schooled at the expense of the state. Rather than disguising his instrumental motive, Eliash portrayed baptism as a vehicle of enlightenment and self-transformation for Jews given the greater educational and career opportunities available to Orthodox youth. He recounted that when his daughter and two older sons converted, he was sad yet above all overjoyed that his children had become useful subjects for their own benefit and for that of their community (*sdelalis' poleznymi sebe i obshchestvu*). One son enrolled in a veterinary and surgical academy in Grodno, and the other worked as a clerk in a police station. Movshe, who had taken the name Ivan and was enrolled in a Vilna gymnasium at his parents' expense, also wanted to follow in his siblings' footsteps by converting. The parents could not continue to pay for his schooling, and hence, Eliash and Malka campaigned for permission for their son to convert and become, in the words of Enlightenment Europe, a "useful person."[104]

Based on the recommendations from local authorities in Vilna that the Berman family was upstanding and that Movshe was capable, Benckendorff, with the agreement of the tsar, approved the baptism and placed Movshe, now Ivan, in the Shturmanskii Cadet Corps.[105] Whereas the compelling factor in the Geiman case was the sincere Christian values of the family, the overriding factor in the Berman case was the unusual circumstance of a Vilna Jewish family promoting the conversion of their children to Christianity and the hope that the Bermans would influence other Jews to convert as well (*ravno dlia primera drugim*).[106] Here the parents' own confession of

Judaism did not arouse concern or threaten to invalidate the son's conversion. In both of these cases, conversion was viewed as a path to enlightenment and socioeconomic advancement, and the state embraced this non-dogmatic understanding of Jewish conversion.

Though the state hoped to use the Bermans as model Jews who acknowledged the value of conversion and as an example of how conversion could benefit the state, the Berman children repeatedly proved themselves unworthy. Records from the Vilna governor-general's office, the Vilna Consistory, and the Third Section of the Imperial Chancellery reveal that the three Berman sons did not do well in school, were not well behaved and sincere in their catechism classes, and were unsuccessful in their careers. In the end, it appears the Berman parents as promoters of conversion were greater assets to the state than their converted children.

The youngest Berman son, despite his father's petition to have him placed in a medical-surgical academy post-baptism, was put in the Shturmanskii Cadet Corps due to his poor behavior and grades in the Vilna gymnasium.[107] Even in military academy, he got into trouble and was transferred to a naval drumming crew.[108] The middle son, Andrei, occupied much of his parents' time even after his conversion. Though he supposedly became a police clerk after conversion, Malka Berman petitioned the state to enlist him into state service and place Andrei's sons into cantonist units.[109] Malka complained to Benckendorff that Andrei had been living at home with his wife and children without any income and so could not provide for his family or his aging parents. Besides being a financial burden, Andrei's presence caused social tensions for Malka, "being that I am an Israelite . . . giving sustenance to my converted children." She stressed that her petition to help Andrei did not stem from "some attempt to better [her] behavior toward Jews," who would have been pleased if she "sacrificed" her heretical children, but rather from financial need.[110] It seems that Andrei was ultimately recommended to work at a post office in Vilna.

The record of the conversion of Yakov, the eldest son, is less clear. He is mentioned by his father as converting before 1838 and enrolling in a Grodno veterinary-surgical academy. No other information about him can be gleaned from the records of the Vilna governor-general or the Imperial Chancellery. An 1834 conversion file from the Vilna Consistory, though, records the conversion of a Kasper Berman, son of Eliash Berman of Vilna, who wanted to enter medical school after conversion. Kasper's conversion was initially postponed due to bad behavior and morals, which came to light during his conversion training. According to a Vilna priest, Kasper left the monastery during training and had to be brought back by the police. The priest implored the Vilna Consistory not to convert Kasper until he finished gymnasium, since he was not mature enough to live on his own. The priest recommended that Kasper be allowed to convert only after he proved capable of supporting himself.

Assuming Kasper is Yakov Berman, we have evidence of three Berman children with behavioral problems and poor academic skills who could clearly benefit from state assistance. As devoted parents of modest means, the Bermans quickly realized the material and academic benefits of conversion. While other Jews may have come to the same conclusion, the Bermans were unique in their unabashed embrace of conversion as parental sacrifice for the future of their children. As Malka Berman told Benckendorff, motherly love forced her to give up her children to the Christian community so they could be educated. In both the Berman and Geiman cases, the parents saw conversion as an instrument of socioeconomic advancement that did not irreparably sever the parent-child relationship. Conversion, in short, had practical benefits and did not require that the parents themselves be baptized.

The wealth of archival material in Russian state ministries about Jewish converts attests to the active and ongoing dialogue between families and converts, facilitated by clerics and governmental personnel. The range of family and communal responses to converted kin reflects the diversity of human experience but also the creativity of family and friends eager to subvert the rigidity of the empire's confessional grid to reestablish parental and communal ties to the convert. Though Jewish memory often reinforced ideas of monolithic confessional communities by excising converts from the Jewish collective—much like the Schneerson descendents did—contemporary Jews struggled with the complex interplay of kinship and religious ties.

❧

While the Russian state under Alexander I and Nicholas I gave institutional support to converts from Judaism, the Schneerson case would have been an impossibility by 1863, by which point the state exited the conversion business for Jews and started to promote Orthodoxy as a resource for Russian nation-building. In 1856 the reformist tsar Alexander II closed the cantonist program in the army. Following Russia's defeat in the Crimean War (1853–1856) and the Polish insurrection of 1863, imperial governance became marked by a greater conflation of the Russian Empire with the Russian people and Russian Orthodoxy, and a desire to assimilate non-Orthodox subjects through cultural and linguistic Russification in the western and eastern borderlands.

Conversion in the post-reform period (1881–1906) was more a result of rising expectations and reduced Jewish rights rather than any concerted conversion policy like the Society of Israelite Christians of 1817 and the Conscription Edict of 1827. Even as the state cut its involvement in missions, institutional supports for Judaism persisted and the confessional choice regime established in 1817 for converts from Judaism continued to set the terms of Jewish conversion through the first Russian Revolution. In 1906 the state amended its freedom of conscience concessions to permit converts to any of the tolerated confessions in the empire to legally reclaim their ancestral religion.

Thus, imperial Russian recognition and support of religious diversity conditioned the terms by which Jews converted to Christianity and the extent to which Jewish communities were invested with power from the state to contest apostasy within their own spiritual domain. The confessional state's ambivalence over conversion not only limited the reach and scope of state-sponsored missions to Jews over the course of the nineteenth century, but it effectively privatized the Jewish missionary enterprise. The proselytizing of Jews became the vocation of native missionaries, parish clergy, and philanthropists who tried to sell a weary confessional state on the merits of converting its Jews. Though the ecumenicism of state culture died with Alexander I, for decades thereafter convert missionaries would attempt to parlay the funds of the defunct Russian Bible Society and the spirit of Alexander I's evangelicalism to coax a hesitant multiconfessional establishment into supporting a mission to the largest Jewish population in Europe.

CHAPTER 2

THE MISSIONIZING MARKETPLACE

IN 1861, at the beginning of the reform period in imperial Russia and just a few years after the closing of the cantonist program, the convert from Judaism and former cantonist Alexander Alekseev published an ethnography of contemporary Russian Jews. Writing in Russian about Sabbath observance and ritual hymns, Alekseev nostalgically recalled the Hebrew song "Ma-efes" (*mayufes*) from his youth, which was the nicest and happiest song sung by Jews on Sabbath evenings. To translate to his Russian audience the spiritual imprint of the song, Alekseev recalled an incident from his days in the army as a boy. During one of Nicholas I's visits to Kiev the tsar requested an audience with Jewish cantonists. Alekseev and his fellow recruits were scared as they approached the tsar, so Nicholas I asked them to sing him a song. With this cue, the boys sang the Sabbath hymn "Ma-efes" with such emotion that they momentarily forgot their sadness and felt as if they were seated at their parents' Sabbath table. Enraptured by the song and imbued with Christian love, the tsar instructed his officials to escort out the cantonists, ostensibly sparing them—at least momentarily—from a coerced baptism.[1]

Alekseev, though a product of the pre-reform state's missionizing of Jews, came of age as a self-styled convert missionary in the reform period when the cantonist program was shut down and the state extricated itself from the Jewish conversion business. In the absence of state sponsorship, as seen in Alekseev's complicated feelings of both fondness and fear of the Nikolaevan

program, Alekseev was pushed to find new means of support for his missionary zeal. He turned to writing and publishing as a way to support himself as
a convert knowledgeable about Jews and interested in making both Judaism
and Christianity intelligible to non-Jews and Jews alike. Alekseev's attempts
to harness a pre-reform imperial mission to Jews together with former state
commitments to publishing missionary materials in indigenous languages
were characteristic of the reform era and post-reform missionary climate.

Ultimately, though, missions to Jews are noteworthy not for their success
but for their story of access.[2] Conversions in late imperial Russia stemmed
from socioeconomic pressures and incentives and were facilitated by everyday confessional encounters rather than formal missions. Missionaries are
noteworthy, though, for their attempt to make Russian Jews objects worthy of the Orthodox Church's attention and to reach Jews in the western
provinces in their native vernacular, Yiddish. Since the details of their lives
unfolded within the force field of confessional politics in the empire, their
individual stories further illuminate how toleration and multiconfessionalism created ambivalence about proselytizing Jews, and how everyday Jewish
encounters with Christianity were mediated by a range of religious groups
beyond just the Russian Orthodox Church. Stories of these converts cum
missionaries are instructive for thinking about how converts navigated the
multiconfessional landscape and were acutely aware of the marketplace of
religion for Jews in a confessional state. As such, native missionaries offered
another space, apart from state programs or everyday confessional intimacies,
from which to view the confessional state and its ambivalent stance on Jewish conversion.

The story of these entrepreneurial converts' initiative and financial
backing begins in the pre-reform era and taps into two parallel developments explored in the preceding chapter. First, in contrast to the sustained
and expensive efforts to reign in Orthodox dissenters, there was no financial commitment by the church to conduct missionary campaigns to Jews.
Nonetheless, since 1826, when Nicholas I abolished the Russian Bible Society
initiated by his ecumenical older brother, a large sum of money remained,
which was earmarked for the translation and dissemination of scripture to
the peoples of the empire. These funds would provide the seed money for
converts from Judaism to promote translation and dissemination of scripture

as a means to convert Jews. As of July 1826, the society's assets (money, property, presses) amounted to roughly two million rubles.[3] Second, the earliest cohort of convert missionaries came of age in the Nikolaevan period and the aggressive state mission to Jews in the army. Emboldened by the state's proselytizing, these converts initiated complementary activities and writings to expand the state's mission into the civilian realm. To convince the imperial government and Jews of the righteousness of their calling, converts exploited confessional politics, and at times even gender politics, to coax Jews and a hesitant Orthodox Church into the missionary arena.

Philanthropy as Mission

As late as 1891, Pavel (né Yosif Yankelev) Dreizin, a Jewish convert to Russian Orthodoxy, lamented that "for all other groups [in the Russian Empire] . . . there are organized missions, but for Jewish delusions nothing is organized."[4] This sentiment was echoed in 1903 by Eugene Smirnoff, a Russian Orthodox priest serving abroad, who wistfully noted that Russian missionaries had yet to proselytize millions of Jews (and Muslims) in the empire.[5] Aside from incentives for conversion provided by the state, there were also unofficial inducements furnished by some diocesan clergy in the form of asylums for converts, akin to the thirteenth-century Domus Conversorum in England and the seventeenth-century Hamburg Shelter for converting Jews.[6] For zealous converts like Dreizin, though, this kind of passive convert philanthropy did not constitute the proactive religious mission he was seeking.

The ambivalence of the state and church about Jewish conversion was the result of several overlapping practical and ideological concerns. Though never admirers of so-called fanatic and separatist Jews, the state and the Orthodox Church were practically much more concerned with Orthodox heretics and schismatics than with the religious beliefs of the tolerated confessions. Thus, regulation of the tolerated confessions to secure the Orthodox faithful and prevent the spread of heterodox faiths proscribed non-Orthodox proselytizing and criminalized the "seduction" of Orthodox believers.[7] Insofar as toleration in the Russian Empire was overwhelmingly instrumental and central to imperial management, there were missionary impulses to wield Orthodoxy as a tool to organize and govern diverse subjects.[8] Despite some underlying interest in missionizing, the state's increasing regulation of conversion in the pre- and post-reform eras (signed statements of voluntary baptism, confirmation of preparation) suggests that conversion was not unproblematic and that the state only desired proselytes who helped to fortify the stability of the empire rather than destabilized confessional coherence. Church and state alike were wary of instrumental conversions, the toxic effects of apostasy, which often resulted from tactical conversions, and the destabilizing effects of missions on heterodox populations.[9] Thus, the state's missionary impulse was more often than not overwhelmed by its recognition and regulation of the tolerated faiths for the sake of stability and as a natural manifestation of imperial ethno-confessional diversity.

Despite Dreizin's and Smirnoff's criticism of an inward-looking Orthodox Church, the church in the reform period did start to galvanize its missionizing. In tandem with the post–Crimean War drive to modernize the empire and the post-1863 Polish insurrection policies to unify the imperial borderlands, the Synod in the era of Great Reforms organized missions in the East to both Christianize and Russify minorities.[10] Under the leadership of Over Procurator Tolstoi (1865–80), the Synod reopened the Orthodox Missionary Society in 1869 and ensured that missionaries and teachers in the East received more money and recruits than before. In 1870 Tolstoi supported the work of Nikolai Il'minskii, a graduate of Kazan Academy fluent in Tatar, who developed the so-called Il'minskii system, a method of proselytizing in native eastern languages. By training non-Russian clergy and opening schools that taught in native languages, the Il'minskii system tried to ensure that Christianization involved study and understanding rather than just simple baptism.[11] Although the Orthodox Missionary Society assisted Jewish conversions to a degree, as will be seen shortly, the Russian Orthodox Church leadership never created a mission to the empire's Jews akin to the Il'minskii system in the East. Such work was undertaken piecemeal by individual converts from Judaism as a way both to satisfy their spiritual needs and make a living.

In contrast to the Il'minskii system, which focused on education, the institutions created by local clerics and lay philanthropists in the Great Reform era aimed to shelter and assimilate Jewish converts into Orthodox society. In some ways like Alexander I's Society of Israelite Christians, these initiatives engaged less in missionary work and more in addressing the perceived material and emotional plight of converting Jews. Some commentators even insisted on describing these projects as less missionizing than "philanthropic" or "humanitarian."[12] The philanthropic bent of Jewish missionary work in cities like Kiev and St. Petersburg in the reform era was characteristic of the growth of philanthropy and a social mission of parish clergy as part of a larger growth of voluntarism and civil society. The rapid growth of voluntary associations under Alexander II, impelled by new concerns for public welfare rather than traditional ideas of charity as individual giving, provided an outlet for clerics and laymen—especially women—to participate in public life. For parish clergy, the revitalization of brotherhoods, a relic of an older parish-based community model, provided a platform for local philanthropic missionizing.[13] Aside from the rise of philanthropy, Russification policies and discourses and the empire's reassessment of its toleration policies, especially in the western borderlands, where the Orthodox Church was viewed as weak in the wake of the 1863 Polish uprising, also shaped local initiatives.

In 1864, a year after the Polish uprising, Kiev clergy with support from local merchants founded the St. Vladimir Brotherhood as a society for the "protection and support of Orthodoxy and of Russian nationality" in the southwest region of the empire, an area populated by Ukrainians, Poles, Jews, and other minorities.[14] At first, the Brotherhood was only minimally involved with converts. Then, in 1871, it received 1,500 rubles from the Kiev branch of the Orthodox Missionary Society (OMS) to open a temporary shelter for converts from Judaism.[15] The OMS, after its 1869 reorganization, was officially charged with raising money for Orthodox missions through extensive fundraising and membership drives among lay Christians throughout the empire.[16] The Brotherhood's increasing financial and operational focus on Jewish conversion forced it to apologetically state in its 1872–1873 annual report that it was not "exclusively engaged in converting Jews, but [tried] in all ways to help Catholics join Orthodoxy."[17] Nonetheless, the Brotherhood opened an elementary school in its orphanage exclusively for preparing Jewish children for conversion. The school opened with about fifty students, ages seven to twelve, who came from near and far. According to published reports, the Brotherhood baptized 617 Jews between 1870 and 1889. In the context of empire-wide conversion statistics for those years,

the Brotherhood on average influenced 5.6 percent of yearly Jewish converts to Orthodoxy.[18] Judging by the names and ages of the Brotherhood's
converts from 1879 to 1882, most Jews who came to the Brotherhood were
young, single women, the majority from villages in Kiev Province.[19] Some
converts, though, came from as far away as Lithuania, Belorussia, and Poland. Brotherhood reports from 1881 and 1882 describe the Jewish converts as
"simple people, illiterate and poor, but diligent" and as being predominantly
from the lower classes, "mostly artisans."[20] The Brotherhood provided icons,
crosses, belts, and shirts to the new converts, as well as food and money.[21]

The Brotherhood's location in Kiev was both a boon and impediment to
its success. Although Jews were legally permitted to live in Kiev Province, the
city of Kiev was excluded from the Pale of Jewish Settlement. Special privileges and selective integration allowed some Jews to legally reside in Kiev,
but on the whole, most Jews could only stay temporarily or visit for business.[22] As a result, authorities scrutinized each convert's application for any
hint of religious insincerity, especially conversion to evade residential restrictions. For example, in 1904 a thirty-six-year-old widow, Rosa Gross, and her
three children were denied entry into Kiev for the purposes of preparing for
conversion with the Brotherhood. The provincial authorities rejected her petition for residence on the grounds that conversion preparation could be done
elsewhere.[23] The Kiev governor's objection in this case is curious, because
forty-six other applicants that same year received temporary residency rights
in Kiev in order to prepare for conversion. The typical petitioner was granted
a fourteen-day stay. Though unevenly applied, the governor's argument suggests that regional authorities were well aware of the choice location of Kiev.

The Brotherhood's shelter for Jewish converts was inspired by the example
of the convert from Judaism Pavel Dzhagiler, who in the mid-1860s helped
found a private shelter for Jewish converts in St. Petersburg, later called the
Mariinsko-Sergievskii Shelter.[24] Over time, this convert-led initiative gained
ecclesiastic leadership and even the patronage of the imperial family. According to its founding narrative, the St. Petersburg shelter was the brainchild of
Dzhagiler, a former teacher at a Jewish school in Minsk who converted to
Orthodoxy with the assistance of Yakov Brafman, a notorious convert whom
we will meet shortly. In 1862 Dzhagiler relocated to St. Petersburg where
he enrolled in the local seminary alongside other Jewish converts who also

hoped to proselytize their former coreligionists. In 1864 Dzhagiler returned to Minsk to reclaim custody of his four-year-old son from his former Jewish wife in order to baptize him in the capital. Back in St. Petersburg, Dzhagiler asked a local Anglican woman, Mariia Noevna Birch, an English missionary in the St. Petersburg Missionary Society, to care for his son. At the same time, another converted Jew, Lipkin, asked Birch to care for his son as well. Birch asked a fellow female philanthropist, Ekaterina Nikiforovna Sheremet'evska, to assist her, and in 1865 the two women rented a three-bedroom apartment to take care of the boys. Over time, the women collected donations from philanthropists in St. Petersburg and Moscow, and other Jewish converts sought their assistance. By 1866 the needs of the orphanage grew and Birch felt unable to maintain it; Dzhagiler asked the OMS to take over the shelter's fundraising and governance. Under the OMS, the orphanage garnered attention and support from St. Petersburg clerics and additional donors. It still lacked steady support and maintenance, though, until 1867, when the philanthropist Tat'iana Borisovna Potemkina gave a substantial grant to the shelter and brought in a steady guiding force, the St. Petersburg archpriest Nikandr Briantsev. The shelter then took over a ten-bedroom house where converts were provided shelter, meals, and clothing; the orphanage even boasted a garden.

From 1867 to 1870 the shelter housed around eighty converts for varying lengths of time, from weeks to years, and gave financial assistance to some converts who were unable to live in the shelter.[25] Aside from conversion training, the shelter provided education for children, vocational training for teenagers, and assistance for adults in finding jobs or pursuing education in the professions.[26] Like the Society of Israelite Christians, the shelter saw itself as functioning in both familial and educational realms—acting as a surrogate family and religiously and vocationally training the neophytes to be productive imperial subjects.[27] In 1870 the shelter garnered the patronage of a few of Alexander II's children, who even served as godparents for some of the converts who were baptized in the imperial family's church.[28] Under the auspices of the Imperial Philanthropic Society, the shelter came under tighter bureaucratic control and evolved into a modern philanthropic institution adhering to strict legal rules and generating official statements of its mission and activities.[29] The shelter averaged twenty Jewish converts a year between 1874 and 1877, and the average annual cost of convert aid ranged from 2,100 to 3,300 rubles.[30]

Though founded by converts and Christian philanthropists, the shelter became very closely associated with the St. Petersburg archpriest Briantsev, who took over its administration at the behest of lay activists. In the words of a St. Petersburg school director, Father Briantsev was so concerned with Jews that if it were possible, he "would convert all of Petersburg's Jews."[31] In 1888 *Novorossiiskii telegraf* (New Russian Telegraph) characterized Briantsev as the lone Russian cleric interested in missionizing to Jews. In his thirty years of missionary work, Briantsev baptized over a thousand Jews. Yet, echoing the general ambivalence of converting heterodox subjects in the empire, Briantsev supposedly lamented that only twenty to thirty of his converts were believing Christians. For all of his missionary zeal, he reportedly called the majority of converts from Judaism "bad Christians" (*plokhie khristiane*).[32]

Aside from Father Briantsev, most of the shelter's leaders and missionaries were converted Jews, including the founders of the shelter, Pavel Dzhagiler and Yakov Brafman. Dzhagiler was also active in convert training. From 1868 to 1869, because of Briantsev's busy schedule, the monastic priest Beniamin, also a convert from Judaism, led most of the prayer services at the shelter.[33] In 1876 the convert Alexander Shkopel' received ordination in St. Petersburg as an Orthodox priest, with the intent to serve as a missionary to Jews at the St. Petersburg shelter. A former student at the Vilna Rabbinical Seminary, Shkopel' moved to the capital to missionize, and he married Dzhagiler's daughter Maria.[34] In 1876 *Strannik* (Pilgrim) hailed his ordination as a boon to the Orthodox Church, whose theoretical monopoly on proselytizing in the empire was broken by Anglican missionaries, who had both the knowledge and proper Yiddish missionary texts to proselytize Jews.[35] Aside from these convert leaders at the shelter, the convert from Judaism O. Brin wanted to join the shelter's staff, but he was denied permanent residence in St. Petersburg.[36] Indeed, the shelter represented an unprecedented institutional attempt to support Jewish conversion, but the profile of its religious leadership suggests that Jewish missionary work was still marginal in the eyes of the Orthodox Church and that it necessitated private organization and financing.

The baptism of an underage Jewish boy, Sergei Griner, led to a scandal that delegitimized the shelter's Jewish conversion work. According to an 1862 Synod decree, the baptism of a child under fourteen required written permission of the parents or legal guardians. In the case of Sergei Griner, a priest at the shelter, Vasilii Glebov, permitted the baptism of Griner with the written consent of the mother alone. Glebov did so based on the testimony of the mother and two witnesses who declared that the father, Abram Griner, had disappeared. The St. Petersburg Ecclesiastic Consistory complained that Glebov had not exercised due diligence to confirm that the father had disappeared. Outraged by the failure to follow legal procedures, the consistory in 1876 warned the shelter committee that all Jewish conversion work had to be directed by Archpriest Briantsev, who adhered to the 1862 ukase.

Following heated correspondence between the shelter and the diocese's administrators in October 1877, the shelter's leadership voted to revamp its Jewish missionary work. Relegating the power struggles over Jewish conversion to a secondary cause, the committee reported that it decided to change the focus of its missionary work since years of experience had shown that most Jews converted for "purely selfish goals, and, consequently, they exploit the protection and monetary aid of the shelter."[37] The committee decided to remake itself as an orphanage dedicated to sheltering and assisting minors—especially children of Russians killed or wounded in war. This was deemed far more important and "closer to the heart of the Russian person" (*russkii chelovek*).[38] Thus, the shelter's leadership publicly disavowed its Jewish mission and adopted a racializing discourse about inborn Jewish characteristics (selfishness, materialism, sloth, parasitism) that could not be washed away by baptismal waters. Concurrent with this scandal, the Imperial Philanthropic Society tried to coax parish charities in St. Petersburg to cooperate with it in coordinating charity in the capital. Most parish charities reacted hostilely, fearing that this was an attempt to take over their management.[39] Perhaps the struggle between the St. Petersburg Consistory and the shelter was a byproduct of the larger philanthropic contest between state oversight and relatively independent parish and lay management. Following this debacle, the shelter continued to assist Jewish converts, though with the death of Briantsev in 1887, it ceased to give them priority.

The St. Petersburg shelter and the history of its founding and endowment highlights the overlapping spheres of mission and philanthropy that typified late imperial investments in converting Jews. Rather than Synod or diocesan funds, it was lay Christian philanthropic money that financed assistance to converts from Judaism. This kind of missionary activity in the form of charity was part of a larger phenomenon of late nineteenth-century and early twentieth-century Christian missionary work, which induced Jewish communities to ramp up their communal welfare programs to prevent vulnerable members from converting.[40] The dearth of Jewish foundling homes was highlighted in a sensational court case in Vilna in 1890 when a Jewish baby farming ring was charged with the murder of newborns. A group of Jewish women took advantage of poor and vulnerable Jewish mothers and their illegitimate offspring by providing newborn care for the desperate women in exchange for hiring the mothers out as wet nurses and domestic servants and extorting their salaries.[41] In the absence of official Jewish welfare programs for unwed women and their illegitimate offspring in Vilna and elsewhere, unofficial and predatory schemes like this both took advantage of and temporarily solved a growing social problem.[42] The weak infrastructure of social services for Jews was cited in 1894 by the Society for the Promotion of Enlightenment among the Jews of Russia (OPE), a Jewish educational and civic association based in St. Petersburg, as a reason to reform the Russian rabbinate so that modern rabbis could both thwart conversions from Judaism and press for social work within Jewish communities.[43] By the early twentieth century, even with the expansion of Jewish philanthropy, especially among wealthy urbanites, many Jews "could and did turn to general charities for various types of assistance."[44] Thus, the uniqueness of the St. Petersburg shelter and its location in the capital, far from the provincial heartland of Russian Jews, was a source of concern for contemporaries interested in Jewish missionary work. Though located in the imperial capital, close to wealthy philanthropists, it was far from the demographic heartland of Russian Jewry.[45] As contemporaries noted, and as many self-made convert missionaries would attest, the tepid missionary impulse in the Orthodox Church was put to shame by the industry of foreign missionaries, who set their sights on the large and relatively literate Jewish population of imperial Russia's western borderlands.

Foreign Missions

For all of the efforts by activist clergy and philanthropists to assist converting Jews in the late imperial period, the only real, consistent Jewish missionary work was by foreign evangelical groups.[46] According to Reverend W. T. Gidney, secretary of the London Society for Promoting Christianity amongst the Jews, evangelicals were much more active in Jewish missions than were Catholic and Orthodox Christians. As a result, European Jews associated the term "Jewish mission" with evangelical Christianity.[47] Indeed, Jewish conversion plays a central role in evangelical eschatology. As such, compared to Russian Orthodox missionaries, evangelicals considered missionizing Jews to be an urgent need; for evangelicals, the end of days was contingent on the Jewish people's conversion and this holy cause demanded the utmost human and financial resources. What makes Gidney's statement remarkable in the imperial Russian context is the legal monopoly on proselytizing by the Orthodox Church as the state religion.

Of the many nineteenth-century evangelical missions to Jews in Europe—most of which originated in England—several took up the cause of Russian Jewry.[48] The Third Section of the tsar's Chancellery issued several permits in the 1860s and '70s for evangelical pastors from Berlin to come to Russia for religious study and Jewish missionary work.[49] In 1876 the London-based Mildmay Mission to the Jews was established by Rev. John Wilkinson to spread the Gospel to world Jewry and disseminate copies of the New Testament. It established numerous centers in imperial Russia: Odessa, Minsk, Warsaw, Vilna, and Berdichev. Also, the British Society for the Propagation of the Gospels amongst the Jews maintained two missions in Russia.[50] The largest and most successful group by far, though, was the London Society for Promoting Christianity amongst the Jews. Founded in 1809, it maintained fifty mission stations across Europe and employed 184 missionaries. Committed to proselytizing through disseminating religious texts in native languages, the society published a Hebrew translation of the New Testament in 1817 and a Yiddish translation in 1821, and distributed over 250,000 copies of the New Testament to European Jews over the course of a century.[51]

Even as late as 1900 Reverend Gidney lamented that the evangelization of the Jews in Russia posed a "problem weighty enough to rivet the concentrated attention of all Christian people," and yet, "here, indeed, is a vast mission field, practically unoccupied."[52] The original London Society mission to Russian Poland began in 1818 with the enthusiastic support of Tsar Alexander I, and it set up its headquarters in Warsaw but proselytized throughout the Pale of Settlement.[53] As evidence of the positive reception of the London mission in Russian Poland, Gidney notes that Grand Duke Constantine Pavlovich, de facto viceroy of Congress Poland, served as godfather to a Jewess baptized through the mission and hosted the widely anticipated event at his palace in 1825.[54] Under Nicholas I, the London Society's missionary work was curtailed to Congress Poland, and in 1830, the state placed the mission under the jurisdiction of the General Lutheran Consistory.[55] Until 1854, when foreign missionary work was barred from the empire due to the outbreak of the Crimean War, the society boasted the baptism of 351 Russian Polish Jews and "a milder disposition towards Christianity" of countless others, many who converted in other churches.[56] After a few unsuccessful petitions to restart its work following the Crimean War, the society received imperial permission in 1874 to preach in Congress Poland and provinces of the empire where there was a "settled Jewish population."[57] In its second life, the society sponsored work in Russia proper through the Kishinev Lutheran pastor Faltin, who facilitated 142 Jewish conversions between 1874 and 1890, and the society embraced, without overtly underwriting, the work of the convert from Judaism Joseph Rabinovich.[58] In 1886 the Volynian Orthodox press noted that the society's missionary in Warsaw had come to Vilna and Kovno provinces to missionize in the northwest. Despite great effort, Anglican missionary work, according to the Orthodox press, fell on deaf ears because of Jewish "fanaticism." The missionary attracted to Christianity only one Jew, who ended up robbing him.[59] Faltin's mission in Kishinev did produce one notable convert—the rabbi turned head Lutheran pastor in Latvia, Chaim Rudolf Hermann Gurland (1831–1905).[60]

It is clear from conversations in the Russian press, both ecclesiastic and secular, that it was generally recognized that English missionaries dominated proselytizing in the empire. In 1888 *Sankt-Peterburgskie vedomosti* (St. Petersburg Gazette) reported that Anglican missionaries had settled in Vilna the year before and spent lavishly on missionary work by distributing free copies of the New Testament translated into Hebrew and Yiddish. A few of the missionaries were doctors and took advantage of their profession by offering free medical care to poor Jews and discussing Christianity with them.[61] As a result, there was widespread Orthodox envy of evangelical missions. Both *Golos* (The Voice) and *Strannik* celebrated when the convert from Judaism Alexander Shkopel' was ordained an Orthodox priest in St. Petersburg in the 1870s and took office in the church of the Mariinsko-Sergievskii Shelter for Converted and Converting Jews. Their hope for leveling the missionary playing field, though, was dampened as they recognized that English missionaries boasted more material resources for proselytizing Jews.[62]

Overall, the lack of state or synodal missions to Jews combined with sustained imperial institutional support for Judaism (state Jewish schools, rabbinical seminaries, the crown rabbinate, the Rabbinic Commission) underscores the fact that nineteenth-century imperial confessional politics was more concerned with bolstering orthodox religion among the so-called foreign confessions than bringing the empire's minorities into the Orthodox Church. At no point did the Orthodox Church's interest in Jewish converts meet the missionizing fervor or lavish financial outlay of the evangelicals.[63] And yet, statistics reveal that the majority of Jewish conversions in the Russian Empire still took place in the Orthodox Church. While missions were not the conduit for the bulk of conversions from Judaism, they do provide a window unto the political and social conversion landscape. In the absence of a coherent imperial policy toward the religious assimilation of Jews, entrepreneurial converts from Judaism came forward to sell the importance of a Jewish mission to the Orthodox Church.

The Gospel in Yiddish:
The Former Russian Bible Society Pays It Forward

Most work to convert Jews was channeled through entrepreneurial converts, like Alexander Alekseev, mentioned at the opening of this chapter, who on their own initiative proselytized former coreligionists. In this way, proselytizing in Russia was a "Jewish" affair, in that it was conceived by former Jews, concerned with Jewish language and literacy, and turned not so much on Jewish-Christian polemics, but on introducing the Russian Orthodox Church to the missionary philosophy and translation/publication apparatus of Protestant groups in the West. For converts, missionary work legitimized their religious apostasy and gave them a profession. For the state, it remedied the particular difficulties of proselytizing Jews.

Officials maintained that Jews tended to be more literate and religiously knowledgeable than many other of the heterodox groups in the empire. In an 1843 proselytizing manual for military priests who preached to young Jewish cantonist recruits, the Synod warned priests that they must be well versed in the Old Testament and prepared to answer Jewish students' questions about conflicting Jewish and Christian biblical interpretations on topics such as Sabbath observance, the rite of circumcision, and the doctrine of the trinity.[64] Similarly, the *Law Digest of the Russian Empire* on the crime of deviation from Orthodoxy treated converts from Judaism much more strictly than converts from Siberia. For the latter, the law disregarded their actions as innocent and unthreatening, ostensibly a comment on their seemingly uncivilized and unenlightened state. For Jewish and Muslim converts to the ruling faith, however, Orthodox Christian neighbors were encouraged to observe converts' religious practices and alert parish priests of any laxity or observance of alien religious customs. For these converts—literate and in conversation with Western religion—any sign of deviation from Orthodoxy warranted ecclesiastical admonition and a thorough investigation.[65]

Whereas evangelicals invested copious amounts of time and money in translating the Gospel into native languages, including Yiddish and Hebrew, the Russian Orthodox Church zealously guarded translations of the Bible and the New Testament from Church Slavonic into the vernacular, fearing even a Russian translation project.[66] With an interest in maintaining hierarchical authority and deemphasizing Bible reading in a church with a majority of illiterate peasant adherents, Synodal authorities for much of the nineteenth century resisted translation projects and broad dissemination of the Old and New Testaments.[67] More than it prioritized accessibility and outreach to the foreign faiths, the Orthodox Church valued its specific iteration of Eastern-rite Orthodoxy in Church Slavonic and did not attempt to bring scripture into the modern marketplace of ideas, knowledge, and mass literacy. Converts from Judaism found fertile ground for pitching their Jewish knowledge and language skills to a church that had paid little attention to the possibility of converting Jews through a Gospel in Yiddish.[68]

Already during the pre-reform period entrepreneurial converts tried to leverage the state's investment in missionizing to make a case for launching a similar imperial project in the civilian realm. Church officials responded positively when two Jewish converts came forward in the 1830s and '40s to tout their cultural and linguistic skills as former Jews to proselytize to the large population of Jews in the Pale of Jewish Settlement. Converts Asher Temkin and Avram Hirsh Levison successfully introduced Jewish civilian missionary work onto the agenda of the Russian Orthodox Church and onto the ecclesiastic payroll, both of them emphasizing the need for translation work and dissemination of missionary materials in Yiddish and Hebrew. Through their initiatives, the defunct Russian Bible Society funds were spent on translation projects for Jews.

Asher Temkin was born in the beginning of the nineteenth century in one of the northwest provinces and was orphaned at a young age. Parentless, he wandered among the Lithuanian yeshivas and even attended a Chabad Hasidic school for a time. In his teens, he married a woman from a wealthy Mogilev family. For years, as he studied for the rabbinate, Temkin and his wife lived on *kest* (free room and board) from his in-laws, who leased a watermill outside of town. When the family business foundered, Temkin was left to support his own family. He asked local Mogilev rabbis to give him *semikhah* (rabbinic ordination), but they found his Jewish legal knowledge lacking. Shmuel Leib Tsitron argues that this profound disappointment and Temkin's precarious finances led him to spurn the rabbis and publicly criticize and denigrate the rabbinate. Ostracized by the Mogilev Jewish community, Temkin became an inveterate Jew-hater.[69]

After his unsuccessful bid for ordination as a rabbi in Mogilev, according to Tsitron's anecdotal narrative, Temkin began to mingle with local Christians and frequent the local bishop. He relocated to Vitebsk, where he authored his first anti-Jewish tract in Hebrew, *Derekh selulah l'yediat amitiyut ha'emunah* (A Trodden Path to True Knowledge of Faith). In this essay, Temkin condemned rabbinic and kabbalistic teachings as harmful and characteristic of the danger of Judaism. His writing caught the attention of the governor-general of Vitebsk, Mogilev, and Smolensk.[70] Temkin presented himself to the governor-general as a Hasidic rabbi, and asked him to support the publication of this propagandistic tract as a means of spreading Christianity among Jews.[71] The governor-general asked the support of Nicholas I, who agreed to finance the publication and Russian translation, pay Temkin 1,000 rubles, and appoint him as Jewish censor in the western provinces.[72] This last stipulation could not practically be fulfilled, though, since only two Jewish censor positions existed, and one was already filled. The second position, by law, was reserved for a Jewish apostate. By the time Temkin converted, the position had been filled. Instead, he embarked on a career as a Jewish missionary in the western provinces.

According to the Synod's archives, the converted Jew Egor Temkin took holy title on March 2, 1835, as a missionary to Jews in Belorussia.[73] For his proselytizing, the Synod used funds from the former Bible Society to pay Temkin an annual salary of 800 rubles, plus a living stipend of 120 rubles, and a travel stipend of 400 rubles, totaling 1,320 rubles per annum.[74] By January 1838 the Mogilev bishop reported to the Synod that Temkin had been unsuccessful because the Jews hated and distrusted him. The Synod transferred Temkin to the southwest region to proselytize the large number of Jews living in the provinces of Volynia, Podolia, and Kiev. Temkin still was paid a salary and living stipend, but the Synod ended the travel stipend, deeming it unnecessary. In July 1839 Metropolitan Filaret of Kiev reported to the Synod that Temkin's work was unnecessary. First, the Jews of the southwest appeared unreceptive to Christianity, and second, Temkin lacked talent as a missionary. The Synod summarily discharged Temkin.[75]

The archival evidence paints Temkin as a convert with a cause but lacking the skills and personality to endear himself to his former coreligionists. Though Temkin's failure to convert many Jews is not necessarily surprising, his church backing and generous remuneration is reason for pause. Presented with the right package of a Jew cum Christian apologist, the Synod happily allotted some of its Bible sum (*bibleiskii summ*) for the Christianization of Jews. The Synod's Bible sum is also referred to as the sum from the former Bible Society (*iz summ byvshego bibleiskogo obshchestva*).[76] Thus, it appears that the defunct Russian Bible Society's assets were the source of Temkin's income.

The Synod's records on Temkin gloss over his corruption as a critical aspect of his dismissal. A May 1838 report from the governor-general of Smolensk, Vitebsk, and Mogilev to the Mogilev archbishop revealed a host of damaging accusations against Temkin and recommended that he be fired. During his time in Belorussia, Temkin reportedly converted two Jews— Sizenkov and Stekolshchik—to Orthodoxy. Temkin then sent them to his friend Ivanov, a convert from Judaism and former Smolensk guard, who illegally offered them as Jewish recruits in 1836.[77] According to the governor-general, Temkin entered missionary work for the very irreligious reason of making money. An investigation revealed that Temkin had a proclivity for heavy drinking, bad behavior, and domestic abuse. According to complaints lodged by his wife, Temkin and two other misfits often stole from her, beat her, and threatened to kill her. A Mogilev police chief verified that police daily broke up the domestic fighting.[78] After his relocation to the southwest, Temkin was censured by Metropolitan Filaret for opportunism and denigrating the missionary calling.[79] Nonetheless, Temkin's dismissal from the Synod's mission was officially attributed to the unenlightened state of Russian Jewry; Temkin's depravity was considered a separate issue. Despite his failure, Temkin reached out to the Synod again in 1850 to recommend the appointment of Alexander Antovil'skii, a recent convert from Judaism, as a missionary to Jews in the western provinces. Having learned a lesson from the Temkin debacle, the Synod checked into the candidate's background, found him incompetent and unskilled, and decided not to hire him.[80]

Though the Synod initially thought it had co-opted a member of the Jewish elite, Temkin proved to be persona non grata in the Jewish community. His replacement, Avram Hirsch Levison, had by contrast the authentic cultural credentials of a legitimate rabbi, but he was a geographic outsider. Levison (b. 1807) hailed from the Grand Duchy of Saxe-Weimar-Eisenach and served as rabbi and preacher there. He was the son of a provincial chief rabbi (*Landesrabbiner*) in the Hesse-Kassel region. Levison was educated at a Jewish school in Frankfurt am Main and then attended university in Göttingen and Würzburg. In 1829 he became a rabbi.[81] According to Levison's 1838 conversion petition to the Russian Orthodox Church and later writings, he became enamored of Christianity while pursuing a university degree alongside his rabbinic and preaching duties. Levison describes how his religious views assumed a rationalist bent such that he considered Mosaic law and even the Talmud as ancient texts, historically compelling but only symbolically relevant in modern times. Levison joined the rabbinate in the early years of the religious reforms, just as sermons in the vernacular and an emphasis on Jewish catechisms were gaining strength. With the emphasis on rabbis as orators, German rabbis needed to be educated in the art of sermon writing and oration. It was through the need to acquire these skills from German pastors that Levison first became acquainted with Christianity.[82] Convinced of the truth of Christianity, Levison admitted that his "heart and conscience were in contradiction with [his] position as rabbi, and [he] steadfastly resolved to openly convert to Christianity."[83] As with Temkin, the translation of Christian texts into Yiddish was a key platform of Levison's missionary proposal and perhaps the only tangible—and billable—product of his proselytizing.

Levison offered practical and theological arguments for his choice to convert to Russian Orthodoxy and proselytize Russian Jews. On a practical level, he viewed Christianity as a vehicle to civilize Jews and make them into patriotic subjects. Because religious and civic duties were intertwined in his worldview, Levison saw the unity of church and state in imperial Russia as ideal—intellectually and financially—for his missionizing goals. Russia attracted Levison since it was wedded to Eastern rite Christianity and was home to the continent's largest Jewish population, which was more "immersed in kabbalistic, Talmudic, mystical, and pharisaic delusions" than Western Jews and wholly lacking in moral and civic education.[84]

Levison's theological arguments for the superiority of Orthodoxy reflected his own confessional journey. According to Vasilii Kutnevich, chief priest of the army and navy and Levison's Synod-appointed mentor, Levison initially wanted to convert to Catholicism and then to Lutheranism, but could not find spiritual satisfaction through them. "The first with its ecclesiastic predominance, intolerance and persecutions; the latter with its striving towards reform . . . and its continuous splintering into new regiments (*polk*), aroused in him distrust. Turning to the history of the Orthodox Church, to his comfort he saw that this church throughout time maintained its independence without wanting to predominate, guided by a spirit of sensible moderation, free of fanaticism and indifference, constantly following those teachings and rites that it adopted from the Apostles and Church Fathers."[85]

Levison also reflected on his own German Jewish background when explaining his turn to the Russian church. Citing the eighteenth-century German Jewish philosopher and father of the Jewish enlightenment Moses Mendelssohn, Levison claimed: "If already Mendelssohn did much to benefit Christianity through his inconsistencies, so-called authentic Mosaicism, such that now thousands of Jews in Germany are converting to Christianity, then how much can possibly be done through Christ's pure teachings on God, virtues and eternality."[86] In implicating Mendelssohn in a wave of Jewish apostasy, Levison parroted critics in the Jewish community who censured Mendelssohn for reducing Judaism to rational principles that later served as a springboard for his disciples to reject Judaism's ceremonial laws and embrace a more universal expression of ethical truths as embodied in Christianity. Based on the Russian state's affinity for co-opting enlightened Western Jewish leaders to help modernize its Jews, Levison clearly thought that Mendelssohn was a figure well known to, and even admired by, Russian officials.

According to historian Shaul Ginzburg, the Russian bureaucracy was familiar with Mendelssohn, the celebrated Jewish Socrates of Berlin. According to an anecdote, the tsarist Jewish Committee in 1850 was casting around for a good polemical work to help Jews see the truth of Christianity and the falseness of the Talmud. Through a complex chain of events, Mendelssohn's *Bi'ur* (German translation of and commentary on the Bible) was brought before the committee, who then eagerly sent it to the Synod for approval. The Synod passed it to Levison, then a professor of Hebrew at the St. Petersburg Theological Seminary, who vetoed the idea and explained that it was not missionary material, but rather Hebrew scripture in the vernacular.[87] Thus, in casting himself as imperial Russia's Mendelssohn, Levison may have attempted to tap into the Nikolaevan regime's cooptation of German Jews for Jewish reform projects to make his own German origins and thus enlightened background a selling point.[88] Levison may also have identified with Mendelssohn's own scriptural translation project, the controversial *Bi'ur*. Levison's missionary philosophy rejected slandering Judaism to sell Christianity in favor of using Jewish texts to "prove the truth of Christianity."[89] Levison hailed translation of scripture into the vernacular as a key vehicle for both Enlightenment and mission, a Protestant ideal he was trying to sell to the Orthodox tsarist state.

Despite Levison's defense of the integrity of his confessional choice, the Synod's lingering doubt of his sincerity was animated by a broader suspicion of foreign Jews using conversion as a way of entering the Russian Empire. Though the empire inherited nearly a million Jews over the course of three successive Polish partitions at the end of the eighteenth century, a 1740 imperial decree prohibiting Jews from moving to Russia was technically still in force. Thus, when deciding three separate cases in 1830 of foreign Jews petitioning for conversion and naturalization in the empire, the Jewish Committee under the auspices of the MVD cited the 1740 ukase as a "fundamental law" that continued to guide Jewish policy nearly a century later. Under this law, Jews could enter Russia only if they converted to Russian Orthodoxy. Thus, the Austrian Jews Solomon Finkelshtein, Yakov Grabias, and Mendel Goldman, all living in New Russia, were to become Russian subjects if they converted to Russian Orthodoxy.[90] Levison, a foreign Jew seeking both conversion and naturalization, was thus subjected to careful Synod scrutiny to ascertain the sincerity of his Orthodox baptism.

Levison was baptized in St. Petersburg on October 21, 1839, with the Christian name Vasilii. With the tsar's approval, he was granted a position in the Orthodox Church's spiritual administration (*dukhovnoe vedomstvo*) as a missionary to the empire's Jews.[91] The tsar declared that the salary and living stipend of outgoing missionary Temkin, 920 rubles a year culled from the coffers of the former Bible Society, should be transferred to Levison.[92] Nonetheless, it appears that Levison's desire for an official mission to Russian Jews was never fulfilled. As late as 1863, Metropolitan Filaret of Moscow unsuccessfully encouraged the Synod to give Levison a missionary post. Filaret wrote in exasperation, "why has the idea of conversion of the Jews to Christianity remained so long without realization?" Based on this, Soviet scholar Mikhail Agursky argued that, aside from the cantonist episode, the Russian state was never interested in creating or supporting a church mission to Jews.[93]

In 1840 Levison was officially awarded an extraordinary professorship in Hebrew language at St. Petersburg Theological Seminary. The seminary seized on this rare opportunity to fill the chair in Hebrew language with a man who combined "the knowledge of teaching with the knowledge of a native Jew."[94] He subsequently began teaching Hebrew at the St. Petersburg Catholic Academy as well. In his academic post, Levison translated the New Testament and Orthodox liturgy into Hebrew, the first an improvement of the British Bible Society's translation from 1813, and the latter his own innovation.[95] In 1852 Levison, in his role as seminary professor, signed a petition on behalf of two Jewish sisters originally from Riga who wanted to convert to Orthodoxy in St. Petersburg but were unable to write the petition themselves in Russian.[96]

Levison and Temkin, though radically different in orientation and levels of success, came of age in the pre-reform era when the Russian state was engaged in proselytizing Jewish soldiers. Drawing on this missionary impulse in the empire combined with financial reserves from the era of Alexander I to use the printed word as a missionary tool, Temkin and Levison were both able to tap into the resources of the defunct RBS to publish missionary material in Jewish languages and encourage the regime to try to match the zeal of foreign evangelicals. Levison and Temkin were unique in that they were both outsiders to the Nikolaevan missionary apparatus—neither were military recruits, and Levison hailed from abroad and cited German missionary societies and Moses Mendelssohn as his inspiration rather than the state's own in-house mission in the military. Jewish cantonist recruits who were subjected to a state mission would style their entrepreneurial, missionary careers in a different light.

Literary Missionaries: Return of the Cantonists

The conversion stories of the former cantonists Alexander Alekseev and Nikolai Kuznetskii, later Archimandrite Nafanail, reveal that the Russian state's engagement in Jewish conversion work in the pre-reform period was a key motivator for official and unofficial missionary work among converts in that era and beyond, even after the state ended its cantonist conversion program. Alekseev (1820–1895) was born Wolf Nakhlas in the small town of Nezarinets (Podolia Province) to a poor Hasidic family.[97] Vulnerable to conscription by the kahal who strategically recruited poor or marginal members of the community, Wolf was selected as a child recruit and sent to a cantonist battalion first in Kazan and then in Vol'sk (Saratov Province), where conversion rates of Jewish cantonist recruits were particularly high. As Wolf and the other Jewish conscripts were being taken to Kazan, a rabbi beseeched them to follow the teachings of their parents and rabbis and not to convert. It was this young Jewish recruit who nostalgically recalled the Jewish Sabbath and belting out a Sabbath hymn for the tsar.[98]

From his own conversion narrative, Alekseev describes how he became a fervent Christian and began proselytizing fellow Jewish cantonists.[99] Alekseev particularly relished the memory of having assisted in the mass baptism of over a hundred Jewish cantonists in the Vol'sk unit that took place in the Volga River. With a large audience and musical accompaniment, the scene was apparently so memorable that a picture was painted and sent to the War Ministry and the tsar.[100] Alekseev's personal missionary work was recognized by the army—he reportedly helped baptize over five hundred cantonists in total—and in 1848 he received an imperial monetary reward and was appointed a noncommissioned officer. He was then transferred to an educational division of a carabineer regiment to serve as a missionary. He asked the army to petition the Synod on his behalf to receive a holy title, but a sudden onset of paralysis caused him to be discharged from service.[101]

Since the military was the only imperial institution underwriting Jewish conversions, Alekseev was left to find other means of support for his missionary work. An accusation of Jewish ritual murder in Saratov in 1853 gave him a start as a Jewish "expert," from which he launched a career in Novgorod as a biographer of imperial Russia's Jews and a prolific writer of popular theology. Between 1859 and 1895 he wrote at least eleven books and numerous articles in Russian journals—*Dukhovnaia beseda, Novgorodskie gubernskie vedomosti,* and *Domashnaia beseda.*[102] As in his debunking of the Saratov blood libel, Alekseev's publications showed that Jewish law did not permit ritual murder. For example, when discussing the holiday of Passover, Alekseev repudiated accusations that Jews prepared the ritual matzo with the blood of Christian children.[103] Based on this one positive contribution of Alekseev's writings, historian Yulii Gessen backhandedly complimented Alekseev for his ability to write in an oversimplified and crude manner that appealed to the average uneducated reader.[104]

What is remarkable about Alekseev's oeuvre is that for the most part it was self-published. As a result, Alekseev needed to promote his work and convince the native-born Orthodox elite of its value. In 1873 Alekseev wrote to Moscow theology professor Nikolai Sergievskii to promote his 1872 essay "Conversations of an Orthodox Christian of Jewish Origins." Alekseev explained that, because of leg problems, he was a sedentary missionary and that writing was his only vocation. The essay contained Talmudic references to Jesus and rabbinic discussions about prophecy regarding the life of Christ.[105]

As a missionary to Jews, Alekseev employed two main proselytizing strategies. He attempted to demystify Christian ritual and dogma by drawing comparisons to Jewish custom, and he acknowledged his own moments of religious weakness as a new convert, thus depicting conversion as a long process of study and practice that extended far beyond baptism. In trying to counter Jews' innate discomfort with churches, Alekseev likened the church service to the ancient Jewish temple and the rites performed there.[106] He compared the veneration of saints to Jewish supplications in the "merit of the forefathers" and the mourner's prayer for the dead, the kaddish. He noted the popular practice of Jews giving charity to young boys studying Torah in the land of Israel in the name of the famous Tanna Rabbi Meir, the miracle worker, ostensibly called on for his saintliness.[107] To counter Jewish discomfort with icons and holy processions, Alekseev noted the iconography of cherubim in Jewish tradition and the biblical story of the ancient Israelites conquering Jericho after marching around the city's wall seven times with Torah scrolls in hand until the wall miraculously fell.[108] Finally, Alekseev demonstrated that even Jews acknowledged the power of Jesus. Referring to the Jewish custom of *blinde nacht* (blind night), Alekseev argued that this tradition of refraining from Torah learning on Christmas eve grew out of the Jews' fear that Jesus roamed the earth that night looking for holy places to rest, especially in yeshivas. Jews feared that Jesus' touch could cause blindness. If Jews dismissed Jesus as a false messiah, argued Alekseev, why did they impute so much power to him and prefer card playing over Torah learning on the night before Christmas?[109] By both familiarizing Christian ritual and belief and acknowledging the long-term process of converts overcoming Jewish prejudices and beliefs, Alekseev tried to encourage and solidify Jewish conversions.

Aside from writing missionary tracts, Alekseev also engaged in ethnographic writing about Jews. He considered his ethnographies to be like his missionary works in that both served a holy purpose—to educate Christian missionaries about contemporary Jewish life. His ethnographic work appears to have enjoyed a rapt Russian audience—in the third edition of his earliest ethnographic text, *Bogosluzhenie, prazdniki, i religioznye obriady nyneshnikh evreev* (Worship, Holidays, and Religious Customs of Contemporary Jews) (1861), Alekseev explained that he responded to readers' feedback and their interest in "contemporary Judaism" by adding an updated section on "Jewish sects."[110]

In his thick descriptions of daily Jewish life, Alekseev wrote himself into a genre of Christian polemics that developed in the sixteenth century in the German lands among secondary Jewish elites who converted to Christianity and trumpeted their Jewish insider knowledge as missionaries and Christian polemicists. Converts from Judaism like Victor von Carben developed a new direction in Christian anti-Jewish polemics, moving from critique of the Talmud to the intricacies of Jewish ritual life that defied any biblical moorings.[111]

In this new genre of polemics, converts from Judaism were well positioned to offer an authentic ethnography of Jewish life that could not be gleaned from Christian Hebraism. These thick descriptions of Jewish ritual brought women into the mainframe of Jewish life, scrutinized their piety and at the same time argued that Judaism theologically marginalized their value in the religious collective. In this way, gender polemics functioned as a strategy of native missionaries to proselytize to marginalized members of the community.

In this vein, Alekseev produced ethnographies on the domestic and communal life of Jews, focusing on rituals, life cycles, and festivals.[112] He highlights the Talmudic origins of daily religious life, and the ways Jewish practice came to life in the context of the *kehilah* (community). His work is often structured autobiographically, using his Jewish past as a template for Jewish living. Throughout his ethnographic writings, Alekseev underscores the male-oriented world of Judaism in which he was reared and educated, and the secondary role of women in the domestic sphere, far from the spiritual domains of synagogue life and Torah study. Thus, like native missionaries before him, Alekseev seized on the generally inferior status of women in Judaism as a means of attracting them to Christianity.[113] Along these lines, Russian Judeophobes in the late imperial period diagnosed the high rates of Jewish female conversion as a reaction of women against their humiliating status in the Talmud and in the Jewish community.[114]

Alekseev opens his 1882 missionary ethnography, *Ocherki domashnei i obshchestvennoi zhizni evreev: Ikh verovaniia, prazdniki, obriady, talmud, kagal,* with the story of his birth, and the celebration of his parents and members of the community, who rejoiced over the birth of a son, yet another Jew added to the nation of Israel. Alekseev notes that "Jews" (by which he meant Jewish men only) also daily praise God for not making them women, "who are considered lower than men" and are only supposed to be man's helpmate.[115] In his 1861 ethnography, Alekseev comments on the domestic, enabling role that women play in all facets of Judaism, from prayer to holidays to daily religious rituals. In discussing prayer, Alekseev explains that "all Jews, excluding of course women," take part in formal, institutionalized prayer.[116] Rather than being found in the synagogue, women are purveyors of food who bring bread to the prayer house every morning so that their husbands can eat after the long morning prayer, which lasts around two hours, followed by Talmud study.[117] On Friday afternoon at sundown when the local *shamas* (sexton) cries for everyone to *geid in shul* (Go to synagogue), men run to pray and women stay home to greet the Sabbath.[118] On Yom Kippur, the Day of Atonement, men bring candles to the synagogue in memory of the dead while women light candles in every room at home.[119] He notes that women are exempt from living in booths on the holiday of Sukkot, and that when families search their homes on the eve of Passover for leavened bread, the head of the house specifically asks a mature male to assist in the search since women are hasty and more talkative.[120] There is a more elaborate ceremony over the birth and naming of a boy than a girl, as seen in the longer prayers and formal ceremony. "Let's take note, that for a girl, they do not make such a feast, and why is this so? Are not all people equal, whether a girl or a boy? According to Jewish thought, not all are equal: men of every century thank God every morning in prayer that God created him a man and not a woman. Even women recognize that men's value is far greater than theirs."[121] Alekseev repeatedly notes that Jewish women explicitly acknowledge that men are greater since they have a larger share of divine commandments.

Alekseev also pays attention to gender roles in Jewish marriages. He notes that women act more "modest and obedient" on the Sabbath. If for some reason the men cannot get to the synagogue for prayer, they may pray at home as long as women are not present; a woman should listen at a distance.[122] On Simchat Torah, the joyful holiday marking the annual completion of the communal reading of the Five Books of Moses, wives happily great their husbands after synagogue and feed them special food even though men are typically drunk. Every woman "implicitly carries out the will of her husband."[123] On Purim, another joyous Jewish holiday, husbands playfully tell their wives, "I see in you Queen Esther," and women treat their husbands like kings.[124] It is this master-helper role playing, even beyond the holiday of Purim—a Jewish version of carnivale—that Alekseev claims is at the heart of rabbinic Judaism, which dupes women into thinking they are Queen Esthers when in reality they are but domestic help.

Like in his gender polemics, Alekseev's descriptions of Jewish life recognize no separation between law and custom or between rituals and their various interpretations and meanings. In line with the ethnographic-polemical genre, he repeatedly emphasizes the gap between Mosaic law and rabbinic law, the crux of his critique of rabbinic Judaism. For example, in discussing the synagogue and daily prayer services, Alekseev notes that Jews purchase synagogue seats, with the choicest being those on the East.[125] He repeatedly emphasizes rituals for the dead, and the different ways Jews attempt to ward off the devil. Alekseev claims, for instance, that the mezuzah, or doorpost scroll, is an amulet to protect Jewish homes from the devil.[126] He details different Sabbath preparations Jews undertake either to ward off the devil or to help sustain the souls of the righteous in the afterlife.[127] He notes that the quality of the sound of the shofar, or ram's horn, blasted on the Jewish New Year could augur either a good year or a bad one. He connects the timing of the shofar blasts leading up to the High Holidays to an elaborate ruse to confuse the devil so that he cannot distinguish which day is Rosh Hashanah and lobby God about the bad deeds of each Jew who prayed for atonement on that day.[128] Thus there is a strong emphasis on Jewish superstition and the ways Jews perceive a thin line separating the living and the dead. In many places, Alekseev cites the source *Eẓ Hayim* (Tree of Life) for its detailed exposé of Jewish life.[129]

In addition to cataloguing daily Jewish life, Alekseev provides an overview of contemporary Jewish sects, another avenue for undermining Jews' purchase on religious truth. He surveys Jewish sectarianism through the lens of the New Testament disavowal of Pharisaism, but he also incorporates the historical writings of Josephus to retrace the landscape of the Second Temple period—specifically, the rites of temple worship, the Roman siege of Jerusalem, and sectarianism.[130] Alekseev surveys the modern sects of Hasidim and Mitnagdim (lit., "opponents" of Hasidim), and he conflates the former with the Pharisees of old who, according to the Gospel of Matthew, only "carry the mask of holiness." According to Alekseev, "they sit for days and nights in the synagogue in front of their Talmud, fast two times a week, on Monday and Thursday, not eating or drinking anything until the stars come out . . . and during prayer they exude such strangeness (*vydelyvaiut takiia strannosti*), which even perplexes other Jews. Frenzied shouts, wailing, jumping, and affectation accompany their prayer."[131] Moving beyond the staple anti-Hasidic polemic of contemporary Mitnagdim, Alekseev surveys Karaites, Sabbatean sects, "Tsadikism," and what he labels the sects of "Sephardim" and "Ashkenazim." He positively appraises the contemporary Karaite communities in imperial Russia, concentrated especially in Kherson Province and Crimea, and commends the Karaites for being honest, hospitable, frugal, moral (in that Karaites allow divorce to protect the woman, whereas rabbinic divorce laws empower the man), peaceful, and law-abiding.[132] Alekseev recounts the story of the seventeenth-century false messiah Sabbatai Zevi, who converted to Islam, and mentions the Sabbatean sects that persisted even after their leader's death. Alekseev views the Hasidic movement founded by the Ba'al Shem Tov in eighteenth-century Poland-Lithuania as a Sabbatean-inspired sect.[133] Though the role of the *tsadik* (righteous person) as a leader was integral to Hasidism, Alekseev, like other critics in imperial Russia, viewed "tsadikism" as a distinct Jewish sect that venerated *tsadikim*.[134] Lastly, Alekseev vaunts the Sephardim as highly educated, successful international traders, while he portrays the Ashkenazim as uneducated, poor, petty traders.[135] Thus ends Alekseev's survey of contemporary Judaism, informed by his own Jewish nostalgia and purchase on internal Jewish discourses, and inflected with his newfound Christian criticisms of Jewish sectarianism, legalism, and spirituality.

In his writings, Alekseev several times mentions a fellow cantonist recruit in Vol'sk who converted and went on to a successful missionary career.[136] Nikolai Kuznetskii (1820–1887) was born as Isaac Borodin in the town of Teofipol' (Volynia Province).[137] Orphaned at a young age, Borodin was conscripted and sent to the cantonist battalion in Vol'sk. Though he began as a leader among the Jewish boys who protested against a particularly nasty priest who preached to the Jews, he became influenced by Christianity over time. He attributed his conversion to the popular eleventh-century work *The Golden Epistle of Rabbi Samuel*,[138] which was first translated into Russian in the late fifteenth century and used to counter Judaizing heresies in Muscovy.[139] In this work, a medieval Moroccan rabbi proves the truth of Christianity through the prophecies of the Hebrew Bible in explaining to a fellow Jew why he desired baptism. In Russia, this work was a prime book in disputations with believing Jews.[140]

In recognition of Kuznetskii's assistance in converting many cantonists (Agursky cites about a thousand), he received 200 rubles and was appointed to the missionary wing of the army clergy. In 1845 he enrolled in the Kazan Seminary, from which he matriculated into the Kazan Academy and graduated in 1853 with a degree in theology. Kuznetskii then received a missionary post in Poltava Diocese. This was the first church-initiated job for a missionary to the Jews in the Pale of Settlement; the second and last would be the position of Pavel Dreizin in Vilna in the 1890s.[141]

In 1878 Kuznetskii became a member of the Orthodox Ecclesiastic Consistory in Poltava and a teacher of Hebrew language in a seminary. In 1884 he was ordained a monk/archimandrite, with the name of Nafanail, and took over as head of the Gustynskii Monastery in the town of Lubny. According to Archimandrite Nektarii, who encouraged Kuznetskii to missionize to local Jews, Kuznetskii converted about three thousand Jews, of which a thousand were in Poltava. Kuznetskii died in 1887 at the age of sixty-seven, having reached the highest ecclesiastic rank of all Jews before the Bolshevik revolution.

In 1862 Kuznetskii used the pages of *Strannik*, an educational and literary journal of the Orthodox Church, to dispel the notion that Jews converted for instrumental reasons. "It is common to hear unflattering opinions about new converts from Judaism, that, apparently, every one of them, of course, decides to convert to Christianity for some selfish (*korystnyi*) reason, not having any belief in the truth of the Christian faith."[142] Highly attuned to the emotional, spiritual, and physical difficulties of Jewish conversion, Kuznetskii nonetheless sought to counter the widespread skepticism toward Jewish converts by showcasing stories of sincere, religiously inspired converts. He introduced Orthodox readers to Vasilii (formerly Chaim) Grinblat from Berdichev, a devout Hasid, who converted at the age of thirty-five after eight years of serious Christian study. Over the course of five months before his early death, Grinblat succeeded in writing two missionary texts in Yiddish and translating key catechisms and Orthodox prayers into Hebrew.[143] Besides publishing Kuznetskii's sketch of Grinblat, the Russian press also presented short biographies and autobiographies of Yakov Brushlinskii, Georgii Klei, Alexander Shkopel', and O. Brin, all sincere Jewish converts who countered the widespread belief that Jews violated the sanctity of the church by converting for material gain.[144]

Alekseev and Kuznetskii, as cantonists cum missionaries, were personal beneficiaries, so to speak, of the pre-reform state's aggressive mission to Jews in the military. They then attempted to harness the state's missionizing to the civilian realm. From Alekseev in particular, and his prodigious missionary publications, we get a snapshot of some of the battle lines for native missionaries in the reform period, especially gender and sectarianism. Alekseev used the marginalization of women and the persistent splintering of Judaism into the modern period as polemical devices to sell the merits of Christianity to a Jewish population still reeling from the coercive state mission of the pre-reform era. In Kuznetskii's reunion with his sister in Teofipol' in 1865, the sister assailed her brother for reneging on the oath he took when he entered the army not to forsake the faith of his family. "Is it all too little to you that you let yourself be baptized," his sister asked in dismay, "will you also baptize us?"[145] In addition to Alekseev and Kuznetskii, who came of age in the reform period as native missionaries, the notorious convert Yakov Brafman also entered the missionary scene at this time and engaged in publishing schemes similar to those of Temkin, Levison, and Alekseev, to prod a hesitant Orthodox Church to follow the example of the Protestants and missionize through publishing.

Yakov Brafman and the Conversion of the Kahal

Of all the converts from Judaism who conversed with the tsar or the Synod and attempted to reshape the future of Russian Jews, only Yakov Brafman as a promoter of Judeophobia in late imperial Russia has really endured in historical memory as a native missionary. Ironically, the mission for which he is notorious was not work to convert Jews, but his later attempt to convince the imperial bureaucracy that Russian Jews were conspirators. During his lifetime, though, Brafman also tried to sell the Russian bureaucracy on the merits of a Jewish mission. Ironically, the evolution of his career from missionary to anti-Jewish demagogue actually turned the imperial conversation on the Jewish question away from rapprochement between Jews and Christians via conversion to the abolition of the kahal via anti-Jewish legislation that increasingly disenfranchised converts as well as professing Jews.[146]

Brafman was by all accounts a marginal Jew. He was born into a poor family in the small town of Ketsk (Minsk Province) in 1824, and was orphaned at a young age. He often clashed with Ketsk communal leaders, especially after his young daughter's death and his inability to pay the burial society (*hevra kadisha*). According to one source, a member of the *hevra kadisha* snatched a pillow from his deceased child's bed as collateral for Brafman's debt.[147] Due to his rebelliousness and marginal economic position, Brafman was a prime candidate for recruitment by the kahal to meet its conscription quota. To evade the draft, Brafman ran from his hometown. After several unsuccessful attempts to launch a career, he converted to Russian Orthodoxy in 1858 in Minsk, even though he had earlier converted to Lutheranism in Kiev.[148] Brafman became a missionary in Minsk and seized upon a visit by Alexander II to gain imperial sponsorship for his proselytizing agenda.

In a petition to the tsar in September 1858, Brafman suggested that missionary work in Yiddish together with a Yiddish translation of the New Testament would be the most effective means of converting Jews. He drew on his own road to baptism, obliquely referring to the fact that he first gained access to the New Testament in German, perhaps connected to his initial baptism, as a Lutheran, in Kiev. He noted that at thirty-four he started to question Judaism, but he had little access in his strict Jewish home to information about Christianity. It was not until he read the New Testament in Yiddish, through a copy given him by the London Missionary Society, that the words of the text soaked through. "The voice of heavenly truth harmoniously called out in my soul and the sounds of my native tongue," recalled Brafman, and only then "compellingly and warmly started to spread the truth in my consciousness."[149]

Underscoring the need for Jewish missionary work by those fluent in Yiddish and knowledgeable of Jewish life and rhetoric (including Talmudic dialectics and debates), Brafman proposed the creation of a missionary society in the western provinces that would be operated exclusively by Yiddish speakers familiar with Judaism who could understand and interact not just with Jewish men, but with women and children as well. Intimacy and access coupled with a Yiddish translation of the New Testament would make for a perfect Jewish mission, all in the interest of "Christianity, the Tsar, and the Fatherland."[150]

His letter was forwarded to the Synod, and he was granted an audience in St. Petersburg the following year to pitch his missionary vision. It does not seem that Brafman's idea got off the ground. He was appointed to the post of Hebrew teacher at the Minsk Theological Seminary in 1860. According to Brafman's own reports, his missionizing—whether independent or nominally funded by the Synod—was amply rewarded: he assisted forty conversions in a six-month period. In 1866 Brafman took a hiatus from teaching and went to Vilna to push his missionary work in a new direction.

Rather than focusing on actual conversion work alone, Brafman ventured into the discussion of the "Jewish question," which framed the issue of the desirability and possibility of Jewish integration. In an inventive twist on the classic Judeophobic denunciation of the Talmud as the cornerstone of Jewish fanaticism, Brafman developed an alternate theory that isolated the kahal as a "Talmudic municipal republic" that used Talmudic teachings to secretly control Jews and indoctrinate them in absolute obedience to the ruling Jewish elites. According to the historian John Klier, Brafman's success rested on the simple yet far-reaching implications of his argument. He reoriented the Jewish question to show how "religious fanaticism, economic exploitation and social alienation . . . could now all be viewed as deriving from the same first principle, the kahal."[151] Through successive iterations of this idea in journals and published works, Brafman took an upward career path from censor of Jewish books in Vilna to censor in St. Petersburg in the Chief Office for Press Affairs. As censor in Vilna, Brafman was given a stipend of 2,500 rubles, underwritten by the Vilna Educational District and the Ministry of Public Enlightenment, to finance the translation and editing of the documents (supposedly taken from the minute books of the Minsk kahal) underpinning his theories of the kahal as a state within a state.[152] His handsome remuneration and state posts, however, did not produce any Jewish converts. Rather, his influential writings helped convince the Russian bureaucracy that the Jewish question was a function of an intractable and unassimilable kahal that lived on despite its official dissolution by the state in 1844. Brafman's overall missionary career was predicated on rejection and denunciation of an elite Jewish communal leadership at whose hands he suffered as a poor, vulnerable, and marginal Jew.[153] In sum, his professional climb up the state bureaucratic ladder was more a product of his sensationalist Judeophobic claims than a recognition of his missionary goals.

During the brief period in which he tried to make a career as a native missionary, Brafman held up foreign evangelical publications of scripture as a model for how the Orthodox Church should engage Jews. He made a case for publications in Yiddish and for missionaries who could speak the language of Jews—both linguistically and culturally. Brafman briefly dabbled in missionary work, during which time he met Pavel Dzhagiler before the latter moved on to St. Petersburg and founded a shelter for Jewish converts.

Though Brafman did not go far with his proselytizing agenda, there was one more convert from Judaism in the late imperial period who tried to leverage foreign evangelical work as a tool to coax an increasingly nationalist church into acting on its legal monopoly on heterodox conversions.

Pavel Dreizin and Evangelical Orthodoxy

In May 1891 Yosif Yankelev Dreizin, a graduate of the Zhitomir Rabbinical Seminary, petitioned the Lithuanian Consistory for permission to be baptized together with his three children in the Orthodox Church.[154] Dreizin is an interesting case of a state co-opted Jewish leader in that both before and after conversion he was on the state's payroll, first as a Jew, then as a Christian. Before baptism, Dreizin was an official town rabbi of Bela, and, as of September 1889, the interim rabbi of Slavazhych, with a state salary for both appointments. Following baptism, Dreizin petitioned the Orthodox Church essentially to continue funding his teaching and preaching, but now in the promotion of Russian Orthodoxy among Jews.

To convince the Synod to fund his translations of Christian texts and Orthodox catechisms into Yiddish and his missionizing work in the northwest region, Dreizin focused on the bilingualism of Russian Jewry and the need for Christian propaganda in Yiddish, so that Jews could actually comprehend Christian dogma rather than just superficially read it in Hebrew.[155] By July 1891, a month after his baptism, Dreizin had already begun translating into Yiddish the New Testament, the lives of the apostles, and other works of the church fathers. Dreizin attached to his petition a completed Yiddish translation of the catechism of the Moscow metropolitan Filaret and a short exposition on the Old and New Testaments. In addition to requesting the Synod to officially sponsor him as a missionary, Dreizin also asked it to cover the cost of printing his Yiddish translations.

Officially, the two missionary posts in the Lithuanian Diocese were for missionaries to all non-Orthodox confessions. Dreizin needed to present a persuasive argument as to why a missionary to Jews in particular was necessary and worthwhile in the northwest. He pointed to lower-class Jews as prime material for conversion since they did not worship Mammon (money) or practice Judaism as a way to get ahead. He chose to focus his proposed missionary work on artisans, traders, and the poor, the "simple nation" who were more amenable to missionary work than intractable Orthodox groups like the Stundists and Schismatics, to whom the church allotted significant human and monetary resources.[156] Dreizin's lament "for all other groups . . . there are organized missions, but for Jewish delusions nothing is organized,"[157] is a remarkable statement for the 1890s, when the head of the Synod, Konstantin Pobedonostsev, was notoriously feared in Jewish circles as a "Grand Inquisitor" who supposedly wanted to solve the Jewish question in three ways: conversion, expulsion, and death.[158]

Having located a segment of Jewry amenable to Christian teachings, Dreizin then took advantage of Orthodox anxieties about its hegemony in the empire by playing the confession card. He alerted the church to the various foreign missions operating in the western part of the empire converting Jews to foreign Christian confessions. Dreizin named three specific British Bible Society operatives in Vilna who spent considerable sums of money on publishing Yiddish translations of Christian writings, based on the fact that most Jews only understood "jargon" (Yiddish) and not Hebrew. To respond to this foreign intrusion on the Orthodox Church's legal monopoly on proselytizing in the Russian Empire, Dreizin challenged the Synod: "If foreign missionaries exist in Russia secretly and proselytize a fair number each year, then how many more of the masses need God's word, which will be preached openly with the permission of the Synod!"[159] Using competition from foreign missionaries as leverage, Dreizin asked the Synod to support an Orthodox missionary project with Dreizin at the helm.

By June 1892 Dreizin had convinced the Lithuanian Consistory and Synod to grant him the second post of missionizer to *inovertsy* (non-Orthodox) in the Vilna Diocese, even though it was clear that the focus of his work would be on Jews.[160] In the Lithuanian Consistory's file on Dreizin's missionary work, Dreizin's own correspondence about his activities always referred exclusively to "Jews"; a third party later edited all such references to read "Jews and other *inovertsy*."[161] Although church record keepers wanted to formally present Dreizin as an equal-opportunity missionary, in fact his work was exclusively with Jews. The Synod allotted Dreizin annually from the ecclesiastic expenses of the western region 600 rubles in salary, 200 rubles for travel, and 453 rubles 33 kopeks for translation expenses. The Synod also announced that Dreizin would be appointed to the Vilna Holy Spiritual Brotherhood, from which he and his family would receive free lodging until they were firmly established in their faith. The Vilna Brotherhood was the model for the St. Vladimir Brotherhood in Kiev, which vigorously supported and facilitated Jewish conversions in the late imperial period. In addition, the Synod allotted 1,571 rubles from its Orthodox Church and school maintenance fund for the printing of ten thousand copies of Dreizin's Yiddish summary of the Old and New Testaments and translation into Yiddish of Metropolitan Filaret's catechism, *True Faith: The Messiah Has Already Come.*[162]

As a missionary, Dreizin concentrated on formal theological discussions with Jews and disseminating Christian knowledge through printed Yiddish translations. In September 1892 Dreizin sent the Vilna archbishop a proposed program of missionary work in the Lithuanian Diocese to be held in his apartment at the Vilna Holy Spiritual Brotherhood. First, he envisioned a weekly hour-long Sabbath sermon based on an evangelical text explicated with an eye toward comparing the Old Testament prophecies with the New Testament. Following each sermon, Dreizin wanted to invite one or two Jews in the audience to publicly engage him in a disputation or discussion. "Such discussions must be conducted without noise, laughter, without reproach or reproof from any side, and only in the most peaceful way."[163] The sermon and discussion would be held weekly from 4 to 6 pm on the Sabbath, and police would be on alert in case of a public disturbance. Second, Dreizin suggested that occasional discussions be held at his apartment weekdays from 10 am to 5 pm for anyone interested in "contesting the truths of Orthodox faith and searching for salvation." On Sabbaths and weekdays, Dreizin wanted to follow the evangelical example and give every interested participant a gift of a New Testament, donated to Dreizin by Dr. Altgauzen, one of the British Bible Society missionaries in Vilna whom Dreizin previously identified to the Vilna Consistory.[164]

Dreizin painstakingly convinced the Orthodox Church of the need to proselytize Russian Jews, and he was awarded for his efforts. He was able to support himself and his family and he launched a career as a translator. As with his predecessors in the Jewish missionary business, Dreizin recognized that publishing Yiddish translations of scripture was the biggest selling point in trying to convince the church to pay converts to preach to a difficult audience.

The vacuum left by the state's disengagement from Jewish missionary work in the reform era, together with the Synod's ambivalence about missions to Jews and the foreign faiths in general, created a space for entrepreneurial converts along with parish clergy and lay philanthropists to proselytize Jews and create institutions capable of assimilating converts into Russian Orthodox society. Converts spent most of their energy on convincing the Orthodox Church of the merits of proselytizing Jews and the need for the church to reclaim its monopoly on missionizing in the empire, which was often eclipsed by the work of foreign evangelicals. Parish clergy and philanthropists, on the other hand, focused on easing the poverty of converts rather than convincing Jews of the theological merits of Christianity. It is thus in the context of religious toleration and the multiconfessional establishment it created, that converts from Judaism—rather than the Russian state or Holy Synod—sought support for Jewish missionary work and adopted the translation and publication strategies of Protestant missionaries.

Ultimately, the story of converts making Jews a worthy object of an imperial Russian mission can be read as an attempt by Jews or converts to sell the state church on the advantages of the Protestant bible society or mission model—emphasizing text, reading, and the mass circulation of ideas. Hence, the creation of a *Judenmission* in imperial Russia was very much a "Jewish" affair—former Jews, some who had been rabbis, trying to sell the Jewish/Protestant affinity for text and reading as a basis for making Russian Orthodoxy intellectually and theologically accessible and attractive to Jews. If conversion in imperial Russia was not a product of state- or church-led missionizing, then it is essential to look at conversions at the grassroots level and analyze social relationships on the ground. It is to that subject we now turn.

PART II

CONVERSION AND THE SHTETL

CHAPTER 3

SHTETLS, TAVERNS, AND BAPTISMS

FAR FROM the inconsistent policies of St. Petersburg and the entrepreneurial designs of convert missionaries, actual civilian conversions from
Judaism in the Pale of Jewish Settlement were facilitated by everyday
Jewish-Christian encounters and relationships forged before baptism. To
understand Jewish conversion in imperial Russia, it is necessary to analyze
how confessional groups shared provincial space and how Jewish communities constantly tried to negotiate and discipline Jewish-Christian encounters. The multiconfessional makeup of the Pale of Settlement is evident in
the space of the town or rural tavern, often leased by Jews from nobles and
frequented by Christian peasants. More than just a place to sell and con-
sume liquor, taverns in Eastern Europe also functioned as inns and stables
for travelers—typically Jewish ones—and often doubled as a country store,
bank, and entertainment venue.[1] Church and state records of conversions
from Judaism in imperial Russian archives repeatedly mention the local inn
as a space in which Jews and Christians met and interconfessional relationships were nurtured, thus serving as a catalyst for conversion. Spatial
configurations of Jewish experience—shtetl, eruv, galut (exile)—have been
well studied. This chapter, however, is about the less-analyzed everyday experience of space, a social reconstruction of proximity and encounter in the
western provinces of the Russian Empire.[2] From the perspective of everyday interactions—quotidian, hostile, and intimate—conversions were not

sudden, impersonal moves but journeys mediated by the familiar people and institutions of neighboring faiths.

The tavern as a site of Jewish-Christian sociability came to life for Russian-reading audiences in May 1866 when *Pravoslavnoe obozrenie* (The Russian Orthodox Review) reported the conversion of the sixteen-year-old Jewess Rachel-Leah Goldferbova to Russian Orthodoxy in the environs of Brest-Litovsk, in the northwest part of the Pale of Jewish Settlement. An orphan, Rachel-Leah lived with her grandmother, who ran a tavern frequented by clerks from the Pskov Regiment stationed nearby. Vaguely aware that one of her brothers had converted while in the army, Rachel-Leah was intrigued by discussions she had about conversion with soldiers, among whom were converts from Judaism. This dialogue both nurtured her desire to convert and provided the infrastructure for her to initiate baptism proceedings. Although local Jews attempted to foil her conversion by abducting and hiding her in a nearby mill, a regimental priest with help from local troops succeeded in wresting her from Jewish hands and bringing her to the baptismal font.[3]

The Russian Orthodox author of the 1866 article wanted to inform readers about the challenges facing converts from Judaism in the western provinces, just three years after a second Polish insurrection threatened to destabilize the empire's western corridor, and a decade after the abolition of the cantonist program, when the state exited the Jewish conversion business. The author polemically attributed the sparsity of conversions to outsized Jewish power in the region, rooted in the Jews' hold on the local economy and their physical restraint of coreligionists who desired to convert. In this period of resurgent Polish nationalism and state campaigns to neutralize the Polish Catholic threat in the region, the author's invective against a recalcitrant ethno-religious minority in the western provinces echoed the defensive posture of an already embattled Russian Orthodox Church. While the author's overt message conforms to the themes of much Jew-baiting in the late imperial period, the symbolic gender and geography of the Goldferbova story reveals much about the sites and forms of civilian Jewish confessional boundary crossing in the Russian Empire.

The female face of the convert from Judaism in the Goldferbova article is striking in two ways. In lieu of the enlisted male of the pre-reform army, the archetypical convert of the reform period is now cast as civilian and female.

Alongside the new gendering of the convert, the article positions the provincial tavern, in place of the imperial army, as the institution of conversion. In this new context, it is Jews who are physically coercive rather than Christian officers trying to compel Jewish soldiers to convert. Whereas Rachel-Leah's brother converted in the army, she converts through social encounters with soldiers in the tavern. By invoking the brother's conversion, the male army conversion experience hovers just beneath the surface, framing the tavern encounter as a voluntary, civilian site of confessional mobility, the "reformed" mode of Jewish conversion in the late imperial period. Thus, the article suggests that in this new order of conversion, gender, and power, the greatest challenge to neophytes is their proximity to the controlling gaze of family and friends. This chapter explores conversions from a local, provincial perspective by analyzing the tavern as an icon of the shtetl's political economy and a historical-cultural space of interfaith encounter; gender and forms of interfaith sociability; and the problems and opportunities attendant on the proximity of converts to their Jewish kin. The study of conversion in the Pale of Settlement thus offers an opportunity to view the contact and interaction between the empire's religious communities.[4]

The Social World of the Tavern

The ways commercial coexistence bred social interaction between Jews and Christians is best viewed in the institution of the tavern, an iconic fixture of the political economy of Jewish Eastern Europe where Jews were overwhelmingly middle class since they made a living not as peasants or nobility but rather as commercial agents engaged in petty trades, shop- or tavernkeeping, craftmaking, and money lending.[5] According to one scholar, "the Jewish-Christian interaction was arguably played out more in taverns, open every day and at all hours, than even in market squares."[6] Hirsz Abramowicz, in his memoirs about Jewish life in prewar Lithuania, reminisces about "village Jews, innkeepers included, [who] were close to the local peasants and adopted some of their customs, sayings, and songs." This confessional sociability, especially in rural spaces with small Jewish populations, "led not infrequently to conversion and mixed marriage, especially in the case of innkeepers' daughters." Offering a detailed picture of how confessional proximity could engender intimacy, Abramowicz paints the scene of a dark night, when "a girl might steal away from her parents and take the horses out to graze in the pasture where her Christian lover waited. If the fellow had serious intentions, a few God-fearing, well-to-do Christian women would intervene. Eventually, after many reproaches at home, the girl would run away. . . . After her conversion and wedding, the girl might return to the village with her husband and settle not far from where her parents lived."[7]

It was intimate encounters like these that caused many Hasidic rebbes to spurn the village—especially the institution of the rural tavern—as a hotbed of Jewish assimilation, where small Jewish populations necessarily fraternized with local peasants and at times even converted.[8] Speaking to this Jewish anxiety, Hirsz Abramowicz recalls the tale of a rabbi who came to the countryside to collect food and donations and was seen mixed dancing in the village inn. When confronted by Jewish patrons about his outlandish behavior, the rabbi defensively replied, "you must understand . . . it comes with the occupation." This innkeeper's tale takes this premise of everyday interfaith sociability to the extreme, suggesting that intimacy was an inextricable part of rural commerce, and arguably of the political economy of Jews in Eastern Europe more generally.[9]

Jewish tavernkeeping in Eastern Europe goes back to the early modern Jewish-noble symbiosis in the Polish-Lithuanian Commonwealth, wherein Jews helped to manage nobles' estates by leasing aspects of the manor economy. An extremely profitable way to create domestic markets for Polish grain, the production and sale of alcoholic beverages developed into a major industry in Poland-Lithuania and its successor states, including imperial Russia. Jews entered this market through the *arenda* (leaseholding) system, whereby they paid nobles for a variety of market concessions, from leasing toll and bridge taxes to leasing flour mills and taverns. Nobles leased almost exclusively to Jews, such that the term *arrendator* (lessee) came to connote "Jew" in local parlance. For centuries, Polish rulers and landowners had encouraged Jewish settlement to develop markets, and in that role, Jews brought goods to the countryside, lent money, and served as the noble landowners' managers and leaseholders.

Tavernkeeping, which became a major source of revenue on noble estates, was a prominent Jewish occupation in towns and villages. At the time of the partitions of Poland-Lithuania (1772–1795) by its absolutist neighbors—when

Russia's expansion led it to inadvertently acquire some three quarters of a million Jews where previously Jewish settlement was forbidden—about 85 percent of taverns were leased by Jews and roughly 37 percent of the Jewish population was officially recognized as tavernkeepers and their families.[10] After the partitions of Poland-Lithuania, the various absolutist rulers in the region tried to modernize and integrate their Jews by eliminating such pronounced Jewish economic niches as the liquor trade. In 1804, for example, Tsar Alexander I outlawed rural Jewish tavernkeeping, though bans like this were often implemented gradually and enforced sporadically.[11] In imperial Russia, the shtetls, or *mestechki* (small towns) as they were classified by tsarist officials, were defined less by demographics and more by the nature of the local economy or the economic activities in which Jews engaged. The shtetl in its Russian iteration married elements of the old Polish private-town leaseholding economy, with its trade, marketplace, and liquor business run predominantly by Jews, to the taxing powers of the Russian state.[12] Into the nineteenth century, Jews continued to play a prominent role in all aspects of the Russian liquor economy, especially as liquor tax farmers. This would become an issue that fueled imperial Russia's "Jewish question" in the late imperial period.[13] The prominence of Jews in the liquor economy in American history has been partially explained by the culture of tavernkeeping imported by Jewish immigrants from Europe.[14]

Despite various attempts in the nineteenth century to legislate the expulsion from villages of Jewish tavernkeepers, who were blamed for peasant poverty and drunkenness, the Russian state could not remove the Jews from the alcohol economy because it heavily relied on them. By the middle of the nineteenth century, a third of Russia's state revenue came from taxes on vodka.[15] According to an 1872 government memorandum, "Jews controlled 500 of 564 distilleries in the governor-generalship of the Southwest, as well as 119 of 148 breweries. Jewish distilleries produced 288,000,000 *gradus* of undiluted spirits, sold through their 19,000 taverns."[16] In the Congress Kingdom of Poland—a semi-autonomous part of the Russian Empire—in the nineteenth century Jews persisted in tavernkeeping despite repeated attempts by powerful groups in Polish society to drive them out of the trade. Tavernkeepers evaded legal obstacles by surreptitiously staying in the rural tavern business, or by engaging in trades similar to tavernkeeping—e.g., running country stores, hotels, stables, banks, and entertainment venues.[17]

Starting in the 1830s, the political economy of the shtetl began to falter as the Russian state increasingly eclipsed the rights of the nobility.[18] It was in the 1860s, though, and the dawn of the reform period, that the economic viability of the shtetl was upended as the emancipation of the serfs and the abolition of feudal conditions in the empire undercut the small-town marketplace. State-led modernization and industrialization projects combined with a large and now mobile rural labor force shifted commerce to the cities, impoverished many Jews as traditional occupations became obsolescent, and created a large pool of labor hungry for jobs and an education. In this late imperial upheaval, the tavern stands out as a symbol of a political economy undergoing massive change and yielding to new pressures for Jews to convert and leave the dying shtetl. However, the persistence of the tavern also underscores the continuity of Jewish life in the provinces, where long-term patterns of interfaith contact and sociability persisted in many respects until the end of the old regime. Taverns in imperial Russia's western borderlands (including Congress Poland) and in Habsburg Galicia continued to play a significant role in the rural economy until World War II. For example, Jews ran three or four taverns in interwar Jaśliska, Poland, and in the nineteenth century, every tavern but one was run by a Jew. In addition, a third of the Jews in Jaśliska made a living from the manufacture or sale of grain alcohol.[19] Though the shtetl's fortunes were on the decline, the small town and village commercial networks and the Jewish community persisted in large measure through World War I and the de facto abolition of the Pale of Jewish Settlement, formalized by the Bolsheviks in 1917.[20] Thus, Goldferbova's family tavern bespeaks a place slowly losing its economic vitality, yet one that would resist full socioeconomic reinvention until the Soviet years.[21]

As a narrative device in Hebrew, Yiddish, and other vernacular literatures, the tavern has served as a metonym for the rural Jewish encounter with the local Christian population—it is economically generated and culturally conflicted, but socially facilitates quotidian exchanges between Jew and non-Jew.[22] Hasidic rebbes may have feared interfaith intimacy in the remote, unsupervised villages of Eastern Europe, but historians and Jewish and Russian contemporaries more often mapped the phenomenon of modern Jewish conversion onto the city, where institutions of higher education, socioeconomic mobility, and a culture of leisure and consumerism facilitated interfaith mixing and sociocultural integration.[23] Moreover, unlike the remote but family-oriented village, the city was thought to offer choice and anonymity, freeing individual Jews from the controlling gaze of organized Jewish communities.[24] In addition to its urban narrative of modern Jewish conversion, imperial Russian history has tended to focus on the army and university as the twin centers of radical Jewish assimilation, serving as bookends to the reform period and its failed project of Jewish integration. Yet, the urban and impersonal institutional backdrop of modern conversion does not tell the full story of conversions from Judaism. As seen in the historical-cultural space of the tavern, conversions were a product of face-to-face encounters rather than an impersonal, instrumental border crossing. Moreover, by locating conversions from Judaism in the villages and small towns of the Pale of Settlement, we get a picture of voluntary conversions undertaken in the thick of Jewish life, laying bare the myths of Jewish separatism and the social death of the convert following baptism. Commercial coexistence undergirded social interactions between Jews and their neighbors, and it is these interactions, usually "within heavily prescribed roles," that frame the cultural and confessional border crossings analyzed here.[25]

Archival and published stories about female converts and taverns in the late imperial period juxtaposed with conversion stories from the pre-reform period suggest that there were many continuities in the social threads of conversion from the early nineteenth century to the turn of the twentieth century, wherein individual conversions were facilitated by social relationships and cultural fluencies forged before baptism. In this way, the tavern complements such urban meeting grounds as the eighteenth-century salon or twentieth-century coffee house, suggesting that Jewish-Christian sociocultural encounters in the modern age did not occur only in the cosmopolitan centers of Europe.[26]

In July 1871, an eighteen-year-old Jewess, Malka Mendeliovna Lin, with a baby son in tow, was asked to give a deposition before the Grodno police as to why and how she came to the provincial city of Grodno to convert to Russian Orthodoxy. She explained that she had lived with her parents, who were tavernkeepers in the town of Bel'sk (Grodno Province), and in 1870 she decided to convert after a soldier in the 102nd Viatka Infantry Regiment who had impregnated her promised to marry her if she converted. Fearful that her parents would discover her pregnancy, she received assistance from the infantry unit to go to Grodno where she gave birth to a son. As a single mother wary of her family's wrath, Lin asked the unit to petition a local convent in Grodno to give her shelter and prepare her for baptism.[27] Before the convent was able to complete a background check on Lin, she became ill and received an emergency baptism in the care of the army. Lin's shot-gun baptism was approved by the Lithuanian Orthodox Consistory, which then allowed the Grodno provincial administration to follow the usual protocol governing Jewish conversions: a one-time monetary handout (25 rubles in this case), deregistration from the neophyte's Jewish community, and a nine-month window of time in which to choose a new legal social status (*rod zhizni*), namely, a new tax-paying community (*obshchestvo*) and estate (*soslovie*).[28]

The archival evidence of Malka Lin's conversion bears a striking resemblance to the journalistic story of Rachel-Leah Goldferbova that opened this chapter. In both cases, growing up in a tavern with frequent access to, and intimate encounters with, Christians educated Jews about Christianity and facilitated sociability with non-Jews. Although Malka Lin does not explicitly say that she met her lover at the tavern, one can guess that the tavern was the meeting ground for Lin and Private Erokhin. Soldiers were present in both encounters. Significantly, Russian soldiers from the interior stationed in the Pale were the conduits of informal, unscripted Russian Orthodox proselytizing. Though ethnic Russians were present in the western borderlands, and the Russification campaigns of the 1860s following the Polish insurrection attempted to assert Russian Orthodox hegemony, the lands in the northwest of the empire were historically part of the Polish-Lithuanian Commonwealth and continued to be heterogeneously ethno-confessional—Polish, Belorussian, Ukrainian, Catholic, Uniate, Lutheran. The tavern was not just a space of interaction between people of different religions, but also a space where Russians from the empire's interior could meet and interact with the local population. This is conveyed in the memoirs of Russian writer F. V. Bulgarin (1846–1847), where he recounts his journey in the Pale of Jewish Settlement with a Russian captain who came to a Jewish inn near Kovno and fell in love with the tavernkeeper's beautiful young wife, Rivka. The Jewess ended up converting to marry the Russian captain.[29]

In thinking about the tavern and the provincial spaces where Goldferbova and Lin converted, Brest-Litovsk and Bel'sk were by no means remote
villages or places with a small Jewish population. Unlike Hirsz Abramowicz
and Hasidic rebbes, who mapped interfaith intimacies onto village spaces
lacking a Jewish communal infrastructure (such as a synagogue and min-
yan), the women profiled here crossed confessional boundaries in provincial
towns that had Jewish communal institutions and a significant Jewish population. Although Jews made up only 12 percent of the population of the Pale
of Jewish Settlement, they often comprising from a third to a half of the
inhabitants of its small towns.[30] While acknowledging the nuances of interfaith relations in remote, small village settings, close confessional contacts
buoyed conversions in small town settings as well. Although contemporary Jews like Hasidic rebbes and even modern Jewish writers and imperial
officials, as we will see, were intent on demarcating Jewish and Christian
space along town and village lines, the reality was that physical and cultural
boundaries were fluid.

Though Jews are typically seen as having been urban, a consequence of
their role in creating and sustaining markets, the actual space they inhabited
"in central and eastern Europe was overwhelmingly rural and agricultural,
towns were generally neither large nor modern, and communities were still
compact and isolated enough to be encompassed by a network of interpersonal connections."[31] The fluid urban-rural terrain of Jewish life in imperial
Russia caused problems for the state in defining the places of Jewish residence. From the time of the Polish-Lithuanian partitions at the end of the
eighteenth century, the Russian state allowed Jewish businesses in towns
and villages, but insisted that all Jews be registered in a town with a Jewish
community. Thus, the official profile of Jews as urban town dwellers muted
the diverse backdrop of Jewish commercial and domestic life between
villages and towns of various sizes, where there was constant migration
between town and countryside for business and family reasons.[32] The termi-
nological ambiguity of *mestechko* (small town) presented practical problems
for state officials in 1882, following the assassination of Alexander II, when
new legislation forbade Jewish settlement in villages and unleashed a tor-
rent of legal appeals from Jews arguing that where they lived was more
urban than rural. Over the next several decades, officials attempted to define

the places of legal Jewish residence and to sharpen the distinction between the rural and the urban, but as late as 1910 this attempt at classification was still a work in progress.[33] Classification proved difficult because small town and rural space existed in a dynamic "economic-cultural zone, linking Jews to Christians and Jews to Jews," making it impossible to isolate Jews from Christians.[34] The tavern was the preeminent institutional link in this economic-cultural zone.

The role of the tavern in the social world of the convert before baptism comes to life in the 1872 conversion narrative of Sheina Leibovna Dlugolenskaia. Like Malka Lin, Dlugolenskaia requested permission to convert to Russian Orthodoxy in order to marry her lover, Vladislav Stanislav Grabovskii—a Catholic peasant also converting to Orthodoxy. According to Dlugolenskaia's pleas to local police and clerics, she despaired that her conversion would be sabotaged by her Jewish family and community because of the complicated and lengthy conversion process established by the church and state that engaged the Jewish community. To her, these rules and regulations would ultimately undermine Jewish conversions, since the Jewish community was so tight and locally enmeshed as to find out about and filibuster any attempt at apostasy. In her mind, a shotgun baptism was the only sure-fire route for Jewish proselytes.

According to metrical records, Dlugolenskaia was fourteen years old, but she testified that she was at least seventeen. Her family was registered in the Bialystok region, in the community of Knishin, but lived in the Bel'sk region, in the village of Subbotka, where her father managed his brother's tavern. It was in this village that Dlugolenskaia found Orthodoxy and her future husband, Grabovskii. It is not clear why the couple wanted to convert to Orthodoxy, as opposed to Dlugolenskaia converting to Catholicism. Perhaps the local peasants of Kotlov, who rallied the police and local cleric on the couple's behalf, were the main reason. The peasant community pledged to assist the couple's conversion training and "adopt" Dlugolenskaia and guard and protect her from her Jewish family until the baptism was complete. In Dlugolenskaia's petition to the bishop of Brest, as mediated through a priest in Bel'sk, she expressed her frustration about the conversion process: "About three weeks ago, I found it timely to reveal my desire to the peasants of Kotlov so that they would inform the priest of the Grinevich church, in whose parish they lived; . . . a week ago, my parents and relatives having found out about my intention . . . got involved and threw me in a wagon and already started carting [me off] in order to do something to me; but to my happiness, at the time, the peasants of Kotlov were informed of this, they overtook us, snatched me and brought me to the Bel'sk police and told them what happened." Nonetheless, Dlugolenskaia still felt a sense of fear and foreboding. "Even though the state administration . . . promises to give me to these peasants for safekeeping from the Jews, I still fear for my life: . . . a Jew can do a lot—especially those as well off as my father and his brother Gershko Dlugolenskii, who hold a few arendas [leases] in Bel'sk District, including for the village of Subbotka, where my father runs an inn. Besides this, . . . my relatives . . . are workers in chancelleries and know all the tricks in their favor, . . . they already certified to the state administration that I am fourteen years old and promised to confirm this with metrical records of my birth, ignoring the fact that I am already seventeen years old."[35]

In Dlugolenskaia's narrative of vulnerability and fear, the local, intimate village setting fostered conversion, but Jewish-Christian proximity also threatened to thwart would-be converts since conversion could not be kept secret and family opposition was readily present. Dlugolenskaia mentioned "new laws" that stymied conversion, possibly referring to the 1862 law raising the legal age of independent conversion to fourteen, though her insistent claim that she was at least seventeen may reflect the local village understanding of legal practice.[36] As for her Jewish family's influence in local governance and their presence in local "chancelleries," it is possible that one of her relatives was linked to the Bialystok crown rabbi, who certified to the authorities Dlugolenskaia's date of birth.[37] This case, like the others, illustrates the irony that rural settings were shared, fostering inter-confessional relationships and access to conversion, and at the same time close-knit and confined, making crossing religious borders difficult.

In thinking about the tavern as a site of conversion, especially pronounced in stories of female converts, it is important to note the role of Jewish women in tavern culture. Modern Jewish writers from S. Ansky to Joseph Roth to Sholem Asch have evoked the female presence in the tavern, and artistic renderings of the Jewish tavern have prominently portrayed women in the thick of activity in the tavern (see Figure 3.1). The archetypical Jewish tavernkeeper finds a place in Joseph Roth's *Radetzky March*, an interwar ode to the fallen Austro-Hungarian monarchy, where an elderly Galician Jew is cast in this most "traditional" of Jewish occupations. In Roth's nostalgic portrait, the man's daughters are key agents in the tavern economy.[38] On this point, S. Ansky wrote in his short story "In the Tavern" (1883–1886) that Leyb, the tavernkeeper, "thought himself master of the tavern, [but] rarely sat behind the counter; he had his own affairs, serious, important matters. He viewed the tavern with disdain, as a two-bit operation fit only for women."[39] Indeed, in Ansky's story it is Leyb's wife and daughter who manage the tavern and interact with its raucous patrons. Ansky himself, born in a shtetl and raised in Vitebsk, saw his mother run a tavern while his father was increasingly absent as he traveled on business.[40] Evoking the tavern as a site of sociability, Ansky later told another writer, "I was born and lived till age 18 in a tavern,

Figure 3.1 E. Iakovlev, *Zhidovskaia karchma* (Jewish Tavern), 1868. The Miriam and Ira D. Wallach Division of Art, Prints and Photographs: Print Collection, New York Public Library. New York Public Library Digital Collections. http://digitalcollections.nypl .org/items/510d47db-b12d-a3d9-e040-e00a18064a99 (accessed July 15, 2015).

so I know all these poor people and not-so-poor ones very well in this setting and very badly outside of it."[41]

The Jewish tavern women memorialized in conversion files are not like the bar wenches of Western frontier saloons; they are key agents in the political economy of the tavern and Jewish Eastern Europe more generally. They are not cast as loose and their presence in tavern life is not suspect, but in their own stories they do play off of tropes of female naïveté and vulnerability to garner legal support for their confessional choices and to throw blame on their Jewish families and communities for any unconventional contact between convert and kin following baptism.[42]

In the 1874 conversion case of Yevka Mordkheleva Blokh, the tavern functions not as a site of inter-confessional romance or informal mission, but of local information and exchange. In April 1874, sixteen-year-old Blokh escaped from the village of Rotnitsa in Troki District (Vilna Province) to the city of Grodno. She went straight to a convent asking for protection and shelter in order to convert to Russian Orthodoxy. Like Dlugolenskaia, Blokh was upset and confused by the lengthy and detailed conversion process, fearful throughout that her Jewish family could thwart her baptism.[43] Indeed, her father attempted to do so. Shortly after his daughter fled, he informed the Grodno police chief that Blokh stole money and goods on the night of her flight, and that he suspected that local frontier guards or police constables encouraged her to do this so they could profit. In his letter, Blokh's father named three guardsmen whom he suspected of duping his daughter, thus cynically undermining her supposed "religious" conversion.[44] In a rebuttal letter, Blokh acknowledged that the guards lived in surrounding villages, but claimed that she had never met them.[45] In his rejoinder, the father went about interviewing locals who had been at the village tavern the night of her escape to verify her petty theft. One local, Ivan Petrovskii, was at the inn drinking vodka, and he saw her with some money and belongings, but could not say to whom they belonged. A woman at the tavern testified that she saw Blokh take money, but did not know how much.[46] Despite the father's attempt to desacralize his daughter's conversion by linking it to theft, the conspiracy theory rested on close Jewish-Christian relations in rural areas. Indeed, Blokh knew of the men her father named as conspirators, and her conversion escape was witnessed in the local tavern where locals knew her, observed her actions, and later reported on them to her father. Blokh also claimed in her depositions that she was abused and neglected by her stepmother, often causing her to wander around the village looking for shelter.[47] Perhaps this, too, heightened her visibility and intimacy with local villagers. In this conversion case, the tavern serves less as an actual agent of conversion and more as a space of interreligious contact.

The meeting ground of the tavern or the roadside inn could also be a space where converts returned to a Jewish milieu. While the baptized soldiers who patronized the tavern in the Goldferbova story functioned as agents of Russian Orthodox influence, a baptized young woman's presence in a Jewish-run tavern in another case undermined her conversion. In a case from the pre-reform period, Anna Kviatkovskaia converted to Russian Orthodoxy in 1819 in the vicinity of her hometown of Merech (Vilna Province). At some point thereafter, she was in Lida (Vilna Province) and spent a night at the inn of the Jewish tavernkeeper Yankel, who slipped a drug into her alcohol, rendering her unconscious. She was then taken from Lida by her father and the Merech rabbi and shuttled among family and friends in the northwest region (crossing back and forth between Congress Poland) in an attempt to return her to Judaism and keep her from state and church authorities.[48] Kviatkovskaia's long story of capture and return raises doubts about her supposed lack of agency in relapsing to Judaism, but it is nevertheless illustrative of the role of the tavern in facilitating inter-confessional encounters.

It would be shortsighted to single out the tavern alone as an inter-confessional space conducive to intimate social encounters. It is but one example of shared Jewish-Christian space in small towns and villages, an institutional median between the synagogue and the church and beyond the marketplace. Though not a turn to religion, Leon Mandelstam's "conversion" to enlightenment and secular education—as seen in his decision in 1840 to enroll as the first Jew at Moscow University—was nurtured by "conversations with Russian army officers who frequented his father's tavern near Vilna."[49] Thus, the tavern stands as an agent of conversion both as a space conducive to intimate, unscripted, and uninhibited encounters between Jews and Christians, and as a symbol of the daily encounters of diverse cultures interacting in a joint, provincial space.

By studying the social and cultural side of tavernkeeping, a few aspects of the political economy of the Pale of Settlement come into relief. First, commerce produces cultural and social intimacies. Rather than just viewing the Pale of Jewish Settlement in imperial Russia as a commercial zone, it must be cast in larger terms as an economic and cultural zone, especially an inter-religious one.[50] Second, the nature of the leaseholding system and the state's classification of Jews as town dwellers, even if they lived in the village, produced a fluid commercial-cultural zone between town and country. Many Jewish families were registered in a town but lived in a village, and this arrangement could vary and change over time. Thus, when studying provincial Jewish conversions and the social intimacies that facilitated them, it is worth casting a wide net on sites and forms of Jewish-Christian encounters and not overly schematizing the differences between town and country.

Gender and Interfaith Sociability

The predominance of female converts from Judaism in late imperial Russia presents an opportunity to consider the various theaters of everyday life where both women and men came into contact with the multiethnic and multiconfessional population of the empire's borderlands.[51] Modern Jewish conversion stories in the civilian sector—by writers as diverse as Heinrich Heine and Daniel Khvolson—have tended to highlight the urban careerist or cosmopolitan strain of radical Jewish assimilation.[52] In this narrative, tied to glass career ceilings and the desire for social integration, female conversions have required some explanation. Middle-class acculturation of women was actually linked to lower conversion rates, because the adoption of bourgeois domesticity strengthened the role of wife and mother as guardian of home and tradition. In this way, female assimilation—at least among the middle classes—was tempered by a commitment to religious tradition as an anchor of domestic stability.[53]

The anomaly of female conversion, then, has been attributed to poverty and desperation, revolutionary activity, or a lack of Jewish education to shield women from the attractions of modern culture.[54] A combination of these factors has been used to explain the higher incidence of female conversion and intermarriage in Eastern Europe, where women had a prominent role in the family economy yet a culturally subordinate role in Jewish education and communal life.[55] Such an analysis privileges structural constraints on the agency of the female apostate and identifies the city as the locus of Jewish flight in the modern age. Rather than careerists or cosmopolitans, then, female converts were often work-place romantics; as one historian put it, "the typical female convert in Central and Eastern Europe was not the Berlin salon hostess who succumbed to German romanticism or the Krakow housewife who capitulated to Polish culture but the Viennese sales clerk who fell in love with a Christian co-worker or the Lithuanian tavern keeper's daughter who became pregnant by a Russian soldier."[56] In this chapter, we have met this tavernkeeper's daughter and others like her who came to conversion through the shared Jewish-Christian space of town and village life. Beyond an urban work space, the tavern functions here as a site of sociability. Thus, a gender analysis can offer a more nuanced understanding of conversion that probes forms of social and cultural contact rather than just sites of conflict and exclusion.

While much of the scholarship on Jews under Christendom focuses on the economic encounter between Jews and Christians, there has been little research on how small-town and village social encounters nurtured knowledge of, and participation in, the confessional life of one's neighbors.[57] In his memoir, Russian Jewish historian Simon Dubnov recalled a yearly icon procession through his hometown of Mstislavl' that drew a large crowd of Orthodox peasants from the surrounding villages and was a boon to Jewish businesses. The shared space of religious life was not just a shared visual landscape. In March 1882 a Russian Orthodox priest from the Uman region of Kiev Province wrote an article in the Kiev diocesan press to publicize the conversion of a seventeen-year-old Jewish boy in the parish church of the village of Nerubaiki, following the example of his older sister, Anna, who had previously converted to Russian Orthodoxy. The siblings were children of a local Jewish wine merchant. From the priest's partisan viewpoint, "such an inclination for the Christian religion on the part of a Jewish family may not be the one and only in a village parish. The proximity of Jewish children to the surrounding Christian population in the villages, especially to children, the public use by the population of signs of the cross, short Christian prayers, visual ceremonies of burial of the dead, and other visible peculiarities of Christian worship affect children's impressionable minds to the point of renouncing their families, relatives, dead Judaism."[58] In this polemical analysis, the priest posited—perhaps with a tinge of willful determinism—that the combination of sustained Jewish contact with non-Jews in intimate rural spaces and the routine public display of Christian religious rituals that Jews imbibed in these spaces created circumstances ripe for Jewish conversion.

Economic contacts at times spilled over into confessional spaces. The 1824 archival record of the convert from Judaism Alexander Gribovskii attests to Jewish medics working in Catholic monasteries. After his conversion, Gribovskii was given room and board at a Vilna Catholic monastery to study for monastic service. Shortly after his arrival, critics within and without the monastery brought a case to the local authorities assailing Gribovskii's depravity and religious insincerity. Among the critics was the Jewish barber (medic) Abrum Mordukhovich, who attended to priests at the monastery. Gribovskii complained that the Jewish barber avoided serving him and attacked Gribovskii when confronted, but the head priest dismissed Gribovskii's complaints and defended the barber.[59] The routine presence of a Jewish barber in a Catholic monastery is surprising, and invites us to analyze other non-market spaces where economic interactions spilled over into private and religious spaces. The taboo against Jews employing Christian servants was a core provision of laws governing Jewish-Christian contact in Christian states, including imperial Russia. Nevertheless, there is widespread evidence of Christian women in the employ of Jews who became embroiled in legal controversies when breaking the taboo led to the feared consequence—miscegenation or Judaizing.[60] Jewish women also worked as domestic servants in monasteries.[61] In his memoirs, Menachem Mendel Frieden recalls his youth in the town of Kvetki (Kovno Province), where he learned music from the local Catholic church organist.[62]

More often than not, the shared Jewish-Christian cultural landscape bred cultural affinities as well as squabbles; conversion was a marginal but persistent phenomenon that throws into relief the social ties that constantly bridged the yawning cultural and often socioeconomic gap between Christians and Jews. Pauline Wengeroff's memoir recounting her years in the small eastern Ukrainian town of Konotop notes the level of shared culture between Jews and non-Jews in the realm of fashion.[63] Beyond memoirs, recent scholarship on the anatomy of a ritual murder accusation—built on acrimony and gossip among neighbors—of ritual murder in a small town is also helpful for thinking about intimate patterns of sociocultural interaction between Jews and Christians outside of the cities of modern Europe.[64]

The imperial archives house voluminous materials on converts from Judaism, many of whom converted in order to marry a Christian or join a Christian family. These files present a lively picture of interconfessional social networks and help explain how and why many Jews, males included, ventured into a supposedly foreign Christian world. These materials not only shed light on the material and religious reasons for baptism, but also reveal the regularity of Jewish-Christian social engagement in imperial Russia, which created the social framework in which conversion to Christianity became conscionable and logistically possible.[65] Significantly, these stories spanning the nineteenth century and the changes in state conversion policy show how many Jews converted based on close relationships with Christians forged before baptism.

In their conversion petitions, many converts paid lip service to having Christian friends and being influenced by their Christian environment in an effort to prove their knowledge of Christianity and the sincerity of their wish to be baptized—a decision conditioned by years of interaction rather than made on a whim. Converts commonly mentioned having lived among Christians, being acquainted with Orthodox people, and in the case of Jewish students, having attended schools with Christians. The recurrence of such statements points to a narrative of authenticity that converts were expected to produce for civil and ecclesiastic officials. In this narrative, would-be converts explained their commitment to Christianity by invoking the web of Jewish-Christian relationships in the Pale of Settlement. This is clear in several examples from the archives. In 1855 the Jewish teenager Faiba Nakhim from the village of Smorgona in Vilna Province applied for conversion after having begun preparations himself by learning prayers and articles of faith from Christians with whom he had "occasional contact."[66] Malka Kuks, the daughter of a mill leaseholder, ascribed her 1864 conversion to her exposure to Orthodoxy and her acclimation to Orthodox life in her village.[67] Roshka Shmulovna Slovatitskaia from the village of Svenchino (Lomzha Province, Congress Poland) explained to the Vilna Consistory in 1870 that "from a young age, living among a Christian population, I had the opportunity to

become acquainted with their faith."[68] Avram Pinkhusovich, from the town
of Olkeniki (Vilna Province), said he was a good student and took advantage of an opportunity to study in a Vilna school, and he supported himself
by offering courses in Christian homes. Thus, Pinkhusovich claimed in 1896
that he became versed in the teachings of the Orthodox Church.[69] The di-
vorcée Lia Leizerovich, from the Snov Jewish community in the province
of Minsk, stated she was trained in Christianity by Christian children with
whom she socialized. She was illiterate but spoke good Russian and moved
in with an Orthodox family before her 1899 conversion. Her baptismal godparents were army personnel.[70] Masha Teitelbaum, born and raised in Lida
(Vilna Province), declared in her conversion petition that she went to school
with and befriended Orthodox Christians, and sometimes, in secret from her
parents, read the teachings of Christ and even went to church.[71] At the time
of her conversion in 1899, she was living with an Orthodox family. Twenty-
two-year-old Khaika Arievna Volskaia converted in 1900 after having lived
among Christians, visited churches, and come to the conclusion that she
loved Orthodoxy above all. In her conversion request, she acknowledged
that she had lived among Christians of different denominations but was attracted to the Orthodox Church.[72] According to her passport, she worked as
a domestic servant. Benzion Itskov Vinnik (Yablonskii), from the village of
Stepan (Volynia Province), attributed his conversion to growing up among
Orthodox people and becoming impressed by their Christian faith.[73] Mendel' Mirkin stated that his interest in Christianity was sparked at the age
of fifteen by friendships with Christians at school.[74] Though vague and im-
precise, these attributions of conversion to exposure and sociability are an
acknowledgment of the multiple cultural fluencies bred in the multiconfessional spaces of the Pale of Settlement where, as one woman noted, many
different kinds of Christians lived. Far from the image of the shtetl as a place
of Jews alone, the villages and towns these neophytes described were meeting
grounds that opened up the possibility of exploring other faiths.

   The themes of cross-cultural literacy, close confessional relationships, and
public consumption of religion in small-town Eastern Europe find expression
in another genre of convert writing—not just the self-fashioning of converts
found in the police brief, but in native missionary literature. Alexander Alekseev, the cantonist convert turned missionary discussed in the last chapter,

employed his Jewish knowledge to publish both missionary tracts for Jews
and cultural ethnographies of Jews for a Russian-reading audience. It is in
the latter context that Alekseev offers some revealing insights into the entangled lives of Jews and Christians in the small towns of Russia's western
provinces. Alekseev's positionality as a convert must be taken into account
when analyzing his ethnographies of Jewish life, as he is not only selling
his bona fides as an authentic insider and cultural ambassador, connecting
his thick descriptions of Jewish life to his larger literary project of naturalizing Christianity for Jews, mainly from a theological position, but perhaps in
his ethnographies, from a social perspective as well. Alekseev's ethnography
of Jewish life, however, was written to enlighten a Russian audience, and it
is tinged throughout with nostalgic and critical portrayals of his childhood.
Overall, his ethnography is structured around the Jewish calendar and life
cycle, and its references to everyday Jewish-Christian encounters are typically
asides, to draw in the non-Jewish reader to cultural practices familiar but
unintelligible to them.

Alekseev highlights Christian awareness of and engagement with Jewish
rituals, thus complementing the previously discussed narratives of converts
imbibing Christianity in their own communities. In his description of the
Jewish Sabbath, Alekseev notes that Jewish prayer and song were so enter-
taining and distracting that local Christians often stood at home or in church
by windows to listen to the Jews.[75] In addition, he notes that poor Christians
were often hired to put out Jewish lamps on the Sabbath.[76] On a culinary
note, Alekseev adds that a staple Sabbath food was kugel, which was the
most delicious Jewish food and which Jews often shared with their Christian
neighbors.[77] On the theme of Passover, Alekseev references the seder ritual in
which Jews open their doors at a designated time to symbolically welcome in
the prophet Elijah, and he notes that non-Jews were aware of this ritual and
would often play a trick on their Jewish neighbors at this part of the meal
by entering themselves or riding on a goat.[78] Alekseev discusses Christians'
fascination with Jewish rituals, especially those practiced on the holiday of
Simchat Torah, which they referred to as the *beshenyi* (frenzied) holiday, and
the holiday of Purim, when the loud noises to blot out Haman's name made
strange impressions on Christians who entered the synagogue at that time.[79]
In highlighting Christian knowledge of the Jewish ritual calendar, Alekseev's

writings offer another perspective on the multiple cultural fluencies alluded to in converts' explanations of their path to conversion.

Some of the richest indicators of shtetl interfaith sociability are conversions that aroused Jewish complaints of child abduction or coerced baptisms. Invariably, as the cases are fleshed out by police investigations, witnesses' testimonies, and converts' depositions, the social relations between the parties involved turn out to be much more complex than the initial claims of criminal behavior against minors imply. In addition to the rich gender discourse surrounding abduction narratives, which often played to assumptions of female naïveté, the common abduction narrative is also a defensive Jewish narrative to build protective walls between religions that in reality coexisted on a local and intimate level.[80] These narratives claim that Christians and Jews were so alien from one another that only a criminal act could physically bring a Jew into a Christian world.[81] Beyond any specific gendered construction of this argument, the very claim—leveled at boys and girls—argues for an imagined Jewish exclusivity and social insularity. In part, the posture of Jewish disbelief that any Jew would want to be baptized stems from an ongoing Jewish mentality of cultural superiority, as has been described in early modern Poland-Lithuania, or from the ways a confessional minority views itself vis-à-vis its neighbors as an urban borderland majority.[82]

Abduction narratives were a feature of Jewish conversion cases throughout the nineteenth century. In 1815 the father of sixteen-year-old Tsepa Shliomova petitioned the governor-general of Lithuania to return his daughter, who he claimed had been coerced by an outside party to convert to Catholicism. Police records indicated that on three occasions, Shliomova's father and relatives and other members of the community came to the convent in Vilna to convince her to return home. Each time, she claimed she wanted to convert. In a report to the governor-general, the police noted that they would have released the daughter had she admitted she was the victim of coercion or abduction. Shliomova's resolve convinced the authorities to let her baptism in the Catholic Church go forward.[83] Despite the father's repeated attempts to delegitimize his daughter's conversion by casting it as implausible and coerced, the seemingly voluntary nature of Shliomova's conversion suggests that a Jew could willingly migrate across religious borders.[84]

The abduction narrative persisted throughout the nineteenth century, even as the Jewish community began to encounter growing numbers of converting Jews in the late imperial period. In 1858 a Jewish mother from Rossieny (Kovno Province) petitioned a host of local civil and ecclesiastic agencies to return her young daughter, who, she charged, was being forcibly held in a convent to convert to Catholicism. The mother, Yakha Yoseliova, claimed that she had been at the parish in her town of Girtagol', where the surveyor Yanushkevich spotted her seven-year-old daughter, Riska. At some point thereafter, Yanushkevich secretly took Riska and hid her in Rossieny at the house of the district treasury accountant Volodkevich, from where she was then transferred to a Benedictine convent for conversion training. The persistent mother petitioned the Vilna governor-general, at which point the Kovno civil governor was taken to task for not responding to her or cracking down on an underage, coerced baptism.[85]

The Kovno provincial administration furnished a very different account of the story. The daughter, Riska Ruvelevna, was ten years old and willingly left her parents' home, expressing her desire to convert. According to the deposition by Riska in August 1857, she had been in a chapel about a year earlier, which inspired in her a desire to convert. On a Saturday night in August, Riska ran away from home to the landlady Yanushkevicha so that she could pursue her wish to convert to Catholicism.[86] In this version of the story, which satisfied the provincial authorities, Riska's disappearance into a Catholic milieu was not random or sudden; she apparently knew her Christian mentor and she had personally encountered Christian worship. Interestingly, the mother's story also gestures to a casual encounter in a parish church, but she does not interpret this as somehow naturalizing her daughter's interest in Christianity. In Yakha Yoseliova's view, Judaism and Christianity existed in complete isolation from each other, thus an abduction was the only way to account for Riska's communal crossing.

In some conversion cases, local military attachments acted as the link between Jews and Christianity in the countryside. Soldiers sometimes mediated between Jews seeking conversion, usually females, and nearby clerics. In 1864 Malka Leibovna Vulfovichovna Kuks ran away from home to the town of Bel'sk with the aid of a local army ensign whom she sought out to help her convert.[87] Two years later, Rutka Abramovna Movshik came from the Jewish community of Volkovysk to a Grodno convent asking to be taken in and prepared for baptism. In the mandatory deposition about her background and identity, Movshik testified that she was seventeen years old and listed in the last Volkovysk census, but she had no written proof of identity with her save for a free ticket to Grodno given to her a few days earlier by a Volkovysk military administrator.[88] In cases like these, the army served as the local face of Christianity and could provide practical help by shuttling a rural Jew to an urban church or convent.

In a similar case that same year, eighteen-year-old Sora Shenderova Arliukova from Oshmiany sought refuge in a Vilna convent to distance herself from her family and community while she prepared for baptism. In the depositions taken to confirm her identity and her reason for being in Vilna, the Oshmiany military head and the head of the gendarmerie identified Arliukova and confirmed her story.[89] Again, the army as local administrators and defenders of the Christian empire provided a rural point of entry into Christianity.

In June 1870 Roshka Shmulovna Slovatitskaia came to a local regimental commander pleading for help to convert after having petitioned a Bialystok cleric to no avail. The neophyte was registered in the Radzilov Jewish community, but her father was a shoemaker in a local village. In both of her conversion petitions, the eighteen-year-old Slovatitskaia explained her attraction to Christianity: "From a young age living among a Christian population, I had the opportunity to become acquainted with their faith" and developed "an irresistible attraction to baptism."[90] The commander set her up in a Grodno convent where the mother superior took up her cause and repeatedly pleaded with diocesan officials to permit Slovatitskaia to be baptized. With the help of the mother superior and the Princess of Oldenburg, Slovatitskaia was baptized in the Orthodox Church despite reports from the police in the town of Sventsiany that she had been involved in prostitution and theft.[91] In 1874 the Vilna townswoman and young Jewish wife Pera Girsenovich approached a noncommissioned officer to help her petition the Vilna Ecclesiastic Consistory for permission to convert to Orthodoxy. In addition to the officer, who helped her gain access to a Vilna convent for shelter and conversion preparation, a local Vilna woman, Sofia Chevskaia, helped guide her to the convent, visited her, and provided her with some material support.[92]

In some conversion cases, Christian neighbors or friends, both old and new, facilitated conversion. In 1865 Dverka Movshovna, age twenty, was taken in by a Vilna family who then assisted her in her desire to convert. At the same time, the family also took in a Karaite girl seeking to covert to Orthodoxy.[93] In 1874 Sora Lea Taich from Slonim was assisted in her conversion by a friend, a soldier's wife, who encouraged her to run to Grodno to enter a convent at a safe distance from her family.[94] In 1883 the Pinsk landowner Kotov repeatedly petitioned the Kiev committee of the Orthodox Missionary Society to convert the Jewess Meri Zalmanova Yafo. Kotov insisted that Yafo wanted to convert and she had already been accepted as a surrogate daughter in a local Christian community, but her Jewish family restrained her.[95] In 1892 Mira Beker was rescued by Christian neighbors from her abusive mother and stepfather, who, she claimed, tormented her because of her desire to convert. Neighbors facilitated her move to a Vilna convent.[96] In short, although Christian dogma and church prayers and even Orthodox clerics may have been foreign to Jews, Christian neighbors and local soldiers were familiar and accessible, and could assist Jews to convert.

In addition to conversion files and state records, the ecclesiastic popular press provided another forum, though highly tendentious, for convert profiles. In June 1879 the Kiev provincial ecclesiastic newspaper published a story on the life and conversion of Maria Leshchinskaia, presenting it in the first person to capture the way Maria told her story to the editors.[97] Her conversion narrative is detailed and drawn out over the course of almost two decades. Like the archival cases just analyzed, Maria's story also contains many of the central tropes of encountering Christianity firsthand: childhood Christian friends, a helpful Russian soldier, observing Christian religious life up close, and, in Maria's case, reading Russian texts.

Leshchinskaia was born in 1851 in the village of Osechkii in Kherson Province, where her father was a second-guild merchant. The only Jewish child in the village, Maria kept mostly to herself, but she did interact with the daughter of the local landowner. Her father was a Mitnagid (opponent of Hasidism), described in the article as one who did not recognize the Hasidic *tsadik* (righteous one) as a spiritual leader and who scrupulously observed Jewish law. Maria admits that until she was nine she thought all Christians were pagans, but that changed when her mother took her for

an extended visit to relatives in the cities of Kherson, Odessa, and Sim-
feropol. Interestingly, her story of increased sociability happened outside
of her village home, where feelings of socioeconomic superiority alienated
her from the local Christian population—a sentiment not unique to Maria.
In her travels, she became friendly with a variety of Christian children—
Russians, Greeks, Armenians. She chided the local Jews for trying to pass
among the Christian population and for being ashamed of their faith. From
her descriptions, she seems to be referring to the acculturated urban Jewish communities of New Russia. At one point, she recounts mourning for
Jerusalem on a Jewish fast day, one of the ritual fasts commemorating the
Roman destruction of the Second Temple and the end of the Jewish Commonwealth, and she notes that her Jewish teacher told her not to cry and
that Titus—the Roman general responsible for the sacking of Jerusalem—
was actually a good person.

Leshchinskaia returned home at the age of ten, right before her father's
death. Soon after, she procured a New Testament in Yiddish, but she notes
that she knew very little about Christianity. In reading Jeremiah, Maria experienced a revelation. "At noon, it became cloudy, and when it rained, I went
outside for refreshment; the wind rose; it dispersed the clouds, and I saw a
church: the sky was blue, but the church seemed golden." She realized that it
was a mirage, as her village had no church. She admitted to having thought
about Christianity before, but having heard that converts married peasants
and not knowing much about convent life, she was uninterested. Again, her
elision of Christian and peasant life is prominent. After this mirage, the idea
to convert was firmly planted within her, though she would try to suppress it
for more than a decade.

Two more anecdotes from her youth helped Leshchinskaia to flesh out
her encounter with Christianity. When Maria was fourteen, after an epidemic
in her village that left many youth dead, her mother brought her to a local
tsadik to inquire into Maria's fate. Cynically viewing the whole pilgrimage as
a money-laundering scheme, Leshchinskaia recounted that on the way home
her carriage fell in a river, and although many Jews witnessed the accident,
the only brave, altruistic person who helped them was a Russian soldier. She
noted that aside from him, the only Christians she respected were local girls
with whom she could share her love of reading English novels and poetry.

Although she tried to avoid marriage for years, at the age of seventeen she married a Hasid and moved to Mezerich.[98] She was married for ten years, bore five children, and was still unhappy. She attributes her persistent desire to convert during this time to Christian books and to a sighting of Metropolitan Arsenii. Leshchinskaia revealed her wish to convert to her relatives, but they responded as if her words were madness (*bezumstvo*). Seeing that she was depressed, her husband's parents suggested that she convalesce under the care of her mother, in Kiev, where her husband's sister lived. Mirroring stories of young neophytes who steal away from home by night so as to escape their family's controlling gaze, Leshchinskaia notes that she was escorted through the town of Kanev at night so as to keep her conversion from public consumption.

In Kiev, after finally being able to explore Christian ritual life up close—though initially only in Catholic settings—Leshchinskaia desperately desired to convert but was almost dissuaded after the prioress of a local convent rejected her, stating that she would not accept a Jewess. Though the editor interjects here in dismay that a Christian would turn away a neophyte, the upshot of the story is that the St. Vladimir Brotherhood saved Leshchinskaia and her determination to convert, as it enthusiastically welcomed and facilitated her baptism. While the narrative overall is finely drawn by a new convert to castigate Jewish religious life, specifically Hasidism, and to laud the dedication of the St. Vladimir Brotherhood and its role in Leshchinskaia's salvation, it stands as a complementary historical source for thinking about where and how Jews socially encountered Christianity in the provinces of imperial Russia. Her narrative of interfaith sociability in and out of the village, accessing Christian texts in Yiddish and Russian, and being captivated by righteous Christians (the helpful Russian soldier and the upright metropolitan), accentuate the shared landscape of Jewish and Christian life in the small town and villages of the western provinces.

Aside from shtetl sociability as a resource for Jews trying to find their way to the baptismal font, interfaith shtetl romance often was both the conduit and immediate reason for conversion (see Figure 3.2).[99] From a random sampling of 244 conversions overseen by the Lithuanian Consistory from the years 1819 to 1911—42 percent of the converts were women—seven Jews (six women and one man) converted to marry a Christian.[100] Within three

"I knew very well where she was and what they were doing."

Figure 3.2 Illustration by Manuel Bennett of Sholem Aleichem's *Tevye the Dairyman* short story cycle, 1993. The picture symbolically portrays Chava's conversion and intermarriage while her parents, Tevye and Golde, mourn. Source: *Sholem Aleykhem's "Tevye the Dairyman": Complete, Illustrated,* illustrations by Manuel Bennett, design by Joseph Simon (Malibu, CA: Pangloss Press, 1994), 99. Reprinted with permission.

years of Rozali Neiman's conversion to Orthodoxy on November 27, 1864, the convert—now Olga Grigoreva Armeiskova—had married a nobleman serving as a noncommissioned officer in the Don Cossack unit.[101] In 1896 Tsina Gorodishch filed for conversion so that she could marry her Orthodox fiancé, the Vilna townsman Nikolai Adamovich.[102] Although evidence suggests that more Jewish women than men converted to intermarry, there are cases of men converting for love as well.[103] In the wake of the legalization of conversion relapse from Orthodoxy in 1905 and from other tolerated Christian faiths in 1906, at least 684 converts from Judaism petitioned civil authorities for permission to relapse to Judaism.[104] Of the converts who petitioned the Kiev civil governor at this time, two women claimed that they had converted for love, but since their interfaith relationships had broken up, they wanted to reclaim their Jewish confessional status. For instance, Esther-Rosa Berkovna Zhukovskaia, who converted in Kiev in 1906 to marry Feodor, a peasant from her village of Mikhailovke, claimed the couple reconsidered their marriage decision at which point she decided to return to Judaism and to her widowed Jewish mother, who lived in the village of Moshny in the Cherkassy District.[105] Reiza Shpigel' claimed her parents kicked her out of her home one night, and by eight the next morning she was already baptized in another village in the district of Skvira. Within eight days of her conversion, she married a peasant. Emphasizing the hurriedness of her conversion and that she knew little about the faith and rites of Orthodoxy, Reiza petitioned the Kiev governor to allow her to return to the faith of her ancestors.[106]

Conversion growing out of interfaith intimacy in the late nineteenth century appeared in many places in Europe. Historian Rachel Manekin has, for example, documented conversions from Judaism in Austrian Galicia in this period among marriage-age women who preferred local Christian suitors over uncultured yeshiva students, and the Zionist publicist Isaac Remba published an entire volume on East European Jewish cultural and political leaders whose children converted, usually for love.[107] Among the many documents in the archives of Father John of Kronstadt (1829–1908), a celebrated and widely revered Orthodox priest in the late imperial period, is a letter from a Jewish woman born in Siberia who was unhappy in her marriage and had fallen in love with an Orthodox man in Kazan. Torn between family devotion and personal happiness, she asked the priest, "Should I leave for Siberia and go back to my parents, my husband, my children, or should I convert to Orthodoxy and marry the man I love?"[108]

While convert petitions and depositions are self-fashioned narratives that bear the imprint of a missionary agenda and are by no means straight-forward records of historical fact, the trope of Jewish-Christian friendships and encounters in these documents reveals a great deal about the normative relationships and closeness of communities of Jews and Christians.[109] Life beyond the Pale of Settlement was not just imagined or achieved through selective integration or accessed through the local Russian bureaucracy and courts; Jews lived in proximity to and engaged economically and socially with Christians on a daily basis in their own backyards. The ease of Jewish-Christian acquaintance, camaraderie, and support alluded to in these files unsettles the common understanding of Jewish social and cultural insularity in the Pale of Settlement, a holdover from scholarship on the premodern era, which depicts Jewish-Christian relations in purely functional terms and posits an East European Jewish mentalité grounded in the idea of cultural superior-ity. While mentalities could orient behavior, they could not always control it.

Rituals of a Local Affair—
The Western Provinces as a Site of Exit and Return

Aside from relationships forged before baptism in the multiconfessional spaces of the western provinces, a salient feature of provincial Jewish conver-sions was the proximity of converts to the controlling gaze of their Jewish families and communities. Jewish leaders like Simon Dubnov and Mendele (pen name of Sholem Yankev Abramovich) only heard belatedly about their children's conversions and lamented them from afar.[110] Similarly, the father of the historian and literary critic Mikhail Gershenzon (1869–1925) suspected till his dying day that his son converted in far-off Moscow because he had matriculated into Moscow University in the period of *numerus clausus* laws. But parents of children converting in the small towns and villages of the western provinces were aware in real time of their children's movements and, as we have seen, were in a position to react immediately.[111] What is so striking about conversions from Judaism in the provinces is that they were literally rituals of a local affair.

Imperial bureaucrats and foreign missions trying to regulate and seek potential converts tailored their efforts to the challenges of converting Jews in
the thick of Jewish communal life. Laws regulating conversions to Christian
denominations specified that they had to take place in a town church with
as much publicity as possible (preferably on a Sunday or holiday), and that
local parishioners watch converts for possible signs of retreat into their former religious habits and customs.[112] Since conversions were orchestrated as
local affairs, attention had to be paid to the maintenance of Christianity after
baptism inasmuch as converts could very well be pursued by relatives and
driven back into the Jewish communal orbit. It was for this reason that the
Catholic missionary congregation of the Maria Vitae Sisters, which operated
sixteen convents in the northwest provinces, forbade Jewish catechumens
from leaving for fear of relapse.[113] During David Bressel's 1871 conversion
to Orthodoxy in a Vilna church, the thirty-one-year-old single Jewish male
signed a routine statement pledging his eternal loyalty to the church. Following the fairly standard wording of the baptismal pledge, David promised
to go to church, especially on Sundays and on church and state holidays, to
annually attend confession and take communion, and to distance himself
from "non-Orthodox customs" (*inovernykh obychaev*), which surrounded him
in the western provinces.[114] The local orientation of conversion ceremonies
is noteworthy both as a required public display of the abandonment of one's
ancestral faith and as a recognition that the convert's road to baptism was a
local affair, a product of local sociability.

Though conversion was sometimes a means of circumventing Jewish
residential restrictions, imperial law tried to distance actual conversions from
the cities, believing that the sincerest conversions were those executed in
spite of local Jewish opposition. Following the 1835 official demarcation of
the Pale of Jewish Settlement, the St. Petersburg governor and the MVD
in 1837 resolved that intent to convert was not legal grounds for Jews to stay
in St. Petersburg beyond six weeks.[115] (The few shelters for converted and
converting Jews that popped up in the late imperial period were in large
cities like St. Petersburg and Kiev; at least one Russian Orthodox critic
noted that they were geographically misplaced.)[116] That an institution like
the St. Vladimir Brotherhood's shelter in Kiev, which both housed and supported converts from Judaism, was located in a city outside the Pale of Jewish

Settlement presented an obstacle for many Jews seeking its protection. By law, neophytes' requests for permission to temporarily reside in Kiev to visit the Brotherhood were channeled through the Kiev civil governor, who was known to reject applications on the basis that since conversion preparations could be undertaken within the Pale of Settlement there was no need to move to Kiev.[117] Foreign missions like the London Society for Promoting Christianity amongst the Jews, which began operating in the empire under Alexander I, focused its missionary work on shtetl Jewry but strategically placed its center of operations in cities so that neophytes could escape the gaze of their families and enjoy the protection of urban anonymity.[118] Wanting to ensure legitimate conversions yet shelter converts from their former coreligionists, imperial bureaucrats were perpetually plagued by the legal limits of effecting full religious and social transformations in provinces of the western borderlands where Jewish and Christian space was so intertwined.

The imperial Russian conversion phenomenon was both legally and demographically rooted in the Pale of Jewish Settlement, where the Jewish world was dominated by small town and village living. Based on information in a Kiev ecclesiastic journal, the Russian Jewish periodical *Nedel'naia khronika voskhoda* (Weekly Chronicle of "The Sunrise") reported that, between August 1881 and August 1882, the St. Vladimir Brotherhood in Kiev had converted thirty-nine Jews, twenty-four of whom were females. Most of the converts were described as lower class, primarily artisans; the women mainly hailed from villages and intended to become peasants following baptism,[119] presumably meaning they planned to marry Christian peasants. The Yiddish newspaper *Kol mevaser* corroborated this in reports of rural Jewish girls, like Maria Leshchinskaia, who ran away from home to marry their peasant lovers.[120] The Brotherhood's reports confirm that converts were predominantly females. In 1894, fifty-three males and fifty-six females were baptized; in 1905–1906, thirty-four males and forty-six females; in 1912, seven males and sixteen females.[121] Though the reporting in the Russian- and Yiddish-language Jewish presses painted conversion and interfaith romance as a village affair, limited to the unregulated spaces of the countryside where few Jews lived, the reports of the Kiev Brotherhood provide a more complete map of neophytes' origins.

The reports of the St. Vladimir Brotherhood contain rich demographic data on converts and their urban and rural places of official residence. (Soviet scholar Mikhail Agursky used press reports and the published reports of the Kiev Brotherhood to argue that women dominated civilian conversions among Jews in imperial Russia, and that Jewish conversion should be seen as a result of the sociocultural disintegration of traditional Jewish society, not of anti-Jewish legislation.)[122] In 1881, of the fourteen Jews who converted between January and May, eight hailed from places designated as a village (*derevnia, selo, khutor*); two from a small town (*mestechko*); two from a town (*gorod*); and the details of two are missing. All of the converts from villages were female.[123] In the September 1881 newspaper reports on the twenty conversions from May through August of that year, fourteen converts from Judaism are listed, eleven of whom came from within Kiev Province, and at least four from villages.[124] Thus, while village Jews were well-represented at the Brotherhood, converts from Judaism hailed from a range of provincial spaces, urban to rural.

The Brotherhood report issued in November 1881 described the thirty-nine converts from Judaism that year—ten male, twenty-eight female—as "simple, illiterate, and poor" but "industrious." The Brotherhood highlighted this last point by noting that upon conversion, the neophytes who had been enjoying the material aid of the society now worked in Kiev or returned to their hometowns to make a living. Women in particular, who, as we have noted, tended to marry peasants after conversion, were already accustomed to peasant life and thus readily returned to village life and "heavy labor" (*chernyi trud*) after baptism. In emphasizing the work ethic of its Jewish converts, the Brotherhood at once deflected naysayers' concerns that Jewish converts were mercenary and suggested that its conversion training program was both spiritual and vocational. Like the Mariinsko-Sergievskii Shelter in St. Petersburg, which housed and supported Jewish converts in the late imperial period, the Brotherhood sought to both Christianize and civilize Jews, the latter through useful and productive labor.[125] To enhance the story of the Brotherhood's successes in this regard, the report noted that most Jewish converts were formally members of the "townspeople" estate. Thus the Brotherhood underscored the coup of converting unproductive, commercial nonbelievers into productive, hardworking Christians.

A majority of the Brotherhood's converts came from Kiev Province, especially the districts of Kanev and Skvira, but some came from as far as Warsaw to the west, Ekaterinoslav (Kherson Province) to the south, and Kovno and Vilna provinces in the north.[126] The Brotherhood noted that local peasants often guided Jews, both men and women, to the Kiev shelter and helped to support them after baptism, either by adopting the males as family members or by offering the females their men as husbands.[127] The demographic data on the Brotherhood's converts and its reliance on local, especially rural, social ties to support converts after baptism offer yet another perspective on the provincial, social landscape of conversion.

A central figure in the rite of baptism and an often overlooked missionary agent that diocesan personnel recognized as indispensable to Jewish conversion was the godparents. Symbolically, the godmother and godfather played the role of Christian parents to the convert reborn in the baptismal waters. Practically, the godparents were supposed to materially and spiritually support the convert, who had supposedly severed all ties to his or her former coreligionists. Every Jewish conversion record lists the name of the godfather and godmother followed by a signature. Converts often received the Christian name of a godparent and adopted a new patronymic based on the godfather's name. The contribution of godparents to conversion is more often than not silent in the archives. Their role is highlighted, however, when ecclesiastic personnel sounded the alarm about a dearth of lay Christians willing to adopt and take responsibility for converts, and when godparents influenced the course of baptism or assured a wary church of the long-term stability of their new godchild.

Godparents and Christian mentors played a crucial role in personalizing the conversion experience and providing the logistical framework for Jews to gain access to clergy and ecclesiastic institutions. Godparents or other, informal Christian mentors provided the social threads that fostered conversion. In the case of Rivka Varnovitskaia's son discussed in Chapter 1, the state overturned the mother's claim that baptism was not in the best interests of her son or the state. The mother argued that conversion left a child without family or social supports, but the care shown by her son's godparents disproved her complaint. The godparents provided him with an education, vocational training, and close oversight.[128]

In a conversion case much later in the century, Rukhel Volkova Liublinskaia, from Khudiakov (Kiev Province), secretly left her parents' home and approached a nearby Chigirin deacon to convert. The deacon suggested that she go to the St. Vladimir Brotherhood in Kiev, where she could distance herself from her Jewish family and have space and solitude to prepare for baptism. Because she was poor and unable to travel to Kiev, the deacon agreed to shelter her, prepare her for conversion, and find local godparents. The woman who agreed to be the godmother, the wife of a Chigirin notary, asked that the conversion take place locally so that she could properly care for her future goddaughter. The Kiev Ecclesiastic Consistory granted permission for the local baptism, which took place on April 3, 1894, conducted by the Chigirin archpriest Kydritskii.[129] The godmother's role here sheds light on an aspect of cultural contact and social encounter rarely discussed in relation to conversion.

Aside from formal godparents, local landowners or bureaucrats sometimes mentored neophytes or provided shelter while looking for an institution that could support the aspiring convert. This is evident in, as discussed earlier in the chapter, Sofia Chevskaia taking Pera Girsenovich under her wing, and in Kotov, an influential person in Pinsk, helping Meri Zalmanova Yafo. In still another case, the teenager Rakhil Miller, who converted in 1909, was closely tied to Olekhnovich, a worker at the Vilna railroad station, whom Miller intended to ask to be her post-baptism "father," as he was a deeply religious man and had no children of his own.[130]

In and out of the army, the demand for godparents often outweighed the supply of committed Christians willing to "adopt" and provide for neophytes. In 1854, at the height of cantonist conversions, when the annual number of Jewish conversions reached an all-time high of 4,439, the commander of the Kiev Cantonist Battalion issued a call for thirty pairs of godparents to come to the Kiev Pechersk Feodosiev Church on June 6 at 8 in the morning for the conversion of 239 Jewish cantonists; the commander asked the godparents to specify how many recruits they were willing to adopt.[131] In the civilian sector, the St. Petersburg shelter experienced a dearth of godparents between 1875 and 1878. According to Archpriest Briantsev, not enough people wanted to take on the responsibility of supporting and assisting Jewish converts. He specifically expressed concern that two boys and two girls currently preparing for baptism would not have godparents.[132] In the provinces, an Orthodox journalist lamented that conversion assistance too often fell on parish priests alone, and that it was often difficult for them to find godparents who could team up with them in the task of sheltering, supporting, and training neophytes for productive lives as Christians. The author, Pavlovskii, argued that shelters for converts like the Mariinsko-Sergievskii Shelter in St. Petersburg needed to be opened in the southwest region.[133] In 1883 *Kievlianin* ran a piece about the difficulties experienced by the St. Vladimir Brotherhood, citing its need for more donors and more local Christians who could help converts (many with no skills) secure jobs. It noted that one of the Brotherhood's key tasks in assisting converts was locating godparents who could provide for them and ensure that they would have a livelihood after baptism.[134]

A sampling of conversion cases shows that godparents came from all sectors of Russian society—clergy and their wives; soldiers and their wives; local administrators and their wives; nobles and peasants. In this way, Jewish conversion involved native Christians in an immediate and personal way. Converts were not just nameless souls needing salvation; they were people with emotional and material needs who inhabited the same local environs. In this light, Jewish conversion was not just the business of the state or church; it also concerned lay people and hinged on the social and religious consciousness of the local Christian population. As with interfaith social encounters that spawned or facilitated baptism, godparents further grounded the conversion experience in the immediacy of place and the cultural contact between religious communities in the imperial Russian borderlands.

꩜

Returning to the Goldferbova conversion story that oriented where and how Jews in the imperial Russia western provinces found the contacts and daring to convert, one cannot overlook the fact that the provincial tavern was both an exit and (at times) an entrance for Jews to both leave and rejoin the local Jewish community. Many converts like Goldferbova had relationships with neighboring Christians that enabled and often propelled their conversions, but those relationships were grounded in a broader political economy wherein entire Jewish communities were constituted by virtue of the economic coexistence of Jews and Christians in the towns and villages of the conquered former Polish-Lithuanian lands. As such, conversions lay bare the everyday social interactions between Jews and their neighbors that often transpired within one's home or home community, under the controlling gaze of family and friends. It is this aspect of close interfaith interaction—the proximity of convert and Jew—that is the subject of the next chapter.

CHAPTER 4

FROM VODKA TO VIOLENCE

RACHEL-LEAH GOLDFERBOVA, the convert from Judaism to Russian Orthodoxy profiled in the popular press in 1866, was presented as an icon of voluntary Jewish conversion and interfaith sociability in the reform era after the imperial Russian state had exited the military conversion business. Though living in a Jewish community in the northwest provinces with a historically strong Polish Catholic presence, Rachel-Leah found Russian Orthodoxy by socializing with Russian soldiers in her family's tavern. And yet, her conversion was anything but smooth. Her family and community kidnapped her before she could reach the baptismal font. Even before her abduction, local priests in the Brest-Litovsk area refused her request to convert out of fear that local Jews would intervene. Rather than touting provincial sociability as a powerful platform for Jewish conversion in the multiconfessional western borderlands, the reform-era ecclesiastic press used Rachel-Leah's story to warn of Jewish violence.

The tavern sociability that nurtured Rachel-Leah's conversion to Orthodoxy, as discussed in the preceding chapter, was also accompanied by violence, another aspect of neighborly interfaith encounters in the provinces.[1] The Goldferbova story, published in the throes of Russification campaigns in the western provinces following the 1863 Polish insurrection, drew readers' attention to the double-edged nature of close Jewish-Christian living in the imperial borderlands.[2] On the one hand, in the triumphant narrative of the story, the small town tavern functioned as a site of interfaith encounter and exit from Judaism via conversion; on the other hand, in the more pessimistic vein of the article, the tavern—or the confessionally mixed spaces of the Pale of Jewish Settlement more broadly—stood as a site of conflict and territorial dispute, a place vulnerable to convert relapse into a Jewish milieu. Conversions were both rooted in and compromised by place. Conversion as a form of boundary crossing raised anxieties about close interfaith living and became a flashpoint for negotiating the local politics of confessional coexistence and religious toleration.[3]

While the story of Rachel-Leah in many ways set the tone for late imperial discourses on Jewish fanaticism and violence, it cannot be dismissed as a product of top-down Russian Judeophobia. This story and many others like it mask a long history of Jewish-convert tensions that percolated in the small towns and villages of the western provinces. Not only the popular press, but even artists in the late-imperial period linked Jewishness and violence to conversions. In 1900, an obscure drama, *Kontrabandisty* (The Smugglers), produced by A. S. Suvorin, the editor of the popular, right-wing daily newspaper *Novoe vremia* (New Times), debuted in St. Petersburg. Showcasing an array of depraved Jewish characters, the play featured a side plot about a Jewish smuggler's daughter who fell in love with a Russian soldier. With the blessing of a rabbi, the father killed his daughter to prevent her conversion.[4] In 1899 the naturalist Ukrainian painter Nikolai Kornilovich Pimonenko linked Jewish violence and fanaticism to religious conversion in his painting *Zhertva fanatizma* (Victim of Fanaticism) (see Figure 4.1). The painting portrays a young woman convert from Judaism being abused and intimidated by her rural Jewish family and community. Pimonenko explained that his sketch was inspired by a Jewish woman in a late imperial Russian shtetl who converted to marry her Christian lover and was then tormented by her former coreligionists. Contemporary Jews decried the play and the painting as anti-Semitic and protested. Jewish and non-Jewish students in St. Petersburg organized theater riots against Suvorin's production and some Jews appropriated Pimonenko's sketch and another like it for circulation on a postcard with the accompanying Hebrew words *Hameshumedet* (Apostate) and *Habogedet* (Traitoress), thus re-narrating the story to cast blame on the neophyte and legitimize the ire of the Jewish community.[5]

Figure 4.1 Nikolai Kornilovich Pimonenko, *Zhertva fanatizma* (Victim of Fanaticism), 1899. Wikipedia Commons.

Violent images of Jews in popular culture media in the late imperial period, buoying up claims that minority fanaticism was inimical to the peaceful,
tolerant political order, were part of the discourse in post-reform Russia on
Jews as a predatory minority. And yet stories of violence also existed beyond the popular media in the realms of state and church related to issues
of conversion and close confessional living. These stories unfolded in provincial small towns and villages characterized by face-to-face living, where
people knew one another and constantly scrutinized each other's actions. In
these stories of violence in response to conversions, confessional feuds became family affairs—they were fought out within the family, stereotypically
violent and malevolent, but the stakes were empire-wide since the overriding
issue was the breakdown of the imperial, patriarchal family through conversion. We catch a glimpse here of Jewish politics, shaped through empire and
the confessional state, and the ways Jews worked through state documentary
practices to alternatively endorse and resist conversion, and even mimic the
previously violent, coercive practices of the state toward converts.[6] Through-

out the sources is a discursive emphasis on Jewish women's vulnerability to Jewish violence whereby women became lightning rods for male anxieties about conversion and powerful figuring grounds for articulating concerns about confessional coexistence, religious toleration, and the contest between individual religious choice and communal solidarity.[7] These stories attest to ongoing Jewish-convert relations and tensions, rifts within Jewish communities over conversion exploding into violence, and confessional migrations as a way to exert familial agency for unhappy children and spouses.

Some of the stories of Jewish violence and resistance analyzed here are anti-Semitic concoctions and others are well documented. The validity of the stories, though, is less important than the point that violence over conversion—whether rhetorical or physical—was grounded in close interfaith social encounters that animated confessional disputes. These stories of violence also reveal how minorities won state patronage from imperial religious toleration, and how the Russian Orthodox Church—legally privileged as the "preeminent and predominant" state church—articulated anxieties about imperial support for the tolerated foreign confessions. The stories shed light on the dynamic aspects of empire, which opened up a broad playing field for Jewish political activity, from submission to contestation to mimicry. The social threads of conversion and the confessional state's empowerment of minorities are explored here through the themes of violence and fanaticism, communal discipline, and family and gender.

Stories of Jewish Violence

Sociability and violence existed in dynamic tension in the tavern and multiconfessional spaces of the imperial Russian western provinces. As in fictional accounts of the tavern by Jewish writers S. Ansky and Sholem Asch, actual taverns brought people together to chat and seek succor in a common space, but the uninhibited environment, permeated by drunkenness, also fostered violence. Ansky's short story "In the Tavern" describes drunken gangs and the curses and physical fighting between female patrons. In both Ansky's and Asch's stories, male Christian patrons lust after the Jewish female tavernkeepers. In Anksy's story, the patron Abramov flirtatiously taunts Khanke, yelling at her that he wants her to convert, "you accursed Jewess," but at the same time eyes her with adoration.[8] In Asch's novel *Salvation* (Yiddish orig.,

Der tehilim yid), tavern violence turns into an attempted rape by a patron of the tavernkeeper's beautiful daughter Reyzele, whom her mother is always trying to protect from the rowdy clients and their lustful gaze.[9] It is this underside of the tavern and the multiconfessional spaces of provincial life that are given voice in narratives of conversion violence.

Jewish resistance to conversions through petitions or physical coercion is continuously evidenced in state and provincial archives from as early as the turn of the nineteenth century. Reports of Jewish violence filed by converts and ecclesiastic personnel mapped the difficulties of Jewish conversion onto the proximity of converts to their Jewish families in the western provinces. Several converts from Judaism filed complaints with civil authorities against family members and entire *kehilot* (Jewish communities) for attempting to stymie their conversions.[10] In the diocesan presses and in the Synod's communications, parish priests admitted that they shied away from converting local Jews out of fear for their lives.[11] It was sentiments like this that prompted the founding and imperial support of several lay-led shelters for converted and converting Jews that operated in St. Petersburg, Kiev, Vilna, and Odessa in the late imperial period, notably far from the small towns and villages where family dramas of conversion played out.[12] The narratives of violence analyzed here were animated by the state and its empowerment of confessional orthodoxies through metrical record keeping, conscription, taxation, and family and religious law. Imperial toleration empowered minorities to discipline members of their confessional communities.

Press coverage of such cases in provincial newspapers, authored by clerics and converts from Judaism, offered sensational images of Jews coming out in mass to thwart conversions or kidnap the converted. When the convert Klei returned to Volynia Province to proselytize to his Jewish parents, local Jews threatened him to the point that he had to take shelter with a police officer.[13] When the convert Brin returned to Dinaburg to make contact with his estranged teenage Jewish son, Brin approached his sister's house only to be rebuffed by Jewish neighbors, who verbally and physically attacked him.[14] An Orthodox journalist recounted the story of an Orthodox seminarian who was escorting a new convert from church to the seminary when he was attacked by Jews. If not for his ability to repel the Jews with sticks and quickly escape into a courtyard, the Jewish mob would have allegedly snatched the convert.[15] The St. Vladimir Brotherhood in Kiev complained that although it could protect neophytes in its shelter, it could not safeguard them on the streets from Jewish family and friends who came to Kiev to pursue and kidnap them, acts it labeled Jewish "fanatic revenge."[16] These narratives of violence even reached into evangelical presses reporting on missionary work in the Russian Empire. In 1868 the English journal *Scattered Nation* reported on the conversion of Rabbi Gurland, who would later become head of the Lutheran Church in the Baltics. Based on a baptismal ceremony in Kishinev at the time, during which local Jews gathered together "intending to murder the baptized goldsmith on his way back" from church, Pastor Faltin asked Gurland if he wanted police protection at his conversion to stave off "the Jews [who] had been heard to say that when the rabbi was baptized, they would make away with him."[17] Such Jewish violence, whether real or imagined (perhaps to excuse unsuccessful missionary work), was described in spatial terms as a kind of confessional turf war, at once demarcating and policing the borders of religious community.

Though stories of violence overwhelmingly focused on Jews, Jews too partook in charges of religious violence. Stories of convert kidnappings typically originated from either Jews or converts themselves. Jewish families and communal leaders at times claimed that Christians abducted Jewish children in order to convert them.[18] The abduction narrative, in which Jews themselves linked conversion to violence, served to challenge baptisms and rhetorically expressed parents' disbelief that baptisms could be voluntary. Guilty parties named by parents included local clergy, police, and residents, usually peasants. Parents often tacked on charges of theft to emphasize that their children's conversions had little to do with religious conviction. In the abduction narrative female children featured prominently, with parents rejecting the agency of the convert as a kidnapped victim.[19] Yet the voices of litigious parents are often overpowered in archival sources by the complaints of children about forceful and often violent Jewish attempts to return converted kin to the community. These convert-driven stories functioned to underscore the urgency of a neophyte's plea for ecclesiastic shelter or an expedited conversion. Leading up to his 1862 conversion, Il'ia Abramovich Eliovich asked the Vilna Consistory for shelter "in a place safe from the persecution of Jews."[20] At a judicial level, such stories were re-purposed to explain converts' unorthodox relationship with Jews following baptism, and possibly even their temporary relapse to Judaism. Sheina Dlugolenskaia, the adolescent daughter of a village tavernkeeper keeper discussed in the last chapter, linked her fears of Jewish intervention to her concern that conversion was a protracted process and she would need shelter during that time. At one point, she charged her Jewish family and community with abduction, which was thwarted by local peasants and provided the opportunity for the peasants to offer her shelter until the time of her baptism and marriage.[21]

Anna Kviatkovskaia, introduced in Chapter 3, accused her family and community of holding her against her will and of theft in an attempt to explain her very unorthodox contact and residence with Jews following her 1819 conversion to Russian Orthodoxy. In 1825 Anna sent a complaint to Tsarevich Konstantin, accusing her father and the Merech Jewish community (Vilna Province) of coercing her to return to Judaism, robbing her, twice kidnapping her, and forcing her to marry a Jew.[22] After the first abduction, Anna escaped to a local landowner who helped her enter a convent and bring her case to the police. According to the criminal court investigation, Anna "complained about the torment of the Jews," and Tsarevich Konstantin in reviewing the case inquired if Anna had been "shielded from the persecution of the Jews."[23]

The second abduction came in 1823. While working with an acting troupe in Keidany (Vilna Province), Anna's brother Leib found her and forced her to swear under the threat of excommunication from the Jewish community, or *herem*, to renounce Christianity. He then forcibly brought her to Congress Poland and then back to Grodno Province, where she was married to the Jew Eina. At some point thereafter, Anna and Eina were in Vilna and by mutual agreement, Eina gave Anna a Jewish divorce in the presence of a local rabbi.[24] Despite Anna's prolonged relapse and even Jewish marriage and divorce, her narrative of Jewish coercion was backed by the criminal court investigation. Because of confusion among bureaucrats and lack of coordination between the western provinces and the palatinates of Congress Poland there were delays in bringing the guilty Jews to justice. The prolonged relapses in the Kviatkovskaia case—entailing marriage with children, and even her marriage ending only after a proper Jewish legal divorce—provoke some incredulity as to how coerced she really was to return to everyday Jewish life. The case sheds light on the rhetorical gesture to violence as a way to cover up convert-Jewish relations.

Converts' claims to have been abducted often led to criminal indictments against Jews for "seducing" converts away from Orthodox Christianity to Judaism. For example, in 1879 a man identified simply as Pravoslavnyi ("Russian Orthodox") wrote into the Kiev diocesan journal about the attempted abduction by Jews of the convert from Judaism Vera Shpanerova, who was married to the brigadier notary Nikolai Logvinovich and was a mother of two. Baptized in 1873, Vera—originally from Podolia Province—married a Russian Orthodox man and settled in Zhmerinka, Kiev Province. On October 25, 1879, she left home to go to the nearby town of Vinnitsa to do some shopping and never returned. After several days, her husband began searching, but in vain. Then, on November 11, the husband received a telegram from Pravoslavnyi, who reported that the missing wife was in Berdichev (Kiev Province), where her relatives were trying to return her to Judaism. According to Vera's later testimony, she was captured in Vinnitsa (Podolia Province) by her mother and Jews from her Podolian hometown, who then brought her to Berdichev to her sister's home where she was locked up and given the option to go abroad and marry a Jewish man. She refused until conditions worsened. She then agreed to relapse in order to escape surveillance, whereupon she contacted her husband. With her husband's appearance in Berdichev and police intervention, her family and several local Jews were arrested on charges of seducing a Christian woman to abandon Russian Orthodoxy.[25]

In 1888 Shmul and Chava Mintses and an array of friends and relatives were arraigned in a Warsaw circuit court on charges of "seducing" Maria Lysak, née Matlia Mintses, away from Russian Orthodoxy. Matlia had previously converted to Russian Orthodoxy and married Lysak, a medical assistant in the army's Cossack division. Shmul, the father, was apprehended by police in Berlin after kidnapping his daughter on Russian soil, forcibly capturing her, hiding her, and transporting her abroad with the intention of separating her from her Russian husband and returning her to Judaism.[26]

Jewish kidnapping, at times, was cast by converts and the right-wing popular press as a violent stepping stone to the vengeful murder of Jewish apostates. In 1886 a Kiev district court in Chigirin found ten Jews guilty of "seducing" the female convert Yevdokiia Shevchenkova back to Judaism. Seven men were sentenced to eight years of hard labor, and three women were given five years and four months of hard labor. Shevchenkova initially re-

ported to police that her Jewish family abducted her from her godfather with
the intention to kill her. Court transcripts even referred to her Jewish uncle,
who was on the road with her when she reported her case to the authorities,
as her "executioner" (*palach*). For the right-wing newspaper *Novorossiiskii
telegraf*, the Jewish seduction in the Shevchenkova case did not convey the
full truth of the crime, which was nothing short of the "systematic and brutal persecution of a Jewess who had converted to Christianity." Rather than
just reporting the case as one of Jews trying to curb apostasy or a neophyte
regretting her decision to convert, the press intervened to remind readers that
what was involved was violent and systematic Jewish "seduction."[27]

Odesskii vestnik (Odessa Herald) provided a fuller account of the judicial proceedings regarding Shevchenkova's abduction and relapse to Judaism
by retelling both Shevchenkova's initial and follow-up testimony. According
to initial testimony, her Jewish family and other Jewish conspirators abducted her in order to murder her. Jews reportedly rebuked Shevchenkova
for causing her sister "shame," and her father supposedly told his brother, the
"executioner," to take her away so that "my eyes do not see her anymore."[28]
Shevchenkova initially reported that she was tortured and beaten, and that
her Jewish kidnappers pinched her and pricked her with needles—an act
commonly associated with ritual murder. Traces of scratches on her wrists
were evidence of the ultimate goal of her attackers. On the stand, though,
Shevchenkova broke down and admitted she had run away to her family. She
pleaded that she was young and ignorant and loved her parents. She admitted that she concocted the whole abduction story since she was afraid her
godfather would beat her. Her Jewish uncle, one of the key defendants in the
case, confirmed that Shevchenkova wanted to return to Judaism and that, at
the behest of his brother, he traveled around with his niece to find her work.[29]

At the time of the trial, Shevchenkova had been married for three
months to a peasant, from a regiment stationed in Kherson Province. Though
she had said her love for her parents was part of the emotional confusion
triggering her relapse, she later claimed on the stand that her parents did
not love her as they had always made her work from a young age for other
Jews, and they used her hard-earned money to buy a dress for her sister.
Shevchenkova's multiple narratives employed violence as a way to articulate
intracommunal tensions. She tapped into gender stereotypes to legitimize

her relapse as coerced, and she used family tensions and sibling rivalry to distance herself from her family as she stabilized her reentry into Russian Orthodoxy through marriage.

The geographic terrain of the case reflects the interethnic matrix of provincial conversions and illustrates that proximity could breed both intimacy and violence. Shevchenkova converted and settled in the same village as her Jewish parents. After her disappearance, her godfather went to her parents' house looking for her. The proximity between the convert, her family, and her godparents seems to have ignited the multiple self-fashionings of the confused convert, torn between her two worlds. Like the Deborah Lewkowicz case in Austrian Galicia studied by Rachel Manekin, Shevchenkova's conversion was not a one-time decision or communal reorientation but rather a protracted process of circulating between two nearby worlds.

In line with the gendered nature of victimhood in many of the stories of violence presented here, it is not coincidental that most stories of communal kidnappings involve women. Perhaps the communal stakes were higher with female runaways due to family concerns (the status of children), or perhaps female runaways were more common, especially in the late imperial period, when female conversions were on the rise. Or, if we read these stories with due skepticism, the very charge of abduction—grounded in the assumed vulnerability of women—is a gendered trope that female converts marshaled in defense of their unorthodox contacts with Jewish friends and relatives.[30] If the number of Jewish female conversions started to surpass male conversions in the late imperial period, and marriages to Christians often accompanied female conversions, then increased Jewish attempts to foil conversions—especially romantic conversions—would have disproportionately involved women.

The story of Jewish abduction, though, was not restricted to women. In 1842 the Jewish conscript Aizikovich professed his desire to convert to Russian Orthodoxy in the army. In his conversion file, he explained that this was actually the second time he attempted conversion. The first time, he sought conversion in a Catholic monastery, but while he was off grounds on one occasion, his Jewish family snatched him and passed him between various homes in order to hide him from the local gentry. Eventually, he was given as a recruit—perhaps because his wayward behavior made him expendable to the community, which was always hungry for easy recruits. Ironically, enlistment offered him the perfect safe venue for conversion, this time to Orthodoxy.[31]

Fanaticism and Ritual Murder

With the growth of the popular press in the late imperial period and public access to transcripts of jury trials in the reformed legal system, journalists seized on stories of Jewish resistance to their converted kin as a form of intolerant, religious zealotry in the modern era, countering voluntary baptisms with violence.[32] Reports of Jewish violence—physical attacks, kidnapping, and murder—accentuated the proximity of converts to their home communities, and stories of Jewish resistance to conversion provided fodder for casting Jews as religiously intolerant in an empire that officially practiced toleration. Jews' violence toward their converted kin marked them as not just religious but social fanatics—willing to put faith before family. The popular press' circulation of images of Jewish "fanaticism" in the late imperial period came on the heels of coercive baptisms of Jewish cantonist recruits in the pre-reform army and the increased incidence of such converts retroactively challenging their baptisms in the reformed judicial system of Tsar Alexander II.[33]

The Russian press carried a spate of stories in the 1870s and 1880s on Jewish murder of converts. In 1876 a fifteen-year-old female convert from Kiev Province was reportedly found dead shortly before her marriage to a peasant.[34] In 1878, a year after Khayka Prizant's conversion in order to marry her peasant lover, the girl's corpse was found in the charred remains of a local inn. Coroners identified the cause of death as strangulation prior to the fire and they noted that she was five months pregnant. The father was accused of arson and murder; the court acquitted him but surmised that the crime was committed by other Jews seeking revenge.[35] In 1886 the Volynian ecclesiastic press reported the murder of a Jewish girl who left home declaring her desire to marry a Christian; the reporter asserted that she was murdered by her fanatic Jewish family, who preferred death to the blight of intermarriage.[36] It was in light of such publicized acts of Jewish "fanaticism" that the conservative Kiev newspaper *Kievlianin* in 1884 called for more legal protections for married Jewish women who converted and whose Jewish husbands refused to grant a divorce in order to free them to marry a Christian. Though imperial law clearly stated that in these cases any children born to the couple would be considered Christian and had to be raised as such, the press contended that Jewish men did not fear such a scenario since they often refused divorce in order to seek religious vengeance through murder.[37]

The trope of the fanatic Jew willing to murder for the faith took on concrete form when it was marshaled as evidence by the prosecution in the prominent murder trial of Maria Drich, a Christian domestic servant in the employ of a Jewish family in Liutsin (Vitebsk Province). Unlike other reported cases of murder where a Jew took revenge on a convert from Judaism, this case is unique in that Jews were accused of murdering a Christian woman who was romantically attracting a Jewish adolescent to conversion. A new riff on the medieval ritual murder charge, the Drich affair illustrates the web of contacts, cross-cultural knowledge, and neighborly relations that surrounded small-town conversions and structured the narrative of confessional intimacy, irrespective of the veracity of the accusation.

In November 1883 the second-guild Jewish merchant Zimel Abramov Lotsov, from Vitebsk Province, informed police that his Christian domestic servant had disappeared from his house one night after stealing from him and escaping with the help of a wagon that left tracks in the snow. Police searched for the young woman in the Liutsin environs, but could not find her. Then, in March 1884, a local fisherman found a woman's corpse in the river. Medical examiners confirmed that the victim was murdered by strangulation, then bound hand and foot to stakes and carried to the river where her body was tied to bricks and thrown into the water. Coroners identified the body as the missing servant Maria Drich.

Authorities arrested Zimel and his wife, Ester, together with two other Jews—Shmuil Leib Getselov Gurevich and Musa Khaimova Maikh—who were at the Lotsov home the night Drich disappeared. All were charged with premeditated murder and conspiracy to cover up the crime. The initial police investigation found several Christian female acquaintances of Drich who reported that Zimel's eldest son, Yankel, was in love with her and intended to convert to Catholicism to marry her. Witnesses testified that on the night Drich disappeared, a crowd of Jews gathered at the Lotsov home, and that Maria told a friend that she overheard a Jew utter the word "kosher," leading her to fear that she would not live through the night. Though the overheard word does not immediately conjure up murder, it is interesting that Maria was acquainted with Jewish parlance and somehow associated "kosher" with ritual slaughter (signaling her fear of a new kind of ritual murder to end an interfaith romance). One of her friends encouraged Maria to run from the house, but when she tried, the Lotsovs grabbed her hand and blocked her exit. Immediately after Drich's disappearance, the Lotsov family spread rumors that she had resurfaced in a distant village jail with a baby in tow. In the trial in April 1885 the prosecutor argued that these rumors together with Zimel's story to the police about a theft were just ruses by Liutsin Jews to deflect attention from the fact that Zimel, abetted by his wife and other Jews, murdered Drich to prevent their son from marrying a Christian.[38]

The prosecutor linked Drich's murder to the Lotsov parents by contending that Jews reacted violently when faced with a coreligionist's conversion. "You, members of the jury," concluded the prosecutor, "live among a Jewish population, and you are well aware what kinds of counteractions are used by them in cases where some Jew desires to convert to Christianity."[39] Following a guilty verdict, the defense attorney argued for a retrial, pointing out that the only evidence against the four defendants was the Christian stereotype of fanatic Jews: "The prosecutor, in his own words, said that 'Jews who convert to Christianity need to hide or otherwise they disappear.' In this way, accusations are immediately thrown in the eye regarding more than half of the worthy population of Liutsin, that they are capable, for religious reasons, of committing murder."[40] The case was tried a second time, and the Lotsovs were found guilty of murder and the other two Jews were acquitted.

Though in some ways a double fiction, a courtroom narrative buttressed by the trope of Jewish religious violence, the Drich case was built on the reality of close small-town living—intimate interconfessional relationships and visibility. The case turned on Christians and Jews living under the same roof; webs of neighborly relations and involvement in one another's daily affairs that spun tales of interconfessional romance and fear of discovery; and testimony that reconstructed the face-to-face dynamics of small-town living.

The Drich affair became the pendant case of the new Jewish ritual murder accusation, used as a frame of reference in the Judeophobic press, but the case did not stand alone. In 1881 *Kievlianin* reported on a Jewish underground adventure gone awry, ending in the murder of a sixteen-year-old male convert to Russian Orthodoxy. The boy's corpse was found in April 1879 in a river in the village of Vishnevets in the province of Volynia, and an investigation confirmed that this was the same boy who had gone missing from the nearby Pochaev Monastery in September 1878, just months after his conversion. According to the newspaper's account, Abrum Itsko Shmikler came to the monastery to convert in May 1878, and while there, told acquaintances that he feared Jewish relatives and friends, who would corner him every so often near the monastery and inveigh him to return to Judaism—either by threatening violence or offering him money (one Jew promised him 100 rubles collected among Vishnevets Jews if he relapsed).[41] On the night of September 13, 1878, Abrum disappeared from the monastery. According to the criminal investigation, three Jews found him in a garden near the monastery that evening, stuffed his mouth, and threatened to kill him if he screamed. They put him in a prepared cart, hid him in straw, hitched the cart to a wagon, and brought him to relatives in Austrian Galicia. After several weeks, Abrum was able to wrest himself away and approached a local Catholic priest for protection. The priest summoned the local gendarmerie commander, who put Abrum under administrative protection. Initially he had a guard trail Abrum, but the protection weakened and one day in December Abrum vanished. From then until the discovery of the corpse that spring in Vishnevets, Abrum was not heard from or seen. Several Jews were charged with either premeditated murder or knowing about the murder but failing to report it. In the end, the jury found an aunt and two uncles guilty of murder and one other party guilty of not reporting the murder to the authorities.[42]

In another case where Jews were accused of murder, as in the Drich trial the prosecution portrayed religiously inspired violence as a staple of the Jewish politics of avenging apostasy, especially incumbent on close relatives of the convert. By defining violence as a religious duty, the prosecution contributed to a public discourse on informal Jewish power that Judaized small-town space. Unlike Jewish literary representations of small towns that relegated non-Jews into the shadows of shtetl life, here a legal discourse portrayed Jews as practicing a physical politics of obliterating the non-Jew within, in this case Andrei Garun, a neophyte who tried to escape Jewish space. The traditional aspects of the charge of ritual murder were expressed in the description of the corpse: found in a river, bound by rope to stakes, and repeatedly punctured.

In 1889 *Kievlianin* reported on still another case, in this instance attempted murder of a Jewish man who had converted and married a Christian
peasant over a decade before his Jewish family attempted to exact revenge.
The report on the case, more than just repeating the popular trope of Jewish fanaticism, sought to demonstrate just how deep and long Jews harbored
aggression against apostates. On July 10, 1888, a pair of brothers in a village
in Lomzha Province (Congress Poland) were gathering mushrooms when
they came across a man "with a disfigured face and swollen eyes" lying in the
field unconscious. He turned out to be Frants Platovskii, a Jew who converted
fourteen years earlier, married a peasant, entered the military and served in the
Caucasus, and was discharged three years earlier. He lived with his wife and
four children in the village of Bosevo and worked as a shoemaker. To supple-
ment his meager earnings, Platovskii often begged in the surrounding villages.
He had Jewish relatives in the area whom he ran into occasionally, but he had
no relationship with them. On one of his begging trips, he entered the village
of Dlugosedlo, where his uncle David Platovskii and the latter's son-in-law,
Yankel Kokhman, lived. In the evening, Frants met his uncle on the street;
the uncle asked about how he was doing and invited him to his home to give
him some money. At the edge of the village, as they passed a church with a
one-horse cart standing outside, David with Yankel's help grabbed Frants and
carted him away with a bag over his head. In the forest, they dragged him out
of the cart, throttled him, and poured sulfuric acid into his mouth and doused
his face with it. Kokhman then struck Frants on the cheek with the bottle
after which Frants fainted and his relatives covered him with brushwood and
left. Frants stated that this attempt on his life was revenge (*mest'*) by his family for converting. Acknowledging that conversion was a blight on a Jewish
family, Frants noted that his two younger sisters never married as a result of
his apostasy. Frants's Jewish family was arrested that November and Platovskii
and Kokhman were found guilty and sentenced to the deprivation of all rights
and exile with hard labor for six and four years, respectively.[43]

In this story of Jewish fanaticism, revenge, delayed fourteen years, is
linked to the victim's vulnerable sisters, who were still anathema to potential
suitors. Implicit is the charge that Jews would go to any length to excise a
convert, erase the shame he brought down on his family, and sacrifice him for
the religious purity of the community. This, in short, implies that vengeance

murders are normative, even commanded, among Jews. Aside from the role of female vulnerability in this story of religious violence—a criticism of Jewish intolerance of converts, which harmed the neophyte's unmarried sisters—the report is noteworthy for the rural setting of the attempted murder and the proximity of Frants to his Jewish family. Platovskii married a local peasant and settled into a Christian life not far from his hometown, but through routine, local encounters he maintained contacts with Jews.

The Jewish Family as Disciplinary Agent

Although it is hard to ascertain the truth of individual charges of Jewish violence, there is ample evidence of many forms of Jewish resistance to conversion that the absolutist and confessional state enabled through religious toleration and attempts to make its subjects "legible."[44] Stories of violence in part reflected a feeling of religious disempowerment or vulnerability by church and state. Indeed, Jews and converts from Judaism navigated the confessional state for their own ends: to consolidate confessional boundaries in the face of conversion. Through documentation practices, the state tracked Jews. At the same time, Jews played on the state's documentation and tracking practices for their own purposes—to track other Jews and discipline them. In disciplining converts, Jews both subverted and appropriated state domination through documentation, registration, and conscription.

Archival evidence of Jewish intimidation of apostates abounds. In 1862 the mother superior of a Grodno convent petitioned the Vilna Orthodox Consistory to rush its decision on the conversion of nineteen-year-old Sora Efraimova Goldshteinova in order to free the convent from disturbances by Jews trying to thwart her conversion.[45] In 1864 the priest of the Bel'sk Nikolaev Church similarly asked the Vilna Consistory to speed up the conversion of Malka Kuks, fearing that the longer she stayed in the district town of Bel'sk preparing for conversion, the greater the difficulty (*zatrudnenie*) local Jews would pose.[46] Two years later, the nineteen-year-old Oshmiany Jewess Sora Senderovna Arliukova, seeking to convert to Orthodoxy, asked for shelter in a Vilna convent since she feared the reaction of her family and community; permission was granted.[47] In 1870 and 1871 mother superiors in Vilna and Grodno petitioned the Vilna Consistory to provide shelter for young female Jews seeking protection in urban monasteries from Jews

who were pursuing them.[48] In 1892 Mira Beker petitioned the Vilna archbishop, claiming that after announcing her desire to convert to her mother
and stepfather, they tormented her and then moved her to an out of the way
hole-in-the-wall to "destroy" her. According to Beker, it was only because
good Christian neighbors saved her from her parents' abusive hands that she
was able to survive.[49] In 1899 the Jewess Masha Teitelbaum, who was living
with an Orthodox family in Lida (Vilna Province) and under strict surveillance to keep her whereabouts hidden, requested an expedited conversion
from the Vilna Consistory since her Jewish family was searching for her.[50]

Jewish intimidation of apostates even caused some ecclesiastic personnel
to consider rejecting Jewish neophytes or drastically reducing assistance to
them. In June 1874 Pera Girsenovich, whom we first met in the Introduction,
petitioned to convert to Orthodoxy and asked to be accepted into the Vilna
Mariinskii Convent for training and protection from Jews.[51] The mother superior, Igumenia Flaviana, lamented that proselytism among Jews was almost
always accompanied by intrigue such as police searches and charges of theft
against the neophytes. In Pera's case alone, police had already twice come to
the convent to carry out investigations at the behest of Pera's relatives. Pera's
mother formally complained that her daughter stole her mother's possessions
as she ran away to convert, and on these grounds, the mother asked to see her
daughter in order to retrieve the stolen goods.[52] The mother superior concluded that either the convent would persist with its goals and withstand any
unpleasantness from Jews, or it would eliminate such problems altogether by
restricting Jewish converts to a specific length of stay under its protection.[53]

A similar environment of fear of local Jews permeated the Kiev Consistory. In 1894 the consistory permitted a Berdichev Jewess to convert in the
town of Uman. According to her petition to Archpriest Narkiss Oltarzhevskii
of the Uspenskii-Sobornii Church in Uman, Paulina Fried thought that since
she lived in Berdichev, a city "heavily populated by Jews," it would be better
to convert in Uman, to avoid "the unpleasantness that I may encounter due
to their fanaticism."[54] The Kiev Consistory honored Fried's request to convert
in Uman.

Overall, archival records suggest that, short of outright kidnapping, Jewish families frequently pursued their converted kin, intimidating converts and
clerics alike, who feared the consequences of entering into local confessional

politics. While the trope of Jewish pursuit sometimes accelerated conversion proceedings, it is unclear if a physical Jewish presence intimated kidnapping or if a politics of persistent legal intervention to disrupt conversions generated fear. In the case of Pera Girsenovich, it seems that the convent's leaders allowed police to intervene and enter the premises to look into charges of theft that could potentially undermine the Orthodox Church's hold on neophytes. Jews, in this scenario, called in the authorities to take the baptism proceedings out of the jurisdiction of the Orthodox Church and into civil hands. Perhaps clerics' anxiety about the presence of local Jews reflected concern that civil authorities could encroach on the church's authority.

Jewish communities used a variety of state documentation and registration tactics to subvert conversion proceedings—for instance, by withholding identity papers or confounding attempts to ascertain a neophyte's name and age. Jewish communities also took advantage of the taxation system and conscription to thwart and discipline apostates, and, using laws that required conversion to be voluntary, they challenged the moral and mental capacity of neophytes. Central to all of these forms of communal resistance is that the state empowered Jewish clerics to maintain vital records of Jews and invested power in religious communal affiliation as a means of organizing and categorizing its vast and diverse population. Ironically, since conversion at a bureaucratic level entailed a change in one's confession and thus in one's official status, Jewish clerics and community leaders were brought into the process and consulted as the gatekeepers of neophytes' estate registration, identity papers, and statistical information—name, date and place of birth, confession, marital status, family status, criminal record, and so on. The involvement of Jewish community leaders could go as far as a rabbi meeting with a priest at a police station to witness a Jew's application to be baptized.[55] At times, state rabbis or communal spokesmen confirmed critical biographical information and a neophyte's voluntary desire to convert (see Figure 4.2); many times, though, Jews used the disciplinary practices of the state to subvert the state's access to converts.[56] Either way, as the Kiev police chief made clear to Girsh Yankelev Volinskii, who was preparing for conversion in the St. Vladimir Brotherhood's Kiev shelter in 1904, he needed to go to his local rabbi in the place in which he was officially registered in order to obtain the necessary metrical records for his conversion proceedings.[57]

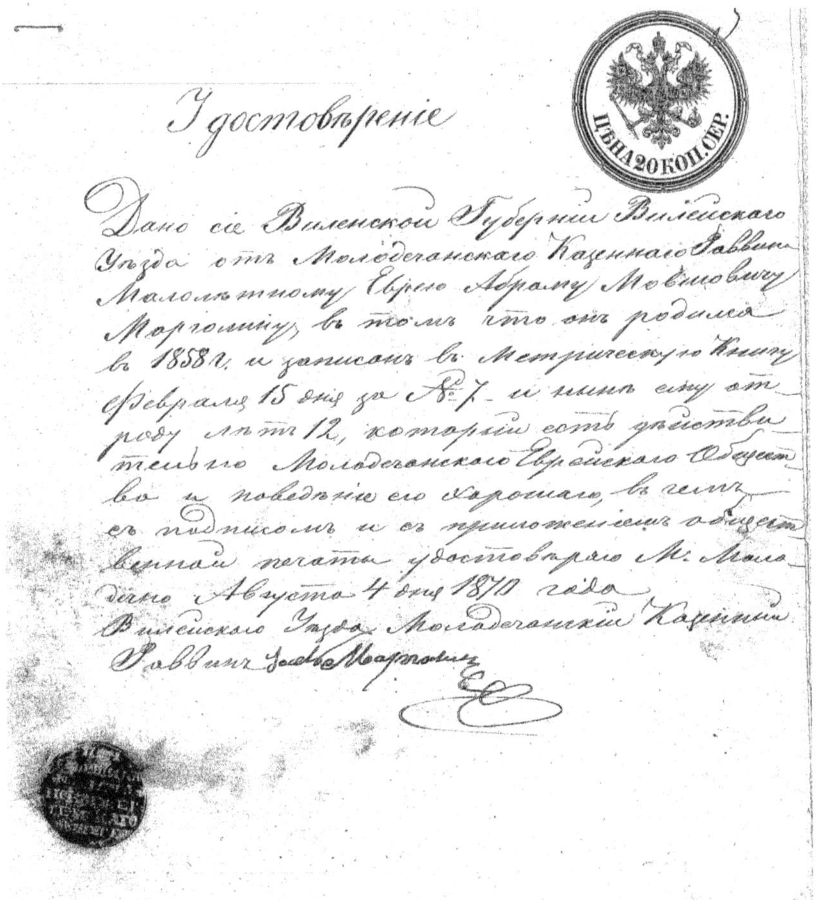

ЦѢНА 20 КОП. СЕР.

Удостовѣреніе

Дано сіе Виленской Губерніи Вилейскаго Уѣзда отъ Молодечанскаго Казеннаго Раввина малолѣтному Еврею Абраму Мовшовичу Морголину, въ томъ что онъ родился въ 1858 г. и записанъ въ Метрическую Книгу Февраля 15 дня за № 7 и нынѣ ему отъ роду лѣтъ 12, который есть дѣйствительнаго Молодечанскаго Еврейскаго Общества и поведенія его хорошаго, въ чемъ съ подписомъ и съ приложеніемъ общественной печати удостовѣряю М. Молодечно Августа 4 дня 1870 года
Вилейскаго Уѣзда Молодечанскій Казенный Раввинъ Іосель Маргалинъ

Figure 4.2 Crown Rabbi of Molodechno (Vilna Province) Yosel Margolin's confirmation of a neophyte's metrical record, age, and behavior, 1870. YIVO RG 46, IV:92, l. 3, Conversion of the Jew Abram Movshovich Morgolin, 1870.

In a case that came to the St. Petersburg military governor in 1823, a convert from Judaism to Orthodoxy, Benedikt Rybakovskii, complained that he could not furnish the necessary papers for his post-baptism relocation to the capital due to the "unavoidable slowness" with which the Jewish community responded to the paperwork of deregistering him from the Vilna townsman estate. Officials in St. Petersburg confirmed that Jewish communities tended to keep converts hostage by continuing to tax them and forcing them to meet other obligations incumbent on registered community members, in addition to "pursuing them" for leaving the faith. Responding to this supposedly well-known situation, the Senate in 1820 instructed provincial administrators in the Pale of Jewish Settlement that they could arrange for converts to be deregistered from their estates without having to go through the Jewish community. In response to Rybakovskii's complaint, the St. Petersburg provincial administration instructed officials in Vilna Province to carry out the estate change despite the Jewish community's delaying tactics.[58] As late as 1876 the Russian Orthodox press was still complaining about Jewish communities withholding metrical records from converts and thus forestalling their conversion.[59]

Although the Senate's 1820 directive to the provinces portrayed imperial will and bureaucratic action as one, fluid continuum, in practice the centralizing pretensions of the autocracy were constantly undermined by the sheer size and scope of the bureaucracy. Although legally converts were supposed to be deregistered from their Jewish communities and issued new identity papers, practical obstacles to communication between provincial officials and local clerics often undermined this norm. In 1871 the Jew Zakharia Stein from Friedrichstadt (Kurland Province) was detained in the district of Bel'sk (Grodno Province) for lacking identity papers. Stein subsequently expressed his desire to convert to Orthodoxy, and a local Bel'sk cleric started conversion training. After some investigations, Grodno officials instructed Bel'sk police to send Stein back to Kurland since he was found to be a draft dodger. Despite clerics' objections, the Vilna Consistory ruled that Stein had to return to Kurland and initiate a conversion petition there, where local clergy could intervene in local registration politics.[60] This case shows the extent to which Jewish communal authority over conscripts could potentially override the Orthodox Church's license to baptize nonbelievers, and the politics of identification and record keeping could operate independently of baptismal proceedings, potentially undermining the independence of the convert from his or her birth community.

By law, converts were not permitted to relocate after baptism without proper identity papers, which were held by their local Jewish community. A 1861 ukase linked the baptismal monetary reward to a convert's post-baptism relocation.[61] The impetus seems to have been a need to further encourage converts to relocate who either did not want to or wished to avoid grappling with the legal obstacles to obtaining their vital records. Converts—whether converting alone or with their families—were encouraged to relocate among Christians in other towns or villages; only after relocation could they receive the 15–30 rubles doled out from the state treasury. In 1816 the expert dyer Moisei Simkin, who had been doing business in the interior of the empire on a special passport issued annually by Mogilev Province, petitioned the tsar's Special Chancellery to let him remain in St. Petersburg and convert to Orthodoxy even though his wife and the Mogilev Jewish community tried to thwart his will by not renewing his passport. The Third Section came to Simkin's defense by going around the Jewish community and asking the St. Petersburg chief of police himself to grant Simkin and his children special papers permitting them to reside in the capital.[62]

In addition to wielding metrical records needed for estate registration and determining one's tax obligation, the Jewish community could furnish (or fabricate) records of births to contest baptisms. There are countless conversion cases where kahal officials or state rabbis sent official letters to civil or ecclesiastic authorities confirming the birthday of a neophyte, which inevitably pegged the convert as younger than fourteen (the legal age of independent conversion as of 1862). In the case of Malka Kuks, when the Bel'sk District police wrote to the head of the Orla Jewish community, Tsukerman, asking for confirmation of Kuks's registration as the daughter of mill landlord Leibko Vulfovich, Tsukerman replied that she was registered in the tenth popular census, which showed that she was currently eleven years old.[63] In the case of Sheina Leibovna Dlugolenskaia, born in the town of Knishin in the Bialystok District, the Bialystok rabbi sent a certificate to Grodno provincial authorities attesting to Sheina's recorded date of birth; the girl was now fourteen years and five days old. Just a month later, Sheina's conversion certificate recorded that she was eighteen years old.[64] In these cases and many like them, the "official" age given by the Jewish community tended to be put aside in favor of the convert's stated age and clerics' own visual assessment of the convert's maturity. Though by fourteen a neophyte was no longer considered a minor and could convert without parental consent, the legal age of adulthood was twenty. In Sheina's case, perhaps the Jewish community wanted to emphasize how very near she came to skirting the law's requirement that converts be capable of independent judgment.[65]

Metrical record keeping as a disciplinary technology of the modern, centralizing state, aimed to identify, categorize, and track individual subjects. Key identifying criteria included the name of the subject and of his or her parents. In most conversion proceedings, ecclesiastic officials began their due diligence into a neophyte's background by confirming the name and census listing of the applicant. As with indigenous groups in other imperial settings playing with names to subvert state disciplinary regimes, Jewish communities in imperial Russia wielded the bilingual nature of Jewish names and the common practice of colloquial diminutives to confound the state's ability to confirm a neophyte's identity and carry out the requisite confession and estate change.[66]

From early in the nineteenth century, when the Russian state invested disciplinary power in the tolerated confessions by having them maintain metrical records, the state was concerned about confusing Jewish naming practices. Jews typically carried double or multiple names (Rukhel Leah, Avrom Itsko Leib), often both the Hebrew and Yiddish variants of a given name (Dov-Ber). In addition, many names spawned a variety of nicknames or diminutives (Sender or Senderel for Alexander), as well as forms of endearment (Leah'le for Leah). As such, official names as recorded in metrical records did not always correspond to the everyday monikers people used. Complex naming practices such as these confounded imperial officials and could be used by Jewish communities to complicate or stymie conversions.

Common Jewish communal subversion tactics included claiming there was no proof of the existence of a particular individual or confusing the bureaucracy by furnishing metrical records with different first names. For instance, two members of the Vilna Jewish community told local police that there was no record of a community member named "Pera" Girsenovich.[67] In

the case of the conversions of two Berdichev Jews to Anglicanism in Warsaw under the auspices of the London Society for Promoting Christianity
amongst the Jews, a rabbi from Berdichev wrote to provincial authorities
that there was no evidence of either neophyte in any metrical records from
the Jewish community between the years 1855 and 1858, when they were supposedly born. Despite this, provincial authorities confirmed to the Anglican
pastor James Ellis that Berdichev authorities had removed the two from the
local Jewish communal tax registry.[68]

Aside from Jewish communities using their powers of record keeping
to forestall conversions, the kahal—even after its 1844 formal dissolution—
had the ability to punish neophytes by getting them conscripted. In 1830
twenty-one-year-old Yosel Abramovich Brukman—from Lepel', the Jewish
community of Kublichi—came to a Catholic deacon in Disna asking to be
baptized after having been thwarted by his Jewish community. The community leaders had decided they would submit him for conscription, and
thus had ordered him to leave the monastery where he had been staying.
In looking into the case, the Department for the Religious Affairs of Foreign Confessions tried to ascertain whether Brukman articulated his wish
to convert before or after the community decided he would be recruited for
conscription. Legally, if a Jew articulated the desire to convert before the
draft, he was no longer subject to Jewish recruitment. The Roman Catholic
College affirmed that Brukman expressed his desire to convert first, pointing to the fact that the community had him removed from the monastery
in order to recruit him, not because he dodged the draft.[69] There are other
cases of communities supposedly kidnapping young Jews on the verge of
conversion and recruiting them, either to fill recruitment slots with disposable community members or to put distance between the neophytes and
their conversion mentors.[70] All of these cases took place during the reign of
Nicholas I and the cantonist legislation, when Jewish communities were responsible for filling recruitment quotas and children could be recruited into
training units.

When recruits subsequently expressed their desire to convert as a way of
evading military service, the Jewish community maintained its right to recruit them. For example, in 1845 a Jewish woman, Ester-Rivka Rosenbergova,
petitioned the governor-general of Kiev, Podolia, and Volynia that her hus-

band, her brother, and three other Jews, were recruited by the Zhitomir Jewish community because they had told some fellow Jews that they intended to convert. The governor-general's office discovered that all five Jews tried to use conversion to evade recruitment, and that all five were drafted due to bad behavior—a decision the governor supported as within the rights of the Jewish community to rid itself of troublemakers.[71]

Another tool available to Jews trying to reign in apostates was the legal right of a spouse to stay in a mixed marriage. The far-right newspaper *Kievlianin* drew attention to this legal quagmire to argue against what it saw as official empowerment of Jewish fanaticism and the "defenselessness of female converts." Focusing on Jewish men as the assumed abusers of this law, *Kievlianin* contended that even though Jews had no legal right to pursue converts, Jewish "fanaticism"—i.e., contesting baptisms—had still achieved a "wide scope" in the empire. The article referenced a recent case in Kiev Province where a female convert to Russian Orthodoxy asked permission to marry an Orthodox man even though she was still married according to Jewish law. The Orthodox Consistory, through local police, contacted the Jewish husband to inquire if he wanted a divorce. The husband repeatedly stated that he wanted to stay married and accepted the terms of the church that his young children were to be baptized and that he would under no circumstances threaten his family's Christian life. As a result, the consistory denied the neophyte's request to remarry. Thus, *Kievlianin* argued, because of this loophole a convert could still be subject to the "despotism of fanatics."[72]

Though inflected by overt anti-Semitism and a belief that Jews conspired to murder converts, the *Kievlianin* article drew attention to the tensions in imperial law over the status of mixed marriages. A deeply contentious issue for many confessions, the laws governing mixed marriages straddled the jurisdictions of imperial law and religious law and brought the principles of religious toleration and Orthodox preeminence into conflict. Marriage according to imperial law was a religious sacrament and thus governed by religious law, which each tolerated confessional community had the right to define and oversee themselves. Since there were no civil marriages in the empire, mixed marriages typically necessitated one spouse to convert, although marriages between Christians of different confessions were legal though highly problematic.[73] In the case of the conversion of one spouse, imperial law honored the religious law that sanctified the initial marriage and only unilaterally annulled the marriage if there were legal grounds to argue for the spiritual endangerment of the converted spouse or children. For Jews, this religious empowerment persisted till the end of the old regime and was formally given shape and imperial oversight through the state rabbinate and the rabbinic commissions that met through 1910 and adjudicated Jewish legal disputes.[74]

Contrary to the *Kievlianin* article's assertion that Jews could always wield the law on mixed marriage to their advantage, the state and church liberally interpreted the clause on danger to the convert to unilaterally annul Jewish marriages and permit converts to remarry a Christian. The Mary Neiding case, discussed later in the chapter, is an example of the state liberally interpreting the Jewish husband's demand to stay married to his converted wife as grounds to fear for her religious well-being and unilaterally annul her Jewish marriage.[75]

Aside from subverting the state's documentary regime to thwart baptisms, Jewish communities at times resorted to character assassination to challenge baptisms, since they were often asked to attest to a convert's probity and lack of a criminal record.[76] Though moral uprightness and mental clarity were not specifically within the legibility regimes of the tolerated confessions, they were pertinent to assessing character and friends and relatives could draw on them to contest conversions. In July 1870, state officials in the Shchuchin region of Lomzha Province (Congress Poland) passed on to the Lithuanian Consistory information they received from "local officials" regarding a neophyte in a Grodno convent. As noted in Chapter 3, information surfaced that Roshka Slovatitskaia, a teenage Jewish girl preparing for baptism, had been involved in prostitution and theft. Despite this red flag, the baptism took place in September of that year. The mother superior of the convent reported back to the Lithuanian Consistory about Roshka's successful baptism, and she noted that Roshka's behavior was excellent. At her baptism, Roshka stated with tears in her eyes that such "slander" (*nagavor*) was perpetrated by Jews to undermine her conversion.[77] In the 1870 conversion case of Solomon Isaakov Vankopp, the Vilna Jewish community declined to pass judgment on the twenty-one-year-old neophyte's behavior and criminal record since he had been temporarily residing in Dinaburg with his father on business.[78]

Though the politics of Jewish contestation of apostasy was local and responded to the entangled lives of Jews and their neighbors in compact, provincial spaces, it was not a phenomenon of isolation, born of local antagonisms and settled in remote, rural spaces. The politics of local communities was profoundly interconnected with the politics of surrounding villages, towns, cities, and beyond. Trade, commerce, and the circulation of people and texts connected small towns to a broad network of people and places. As such, the small-town and village story of Jewish conversion must be mapped within familial and communal networks of Jews across the western borderlands and their imperial neighbors. It was through familial regional networks that some Jews sought to evade the surveillance of the state altogether and shield converts and their offspring from the classificatory powers of the empire.

Imperial law did not necessarily lay claim to the confessional identities of converts in training, but it did claim absolute confessional control over converts once they were baptized, at which point they became subject to the empire's criminalization of apostasy from Christianity. Civil and ecclesiastic authorities demanded that converts adhere to their Christian confession—those who failed to do so and relapsed to Judaism were admonished, sent into exile, or punished with years of hard labor in Siberia.[79]

Thus converts who wished to return to the fold of Judaism, or succumbed to the pressure of their Jewish families to do so, had a strong incentive to disappear. In fact, many neophytes or relapsed converts went missing from the authorities, suggesting that Jewish communities found ways to shelter their Christian kin from the controlling gaze of the state. There was, in other words, a Jewish "underground railroad" or individual family networks for relapsed converts (both those who voluntarily returned to Judaism and those who were coerced by their Jewish families). In a sampling of 192 conversion files from the Vilna Diocese over the course of the nineteenth century held by the YIVO archives, at least 15 case files were closed by the church after the neophyte disappeared and could not be found by ecclesiastic or police personnel. In additional conversion files in the Lithuanian archives, of the 136 converts who applied for baptism in Vilna between 1863 and 1871, 14 disappeared in the course of convert training.[80] For example, in 1845 the seventeen-year-old Jewess Sora Abramova Leibova Ovseiovicha from the village of Veliko-Brzhestovitsa in Grodno Province came to police in

Volkovysk expressing her desire to convert to Russian Orthodoxy. The police contacted the nearest parish priest, who suggested she go to a convent in Grodno for conversion training. While the police waited for permission from the MVD for this move, Sora stayed with a Christian woman in Volkovysk for safeguarding. When the approval came a month later, the caregiver informed the police that Sora had vanished. The conversion file remained active until 1849, when the Vilna Consistory ended its four-year search for Sora.[81] In another case, a young married Jewish woman came to the Catholic church in Minsk asking to be converted. Nineteen-year old Sheina Freida Meier had studied Catholic dogma and prayers and was awaiting official baptism permission from the MVD when she ran back to Judaism, never to be heard from again.[82]

Peshi Tiskevicha, the child of an illicit union (according to imperial law) between a Jewish woman and a convert from Judaism who relapsed from Russian Orthodoxy while on leave from the army, also disappeared. According to imperial law, the father's Christian status automatically devolved on his young offspring. But since Peshi's father was obstinate in his apostasy and his wife was Jewish, the Orthodox Church decided to take Peshi, then seven years old, from her parents and make her a ward of the church. Thus, in 1843 the Holy Synod issued a warrant for her to be detained. When Bialystok regional authorities came to the mother's house, the mother and daughter were missing. After eight years of fruitless searching, the Vilna Consistory closed the case.[83]

Individual relapse networks not only brought apostates back to the Jewish fold and saved Jewish children from being taken from their families, but they also expanded the borders of Jewish communities. In imperial Russia, conversion did not only mean Jews becoming Christians; it also meant Christians becoming Jews. Judaizing was a crime in the Russian Empire, and had been so at least since the fifteenth century. Thus, that a Christian would willingly convert reveals the power and attraction of Jewish communities. As late as the nineteenth century, many tsarist officials blamed the proliferation of Subbotniks, Russian Sabbatarians, on the nefarious influence of Russian Jews.[84] In 1827 the imperial secret police indicted more than nine Jews for the crime of seducing two Catholic domestic servants to Judaism. According to the State Senate hearings, the conversions took place in 1817 in two Jewish communities in Vilna Province. The courts found that the two Catholic maidens were working in Jewish homes, where they were enticed to convert to Judaism. To escape notice, the servants were brought to the Jewish cemetery where the conversion ceremony was started, and then were shuttled between Jewish homes in the area. After conversion, one of the women was married off to a local Jewish man, after which both women were taken to Kurland Province.[85] After the Jewish husband abandoned his converted wife in this distant province, the women pleaded with Catholic authorities that they be allowed to return home. Judaizing was a rare phenomenon in nineteenth-century Russia, but that it happened at all shows that Jews could tap into extensive communal and super-communal networks to evade the Orthodox Church's monopoly on missionizing and, more importantly, the state's criminalization of apostasy from Christianity.

Conversion as a Family Affair

As in the Goldferbova story that opens this chapter and in many of the other cases of alleged kidnappings and murder explored above, much of the drama of Jewish conversion revolved around women who become a figuring ground for the male imagination. Conversion, historically the most conflictual of all boundary crossings, raised a host of issues about family breakdown and communal cohesion, and especially in the nineteenth century, about religious toleration and the state's buttressing of tolerated confessions yet legal privileging of one "true" faith. For Orthodox Christians, anxieties over convert relapses and charges of Orthodox religious coercion found expression in the female victim of Jewish fanaticism who suffered on account of intolerant Jews, violent seducers of converts back to Judaism against their will. In the post-reform period, when calls for freedom of conscience began to gain traction, the female victim of Jewish aggression helped to cast Jews as modern-age inquisitors. Like the gendered figure in Pimonenko's *Victim of Fanaticism*, the pre-reform young Jewish cantonist soldier brutally forced by the state to convert to Christianity had now morphed into the post-reform young female convert abused at the hands of her family and former Jewish community.

Ironically, the charge of fanaticism was often leveled against Jewish female family members for supposedly causing the belated or problematic conversion of Jewish men. For instance, Moisei Simkin, mentioned earlier, blamed his wife for obstructing his conversion and kidnapping his children so they too could not be converted.[86] In 1843 the convert Yankel' Nokhim Girshovich Zandman in trying to unsettle his Jewish wife's charges of theft countered that his "superstitious wife" (*suevernaia zhena*), when she found out about his intention to convert, "pursued his every step" in order to bring him to financial ruin.[87] The convert Moshko Blank from Zhitomir—the great-grandfather of Vladimir Ilyich Lenin—blamed his belated conversion in 1844 at the age of ninety on his Jewish wife: "My wife hindered my conversion until now, but, finally she [...] died."[88]

For Jews, the rise of female conversions in the second half of the nineteenth century raised a whole set of issues about marriage, divorce, and child custody. Although Jewish communities paid little attention to female poverty, it sometimes led to prostitution and conversion, if brothels were located beyond the Pale of Settlement.[89] Moreover, female conversion could change the stakes involved in abandoning one's community—women converted not just because they wanted to better their lot in life but also because they were in love. Conversions could also be used by Jewish women as a legal mechanism to escape an unhappy marriage or avoid an arranged marriage.[90] Using conversion as a communal threat, the Jews of Simon Dubnov's childhood town of Mstislavl' wielded a local apostate's tale as leverage in business or family disputes, pointing out that people always had the choice of going to "Pustinki [a local monastery] to be baptized."

The conversion of a Jewish spouse or parent opened a Pandora's box of problems regarding status from the perspective of both Russian imperial law and *halakhah* (Jewish law). For the state, female conversions destabilized Jewish families and called into question the confessional status of young children. Imperial law forbade mixed marriages between Christians and non-Christians, and would accept unions in which one spouse converted to Christianity only on the condition that the converted spouse and the couples' children would be free of the influence of the Jewish partner. For the Jewish community, conversion of a spouse raised a host of issues. Jewish law generally maintained the principle of eternal Jewishness: a person's status as Jew was based solely on matrilineal descent and was unchanged by baptism. Yet, when a Jew rejected *halakhah*, what was involved was not just abstract notions of identity but concrete questions about such things as divorce, remarriage, child custody, and the indeterminate status of *agunot*, women chained to their marriages because they did not received an official Jewish divorce from a living spouse. For instance, a woman whose husband died childless was, according to Jewish law, obligated to enter a levirate marriage. If the brother-in-law had converted, he was still obligated to either marry her or perform the rite of *ḥaliẓah* (levirate divorce). A convert's refusal in such cases left his brother's widow an *agunah*.

The vigorous discussion of the Jewishness of converted males stemmed largely from Jewish women's legal reliance on men for their own personal status as married, divorced, widowed, or *agunot* (chained). Thus, when Leib Mordukhovich Gol'dberg converted in 1870, his Jewish wife, Perla, had no other legal recourse for a Jewish divorce than to petition the Vilna bishop to order Gol'dberg to give her a *get*.[91] The MVD convened a special Rabbinic Congress in 1910 to consider the problem of conversion in the context of marriage and the various unsuccessful attempts by Jewish leaders to impress on Orthodox authorities the urgency of a Jewish divorce in the event of the church's dissolution of a mixed marriage. Jewish leaders in Warsaw and Pol-tava reported they had failed in their appeal to clerics and local government officials about the need for converts to issue their Jewish wives a divorce. The congress acknowledged that the only option in case of a spouse's conversion was to appeal to the state to have pity on *agunot*.[92] By contrast, when women converted, Jewish law was no longer interested in their status, because their menfolk were considered to be independent actors. The discussion of the legal issues involved in the case of female Jewish converts in imperial Russia thus moved from the rabbinate to imperial jurists, who had to consider the effects of female religious independence on the stability of the home and the rearing of children.[93] On the one hand, female converts to Christianity were looked upon favorably, because they had chosen the true faith. On the other hand, in forging their own religious path, female converts asserted an inde-pendence out of step with the patriarchal social structure of the empire.[94] In this way, female converts could exploit gendered tropes of Jewish victimhood and use conversion as a means to assert agency in crafting their own legal status. Like *halakhah*, imperial law subsumed women under the status of the male head of household. For a single woman, this was her father; for a mar-ried woman, it was her husband. If a woman legally separated herself from the head of household through conversion, how was she to be governed? If she had children, who received legal custody and could the children be converted with her?

The question of a wife's status after conversion was brought to the fore in the case of Mary Neiding, who converted to Roman Catholicism in 1869. The wife of a Jew in Warsaw and the mother of three Jewish children, Neiding desired to leave the Russian Empire and her family following her baptism. In her petition to the state, Neiding requested to be freed of Russian sub-jecthood (*russkoe poddanstvo*). The problem was that according to imperial law, a wife assumes the legal status (*sostoianie*) of her husband. In this case, her Jewish husband was and wanted to remain a Russian subject.[95] Hence, Neiding could be released from subjecthood only if she was first released from her Jewish marriage. In her case, straddling the Jewish and Catholic worlds, two different bodies of religious law governed her marital status. According to Jewish law, her Jewish marriage remained in force, because her husband wanted to stay married to her and would not divorce her. According to Catholic law, if her unconverted spouse harassed her because of her reli-gious beliefs, her former marriage would be considered void and she would be eligible to remarry a Christian.[96]

The Department for the Religious Affairs of Foreign Confessions de-ferred to the Roman Catholic clergy in this matter, citing the lacunae in imperial law on mixed marriages of a non-Christian to a non-Orthodox Christian of the tolerated foreign confessions.[97] In this case, imperial law was subordinated to the imperial commitment to religious tolerance that granted each confessional clergy freedom to govern their own religious affairs. Ac-cording to the Mogilev Archdiocese bishop Stanevskii, Roman Catholic law on mixed marriages was similar to the one articulated by the Synod and codified in imperial law. Mixed marriages were tolerated if the unconverted spouse desired to remain married to the convert and promised not to com-promise the religious integrity of the Christian spouse and children.[98] In the Neiding case, the Jewish husband clearly wanted to stay married. The question the MVD had to resolve was whether the Jewish husband posed a religious threat to his converted wife.

According to Bishop Stanevskii, all the journalistic publicity surround-ing the Neiding case ignored the uncompromising position of the Jewish husband. Mr. Neiding, in the words of the bishop, "demanded retention of his marital rights (*sokhraneniia za soboiu napred supruzheskikh prav*) over her, and expressed his desire to live with [his wife] as before."[99] Although these words do not constitute an overt threat to the new religion of the wife, both the Catholic church and MVD interpreted the husband's response as a green light for annulling the Jewish marriage and allowing Mary Neiding to re-marry a Christian. Since Mr. Neiding wished to stay married to his converted wife, the church's decision to annul the marriage had to hinge on his demand to retain his "marital rights," an admittedly unclear expression. Was Neiding's language too aggressive and thus considered threatening? Was his demand an assault on Mary's religious freedom? Or did the problem hinge on the fact that he would not allow her to travel abroad, something she linked to her conversion to Catholicism? Since the Neidings lived in Warsaw, a pre-dominantly Catholic city, her wish to leave the Russian Empire could not have been because she wanted to escape from a place inhospitable to her new religion. It appears Mary petitioned to emigrate in order to put her Jewish marriage outside the reach of *halakhah*.

In this case, Mary Neiding succeeded in using conversion to escape the patriarchal bonds enshrined in both Jewish and imperial law. Baptism al-lowed her to leave her life as a wife and mother and start over in a new environment. It is clear from the file that she had no immediate intention of remarrying a Christian; she simply wanted permission to leave Russia, and by extension, her paternalistic Jewish marriage.[100]

The Neiding case only dealt with the fallout of conversion as it related to marriage; it did not address the issue of children and custody. The MVD took this up in the case of Elizaveta Alekseeva, a Jewish wife and mother who converted to Orthodoxy in 1858 and petitioned the St. Petersburg Ec-clesiastic Consistory to dissolve her Jewish marriage so she could marry a Christian.[101] Since her Jewish husband, Chaim Beniaminovich, was a bu-gler in the army, the problem of Elizaveta abandoning her Jewish family and the status of her Jewish children was left to military officials to resolve, since her children, born to a soldier, were legally cantonists. The couple had four sons—Beniamin, age fifteen; David, seven; Moshe, six; and Me-nashe, four—and a daughter, Fima, ten. Also, after the mother was baptized and the couple separated, she gave birth to a boy, Alexander, who was considered Christian. Since the military could find no obvious imperial law dealing with child custody in the case of the dissolution of a mixed marriage, it asked the MVD to rule on the status of the children: were the children considered orphans entrusted to the military for support? In this case, the MVD ruled that, indeed, the children of a Jewish couple who divorced after the conversion of one spouse were considered like children with one deceased parent; that is, they were eligible for military assistance.

In addition to considering the effects on children of divorce and parental estrangement after conversion, the MVD also believed that it was the government's duty to encourage Jewish conversion to Orthodoxy (*chto pravitel'stvo dolzhno pooshchriat perekhody v pravoslavie lits evreiskago zakona*).[102] In this case, military subsidies to children of a Jewish couple whose marriage was dissolved after the wife's conversion to Orthodoxy constituted state assistance to Jewish converts. Since the mother had already converted and remarried, it is strange that the MVD considered this belated child assistance as encouraging conversion. The tsar personally approved the legal innovation of considering children of a Jewish divorced army officer (in the case of a marriage dissolved after a spouse's conversion) like orphaned children.[103] This legal maneuvering placed the state in loco parentis to help stabilize a family that had actually been destabilized by the state's lenient divorce laws governing mixed marriages.

According to an 1842 Senate decree, made in consultation with the tsar and the Ministry of State Domains, if a Jewish parent converted, all children of the same gender ages seven and younger could be converted by that parent.[104] In the case of intermarriage, when a convert from Judaism married a Christian, the laws regarding child conversion were stricter. All eligible children were required to be converted together with the spouse desiring intermarriage and these children were required to be reared as Christians. Clerics were advised to make sure that both parent and children attended church, followed church laws, and took communion.[105] The laws for conversion by children between the age of seven and the legal age of majority without a parent are unclear. Imperial law stated that a minor needed the permission of the parents, but the form this was supposed to take was disputed.[106] Sometimes it was understood as requiring the permission of both parents; other times, just one.[107]

For example, in 1847 a noncommissioned officer married to the convert from Judaism Daria petitioned the archbishop of Vilna to return to his wife her eight-year-old son, Berko, the offspring of her previous Jewish marriage.[108] Apparently, the son had lived for a time with his mother in Shchuchin after her conversion and remarriage, but his father, Ari Leibovich, together with other Jews bribed a local official to take Berko from his converted mother in exchange for offering Berko as an army recruit. The Vilna archbishop instructed the Vilna provincial administration to facilitate the return of Berko to his mother. Local authorities in the Lida District, who oversaw the Vasilishki Jewish community, where the father resided, reported that the kahal claimed that Berko had died in the army, and furnished a death certificate signed by the local crown rabbi.[109] The mysterious death further dramatizes the custody battle and the contentious issue that lay at its heart—the conversion of a minor. Although not stated outright in the archival records, the attempt to separate Berko from his converted mother, even at the price of conscription, and the Vilna Consistory's immediate attention to the case suggest that custody of the child would practically determine his religious ascription.

While in the first half of the century imperial laws governing child converts and custody in the case of a parent's conversion were nebulous, and church and state officials tended to heed conversion requests of minors from just one parent, legal protection of minors became more rigorous in the latter half of the nineteenth century. It was over this issue that the St. Petersburg shelter for baptized Jews and Jews seeking conversion limited its assistance to Jewish converts in the 1870s. After a resident priest baptized the minor Sergei Griner with the consent of his mother alone, the St. Petersburg Ecclesiastic Consistory took the shelter to task for irresponsibly baptizing a minor and not heeding synodal law, which by 1862 defined the age of majority as fourteen and required that any minor desiring conversion receive written permission of both parents or legal guardians.[110]

Beginning in the reform era, imperial law upheld minority religious rights and the state did not conduct any consistent or vigorous missionary campaign to Russian Jews. Yet, when a spouse converted or a Jewish family was destabilized by divorce and conversion, there was much more legal maneuvering to allow for the ascendance of Christianity and the encouragement of conversion.

Violence in imperial Russia was the "background static" of small-town life that allowed the resolution of tensions.[111] The violence that accompanied Jewish conversion bespeaks a Jewish politics of intimidation and of contestation of voluntary baptisms—especially by women—in the multiconfessional spaces of the western provinces. Contestation in the context of empire and toleration functioned as a means for Jewish communities both to undermine state classification regimes and to mimic the power of the state to missionize and criminalize apostasy.

The cases discussed here highlight both the increased access to conversion in the face-to-face encounters in provincial communities and the difficulties of crossing religious borders in familiar spaces. Conversions were fostered by intimate, neighborly relations, and stories spun about family and communal violence were based on the publicity of small-town and village conversions and the inability of neophytes to escape the controlling gaze of their communities. Preemptive attacks on potential converts, abductions and murders of neophytes, and priests wary of provoking Jewish wrath were all predicated on the web of interpersonal relations in small towns and individual, regional, familial networks that made visible and open to scrutiny individual behavior, relationships, and whereabouts.

Women in these stories were a lightning rod for anxieties about interfaith sociability, intimacies, and toleration, all of which undermined Orthodox hegemony. Yet, more than just passive symbols of confessional power politics and local fears of miscegenation, women were agents who, by converting, unsettled the patriarchal structures of Jewish and imperial classificatory and status regimes. With minority appeals in the late imperial period for freedom of conscience alongside Russification campaigns in the western provinces and civilizing campaigns in the East to unify the empire under the banner of Russianness and Orthodoxy, religious toleration became a central site of contesting the terms of imperial diversity. For conservatives looking to shore up Russian Orthodoxy as a basis of state-building, the rhetoric of fanaticism and convert victimhood helped to undermine the foreign confessions and their right to be tolerated, let alone individuals' right to freedom of conscience.

Thus, the study of conversion in the Pale of Settlement offers a lens with which to view the contact and interaction between religious communities in the Russian Empire. Conversion is just one manifestation of the thoroughly intertwined geography of Jews and Christians in the western provinces, where the confessional balance of power was locally constructed and maintained (not necessarily in line with the tsars' established church and its prerogatives), and where sociocultural borders were fluid and permeable though reified and contested at moments of conversion. From this perspective, we can read modern Jewish conversion not only as an elite form of adopting European or national culture, but as a product of local confessional sociability, access, and intimacy.

Confessional intimacy in small towns could operate between religious communities and could govern the relationships between apostates and their former coreligionists. The documents and stories culled here about violence, especially convert abductions, do not necessarily tell a straightforward story of Jewish coercion but at times hint at converts' need to cover up moments of doubt or relapse into the orbit of Jewish communal life. Many of these stories point to ongoing Jewish-convert relationships and reveal the elaborate channels Jews and converts used to keep close encounters beyond the reach of the state.

In reality, religious communities were knowledgeable of and enmeshed in each other's practices, taboos, family relations, and social networks. Such knowledge and access could breed intimacy and sociability, but they could also breed hostility and rivalries when conversions subverted the disciplinary power and tacit boundaries within small towns and villages. In this way, intimacy and intimidation were two sides of the same coin of face-to-face provincial living.

PART III

CONVERTS ON THE MOVE

CHAPTER 5

RELAPSED CONVERTS
AND TALES OF MARRANISM

IN THE SPRING of 1872 a Bialystok peasant, Mikhail Petreshevich, informed police of a theft by the convert from Judaism Ivan Bondarev. Upon searching the convert for the stolen goods, local peasants testified that they found *zizit* (a fringed ritual garment) and a *sidur* (Jewish prayer book) in the convert's pocket along with 98.5 kopeks. According to the testimony of witnesses, Bondarev explained that even though he was baptized "he was still a Jew and prays to the one God so that God gives him health."[1] When the Bialystok police took over the case, they interrogated Bondarev and received a more apologetic explanation. He claimed to have found the *zizit* and *sidur* at a local bazaar, but he attributed no religious meaning to his having them. He tried to convince the police that he was a proper Christian even though he was often seen with his "nation," that is, local Jews.[2]

Bondarev's hybrid Jewish-Christian identity warranted a police investigation because apostasy from Christianity was a criminal offense in the Russian Empire punishable by exile and hard labor. A tenuous attachment to Orthodoxy like Bondarev's was common among converts from Judaism in nineteenth-century imperial Russia. As a result of the benefits for conversion inscribed in imperial law and state-sponsored conversions of young Jewish recruits in the pre-reform army, the Russian church and state grappled with the issue of insincere converts. Official anxieties about instrumental baptisms found expression in criminal proceedings against converts suspected of relapsing to their original faith and against Jews suspected of "seducing" converts back to Judaism. Apostates from Orthodoxy were legally considered to have been "seduced" from the true faith, on the assumption that deviance was instigated by an outside party rather than stemming from individual choice. Suspected relapsed converts were subject to ecclesiastic admonition until they recanted their "alien" customs, and seducers were subject to criminal proceedings with a guilty sentence for both parties entailing exile and hard labor.[3]

The criminality of Orthodox deviance was tempered by Nicholas II's freedom of conscience laws issued in the wake of the failed 1905 Russian revolution. One such law, promulgated in April 1905, permitted converts to return to their original faith if they could prove their religious ancestry and their insincerity toward their adopted confession. As a result of this legislation, between 1905 and 1912 at least 684 Jewish converts to Orthodoxy and other Christian confessions returned to Judaism.[4] Actually, a small but steady stream of converts, like Ivan Bondarev, relapsed to Judaism well before it became legal in 1905. The substantial evidence on relapsed converts before 1905 and shortly thereafter illuminates the complex relationship between religious identity and confessional affiliation in an empire that promoted Russian Orthodoxy while extending religious toleration to all subjects. Imperial sponsorship of Russian Orthodoxy combined with the criminalization of deviance from Orthodoxy created an environment in which Jewish converts often lived in the interstices of communal and confessional life, defying clear religious categorization.

Stories of converts' braided identities and multiple cultural fluencies in the popular press and published trial transcripts of relapse cases in the late imperial period reveal the fluidity of identities and the problem of using confessional ascription to undergird imperial stability. Relapsed converts and their tales of marranism, or secret Jewish practice, called into question the confessional state's strategy of mapping identity and community onto confessional ascription—especially following the era of coerced cantonist baptisms when legal and chosen religious identities were often at odds. As church and state officials grappled with these difficulties, relapsed converts and their defenders tried to inscribe their cultural mobility into imperial law through freedom of conscience measures.

Relapsed converts' tales of marranism, a term originally referring to the mass forced conversions of Jews in medieval Iberia and their suspect status for generations thereafter, joined an incipient public discourse in late imperial Russia in which the tolerated faiths used coerced baptisms to argue for the right to freedom of conscience. Like Baltic Germans, who used the argument of freedom of conscience to petition for the right of coreligionists forcibly baptized by the Orthodox Church to legally relapse, Jews and other foreign confessions in the late imperial period sought to expose the inconsistency of religious toleration in the empire and the need for the protection of freedom of conscience.[5] Jewish claims for justice were not aimed just to right the past injustice of the cantonist system, but to ease the mounting pressures on Jews to convert in the late imperial period even in the absence of state violence. State-sponsored industrialization in the late imperial period accompanied by railroad building and urbanization undercut the economic viability of small towns, once home to a majority of Jews in the western provinces. In addition, the terms of selective integration and reforms under Alexander II induced many Jewish youths to aspire to attend university and get a professional degree to insure their future socioeconomic well-being. These pressures and inducements for young Jews to leave home and educationally and linguistically integrate added significant pressures to convert, especially in the post-reform period when quotas on Jews in institutions of higher education and the liberal professions practically forced them to convert for survival.

The courtroom conversation on relapsed soldiers and civilians, though, did not exist in isolation. After the 1863 Polish insurrection and picking up steam in the reactionary political climate of the 1880s, an opposing discourse started in the public press that invoked Jewish fanaticism as a reason to exclude Jews from toleration and to question the efficacy of baptism. "Fanaticism" and other Jewish characteristics (such as cultural separatism and economic parasitism) were increasingly cast as innate and impermeable to baptismal waters. In countering the language of toleration and reform that framed the "merging" of the Jews into the empire, commentators and bureaucrats invoked the language of heterodox "fanaticism" to argue that the tolerated faiths, because of their backwardness, were not worthy of toleration since they themselves did not tolerate religious freedom within their own ranks. The

Russian press increasingly referred to conversion and its discontents to attack the notion that legal privileges should be extended to Jews. In this concert of conversations in the courts and the press, supporters of freedom of conscience reclaimed the slur of "fanaticism," repeatedly used to denigrate the foreign faiths, and argued that fanaticism constituted resistance to coercive baptisms, and thus blazed the trail to true religious freedom in the empire.

Thinking with Marranos

The conceptual similarities between illegally relapsed converts in imperial Russia and late medieval Iberian marranos, or new Christians that the Inquisition tribunals suspected of Judaizing, provided polemical fodder for imperial policymakers and Russian Jewish leaders who grappled with the phenomenon of Jewish conversion in an empire in which religion was highly politicized. In an undated memorandum from the Third Section of Nicholas I's Imperial Chancellery, an imperial official proposed that the empire encourage Jewish conversion and rapprochement (*sblizhenie*) with the native population. In defense of his proposition, the writer extolled the Russian Empire's "sensible" treatment of the Jews in contrast to the barbarism of medieval Spain and Portugal. "If the fanaticism in Spain, Portugal, and other Catholic lands ignited a fire for [the Jews], then the sensible and common politics among my nation dedicated to tolerance has restricted their commerce, constrained residential rights and completely expelled them."[6] Although both Catholic states and the Russian Empire viewed conversion as a way to contain their Jewish populations, this imperial Russian official boasted that his country did not overtly pursue a violent and intolerant policy toward minorities. Tsarist Russia, in his opinion, sought to contain and modernize the empire's Jews through legal policies and encourage conversion through material and legal incentives. The rhetorical distinction between Christian confessions in this memorandum is loaded with a Catholic-Orthodox polemic, as well as a value judgment of modern imperial sensibilities in tolerating imperial diversity versus premodern religious chauvinism and barbarism (e.g., burning at the stake) in handling unwanted subjects.[7]

Comparing the conversion tactics of Catholic Iberia and imperial Russia was something that Jews did as well. Nineteenth-century Russian maskilim, artists, and early twentieth-century Jewish historians invoked Iberian marranos as the predecessors of Russian Jews who converted under duress in the imperial army of Nicholas I, or, later in the century, converted in order to get a higher education or work in the city. Maskilic writers suggested that just as many marranos never fully embraced Christianity but instead lived a hybrid, secret Jewish-Christian life, Russian Jews similarly endured religious persecution without losing their Jewish identity.[8] The late nineteenth-century Jewish artist Mosei Maimon painted his famous *Marranos and the Inquisition in Spain* (*Marrany i inkvizitsiia v Ispanii*, 1893) in response to a traumatic episode he witnessed in the 1880s as a student while enjoying a Passover seder in St. Petersburg with a local Jewish family. During this gathering, police stormed in and demanded to see the registration papers of the host documenting his privilege to reside beyond the Pale of Jewish Settlement. Lacking such papers, the man was promptly expelled from the capital. Years later, Maimon brought this modern Russian scene to life through the imagery of a medieval marrano seder violently disrupted by Inquisitors (see Figure 5.1).[9] For late imperial Russian Jewish historians like Simon Dubnov and Ya'akov Halevi Lifshitz, the Iberian paradigm "served as a highly suggestive

Figure 5.1 Moisei Maimon, *Marrany* (The Marranos), 1893. *Evreiskaia entsiklopediia: Svod znanii o evreistve i ego kul'ture v proshlom i nastoiashchem*, 16 vols. (St. Petersburg: Brokgauz-Efron, 1906–1913; facs. ed., Moscow: Terra, 1991), X:657–58.

metaphor" for Russia's conscription and coerced baptisms of Jewish minors and the dispersion of Russian Jewry across the world in the last decades of the nineteenth century and the early decades of the twentieth century.[10] The image of the Jewish conscript as martyr fortified the thesis that the history of Jews in Russia was conditioned by a state bent on ridding itself of non-Christians through forced conversion.

Although state and Jewish invocations of the Iberian Inquisition and marranos were polemical and of dubious historical accuracy, the parallel is analytically useful for unpacking the complicated Jewish encounter with imperial Russia and how Jews negotiated the covert and overt imperial inducement to be baptized and how they dealt with their Jewish past as new Christians. Their fragmented identity was as much about their own liminal experiences as about Christian society's suspicion and persecution of the lingering "otherness" of converts from Judaism.[11] The two compelling historical parallels between marranos and Russian Jewish converts are the political settings that linked conversion to the ruling faith with opportunity and the imperial church-state alliances that made Judaizing a crime.

These provocative points of convergence by no means imply that nineteenth-century Russian Jews were reliving the fate of their ancestral coreligionists. Indeed, the comparison breaks down when we consider that imperial Russia never gave its Jews an ultimatum to convert or leave, even though nineteenth-century Russian Jews construed state-led Jewish reforms as veiled conversion campaigns. Also, even though the state discriminated against Jews, it was poverty that mainly drove Jewish emigration in the late imperial period. Fear of pogroms also played a role, but the violence was on a different order than that which propelled the huge marrano emigration from the Iberian peninsula in the decades after the institution of the Inquisition tribunals and the *limpieza de sangre* (purity of blood) laws that disenfranchised subjects of Jewish origin. Moreover, that marranos received most of their education in Christian schools was much more revolutionary in early modern Iberia than state education was in nineteenth-century Russia. At a time when Jews were not admitted to universities, marranos were unique in that they were schooled in Western philosophy, science and theology.[12] The same cannot be said of Russian Jews centuries later, when attending universities and state-sponsored Jewish schools had become more commonplace, though still not the norm for the majority of Jews in the Pale of Jewish Settlement.

The comparison between Catholic and Orthodox policies toward Jews is closer when it comes to the criminalization of religious deviance and discriminatory laws against new Christians. Like the Inquisition tribunals in late medieval and early modern Iberia, Russian courts punished Jews suspected of religious deviance. In imperial law, church and society were the eyes and ears of the state in surveilling new Christians. Neighbors and parish priests were instructed to look out for signs of religious and cultural deviation and to note converts who failed to appear in church regularly for confession and communion.[13] Judging from evidence in seduction cases, many priests kept records of Christians, at least new converts, who attended confession and took communion.[14]

In addition to facing surveillance, the Iberian marranos and imperial Russian converts from Judaism similarly encountered discriminatory laws that stigmatized them as new Christians. Like the *limpieza de sangre* laws in medieval Spain that barred converts of Jewish origin from various professions, imperial Russian laws in the second half of the nineteenth century also discriminated against Jews. In 1850 the state mandated that Jewish converts to Christianity retain their Jewish surnames.[15] It does not appear that this law disenfranchised converts, although it did stigmatize them. Under Alexander III, however, laws regulating university admissions and the legal profession disenfranchised Jews and converts of Jewish origins. These laws have been interpreted as measures to break the cycle of Jews converting to escape discriminatory legislation and as political and economic expedients to keep revolutionary politics (commonly associated with Jews) and economic competition at bay.[16]

Whether these laws had a basis in racial theory is contested; however, it is incontrovertible they questioned the efficacy of baptism and linked converts from Judaism to Jews based on extra-religious criteria. Despite the scientific discourse on race in late imperial Russia and its popular, xenophobic appropriations, historians have established that racial theory did not influence late imperial policy or policymakers.[17] Records of the legislative debates following the failed 1905 Russian revolution regarding discriminatory legislation against converts repeatedly called attention to lawmakers' concern for the sincerity of new converts and their questioning about at what point converts and their descendants completely assimilated—politically and economically—to Russian society.[18] "Racial" laws against converts from Judaism did not signal an end to the politics of Russification nor the interest in Jewish conversion but a concern with establishing how soon political and cultural assimilation followed religious assimilation. Nonetheless, there was a growing discourse in the reform and post-reform periods on the challenges of Jewish conversion in which Jewishness was increasingly racialized, thereby calling into question the efficacy of baptism and the legal rights of converts.[19]

Return of the Oppressed: Cantonist Mutinies in the Reform Period

Imperial Russian bureaucracy had no legal classification for unaffiliated or atheist subjects.[20] The empire managed its diverse population through the reigning Orthodox Church and the religious institutions of the tolerated foreign confessions. Thus, religion was not just a spiritual or social commitment; it was an organizational necessity and one's personal legal status depended on it. Imperial law did not permit interfaith marriages; all marriages were considered sacraments to be officiated by religious law, and there were no civil marriages. Thus, a lover who converted to Christianity in order to marry had no legal means to uphold his or her prior religious commitments; and subjects who converted to improve their social or material status had no legal space in which to maintain ties to their former faith.

Imperial law encouraged converts to Orthodoxy to leave their former coreligionists and relocate to Christian communities. For Jews in particular, this desire to alienate convert and kin stemmed in large part from a long-standing fear of Judaizers.[21] Aside from supposedly Judaizing sects like the Subbotniks active in nineteenth-century imperial Russia, there were, as discussed in earlier chapters, Christian converts to Judaism whom church authorities claimed were "seduced" by Jews.[22] Historians have debated the extent of Jewish involvement in early modern Judaizing heresies, but the Russian Empire deemed all Jews a potential religious threat to its indigenous Orthodox population and to new Christians.[23] Thus, imperial law regulated Jewish-Christian interactions, and even paid converts to move away from their native Jewish communities.[24] Because the population of Jews in the Pale of Settlement was large, and was concentrated in cities and towns, when converts relocated within a province it was often to another Jewish area.[25] The state recognized its inability to fully control Jewish-convert relations; the two-fold crime of religious deviance—for which both the seduced and the seducer were punished—evidenced the state's suspicion that any convert who deviated from Christianity was the victim of local, alien influences. The legal term for criminal deviation from Christianity was *sovrashchenie*, meaning corruption, or seduction, often used to connote sexual temptation.[26] The conspiratorial nature of the crime and the equation of heresy with sexual temptation cast the crime as non-spiritual; apostasy from Christianity was not thought to stem from individual choice or spiritual conviction, but rather from weakness of the flesh.

Ultimately, religiosity and deviance in imperial Russia were measured by religious performance rather than faith or doctrinal orthodoxy. Imperial law called on all Christians and parish clergy to make sure that converts at a minimum took communion yearly and annually went to confession.[27] Deviance was legally defined as following "alien customs." In contrast to this emphasis on religious action, preparation for baptism revolved around learning the creed (*Simvol very*) and basic theological tenets. After baptism, though, the only practical gauge of a convert's sincerity was at the level of practice. Thus, cases brought against converts who relapsed were founded on the notion that religiosity is behavioral, and one's actions reflect the sincerity of one's faith. Although lawmakers in the reform era began to conceive of religion as faith (*vera*) more than law (*zakon*), or a matter of personal choice rather than legal ascription, imperial law on the crime of deviation did not embody this new conception until after the revolution of 1905 and even then apostasy was judged solely on the basis of one's behavior.

One of the earliest cases of relapse among Jews in the Russian army came in 1835 with a petition from a veteran asking to be legally reregistered in his native Jewish community. Nikolai Tiskevich, formerly Itsko Mortkhevich, of Bialystok, converted to Russian Orthodoxy in 1830 at about the age of nineteen. At that point, he had been in the military for three years. In 1834 Tiskevich was discharged due to ailing health. Immediately thereafter, Tiskevich lived among Christians in the Bialystok region. According to witnesses, Tiskevich did not have any Christian acquaintances, he engaged in the liquor trade at inns, and he did not keep the Jewish Sabbath. From these accounts, it appears that he was a loner. Tiskevich was socially removed from his Christian neighbors and religiously distanced from his previous faith. Although his way of making a living did not raise concern among Christian villagers, he engaged in a trade that was heavily dominated by Jews in imperial Russia and perhaps served as the trigger for his relapse.

In 1835, a year after the discharge, Tiskevich returned to his home community and married a Jewish woman with whom he fathered a daughter. According to his own testimony, Tiskevich came home from the army still dressed as a soldier but he discreetly wore a yarmulke underneath his military cap. He did not divulge his conversion to his family or community. Jewish onlookers assumed that he had continuously professed Judaism; Christian acquaintances and army personnel assumed by his dress that he was Russian, namely Orthodox. It was Tiskevich himself who ended this confessional tightrope walk and alerted authorities to his relapse when he voluntarily came to local administrative offices and asked to be registered as part of the local Goniondz Jewish community (Grodno Province). He was promptly arrested and indicted on charges of "seduction" from Orthodoxy.

Tiskevich offered two reasons for his abandonment of Orthodoxy. Practically, he strayed from Orthodoxy because, in his words, he could not possibly support himself in a Christian community. Philosophically, Tiskevich claimed that he had never sincerely accepted Christianity but converted out of fear of his zealous unit commander. He claimed that coercion undermined the legitimacy of his Christian status and sincere religious conviction legitimized his return to Judaism. Tiskevich's arguments were ignored and a decade-long criminal proceeding against him and his Jewish "seducers" ensued.

Local Jews, including his father, his future brother-in-law, and the communal rabbi, pleaded ignorance when asked about Tiskevich's relapse. They claimed that they did not know of his conversion, nor did they witness him engaging in any particular Jewish rituals (e.g., attending synagogue) that would substantiate the criminal charges against him. From the farfetched nature of the latter claim, it appears that Tiskevich's family carefully testified so as not to provide evidence of actual deviant behavior. A police investigation later discovered that when Tiskevich returned home from the army, his father, his future brother-in-law, and his future wife read his discharge papers and learned of his conversion.

After a long prison sentence and futile pleas from parish and diocesan clergy inveighing him to renounce Judaism, Tiskevich was exiled to Siberia and his young daughter was ordered to be taken from her Jewish mother and put in an orphanage where she would be reared as a Christian. For eight years the Bialystok regional administration unsuccessfully looked for Tiskevich's wife and daughter. In 1851 the Lithuanian Consistory that oversaw the Bialystok region called off the search for the daughter and closed the case.[28]

In this case, a state bent on protecting the supremacy of Orthodoxy and committed to confessional compartmentalization as a means of imperial management was unable to suppress social and economic ties between a convert and his community. The one-year hiatus between the time Tiskevich left the army and returned home suggests that he did not originally decide to return to the Goniondz Jewish community. It appears that he tried to live as a Christian outside of the army, but social isolation and financial difficulties led him back to his hometown. At home, friends and relatives in the know turned a blind eye to his conversion, and the rest of the community had no reason to doubt that he was a Jew. After marrying and fathering a child, Nikolai sought to make his Jewishness official. Perhaps he believed he could legitimize his crime and unsettle the state's rigid policy on confessional identity. Imperial law, though, had the upper hand.

Whereas Tiskevich's relapse in the 1830s was a novelty, there was a spate of religious mutinies in the imperial Russian army between 1855 and 1860 launched by former Jewish cantonists who claimed they had been forcibly baptized as underage recruits. In his work on Jews in the Russian army, Yohanan Petrovsky-Shtern documented five such cases, involving around 197 cantonists, who collectively contested their religious ascription.[29] Notably, most attempts at relapse were staged when cantonists entered an adult army unit or after they were discharged. The chronology of these relapses suggests that cantonists who succumbed to baptismal coercion accepted their fate as a temporary evil that could be rectified once they moved up into adult units where Jewish soldiers enjoyed religious protection or when they were discharged and hence no longer subject to the military drive for imperial unity, including confessional unity.[30] The issue of coercion dominated the

Department of Military Settlements' investigation of these cases of relapse and mutiny. These cases brought into stark relief the disjuncture between Nicholas I's decrees to carry out cantonist conversions meekly, without any force, and the reality of coercive commanders. In most cases, the Department of Military Settlements ordered local military authorities to neutralize religious rebels through ecclesiastic admonition or relocation to distant military settlements, far from Jewish influences. Although the department at times privately censured zealous commanders for their brutal conversion tactics, it publicly proclaimed the innocence of military commanders and the guilt of cantonists who fabricated accounts of being forced to convert when in fact they had "freely" submitted to baptism. The archival records of these cases lend legal weight to cantonist memoirs that depict the often violent and brutal inducements to baptism for Jewish cantonist recruits. These cases also shed light on the religious lives of converted cantonists who publicly confessed Russian Orthodoxy but privately maintained their Jewish identity.

The religious mutiny of 108 cantonists in the navy in 1855 reveals the marrano-like existence of cantonist converts. In August 1855, Jewish cantonists from the Arkhangel'sk Regiment arrived in St. Petersburg on their way to adult service in the Kronstadt fleet. In St. Petersburg, 92 cantonists, followed by 16 others, declared to the Ministry of the Navy that they were forcibly converted to Russian Orthodoxy as cantonists. The ministry called for a special commission to be set up in Kronstadt to investigate the charge.[31] The Kronstadt commission wanted to know who seduced the neophytes to renounce Orthodoxy and how these cantonist converts, sequestered in the navy, obtained the knowledge and ritual objects to perform Jewish rites. Some of the cantonists testified that in St. Petersburg, while awaiting transit to adult service in Kronstadt, local Jewish elders approached them at the Arakcheev barracks and urged them to renounce their conversion. To coax the converts, the Jewish men "gave many of them money and sweets and showed them how to lodge a claim."[32] Other cantonists testified that adult Jewish crewmen in their midst taunted the converts and urged them to "strongly defend their old faith and deny their new faith."[33] As for access to Jewish ritual items, the converts explained that before they arrived in Arkhangel'sk, they heard from graduating cantonists that the navy confiscated Jewish books. Therefore, the converts buried their books and ritual objects outside of Arkhangel'sk and retrieved them on their departure to St. Petersburg. A few claimed that Jewish books and ritual objects were bought in St. Petersburg and Kronstadt.[34] In reviewing the Kronstadt commission's findings, the naval Judiciary Standards Department, in addition to meting out punishments, ordered that all books and articles on Jewish law gathered from recruits be destroyed.[35] Books and ritual objects confiscated from the converts included a pair of *zizit*, a talit, letters written in Yiddish or Hebrew (*pisannoe po evreiski*), writings on the Ten Commandments, Sabbath candles, a yarmulke, and prayer books.[36]

In addition to this mutiny, twenty-three of the thirty cantonists promoted to the machinists' crew declared that they had been forcibly converted as cantonists and no longer wanted to remain Christians. They asked to use their Jewish names and to never again attend church. They confided that even as baptized cantonists, they secretly left their barracks to attend Jewish prayer services. In line with the legal definition of apostasy as involving conspiracy, the unit commander contended that these boys' relatives and other Jews were to blame for their deviance. He surmised that Jewish families threatened to withhold inheritance money from their boys if they converted.[37]

Though the navy quickly dealt with this mutiny just as Alexander II ascended the throne and shut down the cantonist units, individuals continued to protest against coerced underage baptisms in the reform era. Nikolai Epel'man declared to the Ministry of War that he had been converted to Orthodoxy against his will and wanted "to confess, as before, Jewish law" (*khochet po prezhnemu ispovedyvat' evreiskii zakon*).[38] Epel'man claimed that a sergeant-major forcibly baptized him in 1851 when he was in the Kungur Cantonist Battalion. After ecclesiastical admonition and over a year in a monastery, Epel'man requested a military tribunal to adjudicate his case. He was then transferred to the Vologda Battalion and kept under constant ecclesiastical supervision.[39] The case came to a head in 1869 when Epel'man told the Ministry of War that he had married a Jewish woman, Rachel, according to Jewish law. When admonition proved futile, the Vologda Ecclesiastic Consistory notified provincial authorities of Epel'man's apostasy. The case file closed with Epel'man being deprived of his personal possessions and sent to religious authorities for further sentencing.

In another case, a sailor who continued his quest for the right to relapse for two decades had more success. Mikhail Beilin, formerly Nokhem from

Vitebsk Province, was drafted into the Arkhangel'sk cantonist unit at the age of fourteen and baptized in 1853. Upon reaching adult service in 1855, Beilin told his commanding officer that he had been forcibly converted as a minor and now wanted to contest his confessional ascription. The 1855 apostate mutiny, including Beilin's relapse, was kept an internal navy affair, and all participants were either admonished to recant their apostasy or were punished. Despite the threat of punishment, Beilin persisted and in 1874 he started to search out avenues for justice outside of the military, especially as he was retiring and wanted his veteran papers to document that he had reclaimed his status as a Jew. In 1874, after admonishing him in vain, the St. Petersburg Ecclesiastic Consistory brought him to a criminal court in the capital on charges of apostasy. Reviewing the evidence of Beilin's coerced underage baptism, the court acquitted him on the grounds that he was not legally a convert according to the criminal code's description of apostasy. Though this was a remarkable legal coup, the court had no power to legally change Beilin's retirement papers. In 1876 the Synod itself took up Beilin's petition, and, in 1877 it permitted him to mark "Jewish" as his confessional status on his discharge papers.[40]

In choosing to announce their apostasy publicly, these former cantonists tried to change their religious ascription based on their actual religious practice. Their detailed accounts of Jewish learning, practice, and social engagement attest to the existence of crypto-Jews who began to clamor for confessional recognition during the reformist reign of Alexander II.

Aside from active soldiers and sailors who relapsed in the 1850s, there was a slew of veteran converts in the 1870s who retroactively challenged their conversion as cantonists some two decades earlier. For many veterans, the belated legal challenge came on the heels of their discharge from the army and their early confrontation with the social realities of living as marginal new Christians outside of the army. For those who had been discharged many years earlier, reintegration into their pre-army lives drew them back into the orbit of Jewish living and their confessional duplicity was only discovered accidentally, if at all. In addition, the increase in the number of official relapses in this period can be linked to the judicial reforms of 1864, which eased relapsing by bolstering judicial review in lieu of administrative procedure.[41] The military reform of 1874 instituting universal conscription does not appear

to have affected the rate of relapse or the implicit link between Orthodoxy
and loyalty to the tsar among conscripts despite the new conception of the
military as a citizens' army that served the nation, a multiconfessional empire,
rather than the person of the tsar.[42]

In 1869 retired private Nikolai Ryzhkov was walking through Shklov
when a local gendarme randomly checked his passport. The Christian name
on the passport and the Jewish prayer book in his hands raised the suspicions of the gendarme, who detained Ryzhkov and turned him over to the
police on charges of seduction from Orthodoxy. Born in Mogilev Province,
Ryzhkov was drafted into the imperial Russian army as a minor and placed in
a cantonist regiment from which he then graduated to an adult infantry unit.
According to the fact-finding of the Mogilev police, Ryzhkov was converted
against his will in 1841 and discharged from the army in 1851.[43] Although his
baptism predated Nicholas I's official sponsorship of cantonist conversions,
Ryzhkov's charge that he was coerced into baptism still has historical traction.
Even before Nicholas I commanded army officers to convert Jewish cantonists,
he responded favorably to the conversions initiated by zealous army officers
and requested that conversion statistics be sent to him on a regular basis.[44]
With the implicit approval of the tsar to convert young Jewish recruits, zealous army officers often terrorized cantonists until they submitted to baptism.

From his baptism until a year after he was discharged, Ryzhkov behaved like a dutiful Orthodox Christian. He regularly "fulfilled Orthodox
rites" (*obriady pravoslavnoi very ispolnial*), which meant he annually went to
confession and took communion, prayed, and observed all rites and fasts.[45]
According to Ryzhkov's testimony, although he was not a "truehearted"
Christian while in the army, "he did not observe Jewish rites and prayer, and
he did not attend synagogue."[46] Upon discharge, he lived for nine months in
an almshouse in Mogilev where he continued to profess Orthodoxy. Then
he moved to Rudnia (Orshanskii District), where his brother Hirsch lived.
Ryzhkov began attending Jewish school and he soon "began to profess the
Jewish religion" and reclaimed the Hebrew name Zalman. From 1852 until
1869 Ryzhkov lived among Jews, socialized with Jews, and practiced as a
Jew. Were it not for the local gendarme who exposed his duplicity, Ryzhkov
might have continued to live as a Jew unencumbered by the weight of his
past baptism and former life as an Orthodox Christian.[47]

Like Ryzhkov, retired soldier Ivan Bondarev, introduced at the beginning of this chapter, tried to informally resume his Jewish life without informing the authorities. Bondarev converted to Orthodoxy in 1867 at the age of twenty-three while serving in the military. In contrast to Ryzhkov, who was forced to baptize as a cantonist in the Nikolaevan army, Bondarev freely converted as an adult in the reformed army of Alexander II. In 1870 Bondarev was discharged from the army and settled in the Bialystok area. He suffered from epileptic attacks, which affected his ability to find a permanent residence. The testimonies of former landlords and co-tenants reveal Bondarev's panoply of Christian and Jewish acquaintances. Witnesses were asked to comment on Bondarev's religious behavior to help substantiate the police's tenuous case of seduction. According to the Jew Movsha Meyer Rozental, Bondarev lived and worked for him for six months as a gardener. He was well-behaved though constantly sick, and it was not clear what confession he professed. Rozental never saw Bondarev pray, celebrate the Jewish Sabbath or festivals, or go to synagogue. According to a Christian woman, Tsareva, Bondarev lived for a short time in a small storeroom in her home. She never saw what he ate or whether he prayed. On Saturday, she saw him go to work. Yosel Sroliuk, who lived in the same house as Bondarev for two weeks, said he could not figure out Bondarev's religion or whether he prayed, but he saw him go to work with a shovel every day of the week. Bondarev himself claimed that although he was often among Jews in the Bialystok area, he never went to synagogue and he yearly went to confession and took communion. Beyond that, he rarely went to church because he was busy as a day laborer and was in constant need of money to buy bread. The Lithuanian Consistory took up this case and initially sentenced Bondarev to ecclesiastic admonition. By the time the consistory got involved, though, Bondarev had disappeared.[48]

If we read between the legal lines of this case and the concerted police and church attempt to pin down the confessional identity of Bondarev, we find the life of a Jewish convert that evaded imperial legal definition. Bondarev freely interacted with Christians and Jews and he inhabited a space permeated with Judaism and Christianity. Bondarev appears to defy religious classification because he was not a particularly active religious person and he was a social loner. In this case, the unexplained *zizit* and *sidur* in the absence of other religious indicators were taken as evidence of his perfidy.

Bondarev's case is an anomaly in the stream of veteran relapses in the 1870s, the vast majority of which involved coerced baptisms of cantonists. Nevertheless, his case illuminates the experience of converts in the military irrespective of the impetus of conversion or the particular army unit involved. If the imperial Russian army from the time of Nicholas I was conceived of as a homogenizing institution for the creation of patriotic and useful imperial subjects, then irrespective of coerced baptisms, the military championed Russian Orthodoxy as the state religion and hence the patriotic confessional choice. Whether or not Ryzhkov unwillingly converted as a cantonist bending to his commander's will or Bondarev voluntarily converted as part of the larger integrationist goals of the army, both converts took on Orthodoxy more as a set of practices than a system of belief or an identity. As such, their Orthodoxy was coterminous with their army service; after discharge, they appear to have returned to more familiar ethno-confessional terrain.

Church and state officials who oversaw seduction cases were constantly plagued by the state's inability to control assimilation, especially after a soldier returned to civilian life. Legal cases of veterans point to the specter of relapse that haunted converts in the western provinces, where Jewish-convert relations resisted the confessional state's campaign to maintain religious clarity and communal separation. In the case of the relapsed veteran Nikolai Alekseev, who had served in the Arkhangel'sk Battalion, diocesan officials worried that his repeated refusal to return to Orthodoxy was exacerbated by living in Kherson Province among a robust Jewish population seething with "fanaticism." Officials requested in 1878 that Alekseev—with his long-time record of service and profession of Orthodoxy from the late 1820s to 1860s— be moved to a province devoid of Jews in the hope that, once out of Kherson, he could be goaded to return to Orthodoxy.[49]

Naum Kampel', an army veteran and relapsed convert, was likewise sentenced to relocation far from Jews in 1870 when the Synod intervened in his botched relapse case. In 1868 Kampel' was found guilty of apostasy from Orthodoxy to Judaism in Sedlets (Pol., Siedlce, Congress Poland) and admonished, but to no avail. The Warsaw ecclesiastic administration took over the case and, despite hesitating to return Kampel' to his hometown, declared that his birthplace of Terespol' (Lublin Province, Congress Poland) was the best place to receive clerical admonition in that it was not far from

Brest-Litovsk and its robust Orthodox clergy. In the midst of deciding what to do with Kampel', who was under arrest in Warsaw, he was somehow released to a rabbi. At this point, the Synod intervened and transferred Kampel' to the interior province of Kursk. Within weeks of his arrival in May 1870, Kampel' disappeared. He was not heard from until 1896, when he petitioned the Sedlets governor from his residence in Kraków, Austrian Galicia, for imperial amnesty to return to his homeland. Though the MVD was in favor, the Ministry of Justice rejected pardoning Kampel' since his protracted disappearance and perseverance in his relapse suggested that the state would need to take legal measures to counter his deviation.[50]

Whereas these veterans tried to keep their relapses a secret, there were converts who publicly relapsed and petitioned the state for permission decades before apostasy became legal.[51] In 1876 Private Aleksei Iofin asked Kiev officials to mark "Jew" on his army discharge papers. He was recruited to a cantonist unit at the age of nine from Mogilev, where he was forcibly converted to Orthodoxy. Since he had never considered himself Orthodox and he wanted to profess Judaism as a civilian, he asked provincial officials to legally document his chosen confession. When ecclesiastic admonition failed to convince him to drop his request, a criminal case was launched in 1877. In the trial, the defense emphasized that Iofin did not try to conceal his relapse but boldly expressed the idea of subjective religious freedom (*sub'ektivnaia dukhovnaia svoboda*). Iofin's lawyer declared that freedom of faith (confession, conversion, propaganda) reigned in Europe since the French Revolution, while Russia only protected freedom of confession and officially curtailed conversion and missionizing to the Orthodox Church. Based on the 1862 law protecting children from coerced baptisms in order to prevent "religious slavery" (*dukhovnoe rabstvo*), the defense pleaded that Iofin's cantonist baptism be deemed invalid and that the court uphold "civilization and freedom of conscience." The court acquitted Iofin, following the precedent set in the early 1870s of dealing with coerced cantonist conversions.[52]

Irrespective of the inducements for baptism, that the government sought both to control confessional membership and to have that membership dictate personal status created a class of converted Jews whose formal Christian status and informal Jewish social, cultural, and ritual involvement were at odds. For these converts, laws criminalizing Orthodox apostasy rendered them religiously impotent, much like medieval marranos, unable to choose their religious affiliation. Unlike medieval Iberia, where the Inquisition tribunals were unforgiving, imperial Russian courts and ministries did not always punish apostates, but until 1905, neither they did not outright legalize confessional transfers. Thus, crypto-Jews were the product not just of coercion, but of an unyielding legal system designed to preserve Orthodoxy at the expense of individual choice. As heard in the Iofin case, the call for freedom of conscience would increasingly be sounded by apostates to argue for absolute religious toleration, both to and *from* Christianity.

Civilian Relapses

By the end of the ninteenth century the Russian Empire strictly hewed to the letter of the law by prohibiting civilian converts from leaving any Christian denomination. Like the problem of relapse in the army and state interference in identity politics, civilian Jewish converts' practices and affiliations were often at odds with their ascribed confessional status.

Several cases of convert relapse in the first half of the nineteenth century were connected to the Roman Catholic Church, which dominated many areas of the former Polish-Lithuanian Commonwealth recently partitioned by Russia. In one case, according to records of the Roman Catholic College three sons who were converted by their father as children to Catholicism were charged with returning to Judaism in 1800. The case was originally handled locally in Vilna, where the children were found living as Jews. In 1803 the children appealed their case to Justice Minister Lopukhin, claiming that they had been forcibly converted and relocated by their father, Israel Abramovich, now Vincent Novokovskii, upon his discharge from the Polish army, where he had converted to Catholicism in 1793.[53] In 1796, taking advantage of their father's temporary absence, the oldest brother, Kazimir, followed by the other two brothers, Nikolai and Yosif, escaped to their relatives in Vilna.[54] There they reclaimed their Jewish names (Tobiash, Tankhel, and Falk), the eldest son married a Jewish woman and fathered a son, and the younger two sons enrolled in Jewish schools.[55]

The eldest son was named as the main criminal in the case, since he allegedly incited his two brothers to return to Judaism, and he was sentenced to public lashes and hard labor. The middle son was sentenced to lashes and

conscription since he was deemed unable to support himself. The youngest son, then eleven years old, was sentenced to lashes and given to the care
of his mother to learn a trade.[56] The Catholic father was sentenced to fifty
lashes for not immediately alerting the authorities to his sons' reversion to
Judaism. Kazimir's Jewish wife, Khana, was acquitted as an accomplice to this
apostasy scheme, because she testified that she was unaware of her husband's
Catholic conversion. Jews present at Kazimir's wedding were acquitted on
similar grounds. The Vilna kahal was ordered to publicly invalidate Kazimir's
Jewish marriage and revise the communal metrical records.[57]

Although the sons appealed their case based on the fact that they were
converted by their father as children and were only nominally Christians,
the Roman Catholic College upheld earlier local court sentences based on
canonical texts validating child conversions and the need to punish apostates
even if they were converted by force.[58] Coming on the heels of Russia's an-
nexation of Vilna in 1795, this case is an early testament to the empire's legal
support of the tolerated faiths, in this case Catholicism, and the impossibility
of apostasy. It should be noted, though, that just a few years later, in 1801,
an imperial decree prohibited the Roman Catholic Church from "attracting" (*o ne privlechenii*) Jews to the Catholic faith. Thus, the empire tolerated
minority religion but not heterodox proselytizing.[59] Before Alexander I's creation of a department for handling foreign faiths, the Ministry of Justice
turned the case over to the Catholic Church and supported its hard line on
Christian conversion.

In a case from 1826, a female convert from Judaism to Catholicism was
found dressed in Jewish clothes in a Jewish hospital. She claimed that she
had converted as a minor during the politically volatile year of 1794 near
Vilna, and she now, having come of age, wanted to reclaim Judaism.[60] In
another case, in 1830 Konstantin Lovitskii, a convert from Judaism to Catholicism, was indicted on charges of relapse from Christianity. The Vilna
provincial administration asked the Kovno regional authorities in the towns
of Vidzy and Braslav to either conscript him or exile him to Siberia. A Jew
accused of aiding and abetting the relapse was fined with lashes and the two
kahal members and a rabbi complicit in the relapse were to be barred from
any future communal leadership positions. Moreover, Lovitskii's Jewish
children—a son from his first Jewish wife and two young daughters from his

second Jewish wife—were to be located and given to the Catholic Church for their upbringing and future baptism.[61]

A comparative analysis of archival inventories from the Synod and various Orthodox consistories in and out of the Pale of Jewish Settlement reveals a small but steady stream of civilian relapses from the mid to late nineteenth century. The reputation of some of these civilians as a confessional migrant rendered them marginal and disposable in the eyes of the Jewish community, thus making them vulnerable to conscription. Such a scenario came before the governor-general of Lithuania in 1859. In June 1854 the Semiatich Jewish community offered up as recruits several Jews caught in its midst without passports. One was the Jew Abram Yankeliovich Vrubel', who over half a year later informed his battalion that he was a convert from Judaism unlawfully recruited by the Jewish community. The battalion requested Abram's metrical records, and indeed it was found that he had converted to Catholicism in Lublin Province (Congress Poland) in February 1854 and was baptized under the name of Osip. In defending their right to conscript Vrubel' as a Jew, local Jewish leaders insisted that he "was found among Jews, wore Jewish clothes, ate Jewish food, that is, kosher, went to synagogue and prayer houses wearing Jewish religious prayer attire (tsitses and tefilis), in a word, in all of his relations he appeared as a Jew, and so, when he exited the synagogue, he was detained for not having written documentation, and was given as a recruit, since when he was arrested in Semiatich and then transferred to Grodno, he did not declare that he was a convert or even a Christian."[62] According to the kahal leaders, Vrubel's identity when he was conscripted was determined by his Jewish behavior and affiliation—the only visible criteria of his confessional status. In this iteration of imperial religious identity, confession was determined by how people socialized, what they ate, how they dressed, and what kinds of institutions they frequented.

In his defense, Vrubel' acknowledged being "seen" on the Jewish street, but he offered an elaborate explanation as to why he was still operating in Jewish space. After his conversion, Vrubel' recounted, he looked for work and a place to live. In the meantime, he stayed with a Jewish friend, Abram Lederman, who wanted to convert but first had to divorce his wife. Vrubel' understood his friend's situation, as Vrubel' also divorced his Jewish wife before he converted. Hence, Vrubel' accompanied Lederman to the town of

Semiatich to carry out the Jewish divorce proceedings. While there, Vrubel'
was caught without documentation and summarily conscripted into the army.
In his words, he did not have an opportunity to reveal his true identity to any
army officers until after he was inducted into the army. Although he may
have been seen among Jews in Semiatich, Vrubel' claimed he "did not observe
religious rites of the Jewish faith" at any point.[63] The provincial authorities
stopped their investigation at this point, deciding that Vrubel's baptism made
him ineligible to be a Jewish communal recruit. On the issue of apostasy, they
deferred to the Ministry of Interior to initiate criminal proceedings. Vrubel's
belated revelation of his baptism to army officials combined with his "social,"
if not religious, Judaism, made it seem likely that he was a relapsed convert.

Although it is notable that Vrubel and Lederman agreed to divorce their
wives before baptism (which was voluntary in the eyes of the state and church,
and ultimately for the benefit of the wives, who would not be able to remarry
according to *halakhah* without a *get*), the most visible aspect of their religious
crime entailed Jewish sociability. Thus, the boundaries here between Jewish
sociability, Jewish culture, and the practice of Jewish religion are fluid. In the
testimony of the kahal and in the eyes of the authorities, all were intertwined
and inseparable. Acting Jewish went beyond religion alone—it was enmeshed
in the dynamics of a confessional community that fused religion and culture.

Although many civilian relapses were secretive, like Vrubel's, as we have
seen, a few individuals openly petitioned for official permission to relapse.[64]
Based on a review of a few dozen Kiev Ecclesiastic Consistory and Volynian Ecclesiastic Consistory inventory records from the reigns of Alexander I
and Nicholas I, consisting of several hundred folios, there is no explicit reference to Jewish convert relapses in this period.[65] During these years, the Synod
archives record just a few instances of civilian male "deviations" from Orthodoxy to Judaism.[66] Archival records from the late imperial period document
noticeably more cases of civilian relapse. Between 1893 and 1903, thirteen Jewish converts—ten men and three women—relapsed in the Kiev Diocese. Of
the ten men, two were veterans. All of the cases are categorized as seduction
(*sovrashchenie*) or deviation (*otstuplenie*).[67] For this latter period, the Synod
archives document the petition of the convert Elena Kirichenko to permit her
return to Judaism, and the Kherson Ecclesiastic Consistory archives record
the relapse of a young woman in Odessa in 1881.[68] The archives of the DDDII

include seven cases of civilian relapse in this period, five of which involved petitions from converts asking permission to relapse just a year or two before the 1905 legislation that legalized relapse.[69] Overall, there are few Jewish civilian relapses recorded by the Orthodox Church compared to the hundreds of Jewish conversions each year. The statistics are significant, though, as an indicator of the phenomenon of apostasy from Orthodoxy even before it was legalized.

As we have noted earlier, there were a few bold relapsed civilians who tried to champion freedom of conscience and the freedom to return to the faith of one's ancestors before the watershed legislation of 1905. Several civilian petitions for legal relapse were sent to the MVD on the eve of the freedom of conscience decree of 1905. For example, Yakov Nikolaev Zhidkov petitioned the MVD on October 3, 1904, to allow him "to profess [the] former law into which he was born and free [him] from the depressing spiritual state in which [his] current confession is not Orthodoxy," even though that was his formal religious affiliation.[70] In January 1905 a dying Orthodox woman who had been baptized four decades earlier as a young orphaned teenager taken in by a Russian family petitioned the MVD to be buried as a Jew. Emphasizing her lack of faith in and understanding of Orthodoxy and her feeling that she was being both a bad Christian and a bad Jew, she asked that the government respect her wish to reclaim her ancestral faith. The petitioner, Fenia Mikhailovna Olovenkova, died just months after her petition, before the MVD had a chance to review her request.[71] In another case, a woman who converted from Judaism to marry an Orthodox man asked permission to relapse since her husband had promised not to intrude on her religious life, but subsequently refused to countenance her non-Orthodox faith and forced her to work on her holidays.[72]

Since many civilian relapses were undertaken secretly and when they were discovered by the authorities it was by accident, it is likely that there were other—probably many more—cases that went undetected. In contrast to converted soldiers and veterans, who boldly petitioned for the right to return to Judaism, civilian Jewish converts tended to be reticent. This may be because soldiers and veterans felt the sting of injustice by being forced to convert whereas civilians as a rule freely and voluntarily chose to adopt Christianity. In any event, this reticence would end in 1905 when freedom of religious choice was inscribed into law.

The Apostate Revolution of 1905

Although the Romanovs survived the revolution of 1905, political and social unrest pushed the state to liberalize its laws in an effort to split the liberals from the radicals and thus weaken their coalition against the autocracy. In addition to creating the State Duma, a popularly elected parliament, Nicholas II agreed in the October Manifesto of 1905 to grant freedom of conscience to all imperial subjects, but this was a vague promise that was debated for years thereafter and remained largely uncodified by the end of the old regime in 1917. One of the few practical freedom of conscience laws enacted in this period was the legalization of apostasy from Christianity.

The 1905 law on religious freedom generally allowed apostasy from Orthodoxy to other Christian confessions, but it permitted only certain relapses from Orthodoxy to non-Christian faiths.[73] (In 1906 the law was expanded to permit relapses from all of the tolerated Christian confessions to non-Christian faiths.) Only converts who could prove they relapsed before the 1905 law and who relapsed to the religion of their ancestors could petition to change their confession. Moreover, the state continued to conceive of religious confession as a natural component of ethnic or national identity rather than something a person could choose.[74] Thus, the 1905 law legalizing apostasy was intended to make possible a retroactive legal resolution of predominantly nineteenth-century undesired conversions, rather than to allow converts to leave Orthodoxy.

Baptized Jews who wanted to return to Judaism needed to prove their Jewish ancestry and furnish evidence that they had observed their ancestral religion before the 1905 statute. Ironically, to *legally* relapse, the apostate had to prove that he or she had *illegally* practiced Judaism. In fact, the Saratov provincial government refused Yosif Davidov Fel'dman's petition to relapse since he had converted in 1898 and declared in his petition that he had attended church, gone to confession, and taken communion ever since.[75] Because of the clause in the 1905 law stipulating that petitioners had to prove "continued confession of a non-Orthodox" ancestral faith, Jews' petitions following the 1905 law shed light on the common hybrid religious practices of converted Jews in imperial Russia. While these petitions have been analyzed for what they can tell us about Jewish conversion "strategies," specifically those that backfired and induced some apostates to return to Judaism, I pair these relapse petitions with pre-1905 evidence of seduction to broaden our understanding of the often nebulous religious and cultural zone inhabited by converts from Judaism.[76]

The post-1905 petitions reveal the multilayered social, cultural, and religious lives of Jewish converts formally integrated into Christian communities but informally connected to their ancestral roots. The archive of the Kiev provincial administration, for example, contains numerous petitions from Jewish converts seeking legal relapse following the 1905 granting of freedom of confession (*svoboda veroispovedaniia*). Of the sixteen petitions recorded for the years 1906–1908, all but two were from people who had converted to Orthodoxy either within a decade before the law or even after it had been promulgated. Of the sixteen petitioners, four were female. One petition was rejected outright after an investigation revealed the petitioner had never been Jewish but was born to an Orthodox family.[77] Of thirty-two relapse petitions vetted by the DDDII from 1896 to 1906, two were from relapsed converts who had been baptized several decades earlier—one who converted in 1880, and the other, a cantonist, who had been baptized back in 1851.[78]

The persistence of Judaism in the lives of converts primarily took social/familial or religious/cultural forms. In the first case, legal evidence of ongoing Jewish practice consisted mostly of the maintenance of family relationships, resettlement in a Jewish community, or marriage to a Jew. In the second, evidence of confessing Judaism was mainly found in praying, going to synagogue, and observing the Sabbath. All of the petitions reveal that Jewish society did not consider conversion abnormal and that it readily accepted relapsed converts back into the Jewish fold.

The convert Ester-Rosa Berkovna Zhukovskaia considered Judaism her home and wanted legal recognition of rejoining her Jewish family. According to her petition to the Kiev governor, Ester-Rosa converted to Russian Orthodoxy in December 1906, expecting to marry a young Christian peasant named Feodor whom she met in her home village of Moshny (Kiev Province). Deciding not marry him at the last minute, Ester-Rosa "decided to return to Judaism," even though she had been officially baptized.[79] She moved back in with her widowed Jewish mother, brother, and sister in Moshny, and never went to confession or took communion. In this file, Judaism, or confessional status more broadly, is depicted as a family affair. Ester-Rosa chose Orthodoxy so she could marry a Christian, but Judaism was part of her family status as a single woman. She specifically petitioned the Kiev governor to change her *nationality* and *religious* status, a testament to the fact that these identity markers did not always correlate. Starting at the turn of the twentieth century, converted Jews were legally identified on their passports and other official documents by their Jewish origins (*iz evreev*). The late imperial turn to identification of nationality in addition to confession reflects the state's attempt to find stable measures of identity in light of increasing attention to insincere and forced conversions, which undercut the existential change once naively assumed to accompany baptism.[80] Although population management remained a confessional affair until the end of the old regime, there were subtle administrative and legal attempts to redefine the basis of identity and, hence, personal status beyond religious ascription.

In contrast to Ester-Rosa's family-oriented Judaism, Itsko Khaskelev Nites's religious identification was tied much more to practice. Hailing from the Zhitomir region in Volynia Province, he converted while in the military in 1906. In April 1907 Nites—baptized as Alexander Vladimir after his godfather, the commander of his brigade—entered the reserves. He returned to Zhitomir, where Jewish witnesses testified to his observance of Jewish rites such that they never even suspected he had been baptized. According to these witnesses, Nites was seen numerous times praying at a synagogue in Uman. Others informed provincial authorities that Nites attended synagogue on the Sabbath and Yom Kippur, and that he knew how to pray in Hebrew. Nites substantiated his relapse petition by asserting that he only took communion once following baptism, and that he prayed as a Jew and considered himself a Jew. Family members supported his petition, as demonstrated by the testimony of his father, who furnished evidence of the family's Jewish status and reaffirmed that Nites had professed Judaism since leaving the army by observing Jewish rites and praying in "the Jewish language like all Jews."[81] Nites was twenty-six and single at the time of his petition; his family included his parents and five siblings. Were it not for the 1905 law of religious freedom, these converts would have had no legal recourse to harmonize individual identity and official religious ascription.

Most descriptions of converts' ongoing Jewish practice reflect multiple understandings of or meanings attributed to Jewishness. Nikolai Nemirovskii converted in prison in 1893 after being convicted of blood libel. Sometime after his release, he moved to the town where his Jewish father, Yankel Davidov, lived, and he married a Jewish woman, Sura-Rukhel, with whom he had three children. Having married according to Jewish rites, given his children Jewish names, and circumcised his two sons, Nikolai petitioned the Kiev authorities in December 1906 to formalize his demonstrable—but illegal—Jewish identity.[82] For Nikolai, family, marriage, and practice oriented his confessional affiliation. On the flipside, marriage for some was the prime motivator of conversions to Christianity; when those marriages dissolved or the Christian spouse died, former Jews reclaimed their heritage. Sergei Il'ich Titinger converted to Orthodoxy in 1880 at the age of thirty to marry Ol'ga Kolodetskaia, the daughter of a priest. After his wife died, twelve years before the freedom of conscience ukase, Titinger relapsed to Judaism. In August 1905 he officially petitioned for a change in his confession.[83]

Fedosii Nikolaev Goltsgaker, né Mordko Moiseevich, petitioned the MVD in 1907 to legalize his relapse to Judaism. Mordko converted in the army in 1898, when he was about twenty-three, and then "returned to Judaism, to [his] community" in 1899, when he entered the reserves. According to Mordko, even though he had converted he "never stopped fulfilling the laws of the Jewish religion." According to the Kiev police, no one in Kiev knew Mordko nor could comment on his relapse. The only character witnesses were his Jewish family and the community from his hometown. Although Mordko seems to have been a loner in Kiev and did not make the acquaintance of any Christians, he did not attempt to return to his home community. After the army, he lived in Rostov on the Don, Voronezh, and then Kiev. Mordko's choice to live in Kiev and his voluntary conversion in the army made authorities doubt the veracity of his claim to have relapsed, provoking conjecture that Jews had threatened him, causing him to file the petition.[84] Although Goltsgaker's choice of residence, removed from his Jewish family and community, cast doubt on his supposed return to Judaism, it is significant that the relapse file notes that Goltsgaker asked someone to sign his affidavit on his behalf since he could not sign on the Sabbath. This detail together with his lack of a Kiev social network suggests that he stayed connected to Judaism through family and law, and not necessarily by living in a Jewish community.

So as not to overanalyze these relapsed converts' thought processes and impute a coherent philosophy of religion to apostates and their desire to embrace Judaism, I conclude with the case of Konstantin Uranovskii. In May 1908 Uranovskii petitioned the Vilna governor to allow him to return to Judaism based on the MVD circular of April 1905. The governor forwarded the petition to the Vilna Consistory, the standard pre-1905 procedure in seduction cases. The Vilna clergy exhorted Uranovskii not to deviate from Orthodoxy. In response, Uranovskii wrote, "in matters of religious questions, I am completely ignorant; I do not know the Jewish faith nor Orthodoxy. Having converted to Christianity at age 17, I was hoping through conversion to marry an Orthodox girl, but this marriage never took place." Uranovskii claimed that after he converted he found himself alienated and rejected by both Jews and Orthodox Christians, who instigated several legal claims against him, leading to a few bouts of imprisonment and police surveillance. Uranovskii's life began to straighten out when he became a typesetter for a typographer, where he worked for six years and lived among Jews. With the words "[not to] separate myself from them in any way," Uranovskii explained his choice to publicly reclaim Judaism. Uranovskii concluded, "we workers never talk about religious matters; for us, no matter the faith, we hold onto those rites with which we come into contact. . . . Due to my ignorance of religious matters . . . any exhortation to me is useless, and I petition you not to hold me back."[85]

Whether he spoke from the heart or tried to play the part of a naïf, Uranovskii viewed religion as a tool of communal cohesion rather than an expression of revealed truth. Judaism for him involved cultural belonging suited to his geographic and professional situation. He bluntly detailed his insincere teenage baptism and his ignorance of Orthodoxy. He was a Jew by location, and from his calculation, even a superficial return to Judaism would endear him to the community and secure his economic well-being. Despite his avowedly secular approach to faith, Uranovskii still recognized that in late imperial Russia, identity and belonging were overwhelmingly predicated upon and linked to confessional affiliation. Perhaps this, more than the problem of convert acceptance, induced some apostates to claim they had a right to freedom of faith even before 1905.

Embracing Freedom of Conscience and Jewish Fanaticism

The apostate revolution of 1905 and the introduction of freedom of conscience came only after a protracted struggle in which the tolerated confessions played a role. In the last decades of the nineteenth century relapsed converts defended their right to return to their ancestral faith based on the notion of freedom of conscience. Their voice, which challenged the increasingly venomous Judeophobic screeds in the public press on Jewish fanaticism and violence against converts, became part of a contentious public debate on the terms of toleration and the role of conversion in a state increasingly looking to Orthodoxy as a way to undergird Russian nationalism and imperial unity.

Starting in the 1860s and escalating in the 1880s, criminal cases involving relapsed converts and their Jewish "seducers" captured a great deal of attention in the Russian press. These cases were used to showcase how Jews took advantage of religious freedom to impinge on the religious freedom of other subjects, namely Jews who converted to Christianity. Typifying some of the more occult forms of Judeophobia in the late imperial period, discussions of Jewish fanaticism and supposed ritual murder became an anchor of a growing Russian conservatism born from the optimism of the early reform era and the fallout of rapid socioeconomic change. In the 1870s the popular focus on individual acts of Jewish fanaticism evolved into portrayals of an organized, Jewish communal violence.[86] The popular press, influenced by claims of Yakov Brafman and others that the kahal was an international Jewish cabal, used seduction trials and stories of alleged Jewish religious violence to question the limits and terms of religious tolerance in an empire that granted freedom of religion to all but still claimed a monopoly on absolute religious truth.

In this evolving discourse on Jewish violence against converts, the press latched onto "fanaticism" as an innate Jewish trait that affected both the convert (who was portrayed as insincere and materialistic) and the convert's Jewish family, who would go to any length to thwart a kin's baptism. Thus, the press engaged in a racializing discourse whereby difficulties surrounding conversion—and the questionable viability of the entire imperial toleration enterprise—were blamed on innate and malevolent Jewish tendencies.[87]

Coverage of Jewish conversion—legal developments, missions, biographies of converts, stories of relapse and violence—in national, provincial, and diocesan Russian-language presses was thin in the 1860s and 1870s, with a dozen or so articles each decade. Coverage exploded in the 1880s with upwards of two hundred articles on all things related to converts from Judaism, almost half of which dealt with Jewish-Christian sects that started appearing in New Russia in the 1880s, a subject explored in the next chapter.[88] Journalistic coverage in the 1880s stood out for both the frequency of articles linking conversion and Jewish intolerance and violence to a new accusation of ritual murder—revenge killings of Jewish apostates.[89] Relapsed converts reacted by appropriating the epithet of Jewish "fanaticism" and recasting it as a form of freedom of conscience politics.

Jewish Conversion and Russian Conservatism

With the ascension of the reformist tsar Alexander II to the throne in 1855 and the end of the cantonist program in the army in 1856, the Russian state officially exited the Jewish conversion business. Conversion in the post-reform period was more a result of rising expectations and reduced Jewish rights rather than the outcome of concerted programs such as the Society of Israelite Christians or the Conscription Edict of 1827. Governance changed in the late imperial period, following Russia's defeat in the Crimean War (1853–1856) and the Polish insurrection of 1863. It became marked by a greater conflation of the Russian Empire with the Russian people and Russian Orthodoxy, and a desire to assimilate non-Orthodox subjects through cultural and linguistic Russification in the western and eastern borderlands, although there was no consensus among local and imperial officials over the goals of Russification and what it meant to be "Russian" nor a lasting commitment to nationalist policies.[90]

The reform era witnessed the beginning of the demise of the economic position of Jews in small towns and villages as state-led industrialization undercut the commercial niche of small market towns. This gave birth to a large internal migration of Jews in the Pale of Settlement from small towns and villages to provincial cities in search of education and employment. In this context, religious conversion was increasingly seen as a vehicle of residential and socioeconomic mobility, thus giving birth to the Jewish joke of "baptized passports," whereby individuals underwent "dry" baptisms through schemes involving fabricated passport stamps. Indeed, in the early twentieth-century Finnish evangelical pastors fabricated baptismal certificates for Jews attempting to skirt university admission quotas.[91]

The post-reform period witnessed increasing pessimism about the possibility and desirability of Jewish integration. The assassination of Alexander II in 1881 by revolutionaries ushered in an era of political retrenchment and new

Jewish disabilities that in various measures characterized state politics until the end of the old regime in 1917. The May Laws of 1882 forbade new Jewish settlement in the western countryside, and after 1886 the state imposed quotas on the number of Jewish students in institutions of higher education in provincial and interior cities and of Jews in the liberal professions. In sum, the last three decades of the empire witnessed the rise of a "modern exclusive imperial racism that attempted to limit participation of Jews and individuals of Jewish origin."[92] Sholem Aleichem's novel *Der blutiger shpas* (The Bloody Hoax, 1923) is set in this post-reform period of Jewish student quotas, when a Jewish student and a Russian Orthodox student exchange passports in an attempt to explore success and failure in the empire from an alternative confessional identity.

In addition to rolling back selective integration in the late nineteenth century, the imperial state under Alexander III took an unprecedented step in disenfranchising converts of Jewish origin alongside confessing Jews. This, along with the Jewish quotas, privileged one's origins over one's confession as a salient marker of identity. Several other regulations were debated in this period to restrict converts from Judaism from voluntary associations, unions, and government institutions.[93]

Discriminatory legislation against converts from Judaism in the late imperial period signaled that ethnicity was increasingly supplementing religion as a marker of Jewish difference, or that there was a process of "racialization" whereby popular attitudes and administrative practices constructed and validated a hierarchy of human difference even if scientific racism was not at the core of imperial policy.[94] While the law forbidding converts from Judaism to adopt a new surname had been implemented already in 1850 (and in 1865 explicitly adjudicated to apply to civilian converts), at the turn of the twentieth century many converts petitioned for new Russian surnames, arguing that their Jewish surnames made it difficult to break off ties with their Jewish past and escape the stigma of their origins.[95] In this climate of the stigmatization of Jewishness, the Holy Synod adopted two measures in the early twentieth century to counter instrumental Jewish baptisms in the Orthodox Church. In 1903 the Synod prohibited baptized Jews from relocating out of the Pale unless they had earned the right to do so before baptism. And the church ordered that the phrase *iz evreev* (from the Jews) be stamped on the passports of all Jewish converts to Russian Orthodoxy.[96]

A change in how Jewishness and social difference overall was articulated in the late imperial period is clear in this shift to discrimination against converts from Judaism—a policy that would find expression in the Russian military as well in the wake of the 1905 revolution.[97] Whereas for most of the nineteenth century religion was considered an inheritance from one's forebearers, a key marker of nationality, and a stable maker of one's place in the empire, there was a turn toward ethnicity as an emblem of difference in the late nineteenth and early twentieth centuries. With the anti-liberal shift in late nineteenth-century Russian politics in tandem with social and economic dislocations and the growth of Russian nationalism, flexible ideas about human difference evolved into more fixed and hierarchical conceptions of human difference.[98] Whereas confession could be changed via conversion, ethnicity was increasingly conceived of as a stable and unalterable marker of identity and a reliable means of identifying subjects' loyalty, economic potential, and place in the civic order.[99] Especially in the early twentieth century with the destabilization of religious identities—increasing sectarianism, secularization, legalization of apostasy—confession was eclipsed as a basis of classification.[100] Hence, in this conservative political climate, converts from Judaism could not necessarily shed their "Jewishness."[101]

Race and Conversion

With growing attention to Jewish conversion in the Russian press in the 1880s, journalists increasingly racialized not just the supposed fanaticism of Jewish families but the deceptiveness and insincerity of converts as well. Despite some counternarratives in the religious and provincial presses of sincere converts from Judaism, the main national papers used the assumed insincerity of Jewish converts as a platform for denouncing converts as Christian interlopers, and even worse, undercover Jewish agents intent on destroying Christianity from within—again infusing the discourse on Jewish conversion with a narrative of violence.[102] Inflected in this way, conversion was no longer conceived of as a religious act, but as a means to infiltrate Orthodoxy and destroy it from within.

This argument came to a head in 1888 following an exchange of letters in *Grazhdanin* (Citizen), in which the editor, V. Meshcherskii, proclaimed that Orthodox Christians who believed the Jewish question could be solved by conversion were gravely mistaken. Meshcherskii warned his Christian readers that converted Jews sought to "finally and irrevocably destroy" the church as a means of proving themselves to be God's chosen people and fortifying Judaism.[103] To this argument, *Novoe vremia* responded that from a racial perspective, conversion of Jews over time could spell the demise of Jews as a racially distinct people. Ideally, the paper claimed, Jews should be expelled to a desert far from Christian lands, but since the majority of Russians would not permit the wholesale loss of Jewish credit, the next best solution was through intermarriage predicated on Jewish conversion. In these terms, conversion was desirable not for Christianizing Jews in a religious sense, but for diluting Semitic blood over several generations of mixed marriages.

Unlike *Novoe Vremia*, with its racialized rhetoric, the newspapers *Grazhdanin* and, later, *Novorossiiskii telegraf,* believed that the Jewish problem was a religious one, and as such, an insincere convert took advantage of the system of confessional transfer to rob the church of its sanctity. *Novorossiiskii telegraf* focused its coverage of Jewish conversion and the Jewish question on insincere converts and the religious violation of the Christian church. Noting the common phenomenon of Jews from abroad converting as a means of obtaining Russian subjecthood, the paper lamented that fake Christians were not worthwhile to the state, and, more importantly, they perverted and desecrated the Orthodox Church by their trespassing. The paper contended that real Jewish conversion could only occur at a young age, when the convert could realistically be reborn into the new faith.[104] Hence Jewish converts were denounced as manipulators taking advantage of the empire's commitment to religious toleration and using conversion to compromise the strength and transcendence of the ruling church.

The criticism of Jewish conversion in the Russian press portrayed Jews as crafty subjects who used the law to undermine church and state and to invert the confessional hierarchy of the empire. Equating law-abiding converts with thieves, Russian public opinion seized on conversion as an inherently deceptive act that posed more of an existential threat than a boon to Orthodoxy. Ironically, racialists could overlook this threat since over time intermarriage would render pseudo-Christians impotent. Either way, growing suspicions of Jewish converts combined with growing suspicions of their malevolent Jewish families joined to create a violent discourse on conversion and call into question the confessional state and its toleration policies.

Although censorship of the Jewish press in many respects curtailed Jewish engagement with these discourses,[105] the reformed court system of the late imperial period created an alternative space where Jewish voices could be raised and disseminated through publishing trial transcripts to weigh in on the politics of conversion and religious toleration. In the 1880s there were several well-publicized court cases against Jews who converted in the army and then relapsed to Judaism either during adult military service or immediately after discharge. While cases like these had preoccupied the state, military, and courts since the 1850s, as discussed earlier, they now concerned the public as well due to both publicity in the press and great crowds in the courtrooms. One paper captured the significance of this expanded imperial conversation by casting the actual courtroom experience and the one popularized by published trial transcripts as a drama unfolding on the imperial stage that generated emotion and public opinion regarding an affair once closely guarded and silenced by the state.[106] Reporting on relapse focused on the individual apostates and the extent to which they were victims or victimizers of others in their pursuit to change their religious identity. In the cases presented here, the converts married Russian women before relapse, thus complicating their claim that they had never been sincere Christians and their desire to return to Judaism, which conflicted with family responsibilities. The cases that follow illustrate the consequences of the racializing narrative of Jews as inherently duplicitous.

In 1881 the Jewish paper *Voskhod* (Sunrise) publicized the trial in the St. Petersburg circuit court of retired private Yakov Terentev, né Leib Oralovich Liber, accused of deviating from the Orthodox Church. Conscripted as a minor, Liber joined the Kazan Cantonist Battalion, where he was forcibly converted to Russian Orthodoxy in 1847, at the age of seventeen. In 1862 Liber, now Terentev, married a Christian. He later separated from her and began living with a Jewish woman, though they never officially married. The trial hinged on the circumstances of his conversion, on whether forced conversion constituted a legal conversion, and on whether his marriage to a Russian woman reflected a commitment to Christianity.

Two Jewish witnesses substantiated that Terentev indeed had apostatized. They testified that he started attending synagogue in 1870. One witness knew him before as a practicing Orthodox Christian, and another first met him as a practicing Jew, having no knowledge of Terentev's prior baptism. As for the circumstances of Terentev's baptism, the accused argued that officers in the Kazan Cantonist Battalion forcibly converted underage Jewish conscripts, and that it was impossible for Jews to survive without being baptized. A fellow cantonist in the Kazan Battalion was called by the defense to corroborate that conversions were coerced. As for Terentev's voluntary decision to marry a Russian, he claimed that "he found it better to marry than to fornicate and consider his wife a concubine."[107] Overall, Terentev argued that he never wanted to convert, never practiced as a sincere Orthodox Christian, and was "never in spirit or according to his conscience an Orthodox man." After he was discharged from the army, Terentev was concerned about the salvation of his soul, and he openly returned (*vozvratilsia*) to the faith of his fathers.[108] The court acquitted him.

In 1880 and 1885 two other former cantonist recruits were charged with deviation from Orthodoxy, but in these cases other charges of illegal activity were adjudicated so as to deflect attention from the sincerity of their conversion to the ethics of their behavior as adults. Although the prosecution in both cases sought to center the accusations on immoral behavior and technicalities of the Russian passport system, the defense repeatedly called attention to the era of forcible cantonist baptisms that contemporary jurists tried to silence. Although the *rekrutshchina* (conscription) was not on trial and was only gestured to in the course of trial, the defense made sure that the core issues of religious tolerance and freedom of conscience dominated the jury's consideration.

In 1885 Zelik (Petr Petrov) Grinfelt was tried for three crimes: deviation from Orthodoxy, bigamy, and forgery. Born in Mitav (Kurland Province), Grinfelt was conscripted in 1847 and placed in the Arkhangel'sk Cantonist Battalion at the age of twelve. In 1852, when he was eighteen, he converted to Orthodoxy in his cantonist unit, and later that year joined an adult army unit. In 1859 he married the peasant Ksenia Vasileva, with whom he fathered three children between the years 1861 and 1872, and all three children were baptized in the Orthodox Church. In 1873 he was discharged from service and secretly left his family and moved to St. Petersburg, where he forged his discharge papers to reflect his former Jewish name, his religion, and his status as unmarried. In 1875 Grinfelt married the Jewess Rivka Leibova, with whom he lived until 1879 when a reserve officer, Vulf Gibert (also a convert from Judaism), informed on him to the authorities.[109]

According to Grinfelt's testimony, he experienced coercion to convert as soon as he joined the Arkhangel'sk Cantonist Battalion. He was only converted, though, when he was unconscious in a hospital recovering from a head wound inflicted by a zealous commander intent on converting him. Hence, he never considered himself Orthodox, and throughout his time in the army he observed Jewish rituals. His marriage to a Russian woman was only a ruse so as to deflect attention from his furtive Jewish life. In reality, he never lived with Ksenia nor had children with her; he considered his marriage unconsummated and only a metrical-record fiction. Hence, Grinfelt's subsequent marriage to Rivka was not bigamy but his first legitimate and legal marriage. Upon discharge, he asked an Arkhangel'sk clerk to use his Jewish name and affiliation in his discharge papers, a service for which Grinfelt paid ten rubles.[110]

The defense called as a witness a fellow Jewish convert, Aizenberg, to corroborate Grinfelt's furtive Jewish life (he always wore a cap at work, as per Jewish law), and found a former cantonist to corroborate Grinfelt's contention that officers routinely treated cantonist Jews violently. Grinfelt's own testimony described the violent measures officers employed in their quest to baptize underage Jews. He noted routine lashes inflicted on Jewish recruits, periods of withholding food, lockdowns in heated bathrooms, and trials of walking barefoot on hot irons with hands tied while fed herring and denied water. If cantonists complained, they were given a hundred lashes and then punished still more.[111]

The prosecution's main witness was the informant in the case, Gibert (also called Gibner at times). In the transcript of the trial, he is described in satirical terms, as a typical Jew in appearance and manner of talking, who went to comical extremes to portray himself as a sincere Christian during the trial. When taking the oath at the witness stand, Gibert responded to the straightforward question about his confession with a long-winded response affirming his Orthodox convictions. When coming up to the stand and returning to the audience, Gibert dramatically crossed himself, bowed in prayer, and recited scripture. Gibert testified that he often saw Grinfelt eating and drinking during morning prayer services on the Sabbath, suggesting that Grinfelt feigned being a devout Jew, and hence that his conversion was sincere. Gibert portrayed Grinfelt's first wife, Ksenia, as the love of his life, whom he married voluntarily. Gibert claimed that he informed on Grinfelt out of pity for the latter's deserted wife and children and for Grinfelt's offense against Christianity. Gibert initially tried to locate Grinfelt on his own, but after receiving death threats from Jews, which necessitated his hiding in a monastery, Gibert decided to turn the matter over to the authorities.[112]

The closing arguments of the case rhetorically engaged less with the facts than with the spirit guiding Grinfelt's behavior. The prosecution acknowledged that faith was a matter of "internal conviction, conscience" that could not be thrust upon someone "by external force, physical or psychological."[113] Nevertheless, the prosecutor argued that Grinfelt was legally an adult (eighteen years old) at the time of his conversion and therefore his actions were conscious and thoughtful, and his accusations of cantonist torture appeared to be a fanciful way to cover up his voluntary and rational conversion. Not only dismissing cantonist testimonies of coerced baptisms, the prosecution questioned the very premise of military interest in cantonist conversions. "Who would have an interest if Grinfelt was Orthodox or a Jew? What can Christianity win from the conversion of Grinfelt?"[114] Trivializing Grinfelt's conversion and the very notion of an imperial campaign to baptize Jewish cantonist recruits, the prosecution concluded by censuring the apostate's unethical treatment of his Christian wife. In the prosecutor's words, Grinfelt repaid his wife's love and devotion by abandoning her like some "worthless creature" (*negodnaia tvar'*). The prosecution acknowledged the positive trait of Jewish filial devotion and virtue, but the lawyer argued that it was one-sided and ethnocentric; Grinfelt would do anything for his Jewish wife, but for his Christian wife "he has no lasting feeling."[115] In short, the prosecution portrayed Grinfelt's disloyalty to Christianity as stemming from base, Jewish hostility toward Christians, rather than as a result of a coerced conversion.

The defense attorney, S. A. Rozing, stressed that Grinfelt's behavior should be judged not as selfish but rather as moral and motivated by religious conviction, which is wholly personal and not subject to documentation or corroboration of facts. "Grinfelt is not a criminal, but rather a fighter for religion."[116] The defense portrayed Grinfelt as a victim of religious persecution, a "fanatic" and wholly "unselfish" Jew, who simply desired to profess his ancestral faith. Contrary to the prosecution's depiction of Grinfelt's cantonist persecutions as a fairytale, Rozing grounded the case in the well-documented instances of religious violence toward cantonists in the 1850s and the subsequent imperial legal reforms in the 1860s and 1870s to ground conversion in free will. Rozing stressed to the jury of Orthodox men that this tragic episode in imperial history was an affront to their Christian sensibilities of acting with meekness and love toward their neighbors. In line with articles in the press on Jewish conversion, the terms of the debate in this trial on the merits and foibles of conversion turned on the moral position each side took regarding which imperial confession truly embodied religious tolerance and love for one's neighbor. It is ironic that in nineteenth-century imperial Russia religious tolerance was still alive in a society that attributed absolute truth to the ruling faith, thus undermining freedom of religion as an absolute right, inalienable from the individual irrespective of his or her faith.

Finally, the defense interrogated the whole notion of discrediting Grinfelt as a selfish apostate by laying out the consequences of what could only be construed as Grinfelt's regressive and profitless apostasy. Rather than rejecting the common critique of Jewish conversion as mercenary and instrumental, Rozing embraced it to vindicate converts from Judaism who were sincere enough in their Jewish convictions to give up the benefits of Christian affiliation and risk criminal punishment in order to return to their true faith. In this light, Grinfelt was not an immoral, selfish Jew who carelessly started a Christian family, but rather a persecuted Jew who so sincerely considered himself Jewish that he was willing to forego the rights and privileges granted to Orthodox Christians and return to the disenfranchised status of a Russian Jew.[117] Thus, Rozing engaged the discourse on Jewish fanaticism and used it to support the right to freedom of conscience.

Five years earlier Rozing had defended another relapsed veteran who had been forcibly converted as a cantonist in Arkhangel'sk. In 1880 Movsha Shlemov (Aleksei Antonov) Aizenberg was charged with forging passport documents, not formal deviation from Orthodoxy. Converted as an eleven-year-old cantonist, Aizenberg became a friend of Grinfelt in Arkhangel'sk and upon discharge desired to live and marry as a Jew. He too forged his discharge papers to showcase his Jewish name and confession, and, with Grinfelt's help, he found a clerk to assist him. According to his testimony,

Aizenberg never even told his Jewish wife of his conversion, because he made a promise to himself after discharge "never to lose his way from the Jewish religion."[118] In this case, as well, the prosecution tried to undermine the argument of coerced cantonist conversions (or the "military-missionary system," according to the Jewish press), but the defense reminded the crowded courtroom of the long struggle between Judaism and Christianity and that only out of sincere religious conviction would a fully enfranchised convert to Christianity retreat to Judaism. The jury acquitted Aizenberg.

The annual *Evreiskaia biblioteka* (Jewish Library), which publicized the Aizenberg case in the Jewish press, proudly noted that several Russian periodicals had covered the story as an instance of medievalism in modern Russia. One journal even drew a parallel between Aizenberg and the marrano Uriel de Costa, who was excommunicated several times from the early modern Amsterdam Jewish community for espousing heretical views against rabbinic Judaism. Portrayed as a hero in the face of religious intolerance, de Costa resembled Aizenberg, who suffered in the pre-reform army for his religious beliefs.[119] The Russian newspapers *Golos* and *Molva* (The Talk) were relieved that at least Aizenberg was only tried for forgery rather than for "seduction to Judaism."[120] The Jewish press, though, strongly believed that this case and others like it needed more public attention in Russia and throughout Europe as a warning about the contested terms of toleration and freedom of conscience in the empire.

In 1883 *Russkii evrei* and *Nedel'naia khronika voskhoda* publicized the trial of the Jew Freiman, who was accused of seducing Anna Kazakova to Judaism.[121] Eighteen years earlier Freiman had met the then fifteen-year-old street singer Kazakova, a Christian by birth, and they started an "intimate relationship." Kazakova subsequently gave birth to several children, who were baptized in the Orthodox Church. She and her children later adopted Judaism (the male children were circumcised) and she married Freiman. A neighbor who knew Kazakova and her children were native Christians informed the authorities, at which time Kazakova was taken by clerics for spiritual admonition and Freiman was tried for seduction. The trial attracted a large audience. Freiman argued that he did not know of Anna's Christian origins. From contradictory witness depositions, it appears that Anna's religious affiliation was nebulous. What was clear at the trial and what made a deep impression on the jury, according to *Odesskii listok* (Odessa Leaflet), was Freiman's great love for his wife and children, which he showed with great affection and tears while on the witness stand.[122] According to the papers, the jury reached a verdict immediately, finding Freiman innocent.

While the Freiman case, devoid of clear religious boundaries and lacking violence, drew little attention from the Russian press, cases of seduction involving violence against new converts to Christianity aroused great concern in Christian papers, as explored in the last chapter. The putative zealousness of Jewish family members in these cases was seen as treading on Orthodox prerogatives to maintain a hold on its members, irrespective of the their religious self-identity. In contrast to the Russian press, which condemned what it considered Jewish religious aggression, some Jewish periodicals celebrated the unwavering Jewish national fervor and self-defense displayed by Jews returning converts to Jewish society. When the conservative *Zemshchina* reported with dismay on the murder in Mogilev Province of a Jewish convert to Christianity by his father on the day of the son's marriage to his Christian love, the Russian Jewish journal *Razsvet* defended the father's act: "Can you really deny that the son, who stepped over to the enemy's side, insulted his own father and prompted the murder? This is how any Christian, any Russian would have reacted if their own would have transferred to the enemy's side."[123] Ultimately, though, *Razsvet*'s justification of the father's act was futile; any attempt to maintain inviolable Jewish boundaries in the face of Orthodox proselytizing or eternal church membership was interpreted as a violent intrusion on the church and the tenuous terms of religious toleration in the empire.

～

The very existence of relapsed Jewish converts, both before and after 1905, challenges the idea that conversion offered Jews no more than an escape from Jewish disabilities.[124] Relapse cases offer insight into the politics of confessional belonging and the social and religious forces that structured individuals' lives and sense of belonging. If Jews were perhaps the first among non-equals, but that inequality was the common denominator of imperial subjecthood, then conversion and relapse are best viewed not as a step toward assimilation but as a way to navigate the rights and disabilities of confessional status in imperial Russia that circumscribed the boundaries of a subject's social, economic, romantic, and religious life. Because confessional status influenced or determined one's community, social circle, eligible marriage partners, economic niche, and networks as well as religious practices, conversion and apostasy must be understood as individual decisions contingent on circumstance and hence liable to change. Thus relapse to Judaism looks less like failed integration into Russian society than perhaps a beneficial change in status that could legalize a convert's desired social and religious affiliation. The conflicts between confessional affiliation and religious or ethnic identity among relapsed converts attest to the many layers of belonging tied to religious status in imperial Russia and the variety of considerations conditioning converts from Judaism and how and when they chose the confessional status they considered most beneficial or desirable. Whereas Iberian marranos had no option for Jewish communal membership since Spanish and Portuguese Jews had been expelled, Russian Jewish converts lived in an empire with a large and tolerated Jewish population. Despite laws constraining conversion and penalizing apostasy from Christianity, there were still opportunities for cultural mobility in imperial Russia. In that sense, the 1905 legalization of apostasy was an evolutionary—not revolutionary—step toward freedom of conscience. Even before 1905, relapsed converts tried to reclaim heterodox "fanaticism" as an expression of freedom of religion in the face of strident late imperial anti-toleration discourses that attempted to discredit the foreign faiths.

CHAPTER 6

JEWISH CHRISTIAN SECTS

IN SOUTHERN RUSSIA

IN 1872 the Jewish cantonist turned Orthodox missionary Alexander Alekseev published a set of "conversations" that he wanted to have with converts from Judaism who were weak or vacillating in their new Christian faith. Wary of ongoing Jewish influences on neophytes, Alekseev was actually less concerned about the lingering influence of rabbinic Judaism, since both Judaism and Orthodoxy believed in messianic redemption. Rather, Alekseev warned Jews against the dangers of "progressive" Judaism, which was starting to rear its head in late imperial Russia. According to Alekseev, this new brand of Judaism undermined the whole messianic premise that underlay both traditional Judaism and Christianity and, hence, was the "most dangerous to [neophytes] in the realm of faith."[1] There was little chance a missionary could sell modern Jews on Jesus since they already "completely reject the doctrine of the Messiah" (*vovse otvergaiut uchenie o Messii*).[2]

Thus, Alekseev reacted with ambivalence to the spate of Jewish Christian sects that emerged in southern Russia in the 1880s and undermined the neat lines between Judaism and Christianity, and which many Jews reviled as a Russian iteration of reformed Judaism. Many contemporaries like Alekseev held out hope that these sects could be a bridge from Judaism to Russian Orthodoxy, but they feared that their leaders and adherents were sectarians who undermined the state's investment in orthodox religion and ethno-confessional clarity. Furthermore, some contemporaries viewed these sects as religious reformers who, despite formal or ideological "conversion" from Talmudic Judaism, continued to promote Jewish religious and national difference alongside Christian dogma. While only one sect, Joseph Rabinovich's New Testament Israelites, officially converted to Christianity, the sects in general aroused the concern of the state and public opinion among Jews and Christians about the blurring of confessional lines. The biblicism of Jacob Gordin, the leader of another sect, was denounced as Judaizing intended to seduce Orthodox Christians; and both Jacob Gordin's Spiritual-Biblical Brotherhood and Jacob Priluker's New Israel sect advocated intermarriage, a core taboo in the Jewish as well as the Christian worlds. Through their heterodox doctrines and figural conversions, these sects crossed a host of boundaries—confessional, political, linguistic—and thus sparked a debate in government and among the public about religious reform, sectarianism, and the role of orthodox religion in the empire. At their core, these discussions articulated anxieties about figural conversions of Jews to Christians and Christians to Jews by virtue of adopting the qualities of the other.

Although none of these groups had much success in courting Jews, their interaction with the state, the Orthodox Church, and contemporary Jews offers another perspective on how converts functioned in Jewish and imperial Russian society and questioned the terms of religious identity and communal affiliation. The contest between state and church officials over the legitimacy of Christianizing Jewish sects should be understood in the context of anxieties among officials over revolutionary activity in the last decades of the nineteenth century and an indigenous evangelical movement in the southern provinces that challenged the hegemony of the Russian Orthodox Church. In addition, the imperial management system based on confessional orthodoxies could not tolerate ambiguous religious identities or splinter groups that might destabilize the empire's confessional grid.

Thus, the sectarianism of the 1880s, combined with the marrano narratives of relapsed converts in the reform era discussed in the last chapter, coalesced into a late imperial conversation about conversion, cultural mobility, and the boundaries of imperial confessions. In looking at the state's view of these sects and the Jewish and general public reception through the popular press, we see a range of concerns about conversion and the mobility of identity. In the context of sectarianism, conversion was predicated less on crossing the boundaries between groups and more on appropriating the qualities of another group. In other words, conversion did not require a formal crossing of confessional boundaries but could be undertaken through the circulation of confessional "qualities."[3] Thus, the liminal space occupied by the sects highlights the tension between tolerated confessions and personal faith in the empire and the question of where converts and schismatics communally belonged.

Jewish Sects and the State

Much of the state's concern with Jewish sects in the 1880s centered on attempts to demarcate the boundaries between Christian and Jew. For a state invested in toleration as a means of control, new religious formations tested its ability to maintain order. As Nicholas Breyfogle argued in studying the *Subbotniki* (Russian Sabbatarians), historians must be wary of "assigning clearly demarcated boundaries between 'Jew' and 'Christian'—even if clerics and others at the time aspired to such a dichotomy. Rather than discrete groups in terms of beliefs and practices, Jews and Christians should be understood as forming part of a spectrum of religiosity with the hues and shades of faith and practice often blending with one another and influencing each other."[4] It was precisely this kind of imprecision about Christian Jewish sects that unsettled the state and the Orthodox Church, all the more so since some sectarians officially converted to Christianity. A similar fear of sectarianism animated the polemics earlier in the century surrounding the Frankists in Warsaw, followers of Jacob Frank who converted en masse from Judaism to Catholicism in mid eighteenth-century Poland-Lithuania and whose heterodoxy continued to raise anxiety about their precise religious ascription in imperial Russia.[5]

Inherent in imperial toleration was the naming and regulation of orthodox religion, and hence stigmatization of sects deemed unworthy of imperial toleration and patronage. Though the state increasingly tolerated Protestant sects in the late imperial period in an effort to make their clergy and followers "legible" to the state, it continued to clamp down on Orthodox sectarianism through to the end of the old regime. Nowhere was this more evident than in the state's regulation of the Baptists, which involved recognizing German Baptists as a Protestant sect and persecuting Russian ones (labeled Stundists) as Orthodox sectarians.[6] The official mark of sectarian could undermine a group's legal ability to maintain prayer houses and official records and to officiate at conversions recognized by the state. Interestingly, the *Subbotniki* tried to win official recognition as Jews, in an effort to link up with tolerated groups rather than be seen as sectarians in the eyes of Russian Orthodoxy.[7]

Since the early nineteenth century, the Russian state attempted to find a rubric under which Jewish sectarianism could be classified. In 1804 the state officially recognized the Hasidic and anti-Hasidic split. By 1837 it officially recognized the Karaites as a non-rabbinic Jewish sect entitled to more privileges than Talmudic Jews.[8] In the routine questioning of a Jew petitioning for baptism, Russian Orthodox officials and police inquired about the applicant's faith and "sect." Neophytes typically specified either "Hasid" or "Mitnagid."[9] Thus, the state had become an arbiter of Jewish schism, regulating and legalizing different approaches to Jewish faith, canon, and religious authority.[10] This imperial interest in Jewish sectarianism was expressed in an 1847 publication by the MVD, written by V. V. Grigorev, which traced the history of Jewish sects from the Second Temple period in antiquity to their proliferation in former Polish-Lithuanian lands conquered by Russia. Perhaps as a way to undermine the Jewish purchase on religious truth, Grigorev highlighted the sects of Hasidism, including Beshtian Hasidism (Chabad), which confirmed that Jews were nowhere "in such diversity and fullness of expression" as in the lands "returned" to imperial Russia from Poland.[11] In this 219-page tour de force, Grigorev combed scholarship in German and French from Jewish and non-Jewish writers to explore how Judaism had moved far past Moses and the ancient Israelite religion.

State and church interest in Jewish sectarianism found a ready outlet in the provinces of New Russia—Kherson, Bessarabia, Ekaterinoslav, Taurida— which joined the provinces of the former Polish-Lithuanian territories to make up the Pale of Jewish Settlement. Beginning in 1791, as Catherine the Great opened up New Russia for colonization, Jews and many other groups, lured by tax incentives and the offer of land, poured in. This new Russian territory was a frontier for Jewish society in which new Jewish communities like that in Odessa flourished and became home to growing numbers of enlightened and progressive Jews (especially migrants from Austrian Galicia) and their modern institutional experiments, including reformed schools and liberal newspapers.[12] New forms of Jewish religious expression and the frontier

converged in the conversion story of Maria Leshchinskaia, which was profiled in the Kiev provincial paper in 1879.

As discussed in Chapter 3, Maria's story hinged on her finding confessional clarity in Christianity against the backdrop of a complicated and
alienating Jewish sectarian landscape in New Russia. That landscape included, first, the Hasid-Mitnagid schism, a staple in stories like Maria's.
Second were urban Jews who tried to hide their origins and faith—for example, by adopting Russified names. Maria chided these people for being
"ashamed" (*stydit'sia*) of being Jews.[13] Though written in a missionary vein—
within the generic arc of moving from spiritual and personal darkness to
light—Maria's story in the provincial press is important because it signaled
the changes underway among Russian Jews in the south and popular understandings of the centrifugal forces of sectarianism tearing away at Jewish
religious and communal unity.

Against this backdrop of state and popular concern with Jewish sectarianism came a new form of Jewish schism that evolved in the last quarter of
the nineteenth century in the southern provinces of Kherson and Bessarabia. In the course of the 1880s, three different Christianizing Jewish sects
emerged under the leadership of Jewish laymen. Although the MVD granted
each of them permission to organize, within a decade state powers coalesced
to classify them as sectarian groups dangerous to the Orthodox Church and
the state. Scholarship on these sects has focused on the intellectual journey
of the respective leaders in the context of the 1881–1882 pogroms and the subsequent "widespread ideological reassessment and institutional realignment
in the Russian Jewish community."[14] According to this analysis, the scale
and duration of the pogroms, their alleged government sponsorship, and official assignment of blame on the Jews themselves for exploiting Christians,
deflated most of the optimism of Jewish intellectuals who had championed
the reformist state of Alexander II. In fact, the state moved not toward Jewish emancipation but away from it, adopting anti-Jewish legislation that fed
Jewish nationalism, emigration, conversion, and sectarianism.

The leaders—Jacob Priluker, Jacob Gordin, and Joseph Rabinovich—of
the sects that arose in this time of ideological ferment have been called alternatively apostates, heretics, or religious reformers.[15] All of them, it has
been argued, reacted to the crisis of 1881–1882 by promoting a belief in Jesus

and the need for Jews to assert themselves. This argument, however, ignores the fact that Gordin's Brotherhood began before the pogroms, and all three of these heterodox groups evolved within larger patterns of evangelical and revolutionary ferment in the southern provinces in the last decades of the nineteenth century and within the broad contemporary discourse on Jewish-Christian rapprochement.

The development of these sects and their eventual dissolution by the state and church is connected to the larger development of native Russian sects in the modern period that helped to unsettle fixed notions of a hegemonic, unchanging Orthodox imperial religion and, perhaps, even constituted a belated Reformation in the empire.[16] These sects not only challenged the self-image of Orthodox Russia, but also presented religious, social, and political challenges to the autocracy, the state church, and the cultural "Russianness" of native religious expression, social relations, and behavioral norms. This panoply of indigenous Russian religious expression, though not socially or ideologically isolated from international evangelical movements, included the Skoptsy, who practiced extreme forms of religious expression such as self-castration;[17] the Dukhobors, Molokans, and Subbotniks, who rejected the institutional hierarchy in the Orthodox Church and all forms of social and political inequality;[18] the Shalaputs, Malevantsy, and Ukrainian Stundists, who denied the universal validity of church hierarchies and believed in a priesthood of all believers;[19] and Russian Baptists, who, especially through their adult conversion narratives, challenged the traditional notion of religion as a birthright.[20]

In this context, the Jewish sects that emerged in southern Russia in the 1880s partook of a broader evangelical spirit, but did so, for the most part, within the confessional boundaries of Judaism. These groups—especially that of Rabinovich—were also part of a wider phenomenon of Jews joining evangelical movements in the late empire, especially its last few decades, when the student movement and revolutionary activity created an evangelical wing linking Bible study to political activity.[21] Ultimately, these groups were doubly dangerous to the church and state; they introduced religious choice into Judaism, thus destabilizing inherited religion, and more importantly, they treaded on Christian evangelical turf that further undermined the Orthodox Church and Russian cultural hegemony, and sowed countercultural and subversive political ideas in the countryside.

Of all evangelical and reformist movements within Orthodoxy, the Jewish Christian sects interacted most closely with the Stundists of southern Russia. Stundism in imperial Russia is said to have begun in 1860 when two Ukrainian Stundist leaders who had been part of a German group began their own study circle in the village of Osnova. In this narrative, early Russian Stundists did not want to break away from the Orthodox Church but hoped to maintain a relationship akin to Pietist fellowships within Protestant churches. The Orthodox Missionary Society in the 1870s struggled to contain the spread of Stundism, but the real crackdown began in the late 1880s under Over Procurator of the Synod Pobedonostsev, who used the criminalization of apostasy to wipe out the movement.[22] Though the sect's reformed theology aligned it in many ways with Protestantism, its linguistic and cultural orientation as Russian kept it within the Orthodox confessional sphere, and thus subject to the state's power to discipline schism.

Ironically, each of these three Jewish Christian groups was initially embraced by the state as a progressive Jewish sect. Whereas the beliefs of the Hasidim and their opponents, the Mitnagdim, were variations on rabbinic Judaism, the Jewish sects of the 1880s presented a progressive reformulation of Judaism. One might think that an Orthodox state once committed to baptizing Jewish youth in the military and still invested in providing incentives for Jews to convert to the Russian Church would have celebrated Christianizing Jewish sects. Similarly, it seems logical that the Russian public, convinced of the nefarious influence of the Talmud and rabbinic fanaticism, would have welcomed progressive sects that eschewed Talmudic law. In other words, for an empire built on confessional orthodoxies, and especially those most useful to the state, Jewish sects that embraced the New Testament, rejected Jewish cultural separatism, promoted productive labor, and espoused Jewish integration seemed to present perhaps the ideal form of Judaism. The fact that this was not the case demonstrates that the late imperial confessional state, fearful of reformist and revolutionary activities, was most concerned with maintaining stability and protecting orthodox religion. Thus, since the Jewish Christian sects blurred the lines between Judaism and Christianity, the state considered them schismatic and dangerous. In the end, these sects were silenced by a jealous Orthodox Church and a government wary of an alignment of anti-state revolutionaries and religious nonconformists in the southern provinces. As Alekseev feared, these groups not only obfuscated the clear distinction between Judaism and Christianity, they also undermined the disciplinary power of traditional religion.

Christian Sectarianism in a Jewish Guise

Jacob Gordin launched the Spiritual-Biblical Brotherhood in Elisavetgrad in 1880. Gordin hailed from Poltava Province. His father, who was both a maskil and Chabad Hasid, educated Gordin in the spirit of the German *haskalah*. Gordin developed a passion for literature, and at age seventeen began to write for provincial newspapers. After starting a family and encountering financial difficulties, Gordin briefly worked as a farm laborer and then moved to New Russia and began a career as a teacher and journalist. Influenced by Stundists and Russian Populists in Elisavetgrad, Gordin founded the Spiritual-Biblical Brotherhood, which rejected Talmudic Judaism, espoused Mosaic doctrines, and championed the productivization of Jewish economic pursuits through physical labor. The Brotherhood discarded Jewish laws and rituals, including the marriage ceremony, circumcision, and dietary laws. It initially attracted about thirty followers.[23] Following the pogroms of 1881–1882, many members clamored for emigration to America, but Gordin believed the answer to the so-called Jewish problem required staying in Russia and working the land. He urged Jews to discard their traditional commercial pursuits, which he believed fueled the hatred of Jews as seen in the pogrom violence.

Gordin briefly founded a Jewish agricultural colony, which was shut down because it lacked state approval for the purchase of the land and a dearth of funds; he then labored in a small village for three years. In 1884 he returned to Elisavetgrad and reopened the Brotherhood and, in the same year, established a prayer house in Odessa.[24] This time the Brotherhood applied for state approval, which was granted on January 24, 1885. However, the Brotherhood failed to attract followers and soon disbanded. Over the next few years, Gordin also founded a Tolstoyan colony. Facing increased government repression of sectarians, Gordin immigrated to America in 1891 with high hope of founding a communal agricultural colony. In America the thoroughly Russified and heterodox Gordin found his way into Yiddish theater and became a popular dramatist.[25]

In early 1882 Jacob Priluker founded in Odessa the New Israel sect, which sought to facilitate contact between Jews and Christians through radical religious reform and thus pave the way for Jewish civil emancipation. Infused with a rationalist critique of organized religion, the New Israel religious program embraced Mosaic teachings but rejected the Talmud, *kashrut* (dietary laws), circumcision, and traditional worship. The sect moved the Jewish Sabbath from Saturday to Sunday, instituted Russian as the "native" Jewish tongue of daily life, and forbade usury. As a reward for forging a rapprochement between Judaism and Christianity, the group expected the state to grant them civil equality, permission to intermarry with Christians, and the right to wear a special badge that would distinguish them from Talmudic Jews.[26] It was this mark of distinction that became the focal point of Jewish critics who viewed the sectarians as national traitors. Priluker's reformed Judaism implemented many of the reforms long championed by the state and the spirit of "merging" that informed the evolution of the empire's selective integration policy toward Jews—the remaking of the Jews' linguistic, occupational, and educational profile. In the end, Priluker's movement failed, and he relocated to England, where his Christianizing was embraced by evangelicals eager to proselytize Jews.

The third Jewish Christian sect, the New Testament Israelites, was founded in Kishinev in 1884 by Joseph Rabinovich, a Hasidic maskil who embraced Jesus in the wake of the 1881–1882 pogroms. Rabinovich was fluent in Russian and a prolific writer in the maskilic press. He was a critic of Talmudic Judaism, and aspired to being elected crown rabbi of Kishinev and reorienting Jewish spirituality away from both rabbinicism and Hasidism. Rabinovich's new theology was born out of despair that the future of Jews was in the hands of gentile states. He believed Jews had to regain control of their own destiny, which could only occur once they addressed the age-old mistake of dismissing Jesus. He did not believe that embracing Jesus would or should erase the lines between Jews and Christians; he still championed Jewish nationalism and superiority. According to historian Steven Zipperstein, "he did not seek to win Jews over to a particular, preexisting form of Christianity but promoted a new ideology that was based on an idiosyncratic interpretation of the nature of Judaism and Jesus and which continued to owe much to Jewish nationalism. . . . It was Jesus that Rabinovich embraced in 1883 and not specifically Christianity in any of its forms."[27]

In the 1880s, Rabinovich caught the attention of the international evangelical world. Stories of the Jewish nationalist who had a spiritual "conversion" to Jesus on the Mount of Olives in 1882 stoked broad enthusiasm among evangelicals for a new "Jewish Luther."[28]

In December 1884 Rabinovich received permission from the MVD to establish a Jewish religious sect and a prayer house in his home in Kishinev based on Christian beliefs and a rejection of Talmudic teachings and rituals.[29] Initially, Jews flocked by the hundreds out of curiosity to hear Rabinovich's Yiddish sermons on Jesus. Rabinovich himself boasted that over two hundred Jews were initially attracted to the New Israel sect.[30] His services also attracted others, including police and Christian intellectuals. The services featured a coed choir, hymns, and a combination of Old and New Testament readings. Rabinovich spoke in Yiddish and read the Psalms in Hebrew. However, in the end few Jews accepted Rabinovich's heterodox teachings.

A month after the MVD permitted Rabinovich to organize, a retired general, Shumlianskii, living in Kishinev wrote to the head of the Synod Pobedonostsev alerting him to Rabinovich's sect and its affront to Orthodoxy. Shumlianskii noted that the official "National-Jewish Believers in Christ Movement in Southern Russia" had received the MVD's permission to operate, but he doubted that Rabinovich's group honestly identified itself to the MVD. Whereas Rabinovich described the group as a Jewish sect, Shumlianskii averred that it was "nothing other than a shameless adaptation of all Christian dogma in a Jewish mode (*lad*)"—essentially a sectarian Christian group in a Jewish guise.[31] Shumlianskii suggested that the sect's Jewish orientation was just a ruse to protect it from charges of Christian sectarianism.

In his letter to Pobedonostsev, Shumlianskii quoted from the sect's brochure, printed in German and Yiddish in Germany, which revealed the sect's reformed Christian agenda. The group claimed to believe in Christianity but also sought to preserve aspects of Judaism that were not in opposition to Christianity. It rejected the notion of the Trinity and the Immaculate Conception as inessential to the Christian faith. Instead of communion in church, the group ate a meal with bread and wine in memory of Christ. Ritually, the sect members practiced circumcision and observed the Sabbath. "In general," Shumlianskii wrote, "this program exudes a total denial and a near mockery of all dogmas of Christian faith. This is turning out to be not a schism, not a new Jewish sect, but an audacious reform of Christian religion in a Jewish mode, with the goal of calling *converts to Christianity* and, for this, demanding for themselves civil equality (*grazhdanskoe ravnopravie*)." Shumlianskii warned, "This will only be the beginning: due to the well-known wily nature of the Jewish nation, its vast material resources and its aspiration ... for power, this sect may in time with its propaganda create incalculable difficulties for Christianity; meaning, of course, above all, for Orthodoxy."[32] Shumlianskii exploited anxieties in the Orthodox Church in his attempt to delegitimize the New Testament Israelites. He invoked the threat posed by radical evangelicalism that had been burgeoning in the southern region since the 1830s; he grouped the sect members with insincere converts who adopted Christianity to get ahead socially and whom the church and state had long taken careful legal measures to deflect. And, finally, he played on the contemporary myth of an international Jewish brotherhood bent on world domination to frighten the Synod into banning Rabinovich's sect. Shumlianskii questioned whether a poor townsman, a notary from Orgeev, a small Bessarabian town, could have organized this sect by himself. Invoking stereotypes of the unlettered, unsophisticated provincial white-collar worker, Shumlianskii argued that Rabinovich was just a front man for a skillfully crafted plan by an international Jewish committee. In closing, Shumlianskii presented himself as an upright "Russian subject" who was obligated to defend the fatherland and assist the state in its current difficult situation. The Synod forwarded a copy of Shumlianskii's letter to the Department for the Religious Affairs of Foreign Confessions (DDDII), which apparently dismissed his warnings since the sect was allowed to go on operating.

As it turned out, Shumlianskii may have been partly right. Rabinovich became increasingly close to Protestants both in Kishinev and beyond. In fact, his attraction to Protestantism was so strong that, in March 1885, he went to Berlin to be converted in a Congregationalist church. His decision to convert has been attributed to promises of financial aid to his movement, the excitement of being courted by prominent Christian scholars, and his having been passed over as a missionary for the London Society for Promoting Christianity amongst the Jews because he was not baptized.[33]

In June 1885 the Bessarabian governor asked permission from the MVD to recognize Rabinovich as a cleric who could administer the sect's sacraments and maintain metrical books for the group's followers. Although Rabinovich had no affiliation with any tolerated Christian confession in the empire, the Bessarabian governor supported recognizing Rabinovich and his sect as an independent religious group capable of self-management and worthy of the right of religious tolerance extended to other Christian confessions such as Lutheranism and Catholicism. On the issue of maintaining metrical books, the governor did hedge his request and offered to have the Kishinev municipal authorities maintain the books if the MVD thought that responsibility should not be entrusted to a non-ordained cleric of a fringe sect.

With his request, the governor provided information on Rabinovich's conversion and evangelical Christian connections. Rabinovich's conversion was officiated by Pastor Charles Marsh Mead, former pastor of a Congregationalist church and professor of Hebrew at the theological seminary at Andover, Massachusetts, who came to Germany after he retired and led missions to Jews in Germany. According to Mead's record, he officiated at the conversion according to the "confession—*ikrei emunah*" developed by Rabinovich in Yiddish and translated into German by Professor Franz Delitzsch in Leipzig, a renowned Christian Hebraist, or "Christian Talmudist," noted for his post-biblical expertise, and who himself engaged in Jewish missionary work.[34] In addition to sending Rabinovich's conversion certificate to the MVD, the Bessarabian governor also sent a letter from Professor H. Strack, doctor of theology at the University of Berlin, who offered religious sources for permitting a non-ordained Christian to perform the rites of conversion, communion, marriage, and burial.[35]

The MVD responded to the governor's request by conferring with the Synod, on the grounds that Rabinovich's conversion and subsequent wish to perform religious rites changed a previously fringe and insular sect into a proselytizing group that could potentially affect Orthodox interests in the area. The DDDII asked the over procurator to determine if the sect should be recognized as a tolerated foreign confession and thus granted the right of freedom of religion as set forth in imperial law.[36] The Synod, influenced by local clergy and landlords who complained of Rabinovich's "German" influence in the Russian countryside and religious confusion of Orthodox peasants, ordered police to stop the "anti-Russian" activities of Rabinovich and his sect.[37] In 1886 the police investigated but found nothing incriminating about Rabinovich's behavior. The Synod insisted on banning Rabinovich's sect nonetheless, because it stirred up religious dissent among Russians and defection from Orthodoxy in areas already overrun by sectarianism.

Rabinovich attempted to mollify the Synod; he ceased contact with Stundist peasants and, in 1888, agreed to register the sect with the police and follow the rules of Orthodoxy. From Rabinovich's January 1889 petition to the MVD still asking for permission to operate his sect, we can surmise that the MVD heeded the Synod's ban on the sect. In the spirit of constraining evangelical groups that had proliferated in southern Russia and posed a threat to Orthodox hegemony in the region, the New Testament Israelites were not allowed to officially operate as anything more than a prayer group. Their heterodox theology, independence from any established church, and close ties to foreign missionary groups proved to be beyond the limits of accepted religious difference in the late imperial period. The group died out with the death of Rabinovich. The sect succeeded in converting only a few people; most were from Rabinovich's immediate family.

Gordin's Spiritual-Biblical Brotherhood also encountered obstacles when it attempted to broaden its activities after its official recognition as a religious sect in January 1885 allowed it to establish its own prayer house and appoint a separate rabbi. When the MVD granted Gordin permission to extend the sect's activities to include conversations in private homes with people interested in the Brotherhood's teachings, the ministry stipulated that Gordin could not conduct those conversations in Russian.[38] One can guess that the MVD wanted to prevent the Brotherhood from devolving into something like the Subbotniks, who were a constant source of concern for the tsarist regime. The Subbotniks were indigenous Russian sectarians who to varying degrees embraced Jewish beliefs and practices and identified as Judaizing Christians or as Jews. Many Subbotniks observed the laws of circumcision, *kashrut*, and Jewish holidays, and conducted Jewish prayers in Russian.[39] In 1830 Tsar Nicholas I forced Orthodox sectarians to the Transcaucasian frontier, willingly or not. While the Subbotniks and other sectarians were contained in the South Caucasus, their role as colonizers and the relative religious freedom of the imperial borderland actually increased their numbers and strengthened their institutions. The Subbotniks, with their amorphous Jewish-Christian identity, engendered anxiety in the Orthodox Church and became the object of many Orthodox missions in the southern regions. In this light, the MVD's stipulation that the Spiritual-Biblical Brotherhood refrain from propagating their Jewish-Christian syncretism in Russian signals the state's concern that it not move into the dangerous religious territory of Judaizing Orthodox sectarians.[40]

In December 1888, the Synod expressed its concern to the DDDII that Gordin's Brotherhood was a danger to Orthodox interests in Kherson. The Synod forwarded to the MVD an article from an 1888 issue of the Kherson diocesan periodical entitled "The State of Sectarianism in the Kherson Diocese." The article charged that the Brotherhood, although a state-approved sect, harmed Orthodoxy in the region on two accounts: first, most of its members were not Jewish but Orthodox, culled mostly from local intellectuals; second, its members supported the Stundist claim that the Orthodox Church and its clerical hierarchy deviated from the authenticity of first-century Christianity.[41] As such, the Brotherhood seduced the most valuable members of the Orthodox Church and partook in the anti-Orthodox rhetoric of schismatics in Kherson. After a secret investigation, the Kherson police concluded that charges coming from the Orthodox Church were hyperbolic. The police found that a few Orthodox people had attended some classes of the Brotherhood out of curiosity, but the Brotherhood currently had no Orthodox members. As for the charge that Orthodox people had observed Brotherhood rites, the police dismissed this as a rumor about an Orthodox doctor marrying a Jewish midwife according to the Brotherhood's rites.[42] The MVD overruled the Synod in this case, and the Brotherhood continued to operate in peace. In December of that year, the Ministry of Justice agreed to allow the Brotherhood to register the births of its members separately from the metrical records of Elisavetgrad's Jews.[43]

In June 1890 and again in August 1891, the police, fearing an anti-state alliance, warned the DDDII that the Brotherhood was in contact with Tolstoyans and Stundists in the area.[44] The police chronicled the genesis of the Brotherhood, beginning with a group of Jews drawn to Stundist teachings on socialism and wanting to escape from the class exploitation endemic to Jewish society. Gordin received the state's permission and sympathy to break away from the "dark sides of Judaism," the perceived exploitative economic practices of the mainstream Jewish community. Nonetheless, the police found that his religious sect had become a revolutionary group intent on organizing the intelligentsia into communist agricultural colonies. The police gathered evidence of the Brotherhood's Tolstoyan leanings, based on its recitation of Tolstoyan texts in meetings and sermons. The Brotherhood's activities, according to the police, were not limited to winning over intellectuals; sect members also engaged peasant Stundists in the countryside and offered them advice about farming as a means of extending the sect's influence. In the revolutionary climate of the last decades of the empire, the MVD expressed greater concern about the group's espousal of socialism than its encroachment on Orthodoxy. Although state officials initially praised the Brotherhood for its resistance to Jewish nationalism and religious fanaticism, in October 1891 they closed the Brotherhood out of fear of its involvement with revolutionaries and sectarians and ordered the arrest of Gordin. By then, Gordin and sixty followers had emigrated to the United States.[45]

The heterodox orientation of these three Jewish-Christian sects rendered them subversive in the eyes of the Synod and, eventually, the state as well. Much of the anxiety surrounding the groups was provoked by the blurring of confessional lines—Jews acting like Christians and Christians acting like Jews—without formal conversion. And, while Rabinovich did convert in 1885, his baptism and theology were idiosyncratic and only served to further unsettle his confessional identity and that of his group. In the eyes of the state, these Christianizing sects defied categorization and forced officials typically hesitant to arbitrate heterodox schism into policing the boundaries of sectarianism and political expression. While the state concerned itself with the confluence of evangelicalism and revolutionary foment, the public, as we will see, weighed in on the nexus between religious reform and the so-called Jewish question.

Sectarianism and Religious Reform in the Jewish Press

With the rise of the popular press in Russia in the latter half of the nineteenth century, conversion as a topic of conversation in the empire moved beyond the realm of the state and church to the realm of journalists and writers, who explored conversion and its cultural implications. In the Russian-language press conversation about conversion coalesced around two main flashpoints— the proliferation of Jewish Christian sects in southern Russia in the 1880s, and the violation of confessional boundaries through violence and religious "seduction." In the 1880s, press coverage of Jewish conversion exploded, with about half of all articles engaging the proliferation of Jewish sects in New Russia. In the Russian Jewish press as well, more than half of the articles on Jewish conversion in the 1880s dealt with sectarianism.[46]

The legal organization of the sects under the confessional banner of Judaism led contemporaries to question the definition of Jewish reform and at what point reform could blur the lines between Judaism and Christianity. Since these reformist groups had affinities with Christianity, it bears reviewing the state of the reformation of Judaism in imperial Russia in the late imperial period and the relationship between reform and Christianization.

In 1870 the governor-general of Poltava asked the MVD if "Reform Judaism" was a real and credible Jewish sect.[47] According to both a law adopted in 1804 and the composition of Jewish communities, Russian Jews identified as Hasidim or Mitnagdim, even though the difference was usually lost on non-Jews, who viewed them all as "fanatics."[48] The governor-general's question was prompted by the conversion of a Jew from Austria who had previously identified as a Reform Jew. The governor wanted to know if Reform Jews could receive the one-time state grant given to coverts from Judaism. Despite the presence of modernizing Jewish synagogues and schools in the empire, "Reform Judaism" had not yet entered official imperial legal parlance and it was this void that prompted the governor-general's question.[49] An official in the DDDII responded by explaining that Jews were now split between Orthodox and Reform, the latter stemming from and mainly confined to enlightened and educated Jews in Germany. Reform Jews, the official pointed out, adhered to Mosaic law and were committed to merging Jewish law with civil law, as seen, for example, in some contemporary Jews who observed the Sabbath on Sunday.[50]

Just two years after this exchange, the missionary Alekseev published his concerns about the impact of "progressive" Judaism on Jewish conversion to Christianity, discussed at the opening of this chapter. In his 1872 essay, Alekseev offered a short history of "progressive" Judaism in imperial Russia, citing the nineteenth-century German Jewish historian Isaak Markus Jost's work, *Geschichte des Judenthums und seiner Sekten* (History of Judaism and Its Sects; Leipzig, 1857–1859), which Alekseev had read in its 1864 Russian translation.[51]

Although he relegated it to a footnote, Alekseev concluded his short history of
Reform Judaism from it origins in lay initiatives to its endorsement by rabbis
with the comment that it was dangerous for Jews, even Russian Jews. Already,
according to Alekseev, "the danger of the foreign, anti-religious, progressive
trend is noticed among Russian Jews. Many of them break the holy Sabbath,
making a fire, which is against Mosaic law. They use prohibited food and even
consider circumcision nonobligatory."[52] Alekseev noted that some progressive Jews could be found in Odessa and St. Petersburg.[53] Alekseev warned
new converts from Judaism to avoid conversations with such Jews, who denied the contemporary relevance of belief in the Messiah. Before an apostate
could make the leap from Jewish to Christian doctrine, Alekseev inveighed
his fellow converts to hold fast to the Jewish commitment to and belief in the
Messiah. At this time as well, a two-part article in *Strannik* on the St. Petersburg shelter for Jewish converts noted that contemporary Jews had splintered
into two groups—"law-abiders," or *mitnagdim*, and liberals/progressives, or
apikorsim. It noted that in imperial Russia there were only a few of the latter.[54]

By the 1880s, then, reformed Judaism had appeared in Russia and become part of the discourse about the boundaries of Jewish identity. The
public, however, had not yet recognized that reformed Judaism was not
solely a foreign phenomenon, but had emerged as a vibrant and relevant
movement in Russia as well. Also, much of Alekseev's fear of progressive
Judaism appears to have been a reaction to the movement in Central Europe. There, reformed Judaism could anchor Jews in a German, and often
Protestant, cultural milieu. But in the East, it could not be a bridge to Russianness. This changed abruptly with the growth of Jewish Christian sects
in New Russia in the 1880s. This sparked a debate in the Jewish and Russian
presses over where the reform of Judaism ended and the embrace of Christianity began. For the Russian-language Jewish press in particular, which
tended to be more receptive to integration than the Hebrew or Yiddish
presses, the sects posed a radical challenge to the terms of integration in a
post-pogrom world.

In 1882, responding to Priluker's and Gordin's groups, Emmanuel Ben-
Sion published *Evrei-reformatory* (Jewish Reformers), a public celebration
of the proliferation of Jewish sects in southern Russia.[55] Ben-Sion's polemic
aimed to turn the public conversation in the Jewish press from marginalizing

the founders as mercenary Jews spiritually wounded by the pogroms of 1881–1882, to celebrating them as Jewish intellectuals who boldly espoused Jewish religious reform as a solution to the centuries-long alienation of Jews in Christian Europe. Drawing a timeline of Jewish intellectual responses to religiously and economically motivated anti-Judaism, Ben-Sion viewed Priluker and Gordin as the intellectual heirs of Benedict Spinoza and German-Jewish religious reformers.[56] Though Jewish sects emerged contemporaneously with the pogroms that followed Alexander II's assassination, Ben-Sion argued that these sects were essentially manifestations of Russian Jewry's belated reform and renewal of Judaism as a step toward easing Jewish-Christian antagonisms and carving out a permanent and productive place for Jews in the imperial order. Contrary to Jewish historiography, which excised Eastern Europe from the map of modern religious reforms, Ben-Sion's book applauded Russian Jews who created their own approach to religious reform in the face of Enlightenment thought, emancipation fervor, and pogrom violence.[57]

Jewish newspapers at the time portrayed these sects as marginal or desperate Jewish socioeconomic responses to the violence of pogroms and the perceived need to make Jews earn emancipation and the respect of Christians, even if this meant the Christianization of Judaism.[58] In Ben-Sion's estimation, contemporary Jewish newspapers, with their focus on enlightened Jews and Jewish economic and educational progress, "glanced no more at these Jewish sects than at a sad, amusing incident."[59] Ben-Sion, however, viewed the pogroms of 1881–1882 as a flashpoint in the age-long struggle between Jews and Christians. From Christ-killers to oppressive middlemen in the premodern noble-peasant Polish economy, Jews, Ben-Sion argued, were at once victims of historical discrimination and agents who oppressed gentiles in an attempt to eke out a living. Unlike Jews and Judeophiles who "lull themselves" into believing in their own "angelic innocence" (*v nashei angel'skoi nevinnosti*), Ben-Sion believed all Jews were equally to blame for the Jewish-Christian enmity that kept "the Jewish problem" alive in contemporary Europe.[60] He thus stated, "we need to face the hard truth that our social, economic, and religio-moral relationship to the native population is not normal and we are partly to blame for it. We need to correct our ancestors' mistakes, normalize our relationship with the native population, and not rely on any commission or committee."[61] He argued that both anti-Semitism in Germany and pogroms in imperial Russia stemmed from mutual Jewish-Christian mistreatment, which could only be solved through the reconciliation of Jews and Christians ("love of the nation among whom we live," *liubov naroda, sredi kotorago my zhivem*) rather than through law, especially the political emancipation that Jews hoped for.[62]

Ben-Sion argued that reconciliation required religious reform. What relevance, he asked, could the Talmud have in a modern, enlightened Christian world striving for universal values? Jews living in such a world needed to question whether religiously prescribed separation and exclusion had led them to mistreat the native population. Ben-Sion contended that the Talmud arose in the first century of Christianity, when Jews were dispersed from their native land, lost their unity, and, through academies and commentators, sought to establish religious laws that would give them a sense of chosenness, national unity, and separation from other nations among whom they lived.[63] As a result, Talmud-induced separatism and excessive ritualism created an environment in which it was physically impossible, in Ben-Sion's view, for contemporary Jews to follow the dictates of rabbinic law.[64] Moreover, Talmudic hostility and wariness toward idolaters aroused in Jews from the youngest age a profound hatred of non-Jews, despite post-Talmudic commentators who distinguished between pagans and monotheistic gentiles.[65]

Ben-Sion enumerated several ways the Talmud put Jews in opposition to their surrounding society. For instance, Jews' constant anticipation of the arrival of the Messiah and their view of themselves as only visitors in an alien land, soon to be returned to Zion, alienated them from their host societies. He illustrated this with a story of a Jewish schoolteacher from the village of R. in the northwest region, who often napped in class after lunch. Daily, before his nap, the *melamed* (teacher) warned his students to immediately wake him up if they heard the long-awaited trumpet calls of the Messiah.[66] The geographic setting of this story reveals Ben-Sion's assumption that the masses of unenlightened Jews lived in the northwest region, home to former Polish-Lithuanian Jewry, whom Russia inadvertently inherited through imperial expansion. It was this population of Jews whom Ben-Sion felt were ignored by the contemporary St. Petersburg Jewish press (*Razsvet* and *Russkii evrei*), which reported on progressive and enlightened Jews almost to the exclusion of the Jewish masses, the fervent traditionalists in the northwest, who

were on the front lines of the contentious encounter with the native Russian population. It was these messianic Jews, daily dreaming of redemption,
guided by the Talmud in their worldview, who kept alive the centuries-long
Jewish-Christian enmity. Ironically, Ben-Sion wrote his polemic in the wake
of pogroms in the southwestern provinces, a region he linked with Jewish
enlightenment, detached from the core of Jewish-Christian antagonisms.

Ben-Sion asked contemporary Jews to read the Talmud as literature, a
tale of Jewish survivalism in pagan society, a relic ill-suited for a contemporary world in which universal aspirations trumped religious divisions and
Jewish intellectuals blazed a path to Jewish literacy that did not depend on
deep knowledge of the Talmud.[67] The Talmud as a guide to living should be
abandoned, he argued, and Jews should look to the Bible, Psalms, and Proph-
ets for instruction. In *Evrei-reformatory*, a book that would serve as an anchor
in the public Jewish debate on the sects, Ben-Sion effectively made the sects'
public reception a referendum on the desirability of Jewish religious reforms
moving into the Russian Empire, and which religion should claim sects like
New Israel and the Spiritual-Biblical Brotherhood—Judaism or Christianity.

Converting the Jewish Question

In 1882 the Russian Jewish newspaper *Voskhod*, responding to Ben-Sion's
Evrei-reformatory, published a long article on the proliferation of Jewish
sects in New Russia. In the article, entitled "Attempts at Religious Reforms
by Jews," the author, N.N., a pseudonym for Lev Osipovich Gordon (the
famed Hebrew poet and Russian Jewish enlightener better known as Judah
Leib Gordon), acknowledged that had it not been for Ben-Sion's book, the
Jewish sects that arose in the spring of 1881 during the pogroms would have
been forgotten.[68] Following the themes of religious reform and the resolution of the "Jewish question," which Ben-Sion introduced into the discussion
of these sects, Gordon carefully and thoroughly responded to the fledgling
movements of Priluker and Gordin.

Gordon wholeheartedly agreed with Ben-Sion's diagnosis of contemporary Jews as alienated from the native population, entrenched in ritualism,
and antithetical to the enlightened goals of equality and brotherhood. In theory, Gordon continued to champion religious reform—a topic he published
on in the Hebrew press in the reform era. In practice, though, he strongly

disagreed with the sects' linking religious reform to a resolution of the Jewish question and with their wholesale rejection of the Talmud as a foundation for reform.[69]

Gordon argued that religious reforms could not solve the "Jewish question" and that authentic religious reform should be done for its own sake, not for the reward of citizenship. In the first case, Gordon pointed to Germany, the homeland of the movement for Jewish religious reforms, as proof that reforming Judaism did not quell anti-Jewish sentiment. "For a long time already in Germany," Gordon argued, "Jews have reformed and ennobled their cult; the Talmud for them long ago lost the shroud of divinity, ceasing to be the alpha and omega of all knowledge and the guiding religious codex, and was brought down to the same level as an example of archaeological science, of interest to a few of the elite." Gordon continued, "their temples do not outwardly differ from Christian churches, even as many of these temples affix the desired *magen-david* [star of David]; for some, Sunday has taken the place of the Sabbath, in short, the realization of all the ideas of 'New Israel'; but all of this, however, does not prevent Germany from becoming the homeland of the latest anti-Semitism."[70] For Gordon, German anti-Semitism proved that progressive Judaism was not the antidote to the so-called Jewish question.

A few years later, another *Voskhod* writer, S.B., a correspondent from Vienna, articulated a similar skepticism about the power of religious reforms. Writing from Central Europe—in the author's words, a hotbed of Jewish assimilationism—S.B. averred that the Jewish question had not been solved nor had inroads even been made. Anti-Semites despised assimilated Jews more than non-assimilated ones. The fault line in late nineteenth-century European identity politics was not religion but nationality, an identity that could not be reformed or erased.[71] Thus, trying to convince Jewish citizens to adhere to "the Mosaic faith" was an elusive project that ignored the great pull of nationalism in the modern era. Unlike Ben-Sion, who believed religious reform was the remedy for Jewish-Christian hostility, both Gordon and S.B. viewed the Jewish problem as involving more than religious practice and the relevance of the Talmud.[72]

Beyond questioning whether the Jewish question could be resolved, Gordon also questioned the authenticity of religious reforms that stemmed from a desire to achieve sociopolitical goals. "This reform needs to be accomplished not with base goals—the attainment of earthly blessing—but in the name of higher interests of mankind, for the revival and inducement to a new cultural life of an invalid nation, covered in deep scars, but also in everlasting glory."[73] Gordon argued that the relevance of religious reform extended beyond the political: it was as important for Galician Jews with representatives in parliament as it was for Russian Jews recently attacked in pogroms.

Soon after Gordon's article appeared in *Voskhod*, Mariia Saker, an innovative educator and first female writer in the Russian Jewish press, added her voice to the debate about Jewish sects and religious reforms in the East. Her rhetoric was like Gordon's but more hyperbolic: she disdained New Israel's commoditization of Judaism as a good that could be sold for material benefits and political privileges. If true religion was premised on devotion and belief, then a Jewish sect that operated as an "industrial" (*promyshlennoe*) enterprise promising dividends to its adherents could not be considered a true "religious" movement. Saker's wrath stemmed from New Israel's program to win civil rights for its adherents alone, thus selfishly aggrandizing themselves "against the entire Jewish nation" (*protiv vsego evreiskago naroda*). In Saker's worldview, modern enlightened nations separate religion from civil life, thus rendering Jews who are willing to relinquish their religion for civil acceptance both a historic anachronism and an embarrassment to the modern ideal of "freedom of conscience" (*svoboda sovesti*). Jewish sectarians, in this light, had regressed into a medieval mode of apologizing for their beliefs, thus turning to Christianity against the dictates of their conscience. Saker's disgust with Jews who viewed their identity in purely religious terms reflected her own deeply held understanding of Judaism as both a religious and national ascription that could not be erased through religious reforms or conversion. Furthermore, Saker was incredulous that members of New Israel could display such a tenuous and superficial attachment to the Jewish nation. In her words, people born into a particular religion do not generally equate religious deviation with leaving the nation (*narod*): "Among adherents of ancient religions, it is not only rituals that serve as connecting links, but also the kindred feeling of family (*rodstvennoe chuvstvo sem'i*), which survives through joy and sorrow, persecution and oppression, and the joy of the victory of one's nation."[74] Members of New Israel, in her estimation, were traitors to their nation and profoundly unenlightened in their religious approach to Jewish progress—a contemporary issue pursued by Jews and non-Jews alike in terms of human equality and freedom of conscience.

In a similar vein, *Russkii evrei* (Russian Jew) in 1882 lambasted the sects as Jewish defectors trying to buy residency rights by selling their religion. It compared the sects' leaders to the salon women of Berlin who pursued intermarriage at the turn of the nineteenth century, both "soliciting the right to wear a mark of distinction on their chest" to uplift themselves from their struggling nation. The author, Shael, doubted that "the defectors would manage to moor to a different shore."[75]

Aside from the criticizing the impetus for reforms, Jewish journalists also criticized the nature of the reforms themselves. Gordon positively noted that the sects of Priluker and Gordin were designed as bulwarks against indifference and unbelief rampant in contemporary Jewish society as much as they were a shield against Jewish "fanaticism."[76] Gordon nonetheless questioned the kind of reform espoused by New Israel and the Spiritual-Biblical Brotherhood, which augured more of a Jewish-Christian amalgamation than a distinctive, reformed Judaism. Both Gordin's and Priluker's groups advocated excising the Talmud from the Jewish canon and returning to Judaism's pure roots in Mosaic law. They rejected the Talmud as embodying an outdated Judeo-centric worldview, intolerant and disdainful of gentiles, and even antiscientific. Judging from the main tenets of the sects, which included moving the Sabbath to Sunday, making circumcision voluntary, and promoting intermarriage, Gordon argued that these reformers were not pure Mosaicists but rather adherents to selective aspects of Mosaic law.[77] And, by jettisoning the Talmud from the Jewish canon, the reformers denied the historical significance of the Talmud for Jews in exile and the linguistic importance of the Mishnah in the development of the Hebrew language, which the sects supposedly valued.[78] Moreover, Gordon noted that there were instances in daily life when the Talmud was relevant and a necessary explication of the Bible. For example, it was the Talmud that gave a reasonable explanation (the need to monetarily compensate for physical damages) for the biblical punishment of "an eye for an eye, a tooth for a tooth," an otherwise seemingly barbaric act of revenge. Alternatively, there were instances when it was necessary to reject the Talmud in favor of the plain reading of Bible—for example, regarding the laws of *kashrut*.[79] Gordon concluded that it was not the Talmud that stood as an obstacle to reforming Judaism, but rather the hesitancy of rabbis since the redaction of the Talmud to engage in an ongoing exegesis of the Bible in light of contemporary needs. In place of the haphazard reforms of the sects that followed no fixed principles, Gordon proposed guidelines for reforms that would "renovate" the edifice of Judaism rather than destroy it. The two most important were religious command-ments should be subordinate to the demands of life, and religious behavior should be an individual matter not subject to communal oversight or respon-sibility.[80] In this way, *Voskhod* writers—unlike other Jewish journalists, who were loath to discuss the sects' reforms at length out of fear that it might dignify them—seriously engaged the issue of religious reforms in light of the Jewish sects proliferating in southern Russia in the 1880s.

In 1884 the public Jewish conversation on the sects heated up again, with a new spate of publications reacting to Ben-Sion's essay *Evrei-reformatory* and the ongoing development of the sects. That year, V. Portugalov published an essay supporting Gordin's Spiritual-Biblical Brotherhood, and the rabbi Yosif Vilkovir published a book lambasting Ben-Sion and the sects. Portuga-lov wrote that Gordin's sect had planted the "seed for the brightest future for the Jews."[81] He averred that although Orthodox Christianity and Ortho-dox Judaism were radically different, Jewish and Christian sects had much in common.[82] In other words, while conventional religion bred opposition and isolation, sectarianism led to commonality. Portugalov pointed out the similarities between Gordin's Brotherhood and Anglican missions that also focused on biblical reading.[83] Overall, Portugalov hailed the sect for pro-moting ethical living and a universal vision of humanity free of the Talmud, which could ameliorate the Jews' historic position of exploiting native labor as managers for the privileged class. In his reading of Jewish life and the Jew-ish question, Portugalov believed that Gordin's Brotherhood severed Jews from commerce, materialism, and institutional hierarchies, especially patriar-chy, which subjugated women.

In a radically different vein, Vilkovir, the rabbi of the town Aleshkov, who had been closely following the debate on the sects, attacked Ben-Sion and the sects. Vilkovir conflated the sects in southern Russia with the contempo-rary religious reform movement in Congress Poland, all of which attempted to bring Jews closer to the natives and give Judaism a new "flavor" (*vkuse*) or spark its "regeneration" (*pererozhdenie*). Vilkovir noted parallel developments in Congress Poland, where a new synagogue was built featuring modern sermons and a coed choir in place of the traditional singing of hymns. Putting these late nineteenth-century reforms on a continuum with ancient and medieval religious developments, Vilkovir compared the Christianizing sects to the Sadducees of the Second Temple period, the Karaites under medieval Islam, and the Sabbateans of the early modern period. Overall, Vilkovir added his voice to those in the Jewish press who called for the end to Jewish "nihilism" and "absurdity."[84]

There was, in short, a split in the Jewish press between those who approved of the sects and took them seriously and those who dismissed them as a passing, fringe phenomenon. As the Jewish sects started to weaken and disappear over the course of the 1880s, many Jewish commentators were eager to write their obituary as well as to dismiss their impact on late imperial Jewish society and the conversation over the legitimacy of religious reforms. In 1882, after Gordon's critique of Ben-Sion's book, the weekly *Nedel'naia khronika voskhoda* showcased a "half-serious, half-satirical" ode to New Israel, dubbing its leader a contemporary Luther and wondering: "What have you added to the old faith?/What did you keep back in exchange for everything?" (*chto k vere staroi ty pribavil/vzamen vsego, chto vychel*).[85] In this satirical, dismissive vein, Jewish writers rejected the sects as neither a coherent "movement" nor a genuinely Jewish phenomenon. In 1885 a correspondent called any discussion of an imperial Russian Jewish reform movement "a chimeric daydream." Although Joseph Rabinovich's synagogue in Kishinev opened in December 1884 with great fanfare in the press, F. Ia. Kitover surmised that the attention was only a reflection of the aggravation of the Jewish question, which caused society to be hyper-attuned to all things Jewish. Although Jewish sects had appeared in Western Europe in modern times, Rabinovich's sect recognized Jesus as the Messiah and, hence, was beyond the bounds of Judaism. Kitover deferred to the opinions of the Russian press, especially *Odesskii vestnik*, which closely monitored the proliferation of Jewish sects in southern Russia and which argued that Rabinovich's New Testament Israelites should legally be considered a Christian rather than a Jewish group.[86] Jews reportedly called Rabinovich an "uneducated idiot" and a "snake" who seduced Jewish souls into his sectarian "net."[87] In 1888 a reviewer of one of Rabinovich's sermons published a year earlier called Rabinovich's ideas a "strange mishmash" of Judaism and Christianity that had a readership as meager as the tiny audience in his empty "Bethlehem" prayer house in Kishinev.[88] Also in 1888, another Jewish journalist offered a "tragi-comic" sketch of Joseph Gordin in light of the Spiritual-Biblical Brotherhood's demise in Elisavetgrad. He concluded on a positive note, celebrating the "finale of a reformist tragi-comedy" (*reformatorskaia tragikomediia*), which, like a disease, has "cruelly eaten away at the organism of Judaism."[89]

Looking objectively at Rabinovich's sermons themselves, however, reveals a progressive and critical approach to rabbinic Judaism and its texts. At the start of his sermon of July 5, 1886, Rabinovich quoted the Talmud in Tractate Menachot about the story of Moses dropping in on the Tannaitic Rabbi Akiva's study house and not understanding any of the Torah being taught, whereupon a student's question induced Rabbi Akiva to cite his teachings as coming from the laws given to Moses at Sinai. This text is a classic articulation of the Talmud's legitimation of rabbinic authority and rabbis' own understanding of their exegetical innovations as grounded in the eternal teachings of revelation. Rabinovich starts with this text as a way to criticize the rabbinic project and its attempt to retroject rabbinic Judaism onto biblical religion. Linking these concerns of the Talmud with liberal Jews' struggles with the Oral Law, Rabinovich embedded his Jews for Jesus project within the classic criticisms of Reform Jewry and the reappraisal of the relevance of the Talmud in modern times.[90]

Blurred Confessional Lines

Whereas Jewish journalists in the 1880s increasingly distanced themselves from Jewish sects that explicitly adopted Christian dogma or implicitly sought to strip Judaism of its distinctiveness, many Russian journalists sought to claim the sects for Christianity. While Jews lamented that the state had designated these sects as Jewish, Christians often questioned the rigid confessional lines drawn by the state, distinctions that constricted and suppressed hybrid Jewish-Christian groups. *Sankt-Peterburgskie vedomosti*, after the state shut down Gordin's Spiritual-Biblical Brotherhood, called attention to the beginnings of an "anti-Talmud movement" in southern Russia, citing Joseph Rabinovich's sect and a similar hybrid Jewish Christian sect that had appeared in Moldavia in 1868.[91] The newspaper attributed the Brother-hood's demise to a "police misunderstanding" and assured its readers that Russian newspapers "almost unanimously" called on the state to remove the local "administrative ban" on Gordin's group. This nascent anti-Talmud movement had "the seeds and instincts to destroy the fanatical kahal." The paper attributed the modest size of Rabinovich's movement to his initial fear of spreading his ideas, despite the attention he drew in the local and foreign press. It was only with the encouragement of the German Hebraist Franz Delitzsch that Rabinovich published his sect's ideology and petitioned the Bessarabian authorities for permission to set up a separate prayer house and a separate section in the local Jewish cemetery. In a grand gesture, the St. Petersburg journal welcomed "with best wishes" the new anti-Talmud movement among Bessarabian Jews.

To soften this celebratory note, *Sankt-Peterburgskie vedomosti* warned that imperial law, ironically, obstructed the development of Christianizing sects. Citing the law on mixed marriages, which gave a Jewish spouse the right to stay in a mixed marriage, the paper noted that kahal members actu-ally had state backing to "oppress 'on legal grounds' those renegades from the Talmud, who, severing all ties with its religious organization, would want to place themselves under the protection of the state religion (*gosudarstvennaia religiia*), that is, to pass into the bosom of the Orthodox Church."[92] In both cases—converts seeking to remarry and Christianizing Jewish sects seeking to practice their faith freely—the confessional state and its policy of toleration seemingly privileged the official Jewish community governed by the kahal over Jewish sects that sought a rapprochement with Christianity. The paper cited the Kiev newspaper *Kievlianin* for similarly noting that the state pro-tected Jews who were members of the recognized confession at the expense of Jews on the margins who tried to efface the boundaries between Judaism and Christianity.

On the whole, however, the provincial Russian press was ambivalent about the Jewish Christian sects. *Kievlianin* applauded their rejection of the Talmud and their ethical program, but it lambasted their theology as overly rationalist and even irreligious, more so than the Stundists, who had long been vilified by the Orthodox faithful.[93] The Kherson diocesan press's articles on the sects were full of admiration, and yet also concern about the confessional orientation of the groups, which seemed to be in flux. Whereas the Volynian press noted the Protestant influence on Rabinovich's 1885 conversion, the Kherson press reprinted his *ikrei emunah* (tenets of faith) to show Russian readers that the New Israel sect was not doctrinally Protestant.[94] Nevertheless, the press still held out hope that the sect would eventually "serve as a transitional stage from Judaism to Orthodoxy."[95] In sum, the Russian press in the 1880s hedged their bets on whether the sects would drive Judaism and Christianity still farther apart or bridge the two faiths.

In January 1885, within a month of the opening of the New Israel synagogue in Rabinovich's home in Kishinev, a rumor circulated in Odessa that Rabinovich had been killed. Though the rumor was false, the Kherson diocesan paper surmised that "Jewish detractors are spreading rumors of murder with a preconceived intention to sow discord among them [the Jews] and the Orthodox population."[96] The myth of Jewish ritual murder thus reared its head yet again, impugning Jews for supposedly not tolerating unorthodox beliefs. With sectarianism as with formal conversion, confessional boundary crossing aroused anxiety about the borders of community and the mobility of identity in the modern age.

In his 1895 publication *O religioznom dvizhenii evreev i rasprostranenii khristianstva mezhdu nimi* (On the Religious Movement of Jews and the Dissemination of Christianity among Them), the missionary Alexander Alekseev discussed the reception of the reformist Jewish sects and their long-term import for Christian society. Sects like Joseph Rabinovich's New Testament Israelites, in addition to mass cantonist conversions in the pre-reform army, represented critical steps toward the spiritual merging (*k sblizheniiu dukhovnomu*) of Jews into Christianity.[97] Alekseev stressed, however, that Rabinovich's sect did not belong to any established Christian denomination and that the main influence on the sect was Protestantism, not Orthodoxy, which, in his words, was the proper Christian confession for all Russian subjects, including Jews.[98] Despite the confessional confusion of the sects that confounded state and church administrators and led to the sects being censured, commentators noted that New Testament Israelites and anti-Talmud Jews represented a small, but nonetheless significant, step toward the Christianization of Russian Jewry. Within Jewish society, the confessional ambiguity of the sects suggested that Russian Jews had belatedly embraced the diversity of Jewish expression and reform that had already become a mainstay of Jewish society in the West. Both perspectives on the religious identity of the sects grappled with how to accommodate heterodoxy while maintaining confessional boundaries.

～

In many ways, the challenge reformist Jewish sects of the 1880s posed to the state and its church paralleled that of relapsed converts in the late imperial period whose religious affiliation defied ascription. Relapsed converts and Christianizing Jews hovered in a liminal space that resisted state powers of naming, classifying, and regulating. The Orthodox Church feared indigenous reformist movements within Orthodoxy that seemed to threaten a modern Russian version of the Protestant Reformation. This fear of schism in the southern provinces induced the state to violate its historical legitimation of Jewish sectarianism alongside its general disengagement from heterodox schism and to intervene in what some commentators considered a promising Jews for Jesus moment. Ultimately, the state handed down a negative verdict on the sects and bowed to civil and ecclesiastic fears that they were morally and politically subversive.

In the public eye, sectarianism and conversion created a forum for discussing the terms of religious toleration and orthodoxy in a multiconfessional empire and the existence or fantasy of culturally and religiously isolated communities. Whereas many Russians viewed the Jewish sects in New Russia as way stations on the road to Christianity, Jews ultimately were concerned less with the religious message of the sects than their national disloyalty and reckless attempt to reground modern politics in the religious wars of the past. National identity weighed more heavily on the shoulders of the Jewish journalists than the form or content of Judaism espoused by Priluker, Gordin, and others. Even though the sects were established as Jewish religious groups, their attempt to legally differentiate themselves from Jews and promote intermarriage to hasten emancipation made them, arguably, more reprehensible to Jews than apostates. Whereas converts solely underwent a religious transfer, the new sects, in the eyes of the Jewish press, attempted to remake their national identity by legally separating themselves from mainstream Russian Jewry. By the late nineteenth century, many Jews could admit that one's religious identity was fungible, but the majority adamantly believed that one's national identity was inborn and immutable. Not until the twentieth century, especially in the Soviet period, would Jewish voices emerge to challenge the link between the religious and national components of Jewish identity.

Just as press coverage of conversions revealed evolving conceptions of Jewish identity, it also revealed changing notions of religion and the role of the individual in matters of faith. Whereas much of imperial law defined confessional status in terms of official registration and perfunctory religious acts (e.g., church attendance, taking communion), reports on sects and relapsed converts and coerced cantonist conversions excited great public concern for the individual's freedom of conscience in the realm of religious belief. Both Christians and Jews invoked the right to religious freedom when trying to control the direction of conversions, either to Christianity or back to Judaism. Although this freedom was not recognized by imperial law until 1905, and then only partially, writers appropriated the concept of freedom of conscience as a way to establish a moral high ground when contesting conversions and the right of religious communities to hold onto their flock and the ideology and rites of their confession.

EPILOGUE

Converts on the Cultural Map

CONVERTS FROM JUDAISM in imperial Russia, though few in number, left an outsized imprint on the cultural map of East European Jews grappling with questions of individual and communal identity and the role of religion in the increasingly powerful Jewish secular nationalist ideologies of the late nineteenth and early twentieth centuries. Thinking with converts meant nothing less than contemplating the future of Judaism, the survival of Jews as a community, and the problem (or blessing) of religious choice in an era of rising nationalism. Exploring Jewish attitudes toward baptism, interfaith sociability, and cultural mobility in the late imperial period helps to chart how Russian Jewry went from the largest, most traditionalist Jewish community to the most secular over the course of a century, from shunning apostates to embracing new forms of Jewish ethnicity with or without Jewish religion. Although state cultural politics and avenues for Jewish socioeconomic advancement, including interior migration, were key sources of the ethnicization of Jewish identity over the course of the Soviet century, there was also a more far-reaching internal process underway in the imperial period of out-conversions and a developing contest between individual choice and collective identity among converts and their kin.

Conversions in Comparative Context

Conversions from Judaism ironically increased in the modern period just as emancipation held out the promise of equality. If in premodern and early modern Europe Jews converted for the sake of sheer survival—when the choice often was between converting or being expelled (or murdered)—Jews in the modern period converted for strategic reasons, to escape the stigmatization and burdens of Jewishness that persisted even after the right to citizenship was won. While it is difficult to pinpoint why any particular Jew converted, historian Todd Endelman argues that all converts and conversions were structured and guided by the age-old stigmatization of Judaism in Christian Europe.[1] Though converts ostensibly sought a total break from Jewishness, hence conversion has been described as a form of radical assimilation, baptism often failed to provide relief from Jewish origins. Indeed, with the spread of racial thinking in the late nineteenth century escape from Jewishness became even more difficult.

Since modern conversions were strategic, convenient, and tied to the ambitions and hopes of Jews for full socioeconomic and political equality, converts in Russia—an autocratic regime lacking a discourse of emancipation—resembled premodern converts whose baptisms were coerced or driven by despair and persecution. Moreover, few East European Jews could picture themselves as part of a Christian world, one that frustrated the hopes and ambitions of Western and Central European Jews.[2]

The motivations (arising from the national context, social status, and gender) for conversion in late imperial times were inextricably bound up with the people and confessional communities who facilitated and personalized the conversion experience since conversion was as much a social as structural expedient. The absence of civil marriage in imperial Russia alongside legal discrimination (residential and later educational and professional) structured the horizon of possibilities for Jews. With avenues for mobility closed, conversion became a way out, especially in periods of illiberalism and increased discrimination against Jews (the post-reform period and the rise of Russian conservatism). However, not all Jews who converted did so out of a sense of desperation. Interfaith sociability—relationships between Christians and Jews—forged before baptism sometimes was a key factor pulling Jews toward conversion. Beyond the politics of social acceptance among the educated and wealthy European Jewish elite, where a lack of intimacy fueled frustration, neighborly relations and small-town and rural liaisons facilitated many conversions in the Russian provinces.[3] Whether or not East European

Jews were conversant with Christian theology before baptism, many Jews knew Christians and their relationships with them could stimulate conversions.[4] Indeed, many converts in imperial Russia faced poverty, hardship, and despair (criminal sentences, residential restrictions, abusive marriages, estranged families), but they still chose conversion and strategically used confessional affiliation as a way to navigate imperial status, thus complicating the contrast between conversions out of desperation and out of strategic considerations or convenience.[5]

Historian Todd Endelman argues that in the modern period only a minority of converts were sincere and experienced the proverbial radical transformation documented by scholars like William James and Arthur Darby Nock in their seminal works on conversion and religious experience. In particular, Endelman describes Jewish converts to new-age religions in the late twentieth and early twenty-first centuries whose convictions were less a matter of ideology and more a sincere quest for life meaning and self-improvement. These converts were seekers—due to their individual needs and their response to countercultural currents—whose choice of religion was influenced more by a recruiter or a personal relationship than by ideology.[6] There is much affinity between this kind of people-inspired conversion and conversions in response to the "desperate" circumstances that faced Jews in imperial Russia. Though Russian Jewish conversions were shaped by the restrictions and disabilities imposed on Jews, it was converts' ties to Christians that mediated these material circumstances. Thus, the path to conversion in imperial Russia is as important as the political climate, prospects for socioeconomic mobility, and gender, all of which affected the horizon of possibilities for Russian Jews.

Scholars have interpreted ongoing convert-Jewish ties in West and Central Europe as evidence of increased acceptance of converts in Jewish society—a turn away from the premodern Ashkenazic view of conversion as betrayal to a modern view of conversion as social practice.[7] This was less true in Eastern Europe, where shunning converts continued, especially among Jewish nationalists; evidence of this can be seen in Jewish violence against converts, which was hardly imaginable at the time in Western Jewish communities.[8] Yet, there were increasing numbers of Jews in Eastern Europe who did not shun converts, making it possible for them to lead a normal life in Jewish communities.[9]

Religious communities even in tsarist Russia, where the state was invested

in stabilizing and marking religious boundaries and ascription, were nonetheless permeable. Conversion thus offers a window unto more than just
the failures of Jewish emancipation—an inadequate framework for studying
tsarist Russia. It brings into focus the dynamic interaction between neighboring faiths and reveals how Jews and their neighbors negotiated everyday
cultural entanglements.

Attitudes toward Conversion and
Conversations on the Jewish Future

The issue of the survival of Judaism occupied writers, rabbis, and political
and cultural leaders in the late imperial period. Although all of them wanted
to protect the distinctiveness of Jewish culture, they were divided over what
made that culture different. In the late imperial period conversions from Judaism were so common that some contemporaries accepted them as perfectly
normal while others were so alarmed that they considered them an act of national suicide. Conversion stood at once as a testament to Jewish integration
and as a sign of its abject failure. In 1912, reacting to heightened attention in
the Jewish press to a veritable epidemic of conversions, a commentator called
for national soul-searching for the causes of increased national disaffection
and for a more intensive Jewish nationalist education so that youth would
view apostasy as a form of "national suicide."[10]

The personal toll for conversion could be immense. For example, the
conversion of the renowned Jewish historian Simon Dubnov's daughter
caused her father and many of his fellow Jewish intellectuals to shun her as
an enemy of her people. Ahad Ha'am asked, "how can a man like Dubnov
make peace with the thought that his daughter 'fattens calves for idol worship' and that his descendants will be Gentiles and anti-Semites? In this
situation there is only one way to escape the sorrow that consumes body and
soul, and that is to tear out from the heart in one act all the ties which bind
him to the sinful soul, and to consider her dead and non-existent."[11] As late
as 1917, Rabbi Chaim Ozer Grodzinski issued a *kol korei* (rabbinic statement)
warning Russian Jews that conversion was too often the price of equality.[12]
In responding to the rise of exogamy in the modern Jewish world and the
challenge of maintaining communal borders, famed Russian rabbi Yitzhak
Elhanan Spektor penned a responsum prohibiting the circumcision of a son

born to a Jewish father and a non-Jewish mother, thus privileging the maintenance of boundaries and circumscribing the definition of Jewishness.[13]

For all of the public Jewish outrage and stories of ritual and personal shunning of apostates, not to mention the episodes of violence explored in the book, there is also abundant evidence of the increasing normalcy of religious boundary crossings and a fascination among Jews with converts and their stories of communal migration.[14] Rather than viewing conversion as a severing of national bonds, some contemporaries helped craft a narrative of convert insincerity, which touted the essential Jewishness of apostates. In his memoirs, the Yiddishist and diaspora Jewish nationalist Chaim Zhitlovskii recounts a story of the Jewish family M—n in the village of Efremov (south of Moscow), who suffered a "tragedy" in 1885. A local gentile man fell in love with their adolescent daughter, and she converted in order to marry him. "Remarkably," commented Zhitlovskii, "the family's personal relationships with the converted daughter were not torn apart."[15] Out of the parents' great love for their child, or perhaps due to their liberalism, they did not exclude the daughter from the family, and she regularly visited home. Zhitlovskii concluded from this that, despite the daughter's lack of a Jewish education, she was still deeply committed to Judaism and that her simple Jewish soul (*pintele yid*) still burned within her.[16] While not denying the "tragedy" of conversion in Russian Jewish society, Zhitlovskii was mindful that converts could continue to function in Jewish society. Likewise, the return of Protestant-born Vladimir Medem (1879–1923), a leading ideologue of the Jewish Labor Bund, to Jewish life as a socialist was conditioned by years of sustained convert-Jewish relations despite his parents' formal apostasy.[17]

In addition to stories of Jews' attitudes toward converts in their midst, conversion and radical Jewish assimilation became a topic of fascination (and derision) for Jewish and non-Jewish writers in the late imperial period. These writers explored the malleability of identities (national, religious, and individual) in a time of accelerated Jewish acculturation and public debate on the so-called Jewish question. Even Russian writers like Anton Chekhov used converts from Judaism as a symbol of the mutability of identity in empire.[18] The famed Yiddish playwright Avram Goldfaden, once an admirer of Jews turning gentile as strategy and performance, became a vocal critic of converted Yiddish playwrights for flirting with Christianity and betraying the

Yiddish theater's Jewish "authenticity."[19] In the early twentieth century, two of the most celebrated and popular Yiddish writers—Sholem Rabinovich (Sholem Aleichem) and Sholem Asch—devoted entire novels to the theme of converts and conversion. In 1923, Sholem Aleichem published *Der blutiger shpas* (The Bloody Hoax), a story of an identity swap in which two gymnasium friends, one Jewish and the other Russian Orthodox, explore life in each other's shoes and the benefits of turning Christian in an era of Jewish student quotas and a renewed blood libel. In 1934, Sholem Asch published *Der tehilim yid* (The Psalms-Jew, translated as *Salvation*), which centers on a simple, pious Jew, Reb Yehiel the Psalms-reader, and his intimate confrontation with conversion and intermarriage. Reyzele, a girl he helped bring into the world through his prayers on behalf of her barren parents, falls in love with Stepan Dombrovskii, a Polish Catholic, and escapes with him to a convent where she prepares for conversion. The heretofore integrated shtetl in which the story is set descends into religious war—Catholics versus Jews fighting over Reyzele. Deciding that Reyzele's death is preferable to her conversion, Yehiel kills her before she can convert, and she is thus buried a Jew.[20] These novels are rich sources on the cultural presence of converts in East European Jewish society and the use fiction writers made of conversion to probe the boundaries of Jewish ethnicity and spirituality and the nature of Jewish difference.

Apart from fictional discussions of converts in the early twentieth century, there was a flurry of Jewish scholarly interest in the biographies of actual Jewish apostates. Shaul Ginzburg, Shmuel Leib Tsitron, and A. N. Frenk all wrote anecdotal sketches of *meshumodim* (apostates), personalizing a theme in Jewish history often marginalized, maligned, or silenced.[21] Their publications, together with serials in the early twentieth-century Yiddish press on the theme of apostasy, reflect the remarkable interest in the subject of Jewish conversion, which was not a taboo or necessarily a negative topic.[22] By humanizing converts' experiences and showing the diversity of their interactions with Jews and their ongoing commitment to Judaism, these writers suggested that conversion undermined neither the Jewish nation nor the ethos of its survival in the diaspora.

Jewish commentators attempted to create a hierarchy of converts, sorting out the bad from the good, and the insincere from the sincere, in order to clarify which converts remained part of the Jewish collective. In 1888 an article in the Russian Jewish journal *Nedel'naia khronika voskhoda* rejected out of hand the idea that apostates necessarily became Jew-haters or divested themselves of Jewishness. The writer responded to the lively discussion that year in the Judeophobic press about the desirability of Jewish conversion—since converts supposedly became alienated from Judaism and, over time, became greater enemies to Jews than the native population—by offering a taxonomy of three types of converts from Judaism, only one of whom became a Jewhater. He argued that Jews who converted for ideological/theological reasons and for material benefits still could live in Jewish society and that some in fact used their prominence and status as professionals to help Jews.[23] Thus, the shunning of apostates coexisted with ongoing convert-Jewish relations and an acceptance among East European Jews of converts in their midst.

Aside from attitudes toward converts, conversations on conversion also engaged the theme of baptism as a verdict on Jewish integration. In his short story "Avraam Iezofovich," published in *Voskhod* in 1887, Russian Jewish writer Lev Levanda narrated the travails of a talented young Jew in sixteenth-century Poland who was invited to be the king's financial advisor, provided he converted to Catholicism. The young man succumbed, only to spend the rest of his life tormented by his decision to forsake his people.[24] In the context of Levanda's own misgivings over the project for Jewish integration in the Russian Empire, articulated already in the 1870s and intensified following the 1881–1882 pogroms, the convert's spectacular success drowned out by personal sadness amounted to an indictment of contemporary Jewish integrationist politics and the terms of Jewish futurity.

Sholem Aleichem addressed the topic of conversion in two short stories, "Chava" and "The Lottery Ticket," and the novel *Der blutiger shpas*. As he explained in a letter to a friend, he wrote about conversion since the "theme is a topical one" and readers were interested in it.[25] In "The Lottery Ticket" (1902), a traditionalist and poor shtetl sexton flaunts his son's success in school. Swollen with pride, he dubs the boy "a regular lottery ticket," convinced he will become a great success in life and provide his father with a windfall. With his eyes set on medical school, the son, Benyomchik, converts out of desperation to matriculate into university in an era of quotas on Jewish students. Like Tevye and his wife, Beyomchik's parents sit shiva for their converted child, mourning the spiritual loss of both their son and now their ticket out of poverty.[26]

Isaac Babel's 1913 story "Old Shloyme," the earliest known publication of the Russian Jewish writer and journalist, uses conversion as an act of religious obliteration to frame the breakdown of shtetl life and the vulnerability of Jewish survival in a post-pogrom world overtaken by the revival of the ritual murder accusation in imperial Russia. The story's protagonist, Old Shloyme, hangs himself after his son converts for socioeconomic opportunity. While Old Shloyme acknowledges that he was never a particularly religious man and he recognizes the exigencies of his son's situation, conversion nonetheless symbolizes the destruction of his life and a world that will allow Jews to survive.[27] Converts thus registered prominently on the cultural map of Jewish Eastern Europe and were used by a variety of writers to think through the boundaries of the collective and the possibilities for the Jewish future. For a minority of critics, as we will see, converts as communal boundary crossers suggested that religion as a resource for the emerging Jewish nation need not be conceived of in terms of Judaism alone.

Converts in the Twentieth Century:
The Russian-Orthodox Jew

In the inter-revolutionary period (1906–1917) conversions from Judaism accelerated, even as converts could now legally relapse in the wake of Nicholas II's reforms after the failed revolution of 1905.[28] During the Soviet period as a whole there was an exponential increase in exogamy, and in the post-Stalin period the phenomenon of self-identified Jewish Christians.[29]

Religious conversion as a political act joined Zionism, diaspora nationalism, and emigration as a way to reconfigure the terms of Jewishness and collective survival in a post-pogrom world.[30] If nationalists stressed the ethnic dimension of Jewishness over the religious and émigrés took a portable Jewish religion to more welcoming states abroad, converts embraced a national Jewishness that still made room for adopting another faith. Most famous and contentious in this regard was Mikhail Gertsenshteyn, a converted member of the first Duma, who provocatively entered his religion as Russian Orthodox and nationality as Jewish in a Duma questionnaire.[31] In addition to being a profoundly social act, as explored at length in this book, conversion was also tied up with regimes of power and identification, and it too made claims to the terms of Jewish collective difference.

Within the mainstream of Jewish nationalism, both statist and diasporic, there were many defenders of the legitimacy of converts. Much of diaspora nationalist thinking in the inter-revolutionary period focused on conceptualizing the organs of Jewish national autonomy in the diaspora, in particular a modern *kehile*, or Jewish political community. Supporters agreed that a modern Jewish corporate entity needed to be democratic and open to all Jews, thus prompting a debate among nationalists about the status of converts and the parameters of Jewish national belonging. The majority refused to consider converts as Jews unless they "reconverted" to Judaism. A few nationalists supported including converts in the *kehile* if they submitted a statement of "Jewish affiliation."[32] Vladimir Medem of the Jewish Labor Bund, for example, argued that the requirements for membership in the *kehile* should be secular. Written declarations asking for communal membership would thus allow converts (or children of converts, in Medem's case) to join, while it would permit Jews who disavowed a Jewish national status (such as Poles and Russians of the Mosaic faith) to leave the *kehile*.

While Medem still tacitly acknowledged a fundamental religious component to Jewish nationality (hence the need for converts to establish their Jewishness), some diaspora nationalists defined Jewishness according to language and culture rather than birth or theology. In particular, Yiddishists believed there was a secular Yiddish linguistic core to Jewish national identity. In this camp, Chaim Zhitlovskii, whose memoirs repeatedly reference the normalcy of convert-Jewish relations, even argued that "a Yiddish-speaking and Yiddish-reading Jew could choose whatever metaphysical or religious system he preferred, including Christianity, and remain a Jew by nationality."[33] In a similar vein, though refracted through the lens of Zionism, which privileged Hebrew language and culture rather than Yiddish, Yosef Chaim Brenner in 1910 voiced his contentious opinion that belief in Jesus in no way undermined national Jewishness, even the project of Jewish state-building in Ottoman Palestine.[34]

In the Soviet era, these radically secularist articulations of Jewish nationality fell into step with an atheist state ideology that was vehemently antireligious and supported the ethnicization of Jewishness completely divorced from religious moorings. It was only in the post-Stalin era, though, after the Russian Orthodox Church was revived during the Great Patriotic War to buoy up

Russian nationalism and Khrushchev's thaw alleviated some of the ideological strictures of Stalinism, that a new generation of Jews articulated a Soviet vision of the Russian Orthodox Jew—Christian by religion but nationally Jewish. For some Soviet Jewish dissidents who came of age in the post-Stalin period, Orthodox Christianity, or religious revival in general, offered a spiritual refuge and an avenue for political dissent. For many baptized Soviet Jews, as well, conversion was tied to the charisma of Father Alexander Men', a convert from Judaism who greatly influenced a generation of Soviet intellectuals and opened up the Orthodox Church to Jewish newcomers in the 1960s–1980s.[35]

It was in the post-Stalin era, then, that national Jewishness achieved its strongest articulation in Russia. Many Jewish scientists and historians were drawn to Men's message and his desire to connect the church and secular society, science and religion.[36] Soviet historian Mikhail Agursky came from this milieu, and, in 1975—after years of being refused permission to leave the Soviet Union—he immigrated to Israel and accepted a research position at the Hebrew University. Agursky authored some of the key late-Soviet and post-Soviet studies on converts from Judaism in imperial Russia, and he wrote passionate essays on the cultural affinities between Jews and Russians with an optimistic eye toward interfaith rapprochement.[37] Agursky, an acolyte of Men's, left unedited memoirs that openly discuss his involvement in the Russian Orthodox Church. Yet, he gradually "distanced himself from the Church and was circumcised after coming to Israel," according to his widow, Vera. And his memoirs (posthumously published) were stripped of all references to his Christian activity.[38] Although the baptism of Jews became normative for a growing group of intellectuals in the pre-perestroika period in the Soviet Union, the logic of a Jewish Christian began to break down beyond the borders of the USSR, especially in Israel.

The claim of Brother Daniel, or Oswald Rufeisen, a Jewish convert to Catholicism in Poland during World War II, to national Jewishness was turned down in 1962 by the Israeli Supreme Court, which concluded that his conversion invalidated his eligibility for citizenship via the Law of Return. Rufeisen's case was complicated because he was an avowed Zionist who had converted during the Holocaust, after enjoying refuge in a local convent and risking his own life several times to save other Jews. His loyalty to the Jewish nation alongside his embrace of Catholicism made sense to many Soviet Jews who emigrated to Israel and joined his church in Haifa, but his hybrid identity did not pass muster with Israeli jurists who grounded Jewish identity in religion and viewed conversion as a rejection of the nation.[39] Ironically, according to *halakhah*, which generally holds that "once a Jew always a Jew," Rufeisen was a Jew.

This ethnicization of Jewishness, which reached its apotheosis in the post-Stalin era among baptized Jews, has persisted in some ways even after the fall of the Soviet Union, both in former Soviet states and in the Russian Jewish émigré community abroad.[40] While Judaism as a religion continues to be absent from articulations of post-Soviet Jewishness, which mostly involves ethnic pride and confronting anti-Semitism, Anna Shternshis has shown how religion, especially Russian Orthodoxy, is not entirely absent from post-Soviet Jewish identities. From Jewish women reciting kaddish for a loved one in an Orthodox church to attending church for its beauty, the accessibility of the liturgy (which is in the vernacular), and the opportunity for women to engage in rituals, some contemporary Jews continue to tacitly assert the symbiosis of ethnic Jewishness and Orthodox religion.[41] In part, this embrace of Christianity is a product of Soviet education, which equated and condemned all religions as harmful, thus ironically causing spiritual seekers in the late Soviet period to democratize religious truth. Apart from a worldview that has naturalized the efficacy of kaddish even in a church, the post-Soviet hybrid Jewish Christians connect to a history that stretches back to the late imperial period when the nationalization of Jewishness increasingly made room for Jews to adhere to the nation and yet convert to another faith. Though Russian Jewish Christians were not the majority in the imperial or Soviet periods, in the words of Judith Deutsch Kornblatt, "the significance of their stories is large in terms of the theoretical questions of religion and national identity they raise."[42] Thus, tracing the evolving phenomenon of baptized or church-going Jews in the Russian cultural sphere at home and abroad reveals how religion continues to inform and complicate how Jews imagine and construct the boundaries of community.

Converts from Judaism in the nineteenth and twentieth centuries figured prominently on the cultural map of East European Jewish society and stood at the heart of discussions on the future of Judaism and the formation of a Jewish national collective. And yet, converts did not just exist in the cultural imagination. Conversion as an outgrowth of Jewish-Christian daily engagement—friendships, love affairs, hospitable peasants, philanthropic Christians, and socially active parish clergy—reveals that it was predicated on the social and geographic interconnectedness of Jews and Christians in the empire's western provinces. Conversion narratives reveal the interconfessional social networks that made religious transfer possible, and the close proximity to family and friends who were legally empowered to both confirm and contest confessional transfers. Close Jewish-Christian socioeconomic contact usually did not lead to conversion. But the minority of Jews who did convert raises the question of the terms of Jewish separatism and the diversity of confessional life in the Pale of Jewish Settlement.

By looking beyond the question of what motivated conversion and jettisoning assumptions about imperial designs to baptize Jews, a rich picture of Russian Jewry emerges. Jewish residential restrictions and material inducements to convert greatly influenced a Jew's choice to undergo baptism, but the actual process of conversion was facilitated by local Jewish-Christian networks that introduced Jews to the people and practices of other faiths. Beyond political repression and material attractions, it was shtetl sociability and interfaith romance that occupied center stage in civilian, especially female, conversions. Convert-Jewish relations were not necessarily severed upon baptism. Converts from Judaism lived in a confessional state that institutionally supported Judaism and maintained the rule of Jewish religious law for Jews. In this setting where Jewish life was vibrant and conversions were generally uncoerced, imperial toleration in many ways empowered Jewish communities to articulate and defend the boundaries of the Jewish collective.

Converts in imperial Russia, bowing to the absolute demands of confessional affiliation, experimented in their own way with the terms of modern Jewish identity. In contrast to emancipationist iterations of French or German Jews of the Mosaic faith, many Russian Jewish converts reveal that it is possible to be a Jew of the Christian faith, an idea that would find its fullest expression in the Soviet and post-Soviet eras.

REFERENCE MATTER

NOTES

Abbreviations Used in the Notes

ARCHIVES AND SOURCES

CAHJP	Central Archives for the History of the Jewish People, Jerusalem
DAKO	Derzhavnyi arkhiv Kyivs'koi oblasti (State Archive of Kiev Oblast')
DAmK	Derzhavnyi arkhiv m. Kyieva (State Archive of the City of Kiev)
DAOO	Derzhavnyi arkhiv Odes'koi oblasti (State Archive of Odessa Oblast')
DAVO	Derzhavnyi arkhiv Volyns'koi oblasti (State Archive of Volynia Oblast')
DAZhO	Derzhavnyi arkhiv Zhytomyrs'koi oblasti (State Archive of Zhitomir Oblast')
GARF	Gosudarstvennyi arkhiv Rossiiskoi Federatsii (State Archive of the Russian Federation)
LVIA	Lietuvos valstybės istorijos archyvas (Lithuanian State Historical Archive)
NIAB	Natsional'nyi istoricheskii arkhiv Belarusi (State Historical Archive of Belarus)
PSZ	*Polnoe sobranie zakonov Rossiiskoi Imperii* (Complete Collection of the Laws of the Russian Empire), 3 series
RGADA	Rossiiskii gosudarstvennyi arkhiv drevnikh aktov (Russian State Archive of Early Acts)
RGAVMF	Rossiiskii gosudarstvennyi arkhiv voenno-morskogo flota (Russian State Archive of the Navy)

RGIA   Rossiiskii gosudarstvennyi istoricheskii arkhiv (Russian State
           Historical Archive)
RGVIA   Rossiiskii gosudarstvennyi voenno-istoricheskii arkhiv (Russian
           State Military History Archive)
SZ   *Svod zakonov Rossiiskoi Imperii* (Law Digest of the Russian Empire)
TsDIAK   Tsentral'nyi derzhavnyi istorychnyi arkhiv Ukrainy, Kyiv (Central
           State Historical Archive of Ukraine, Kiev)
TsGIA-SPb Tsentral'nyi gosudarstvennyi istoricheskii arkhiv Sankt-Peterburga
           (Central State Historical Archives, St. Petersburg)
YIVO   YIVO Institute for Jewish Research, New York

ARCHIVAL CITATIONS

d. (dd.)   *delo, dela* (file, files)
eksp.   *ekspeditsiia* (department)
f.   *fond* (collection)
g. (gg.)   *god, goda* (year, years)
kn.   *kniga* (book)
l. (ll.)   *list, listy* (leaf, leaves)
ob.   *oborot* (verso)
op.   *opis', opisi* (inventory, inventories)
otd.   *otdelenie* (section)
RG   record group

Introduction

1. YIVO RG 46, Box III:76, Conversion of Vilna Jewish townswoman Pera Girsenovich, 1874.

2. On the terminology of "confession" in state institutions, see Paul W. Werth, *The
Tsar's Foreign Faiths: Toleration and the Fate of Religious Freedom in Imperial Russia* (Oxford: Oxford University Press, 2014), 53–57. On Russian legal conceptions of religion as
a body of law rather than faith in the pre-reform era (before 1855), see Paul W. Werth,
*At the Margins of Orthodoxy: Mission, Governance, and Confessional Politics in Russia's
Volga-Kama Region, 1827–1905* (Ithaca, NY: Cornell University Press, 2002), 140–45. The
language of "confession" in imperial Russian religious politics recalls the confessional
politics of early modern Europe and scholarly debates over the relationship between
state consolidation and confessionalization, or denominational consolidation. The ter-
minological parallel is fruitful insofar as confessional politics in the Russian Empire
were directly related to Russian state-building and the empire's instrumentalization
(and formalization) of confessional difference for administrative order and control.

3. Aggregate statistics from the Governing Synod of the Russian Orthodox Church
and German missionaries conservatively estimate Jewish conversions to various Chris-

tian denominations in nineteenth-century imperial Russia at 84,500. The annual Synod reports, which were published for the years 1836–1914, are entitled *Vsepoddanneishii otchet ober-prokurora Sv. Sinoda za . . . god* (Petersburg), and the combined data from the reports are used in two collective statistical analyses of conversions: Ivan Preobrazhenskii, *Otechestvennaia tserkov' po statisticheskim dannym s 1840–41 po 1890–91 gg.*, reprint, 1897 (Petersburg, 1901), esp. 46, 53; and J. F. A. de le Roi, *Judentaufen im 19. Jahrhundert* (Leipzig, 1899), 42–45. For statistics on non-Orthodox conversions, see de le Roi, *Judentaufen*, 31–32, 40–41.

4. Gauri Viswanathan, *Outside the Fold: Conversion, Modernity, and Belief* (Princeton, NJ: Princeton University Press, 1998), 16.

5. Saul M. Ginsburg, *Meshumodim in tsarishn Russland* (New York: "CYCO" Bicher Farlag, 1946); Shmuel Leib Tsitron, *Meshumodim: tipn un silueten funm noenten over*, 4 vols. (Warsaw: Verlag Tsentral, 1923–1928); Ezriel Nathan Frenk, *Meshumodim in Poyln in 19-tn yor-hundert* (Warsaw: M.Y. Fried, 1923). Tsitron's series was titled *Meshumodim*, but volumes 3 and 4 were titled *Avek fun folk*. Before the collapse of the Soviet Union, the following groundbreaking articles on conversions from Judaism were published, based on either published sources or small deposits of archival materials preserved in Western libraries: Mikhail Agursky, "Conversions of Jews to Christianity in Russia," *Soviet Jewish Affairs* 20, no. 2–3 (1990): 69–84; Michael Stanislawski, "Jewish Apostasy in Russia: A Tentative Typology," in *Jewish Apostasy in the Modern World*, ed. Todd M. Endelman (New York: Holmes and Meier, 1987), 189–205; Steven J. Zipperstein, "Heresy, Apostasy and the Transformation of Joseph Rabinovich," in *Jewish Apostasy in the Modern World*, ed. Endelman, 206–31. More recently, conversion has been the subject of several important studies on Jews in imperial Russia: John Klier, "State Policies and the Conversion of Jews in Imperial Russia," in *Of Religion and Empire: Missions, Conversion, and Tolerance in Tsarist Russia*, ed. Robert P. Geraci and Michael Khodarkovsky (Ithaca, NY: Cornell University Press, 2001), 92–112; Eugene M. Avrutin, *Jews and the Imperial State: Identification Politics in Tsarist Russia* (Ithaca, NY: Cornell University Press, 2010); Todd M. Endelman, "Jewish Converts in Nineteenth-Century Warsaw: A Quantitative Analysis," *Jewish Social Studies* 4, no. 1 (Fall 1997): 28–59; ChaeRan Freeze, "When Chava Left Home: Gender, Conversion, and the Jewish Family in Tsarist Russia," *Polin* 18 (2005): 153–88; Eugene M. Avrutin, "Returning to Judaism after the 1905 Law on Religious Freedom in Tsarist Russia," *Slavic Review* 65, no. 1 (Spring 2006): 90–110; Olga Litvak, *Conscription and the Search for Modern Russian Jewry* (Bloomington: Indiana University Press, 2006); Yohanan Petrovsky-Shtern, *Jews in the Russian Army, 1827–1917: Drafted into Modernity* (Cambridge: Cambridge University Press, 2009). In addition to this literature, there are several complementary studies on conversions from Judaism in eighteenth-century imperial Russia and the Polish-Lithuanian Commonwealth, as well as studies on Jewish missions and convert missionaries in nineteenth-century imperial Russia, especially Congress Poland. See Viktoria Aleksandrovna Gerasimova, "Kreshchenye evrei

v Rossii v XVIII v.: Osobennosti sotsiokul'turnoi adaptatsii" (PhD diss., Russian State University for Humanities, Moscow, 2013); Adam Kaźmierczyk, *Rodziłem się Żydem . . . Konwersje Żydów w Rzeczypospolitej XVII–XVIII wieku* (Kraków: Księgarnia Akademicka, 2015); Raymond Lillevik, *Apostates, Hybrids, or True Jews? Jewish Christians and Jewish Identity in Eastern Europe, 1860–1914* (Eugene, OR: Pickwick, 2014); Agnieszka Jagodzińska, "Christian Missionaries and Jewish Spaces: British Missions in the Kingdom of Poland in the First Half of the Nineteenth Century," in *Space and Conversion in Global Perspective*, ed. Giuseppe Marcocci et al. (Leiden: Brill, 2015), 103–26.

6. Of the conservative estimate of 84,500 Russian Jews who converted to Christianity over the course of the nineteenth century, roughly one quarter can be characterized as coerced and underage. For an estimate of 25,000 cantonist conversions, see Stanislawski, "Jewish Apostasy in Russia," 193–94. For a more recent estimate of 20,000, see Avrutin, "Returning to Judaism," 95.

7. For a correlation of Synod statistics on Jewish conversion to shifts in tsarist regimes and politics, see I. Cherikover, "Obrashchenie v khristianstvo," *Evreiskaia entsiklopediia: Svod znanii o evreistve i ego kul'ture v proshlom i nastoiashchem* (St. Petersburg: Brokgauz-Efron, 1906–1913), XI: cols. 884–95; Stanislawski, "Jewish Apostasy in Russia," 190–91.

8. On the shtetl as idea and history, see Antony Polonsky, ed., "The Shtetl: Myth and Reality," *Polin* 17 (2004); Gennady Estraikh and Mikhail Krutikov, eds., *The Shtetl: Image and Reality* (Oxford: Legenda, 2000); Steven T. Katz, *The Shtetl: New Evaluations* (New York: New York University Press, 2007); Dan Miron, *The Image of the Shtetl and Other Studies of Modern Jewish Literary Imagination* (Syracuse, NY: Syracuse University Press, 2000); Jeffrey Shandler, *Shtetl: A Vernacular Intellectual History* (New Brunswick, NJ: Rutgers University Press, 2014).

9. Jeffrey Veidlinger, "From Shtetl to Society: Jews in 19th-Century Russia," *Kritika* 2, no. 4 (Fall 2001): 823–24.

10. Michał Galas, "Inter-religious Contacts in the Shtetl: Proposals for Future Research," *Polin* 17 (2004): 41–50.

11. On the heterogeneity of confessional life in imperial Russia and lived religion, see Heather Coleman, *Russian Baptists and Spiritual Revolution, 1905–1929* (Bloomington: Indiana University Press, 2005); Laura Engelstein, *Castration and the Heavenly Kingdom: A Russian Folktale* (Ithaca, NY: Cornell University Press, 1999); Nadieszda Kizenko, *A Prodigal Saint: Father John of Kronstadt and the Russian People* (University Park: Pennsylvania State University Press, 2000); Sergei I. Zhuk, *Russia's Lost Reformation: Peasants, Millennialism, and Radical Sects in Southern Russia and Ukraine, 1830–1917* (Baltimore: Johns Hopkins University Press, 2004); Nicholas B. Breyfogle, *Heretics and Colonizers: Forging Russia's Empire in the South Caucasus* (Ithaca, NY: Cornell University Press, 2005); Werth, *At the Margins of Orthodoxy*; Gregory L. Freeze, "The Rechristianization of Russia: The Church and Popular Religion, 1750–1850," *Studia Slavica Find-*

landensia 7 (1990), 101–36; Vera Shevzov, *Russian Orthodoxy on the Eve of Revolution* (New York: Oxford University Press, 2004); Robert P. Geraci and Michael Khodarkovsky, eds., *Of Religion and Empire: Missions, Conversion, and Tolerance in Tsarist Russia* (Ithaca, NY: Cornell University Press, 2001). For a recent work on religious encounters between Judaism and various forms of Christianity in early modern and modern Eastern Europe, see Glenn Dynner, ed., *Holy Dissent: Jewish and Christian Mystics in Eastern Europe* (Detroit: Wayne State University Press, 2011).

12. Robert Crews, "Empire and the Confessional State: Islam and Religious Politics in Nineteenth-Century Russia," *American Historical Review* 108, no. 1 (February 2003): 50–83.

13. Robert D. Crews, *For Prophet and Tsar: Islam and Empire in Russia and Central Asia* (Cambridge, MA: Harvard University Press, 2006). Mikhail Dolbilov has modified Crews' thesis by positing that there was a tension in confessional politics between state patronage of the tolerated confessions and state attempts to discredit the foreign faiths. See Mikhail Dolbilov, *Russkii krai, chuzhaia vera: Etnokonfessional'naia politika imperii v Litve i Belorussii pri Aleksandre II* (Moscow: Novoe literaturnoe obozrenie, 2010). Paul Werth's recent synthetic survey of religious toleration in the Russian Empire employs both of these theses to analyze Russia's "multiconfessional establishment." See Werth, *The Tsar's Foreign Faiths.*

14. On these institutions and the maskil-state alliance, see Azriel Shochat, *Mosad 'Ha-Rabanut Mi-Ta'am' Be-Rusyah* (Haifa: University of Haifa, 1975); Michael Stanislawski, *Tsar Nicholas I and the Jews: The Transformation of Jewish Society in Russia, 1825–1855* (Philadelphia: Jewish Publication Society of America, 1983); ChaeRan Y. Freeze, *Jewish Marriage and Divorce in Imperial Russia* (Hanover, NH: University Press of New England, 2002); Eli Lederhendler, *The Road to Modern Jewish Politics: Political Tradition and Political Reconstruction in the Jewish Community of Tsarist Russia* (Oxford: Oxford University Press, 1989); Vasily Shchedrin, "Jewish Bureaucracy in Late Imperial Russia: The Phenomenon of Expert Jews, 1850–1917" (PhD diss., Brandeis University, 2010).

15. On metrical record keeping, see Chapter 1.

16. Duane J. Corpis, *Crossing the Boundaries of Belief: Geographies of Religious Conversion in Southern Germany, 1646–1800* (Charlottesville: University of Virginia Press, 2014), 13. On new trends in conversions studies, see Anthony Grafton and Anthony Mills, eds., *Conversion: Old Worlds and New* (Rochester, NY: University of Rochester Press, 2003), introduction; Natalie Zemon Davis, *Trickster Travels: A Sixteenth-Century Muslim between Worlds* (New York: Hill and Wang, 2007), 11–12.

17. Paul Werth, "Lived Orthodoxy and Confessional Diversity: The Last Decade on Religion in Modern Russia," *Kritika* 12, no. 4 (Fall 2011): 849–65; G. M. Hamburg, "Religious Toleration in Russian Thought, 1520–1825," *Kritika* 13, no. 3 (Summer 2012): 515–59; Randall A. Poole, "Religious Toleration, Freedom of Conscience, and Russian Liberalism," *Kritika* 13, no. 3 (Summer 2012): 611–34. On new trends in the study of

religion in Russia, especially Russian Orthodoxy as lived experience, see Valerie A. Kivelson and Ronald H. Greene, "Introduction: Orthodox Russia," in *Orthodox Russia: Belief and Practice under the Tsars*, ed. Valerie A. Kivelson and Ronald H. Greene (University Park: Pennsylvania State University Press, 2003), 1–19.

18. For historical scholarship in the late-imperial and Soviet periods, which dismissed Russian pretensions to toleration and generally read imperial Jewish policies as fronts for baptizing Russian Jewry, see I. G. Orshanskii, *Russkoe zakonodatel'stvo o evreiakh: Ocherki i issledovaniia* (St. Petersburg, 1877), 26–59; Saul M. Ginsburg, *Historische Werk*, 3 vols. (New York: S.M. Ginsburg Testimonial Committee, 1937), II:235–38, III:59; Louis Greenberg, *The Jews in Russia: The Struggle for Emancipation* (New Haven, CT: Yale University Press, 1944).

19. For a recent synthetic treatment, see Todd M. Endelman, *Leaving the Jewish Fold: Conversion and Radical Assimilation in Modern Jewish History* (Princeton, NJ: Princeton University Press, 2015). Endelman pairs conversion as strategy with prior Jewish disaffection; others have paired it with weak Jewish education. See Franz Rosenzweig, "Renaissance of Jewish Learning and Living," in *Franz Rosenzweig: His Life and Thought*, ed. Nahum N. Glatzer (New York: Schocken, 1961), 218; Paula Hyman, *Gender and Assimilation in Modern Jewish History: The Roles and Representations of Women* (Seattle: University of Washington Press, 1995), 21.

20. Stanislawski, "Jewish Apostasy in Russia," 200.

21. Elisheva Carlebach, *Divided Souls: Converts from Judaism in Germany, 1500–1750* (New Haven, CT: Yale University Press, 2001); Marcus Moseley, *Being for Myself Alone: The Origins of Jewish Autobiography* (Stanford, CA: Stanford University Press, 2005); Freeze, "When Chava Left Home."

22. Peter van der Veer, Introduction to *Conversion to Modernities: The Globalization of Christianity*, ed. Peter van der Veer (New York: Routledge, 1996), 10–11.

23. Keith P. Luria, "The Politics of Protestant Conversion to Catholicism," in *Conversion to Modernities*, 25–26, 28–29. For the classic Protestant-inflected theories of conversion, see William James, *The Varieties of Religious Experience* (New York: Longmans, Green, 1902); A. D. Nock, *Conversion: The Old and New in Religion from Alexander the Great to Augustine of Hippo* (Oxford: Oxford University Press, 1933). For more recent works that attempt to broaden the conversion experience beyond the highly ideologized narrative of Paul's individual, internal, and spiritual conversion, and which acknowledge the sociocultural components of conversion and view it as a gradual process, see Ramsay MacMullen, *Christianizing the Roman Empire (A.D. 100–400)* (New Haven, CT: Yale University Press, 1984), 1–9; Lewis Rambo, *Understanding Religious Conversion* (New Haven, CT: Yale University Press, 1993).

24. For a discussion of Jewish conversions to minority faiths in the Russian Empire that complicates the narrative of instrumental baptisms in modern Jewish history, see Ellie R. Schainker, "Jewish Conversion in an Imperial Context: Confessional Choice

and Multiple Baptisms in Nineteenth-Century Russia," *Jewish Social Studies* n.s. 20, no. 1 (Fall 2013): 1–31.

25. Kenneth B. Moss, "At Home in Late Imperial Russian Modernity—Except When They Weren't: New Histories of Russian and East European Jews, 1881–1914," *Journal of Modern History* 84 (June 2012): 449–50. On the Subbotnik story as an example of everyday, rural encounters between Jews and Christians, see Nicholas Breyfogle, "The Religious World of Russian Sabbatarians (*Subbotniks*)," in *Holy Dissent: Jewish and Christian Mystics in Eastern Europe*, ed. Glenn Dynner (Detroit: Wayne State University Press, 2011), 383–84.

26. This approach builds on conversion studies that have emphasized place and sociability in analyzing confessional migrations. See, for example, Agursky, "Conversions of Jews"; Rachel Manekin, "The Lost Generation: Education and Female Conversion in *Fin-de-Siècle* Kraków," *Polin* 18 (2005): 189–219.

27. Mordechai Altshuler, *Soviet Jewry on the Eve of the Holocaust: A Social and Demographic Profile* (Jerusalem: Ahva Press, 1998), 69–76. Compare to statistics on Jewish conversions in Prussia and the surrounding provinces, where 380,000 Jews lived by the end of the century and 13,128 Jews converted over the course of the nineteenth century (de le Roi, *Judentaufen im 19. Jahrhundert*, 8, 15–16).

28. On the threat of conversion as a historical force, see Grafton and Mills, *Conversion*, ix–xvii.

29. Carlebach, *Divided Souls*, 30–31; Avraham Grossman, *Hasidot u-mordot: Nashim Yehudiyot be-Eropah be-yeme-ha-benayim* (Jerusalem: Merkaz Zalman Shazar, 2001).

30. Simon Dubnov, *The Book of Life: Memoirs and Reflections*, trans. by Dianne Sattinger, edited by Benjamin Nathans and Viktor Kel'ner (forthcoming, University of Wisconsin Press), chap. 7.

31. Puah Rakovsky, *My Life as a Radical Jewish Woman: Memoirs of a Zionist Feminist in Poland*, edited and introduced by Paula E. Hyman (Bloomington: Indiana University Press, 2002), 51.

32. Ibid., 38.

33. Benjamin Nathans, *Beyond the Pale: The Jewish Encounter with Late Imperial Russia* (Berkeley: University of California Press, 2002), 206.

34. On the Talmudic dictum "although he has sinned, he remains a Jew" (Babylonian Talmud, Sanhedrin: 44a), and its evolution as a principle in Jewish law positing the eternal Jewishness of apostates in the medieval period and beyond, see Jacob Katz, *Halakhah ve-Kabalah* (Jerusalem: Magnes Press, 1984), 261–69. On the status of apostates in rabbinic law in the medieval and early modern periods, see Yosef Hayim Yerushalmi, "The Inquisition and the Jews of France in the Time of Bernard Gui," *Harvard Theological Review* 63 (1970): 317–76; Jacob Katz, *Exclusiveness and Tolerance* (Oxford: Oxford University Press, 1961), 67–81; Ephraim Kanarfogel, "Changing Attitudes toward Apostates in Tosafist Literature, Late Twelfth–Early Thirteenth Centuries," in *New Perspec-*

tives on Jewish-Christian Relations, ed. Elisheva Carlebach and Jacob J. Shachter (Leiden: Brill, 2012), 297–328; Edward Fram, "Perception and Reception of Repentant Apostates in Medieval Ashkenaz and Premodern Poland," *AJS Review* 21, no. 2 (1996): 299–339.

35. Coleman, *Russian Baptists*; Laura Engelstein, "Holy Russia in Modern Times: An Essay on Orthodoxy and Cultural Change," *Past and Present*, no. 173 (November 2001): 129–56.

Chapter 1

1. On Moshko Blank and his conversion to Russian Orthodoxy, see Yohanan Petrovsky-Shtern, *Lenin's Jewish Question* (New Haven, CT: Yale University Press, 2010). For an in-depth analysis of Moshe Schneerson's conversion record in the context of Hasidism and the contestation of his memory in Jewish history, see David Assaf, *Untold Tales of the Hasidim: Crisis and Discontent in the History of Hasidism*, trans. Dena Ordan (Waltham, MA: Brandeis University Press, 2010).

2. The first work is Shneur Zalman's systematic exposition of his Hasidic philosophy. It is both a work of Jewish mysticism and a practical guide to divine service. The second work is Shneur Zalman's Hasidic reworking of the authoritative code of Jewish law written in sixteenth-century Safed by Joseph Karo.

3. Assaf, *Untold Tales*, 35–36, 38.

4. NIAB f. 1781, op. 2, d. 271, ll. 13, 26–270b., "O rabine Leone Shneere, zhelaiush-chem prisoedinit'sia k khristianskoi tserkvi iz evreev (1820)" [CAHJP inv. no. 8651].

5. RGIA f. 821, op. 45, d. 124, ll. 1–2, 14, "Atlas—narodonaseleniia zapadno-russkago kraia, po ispovedaniiam (1863)." Out of a total population of about 10.7 million in the nine western provinces, 2.6 million were Catholics of various ethnicities, including Polish, Lithuanian, and Latvian.

6. NIAB f. 1781, op. 2, d. 271, ll. 30–33; NIAB f. 1781, op. 3, d. 51, ll. 84–85, Jew Movshe Shneur who wants to convert to Catholicism.

7. NIAB f. 1781, op. 2, d. 271, ll. 3–90b. On the history of Jewish deputies and a discussion of the Schneerson case in that context, see Ol'ga Minkina, *"Syny Rakhili": Evreiskie deputaty v Rossiiskoi imperii, 1772–1825* (Moscow: Novoe literaturnoe obozrenie, 2011), 179–81.

8. NIAB f. 1781, op. 2, d. 271, ll. 40b.–5, 70b., 9.

9. Ibid., ll. 9–90b., 11.

10. Ibid., ll. 16–17, esp. 160b.

11. *SZ* (1832 ed.), vol. I, no. 40–42.

12. Robert D. Crews, *For Prophet and Tsar: Islam and Empire in Russia and Central Asia* (Cambridge, MA: Harvard University Press, 2006), 9–10.

13. Andreas Kappeler, *The Russian Empire: A Multiethnic History* (Harlow, Eng.: Pearson Education, 2001), 141–53.

14. *PSZ* II, vol. II, no. 1360 (August 20, 1827). In 1830 this permission was extended

to Jewish conscripts as well. See RGIA f. 1409, op. 1, d. 1251, l. 36, "O dozvolenii Evreiam, otdavaemym v rekruty, prinimat' Khristianskuiu veru vsekh terpimykh ispovedanii (September 6, 1830)" [CAHJP RU 1275]. In 1833 this law was applied when the Synod was asked if Jews from the former Polish territories could convert to Catholicism in the army (RGIA f. 797, op. 4, d. 17835, "O evreev sluzhivshikh v pol'skoi armii i zhelaiushikh priniat' rimskokatolichesky ispovedanii").

15. RGIA f. 821, op. 45, d. 124.

16. J. F. A. de le Roi, *Judentaufen im 19. Jahrhundert* (Leipzig, 1899), 31–32, 40–45.

17. RGIA f. 383, op. 29, d. 859, Jewish agriculturists in the southern colonies who convert to Christianity, 1826 [CAHJP RU 1312]. According to this file, between 1810 and 1826 eleven such Jewish men converted to Orthodoxy.

18. On the political background of Synod conversion statistics, see I. Cherikover, "Obrashchenie v khristianstvo," *Evreiskaia entsiklopediia: Svod znanii o evreistve i ego kul'ture v proshlom i nastoiashchem* (St. Petersburg: Brokgauz-Efron, 1906–1913), XI: cols. 884–95; Michael Stanislawski, "Jewish Apostasy in Russia: A Tentative Typology," in *Jewish Apostasy in the Modern World*, ed. Todd M. Endelman (New York: Holmes and Meier, 1987), 190–91.

19. *PSZ* III, vol. XXV, no. 26,126 (April 17, 1905). On the 1906 clause permitting relapses from non-Orthodox Christian confessions and its impact on Jewish reversions, see Eugene M. Avrutin, "Returning to Judaism after the 1905 Law on Religious Freedom in Tsarist Russia," *Slavic Review* 65, no. 1 (Spring 2006): 102.

20. CAHJP RU 1592, Files of St. Petersburg Rabbi Katzenellenbogen. A copy of part of this list is in Mikhail Beizer, *The Jews of St. Petersburg: Excursions through a Noble Past*, trans. Michael Sherbourne (Philadelphia: Jewish Publication Society of America, 1989), 184. If the register numbers are indicative, there were possibly over 3,700 relapsed converts in the St. Petersburg community in this period. In 1914, nine of the ten relapsed converts came from Protestant churches (TsGIA-SPb f. 422, op. 1, d. 138, "O litsakh pereshedshikh iz pravoslaviia obratno v iudeistvo [1914]").

21. On this triangular relationship, see Peter Waldron, "Religious Toleration in Late Imperial Russia," in *Civil Rights in Imperial Russia*, ed. Linda Edmondson (Oxford: Oxford University Press, 1989), 104. On bringing the confessionalization paradigm to imperial Russian studies, see Darius Staliunas, *Making Russians: Meaning and Practice of Russification in Lithuania and Belarus after 1863* (Amsterdam: Rodopi, 2007), 131.

22. Paul W. Werth, *The Tsar's Foreign Faiths: Toleration and the Fate of Religious Freedom in Imperial Russia* (Oxford: Oxford University Press, 2014), 4.

23. John D. Basil, *Church and State in Late Imperial Russia: Critics of the Synodal System of Church Government (1861–1914)* (Minneapolis: University of Minnesota, 2005).

24. Werth, *The Tsar's Foreign Faiths*, 6–7.

25. Ibid., 4.

26. Paul W. Werth, *At the Margins of Orthodoxy: Mission, Governance, and Confes-*

sional Politics in Russia's Volga-Kama Region, 1827–1905 (Ithaca, NY: Cornell University Press, 2002), 15–16.

27. Robert Crews, "Empire and the Confessional State: Islam and Religious Politics in Nineteenth-Century Russia," *American Historical Review* 108, no. 1 (February 2003): 50–83"; Andrei Zorin, "Ideologiia 'pravoslaviia-samoderzhaviia-narodnosti': Opyt rekonstruktsii," *Novoe literaturnoe obozrenie* 26 (1997): 71–104.

28. Nathaniel Knight, "Ethnicity, Nationality and the Masses: *Narodnost'* and Modernity in Imperial Russia," in *Russian Modernity: Politics, Knowledge, Practices*, ed. David L. Hoffman and Yanni Kotsonis (New York: St. Martin's Press, 2000), 59.

29. On Jewish conversions to the tolerated confessions, see Ellie R. Schainker, "Jewish Conversion in an Imperial Context: Confessional Choice and Multiple Baptisms in Nineteenth-Century Russia," *Jewish Social Studies* n.s. 20, no. 1 (Fall 2013): 1–31.

30. This prohibition is at play in the case of Korabel'nikov, a rabbinic Jew by birth (whose parents converted to Orthodoxy and then relapsed), who asked the MVD to change his religious ascription to Karaite so that he could register his children as such. See RGIA f. 821, op. 8, d. 202, l. 65–65ob., Letter from the DDDII to the Odessa mayor (October 8, 1904) [CAHJP HM2 8000.17]. Also, when in 1884 a rabbinic Jew petitioned for conversion to Karaism, the DDDII denied the request (Werth, *The Tsar's Foreign Faiths*, 90).

31. Kappeler, *The Russian Empire*, 142–43.

32. Mikhail Dolbilov, *Russkii krai, chuzhaia vera: Etnokonfessional'naia politika imperii v Litve i Belorussii pri Aleksandre II* (Moscow: Novoe literaturnoe obozrenie, 2010). One method of discrediting foreign faiths was through the discourse of "fanaticism," which challenged how a tolerated faith inculcated loyalty to the empire and fostered enlightenment. Hence, "'fanatical' forms of religion were marginalized or repressed as being incompatible with the raison d'être of the enlightened imperial state." See Martin Schulze Wessel, "Confessional Politics and Religious Loyalties in the Russian-Polish Borderlands," *Kritika* 15, no. 1 (Winter 2014): 193–94. The connection between the discrediting of foreign faiths and growing freedom of conscience debates in the late imperial period are explored in Chapters 4 and 5.

33. Paul W. Werth, "Lived Orthodoxy and Confessional Diversity: The Last Decade on Religion in Modern Russia," *Kritika* 12, no. 4 (Fall 2011): 849–65." Martin Schulze Wessel notes the transfer of ideas between Vienna and St. Petersburg on the well-ordered state in the age of Enlightenment and the Romanov indebtedness to the Josephine system of toleration, which was predicated on the disciplinary function of religion. For a comparative discussion of imperial strategies for ethno-confessional minorities in the Josephine system of toleration, the Ottoman "millet" system, and Romanov confessional politics, see Wessel, "Confessional Politics."

34. See, for example, I. G. Orshanskii, *Russkoe zakonodatel'stvo o evreiakh: Ocherki i issledovaniia* (St. Petersburg, 1877), 26–59. Max Lilienthal, a German Jew who advised

the Russian state on Jewish educational reforms in the 1840s, later observed that Nicholas I did everything in his power to promote Jewish apostasy. See David Philipson, *Max Lilienthal, American Rabbi: Life and Writings* (New York: Bloch Publishing Company, 1915), 181, as cited in Werth, *The Tsar's Foreign Faiths*, 3.

35. Werth, *At the Margins*, 151.

36. Olga Minkina, "The Election of Jewish Deputies in Vilna in 1818: Government Projects and Jewish Claims," *East European Jewish Affairs* 43, no. 2 (2013): 206–16.

37. Eugene M. Avrutin, "The Politics of Jewish Legibility: Documentation Practices and Reform during the Reign of Nicholas I," *Jewish Social Studies* 11, no. 2 (2005): 136–69; Paul W. Werth, "In the State's Embrace? Civil Acts in an Imperial Order," *Kritika* 7, no. 3 (Summer 2006): 433–58.

38. V. O. Levanda, *Polnyi khronologicheskii sbornik zakonov i polozhenii, kasaiushchikhsia evreev, ot ulozheniia Tsaria Alekseia Mikhailovicha do nastoiashchago vremeni, ot 1649–1873* (St. Petersburg, 1874), 445, as translated and cited by ChaeRan Y. Freeze, *Jewish Marriage and Divorce in Imperial Russia* (Hanover, NH: University Press of New England, 2002), 349n120.

39. Freeze, *Jewish Marriage and Divorce*, 86.

40. This imperial quest for streamlining confessional management across the religious spectrum has been analyzed in particular for the Muslim case. See Crews, *For Prophet and Tsar*, 10–11, 23–24; see also Werth, "In the State's Embrace?" 441.

41. The DDDII was conceived and structured to administer the non-Orthodox faiths of the empire. On its institutional history, see Erik Amburger, *Geschichte der Behördenorganisation Russlands von Peter dem Grossen bis 1917* (Leiden: Brill, 1966), 176. On the limits of the DDDII's administration in Congress Poland, Finland, Central Asia, and among Buddhists, see Werth, *The Tsar's Foreign Faiths*, 56.

42. On Jewish censors and advisors, see Eli Lederhendler, *The Road to Modern Jewish Politics: Political Tradition and Political Reconstruction in the Jewish Community of Tsarist Russia* (New York: Oxford University Press, 1989), 92–95; D. A. Eliashevich, *Pravitelstvennaia politika: Evreiskaia pechat' v Rossii, 1797–1917* (St. Petersburg: Mosty kul'tury, 1999). On Jewish experts, see Vasily Shchedrin, "Jewish Bureaucracy in Late Imperial Russia: The Phenomenon of Expert Jews, 1850–1917" (PhD diss., Brandeis University, 2010).

43. Charles Steinwedel, "Making Social Groups, One Person at a Time: The Identification of Individuals by Estate, Religious Confession, and Ethnicity in Late Imperial Russia," in *Documenting Individual Identity: The Development of State Practices in the Modern World*, ed. Jane Caplan and John Torpey (Princeton, NJ: Princeton University Press, 2001), 70.

44. Avrutin, "Politics of Jewish Legibility," 157n110.

45. Religious dissenters like the Old Belief and certain distrusted confessional groups like the Baptists were denied clerical record-keeping recognition. The 1905 laws

on toleration belatedly granted Old Belief the right to maintain metrical books. See Steinwedel, "Making Social Groups," 70–73.

46. *PSZ* II, vol. XXXIV, no. 26,752 (March 25, 1817). On the ecumenicism of Alexander I's reign and its legacy of including foreign confessions in imperial statecraft, see Elena Vishlenkova, *Zabotias' o dushakh poddannykh: Religioznaia politika v Rossii pervoi chetverti XIX veka* (Saratov: Izdatel'stvo Saratovskogo Universiteta, 2002). On the Frankist backdrop to Alexander I's acknowledgment of existing Israelite Christians already in 1817, see Paweł Maciejko, *The Mixed Multitude: Jacob Frank and the Frankist Movement, 1755–1816* (Philadelphia: University of Pennsylvania Press, 2011), 260.

47. RGIA f. 797, op. 2, d. 8905, "O priniatom staroobradtsami v khristianskuiu veru Evree Girshe Leibe (1820–1821)." For two cases of Jewish conversion to Old Belief in the Kiev region, see DAKO f. 1, op. 295, d. 21829, MVD ruling on Jews converting to Old Belief, 1838.

48. *PSZ* I, vol. XXXIV, no. 26,752 (March 25, 1817); DAVO f. 361, op. 1, d. 32, Ukase of Alexander I on the Society of Israelite Christians [CAHJP HM2 9637.2]. The translation is mine, loosely based on the Friedlaender translation of Simon M. Dubnow, *History of the Jews in Russia and Poland: From the Earliest Times until the Present Day* (Philadelphia: Jewish Publication Society of America, 1916), I:396.

49. John Doyle Klier, *Russia Gathers Her Jews: The Origins of the "Jewish Question" in Russia, 1772–1825* (Dekalb: Northern Illinois University Press, 1986), chap. 2.

50. Ibid., chap. 6; Janet M. Hartley, *Alexander I* (London: Longman, 1994), 185–97.

51. Hartley, *Alexander I*, 186.

52. Ibid., 187–88; Alexander M. Martin, *Romantics, Reformers, Reactionaries: Russian Conservative Thought and Politics in the Reign of Alexander I* (Dekalb: Northern Illinois University Press, 1997), 160, 186, 190.

53. Max J. Kohler, *Jewish Rights at the Congresses of Vienna (1814–15) and Aix-la-Chapelle (1818)* (New York: American Jewish Committee, 1918), 88–93.

54. RGIA f. 797, op 2, d. 5471, "Po vysochaishemu poveleniiu o vydache iz kabineta odnoi evreiskoi sem'e, priniavshei khristianskuiu veru, 1000 rublei (1816)."

55. Dubnow, *History of the Jews*, I:399–400. Despite the society's failure, the tsar affirmed that he wanted the program and its budget to continue. See GARF f. 109, I eksp., 1827 g., d. 196, Third Section on Israelite Christians [CAHJP HM2 9420.3]; GARF f. 109, I eksp., 1829 g., d. 239, Ekaterinoslav Committee of the Guardianship of the Israelite Christians [CAHJP RU 592].

56. For example, the State Council ukase of September 26, 1829, mandated that a Jew converted to any Christian confession could join a town estate even if the local Christian community objected. Entry into rural state settlements was subject to provisions made for local peasants so that Jewish converts would not impinge on native landholdings. *PSZ* II, vol. IV, no. 3, 195 (September 26, 1829); DAVO f. 361, op. 1, d. 103,

1829 ukase [CAHJP HM2 9637.7]. On the social problems converts encountered when registering in Christian communities, see TsDIAK f. 182, op. 1, d. 44, Excerpt of "On the difficulties encountered by Jews upon converting to Christianity," and a project to alleviate these difficulties, 1840.

57. For a positive evaluation of the manifesto and its conversion program by an 1819 Orthodox convert from Judaism, see V. Levenvald, *Veroispovedanie izrail'skago khristianina* (St. Petersburg, 1832).

58. *SZ* (1832 ed.), vol. XIV, chap. 4, part 2, no. 90. Interestingly, the confessional choice regime ushered in by the 1817 ukase was limited in one application—for foreign Jews seeking conversion and naturalization in the Russian Empire. In this context, the MVD upheld the fundamental law of 1740, which stated that Jews needed to convert to Russian Orthodoxy to live in the empire; here, the 1817 ukase was narrowly construed as offering confessional choice only to Jewish converts on Israelite-Christian land. See GARF f. 109, IV eksp., op. 171, 1831 g., d. 22, "Delo o Egere Gol'dmane, iz'iavivshem zhelanie priniat' khristianskuiu veru" [CAHJP HM2 9561.20].

59. In 1832, the DDDII left the Ministry of Public Enlightenment and became a department in the Ministry of the Interior. See Amburger, *Geschichte der Behördenorganisation Russlands*, 176–77.

60. RGIA f. 822, op. 1, d. 3653, ll. 1–2, "Po predlozheniiu admirala Shishkova o dozvoleniia evreiam prinimat' r.k. veru (1827)" [CAHJP HM2 7919.19]. In this file, a Catholic bishop in the Kamenets-Podol'skii Diocese advocated stricter conversion measures to ensure sincere baptisms, including asking the neophyte to explain his or her choice to convert to Catholicism rather than the "ruling faith" (*gospodstvuiushchaia vera*), Russian Orthodoxy (l. 35).

61. *SZ* (1832 ed.), vol. XIV, nos. 68–96, in particular no. 90, subsections 1–4.

62. On confessional choice and the anxieties it spawned about instrumental and serial conversions, see Schainker, "Jewish Conversion."

63. GARF f. 109, I eksp., 1827 g., d. 196 [CAHJP HM2 9420.3]; GARF f. 109, I eksp., 1829 g., d. 239 [CAHJP RU 592].

64. Michael Stanislawski, *Tsar Nicholas I and the Jews: The Transformation of Jewish Society in Russia, 1825–1855* (Philadelphia: Jewish Publication Society of America, 1983); John Klier, "State Policies and the Conversion of Jews in Imperial Russia," in *Of Religion and Empire: Missions, Conversion, and Tolerance in Tsarist Russia*, ed. Robert P. Geraci and Michael Khodarkovsky (Ithaca, NY: Cornell University Press, 2001), 92–112; Yohanan Petrovsky-Shtern, *Jews in the Russian Army, 1827–1917: Drafted into Modernity* (Cambridge: Cambridge University Press, 2009).

65. TsDIAK f. 533, op. 5, d. 172, Jewish cantonist recruits (1827) [CAHJP HM2 9450.15].

66. Petrovsky-Shtern, following Shaul Ginzburg's lead, concurs that Jewish conscription was not conceived of as a means to Christianize Jews, but over time, the army

proved to be a productive conversion site. See Petrovsky-Shtern, *Jews in the Russian Army*, chap. 3.

67. TsDIAK f. 127, op. 641, d. 157, Synod ukase on measures to enlighten through baptism Jewish cantonists, 1843 [CAHJP HM2 9683.1].

68. *Nastavlenie sviashchennikam voennykh zavedenii, kasatel'no obrashcheniia vospitannikov iudeiskogo ispovedaniia v khristianskuiu veru* (St. Petersburg, 1843).

69. John Klier, "State Policies," 103. For such reports, see TsDIAK f. 127, op. 649, d. 650, Numbers of Jewish cantonists who converted to Christianity, 1847–1848 [CAHJP 9484.16]; TsDIAK f. 127, op. 656, d. 13, Converts in the Kiev cantonist battalion, 1854 [CAHJP 9484.18]; TsGIA-SPb f. 19, op. 44, d. 40, "Po raportu Sviashchennika Konstantina Smirnova o kantonistakh iz evreev po Revel'skomu polubatalionu (1852–1853)"; TsGIA-SPb f. 19, op. 45, d. 5, "Po raportu Revel'skago polubataliona voennykh kantonistov, zakonouchitelia sviashchennika Konstantina Smirnova o razreshenii emu prosvetit' sv. kreshcheniem 31 kantonista evreev (1853–1855)"; TsDIAK f. 127, op. 649, d. 520, Conversions of Jewish cantonists, 1847 [CAHJP HM2 9484.15]; DAmK f. 316, op. 1, d. 210, List of Jewish cantonists in the Kiev Battalion who have expressed a desire to convert to Orthodoxy (1854); RGVIA f. 405, op. 5, d. 11588, Report from Department of Military Settlements, 1849 [CAHJP RU 1238].

70. On the eve of the 1843 directive, the Synod reported 741 Jewish conversions for 1842. In 1843, the number jumped to 1,846. The yearly average of Jewish converts remained in the 1,000–2,000 range through 1857. By 1858 the number had dropped to 659. The largest number of Jewish conversions for a single year—4,439—was recorded in 1854. See Ivan Preobrazhenskii, *Otechestvennaia tserkov' po statisticheskim dannym* (St. Petersburg, 1901), 46.

71. Stanislawski, *Tsar Nicholas I*; Olga Litvak, *Conscription and the Search for Modern Russian Jewry* (Bloomington: Indiana University Press, 2006); Petrovsky-Shtern, *Jews in the Russian Army*.

72. On missions and conversion among these groups, see Werth, *At the Margins*; Robert P. Geraci, *Window on the East: National and Imperial Identities in Late Tsarist Russia* (Ithaca, NY: Cornell University Press, 2001).

73. *PSZ* II, vol. XII, no. 10,135. Yet, an Odessa paper reported in 1881 that converts from Judaism and Islam in Transcaucasia, or the South Caucasus, were to be given a monetary award from special funds allocated in the state treasury. See "Posobiia evreiam prinimaiushchim kreshchenie," *Odesskii vestnik* 151 (1881).

74. *SZ* (1857 ed.), vol. IX, p. 1387.

75. Petrovsky-Shtern, *Jews in the Russian Army*, 74.

76. According to Petrovsky-Shtern, Nicholas I purposely directed a disproportionate number of Jewish recruits to naval service since it was the most demanding service, and hence the most hospitable environment for Jewish "re-education" through the military (*Jews in the Russian Army*, 76).

77. RGAVMF f. 205, op. 1, d. 656, Report of Archpriest Zaushkevich to Admiral Greig [CAHJP HM2 8281.5]; RGAVMF f. 283, op. 1, d. 1587, Whether Jews in the Baltic Fleet should receive rewards upon their conversion, 1830 [CAHJP HM2 8281.11]. According to CAHJP archivist Benyamin Lukin, Admiral Greig was married to a convert of Hasidic background.

78. For the cultural significance of corporal punishment, see Abby Schrader, *Languages of the Lash: Corporal Punishment and Identity in Imperial Russia* (Dekalb: Northern Illinois University Press, 2002).

79. DAVO f. 361, op. 1, d. 66, ll. 421–22, Ukase of commuting sentences of converts to Orthodoxy, 1826 [CAHJP HM2 9637.4]. For another legal decision sent to the State Senate regarding conversion benefits to Jewish criminals, see DAVO f. 361, op. 1, d. 90, Senate ukase, 1828 [CAHJP HM2 9637.6].

80. This was the legal issue at the center of the Kroianskii case involving a young Jewish convert to Catholicism who was conscripted by the Vilna kahal and sent to the Riga cantonist battalion. After verifying the legitimacy of the conversion, the Vilna authorities ordered the convert to be released from the military and instructed the kahal to offer up a Jewish recruit in his place. See LVIA f. 377, op. 1, d. 663, Complaint of the widow Wilhelmina Kroianskaia that the Vilna kahal recruited her son Yakov Kroianskii instead of the Jewish boy Yankel Krasovskii (1829) [CAHJP HM2 9727.1].

81. See RGIA f. 822, op. 1, d. 4561, Report of Bishop Lipskii about permission to convert the Jew Yosel Abramovich Brukman, 1830 [CAHJP HM2 7919.11], in which a Jewish convert to Catholicism claims immunity from Jewish recruitment; YIVO RG 46, Box I:11, Conversion of Jewish prisoner Zakharia Stein to Orthodoxy, 1871; TsDIAK f. 442, op. 78, d. 266, Petition of Zhitomir Jewish townswoman Ester Rosenbergova about the wrongful recruitment of her husband and brother who had expressed a desire to convert, 1845–1851. In this last case, the governor-general of Kiev found Ester's husband and brother guilty of trying to convert to escape recruitment. He added that if they really wanted to convert, they could do so while serving in the army (ll. 11–12).

82. On conversion incentives for Muslims and animists in the Volga-Kama region, see Werth, *At the Margins*, 79–86.

83. *SZ* (1832 ed.), vol. XIV, part 1, chap. 3, section 2, I:45.

84. This rule was applied in the case of the Kaminskii couple; see RGIA f. 821, op. 8, d. 348, Request of the Jew Kaminskii, 1853 [CAHJP HM2 7999.7].

85. GARF f. 109, IV eksp., III otd., 1827 g., d. 176b, ll. 8–90b., "Perepiska deistvitel'nogo statskogo sovetnika M.Ia. Fon Foka po delam evreiskogo komiteta" [CAHJP HMF 830].

86. Ibid., II eksp., III otd., d. 603, ll. 1–30b., Request of Vilna Jew Berman to convert his son Movshe/Ivan, 1838 [CAHJP HM2 9523.3].

87. Werth, *At the Margins*, chaps. 3, 5.

88. NIAB f. 1781, op. 2, d. 271, l. 26–260b.

89. Assaf, *Untold Tales*, 76–96. Assaf notes that Moshe's existence was not ignored

on the whole, rather the details of his life were always shrouded in mystery. Chabad was forced to openly engage Moshe's legacy only when modern historiography took an interest in Hasidic history. Notably, the Chabad Rebbe Yosef Yitzchak Schneerson, in response to the historian Shaul Ginzburg's writings on the subject in 1931, attempted to deny Moshe's conversion. For the emotional toll Moshe's conversion brought on the Schneerson family and its imprint on Hasidic literature, see Don Seeman, "Apostasy, Grief, and Literary Practice in Habad Hasidism," *Prooftexts* 29, no. 3 (Fall 2009): 398–432.

90. *PSZ* II, vol. XXXVI, no. 37,709 (January 22, 1862).

91. Avrutin, "The Politics of Jewish Legibility," 156–59; Werth, "In the State's Embrace?"

92. RGIA f. 822, op. 1, d. 2820, Request of Golitsyn to permit the Jewish girl Feygele to remain in the convent until she comes of age, 1823 [CAHJP HM2 7919.20].

93. ChaeRan Freeze, "When Chava Left Home: Gender, Conversion, and the Jewish Family in Tsarist Russia," *Polin* 18 (2005): 165–71.

94. LVIA f. 378, B/S, d. 184, Police report to Lithuanian military governor, 1815 [CAHJP HM2 9733.20].

95. TsDIAK f. 442, op. 152, d. 745, Petition of the Jewess Rivka Varnovitskaia, 1843.

96. For more cases of Jewish parents promoting the conversion of their children, see YIVO RG 46, Box II:32, Conversion of Jewesses Ester Yankeliova Levinova and her sister Yenta Massovna, 1852; LVIA f. 377, op. 1, d. 663, Complaint of the widow Wilhelmina Kroianskaia, 1829 [CAHJP HM2 9727.1]. Famous cases include the childhood conversions of Russian pianists and composers Anton and Nikolai Rubinstein and the leading Bund ideologue Vladimir Medem. The former were converted in their youth to Christianity at the behest of their grandfather, who wanted to move the family to Moscow for economic opportunity and to escape the oppressive poll tax on the Jewish community. On the Rubinstein family, see Philip S. Taylor, *Anton Rubenstein: A Life in Music* (Bloomington: Indiana University Press, 2007). On Medem, born Russian Orthodox to parents who converted from Judaism, see Vladimir Medem, *The Life and Soul of a Legendary Jewish Socialist*, trans. Samuel A. Portnoy, original pub. 1923 (New York: Ktav, 1979).

97. A merchant's level (e.g., first or second guild) was determined by the value of his business.

98. LVIA f. 378 B/S, 1826, d. 480, ll. 3–50b., Correspondence of Minister of Public Enlightenment permitting Geiman children to convert to Lutheranism, 1826 [CAHJP HM2 9772.12].

99. Ibid., d. 673, l. 210b., Solomon Geiman's receipt of gold medal, 1826 [CAHJP HM2 9772.14].

100. Ibid., 1834, d. 842, Induction of first-guild merchant Solomon Geiman into rank of Commercial Councilor, 1834 [CAHJP HM2 9777.9].

101. Evzel Gintsburg, of the prestigious St. Petersburg Jewish family, was also awarded the title of honorary citizen for his financial successes.

102. LVIA f. 378 B/S, 1838, d. 873, l. 1–10b., Petition of father Eliash Movshovich Berman to place his son in the Medical-Surgical Academy, 1838 [CAHJP HM2 9780.3]; GARF f. 109, II eksp., III otd., 1838 g., d. 603, Request of Vilna Jew Berman to baptize his son Movshe, 1838 [CAHJP HM2 9523.3].

103. The Third Section constituted a secret police force. GARF f. 109, II eksp., III otd., 1838 g., d. 603, ll. 1–30b.

104. Ibid.

105. Ibid., IV eksp., 1839 g., op. 221 (VD), d. 73, Imperial report on petition of Vilna Jew Berman to baptize his youngest son and place him in the Shurmanskii Academy on state payroll, 1839 [CAHJP RU 709].

106. Ibid., II eksp., 1838 g., d. 603, l. 30b. [CAHJP HM2 9523.3]. Also see ibid., IV eksp., 1839 g., op. 221 (VD), d. 73, ll. 7–9 [CAHJP RU 709].

107. LVIA f. 378 B/S, 1838, d. 873, ll. 3–4 [CAHJP 9780.3].

108. GARF f. 109, II eksp., 1838 g., d. 603, ll. 27–290b. [CAHJP HM2 9523.3].

109. Ibid., ll. 21–210b., 25–26. Malka Berman submitted a petition in 1841 and a second in 1842.

110. Ibid., ll. 25–26. The claim insinuated here that Jews prefer to kill converted kin is explored in Chapter 5.

Chapter 2

1. Aleksandr Alekseev, *Bogosluzhenie, prazdniki, i religioznye obriady nyneshnikh evreev* (Novgorod, [1861] 1865), 47. Chone Shmeruk has shown how this classic Jewish Sabbath hymn evolved into a generic song-dance routine that Jews performed for the amusement of non-Jewish audiences in early modern Poland. Associated in Jewish collective memory with the trauma of coercion, or for some, toadying to power, *mayufes* later became a stand-in for Jewish nationalists of the scourge of diasporic assimilation and political powerlessness. Alekseev's narrative about *mayufes* seems to engage both the song as a popular Sabbath hymn and the ways non-Jews (here, Tsar Nicholas I) delighted in commanding such humiliating performances by Jews. See Chone Shmeruk, "*Mayufes*: A Window on Polish-Jewish Relations," *Polin* 10 (1997): 273–86.

2. Todd M. Endelman, *Leaving the Jewish Fold: Conversion and Radical Assimilation in Modern Jewish History* (Princeton, NJ: Princeton University Press, 2015), 226, 247–48. Endelman notes that the sizeable paper trail left by missionary institutions and convert missionaries is disproportionate to their actual numbers or representativeness as everyday converts from Judaism. Endelman focuses on evangelical missionary access to poor, desperate Jews.

3. Judith Cohen Zacek, "The Russian Bible Society, 1812–1826" (PhD diss., Columbia University, 1964), 313. As of 1826, the society had published scriptural translations in over forty languages—but not in Yiddish.

4. YIVO RG 46, Box III:68, ll. 12–130b., Yosif Yankelev Dreizin, wife and three children desire conversion, 1891.

5. Eugene Smirnoff, *A Short Account of the Historical Development and Present Position of Russian Orthodox Missions* (London: Rivingtons, 1903), 73.

6. Robert C. Stacey, "The Conversion of the Jews to Christianity in Thirteenth-Century England," *Speculum* 67 (1992): 263–83; Christopher Clark, *The Politics of Conversion: Missionary Protestantism and the Jews in Prussia, 1728–1941* (Oxford: Clarendon Press, 1995).

7. Paul W. Werth, *The Tsar's Foreign Faiths: Toleration and the Fate of Religious Freedom in Imperial Russia* (Oxford: Oxford University Press, 2014), 33.

8. Ibid., 39–40.

9. Ibid., 74–85, esp. 83.

10. Paul W. Werth, *At the Margins of Orthodoxy: Mission, Governance, and Confessional Politics in Russia's Volga-Kama Region, 1827–1905* (Ithaca, NY: Cornell University Press, 2002), 124–25.

11. Yuri Slezkine, "Savage Christians or Unorthodox Russians? The Missionary Dilemma in Siberia," in *Between Heaven and Hell: The Myth of Siberia in Russian Culture*, ed. Galya Diment and Yuri Slezkine (New York: St. Martin's Press, 1993), 20–22; Robert P. Geraci, *Window on the East: National and Imperial Identities in Late Tsarist Russia* (Ithaca, NY: Cornell University Press, 2001), 47–85.

12. "Priiut kreshchenykh evreiskikh detei," *Golos* 136 (Monday, June 27, 1877).

13. Adele Lindenmeyr, *Poverty Is Not a Vice: Charity, Society, and the State in Imperial Russia* (Princeton, NJ: Princeton University Press, 1996), 106, 119, 129–35.

14. DAmK f. 14, op. 1, d. 1, ll. 1–30b., Act of the opening the Kiev Vladimir Brotherhood, 1864.

15. DAmK f. 286, op. 1, d. 15, ll. 1–2, St. Vladimir Brotherhood receiving money from Kiev Missionary Society to organize a temporary shelter for Jews desiring Orthodoxy, 1871.

16. Smirnoff, *A Short Account*, 25–26.

17. DAmK f. 14, op. 1, d. 35, ll. 20b.–3, Report of Brotherhood, July 15, 1872–July 15, 1873. In those twelve months, the Brotherhood assisted seventeen Jews and thirteen Catholics in converting to Orthodoxy.

18. Yearly Brotherhood conversion statistics come from *Otchet Kievskogo sv. vladimirskogo bratstva* (Kiev, 1889) as cited by Mikhail Agursky, "Conversions of Jews to Christianity in Russia," *Soviet Jewish Affairs* 20, no. 2–3 (1990): 77. Agursky juxtaposes these numbers to the general statistics on Jewish conversions to Orthodoxy according to Ivan Preobrazhenskii, *Otechestvennaia tserkov' po statisticheskim dannym* (St. Petersburg, [1897] 1901).

19. Likewise, women initiated more than half of the petitions sent by Jews to the Kiev provincial administration in 1904 asking for temporary residence in Kiev to pre-

pare for baptism with the Brotherhood. See DAKO f. 1, op. 140, d. 858, Petition of Jews to allow them temporary residence in Kiev in order to convert to Orthodoxy, 1904 [CAHJP HM2 9424.3].

20. Cited by Agursky, "Conversions of Jews," 80. There is some evidence that not all Jewish converts fit this stereotypical lower-class profile. In 1904, for example, two Jewish students (one at a gymnasium) asked permission to temporarily reside in Kiev while preparing for conversion at the Brotherhood (DAKO f. 1, op. 140, d. 858, ll. 6, 48).

21. On the Brotherhood's finances and allotment of resources, see DAmK f. 14, op. 1, d. 35, ll. 30b.–40b.

22. For a history of Jews in Kiev, see Natan M. Meir, *Kiev, Jewish Metropolis: A History, 1859–1914* (Bloomington: Indiana University Press, 2010).

23. DAKO f. 1, op. 140, d. 858, l. 12–120b. (1904) [CAHJP HM2 9424.3].

24. Eugene M. Avrutin, "A Legible People: Identification Politics and Jewish Accommodation in Tsarist Russia" (PhD diss., University of Michigan, 2004), 209. Avrutin notes that similar shelters for Jewish converts were started in Warsaw and Odessa in the 1870s and 1880s.

25. "Chastnyi priiut v S. Peterburge dlia prisoediniaemykh v pravoslavnoi tserkvi evreev," *Strannik* 54 (1870): 68–76. For a similar history of the shelter, see A. Alekseev, *O religioznom dvizhenii evreev i rasprostranenii khristianstva mezhdu nimi* (Novgorod, 1895), 28–42.

26. "Chastnyi priiut v S. Peterburge dlia prisoediniaemykh v pravoslavnoi tserkvi evreev," *Strannik* 189 (1870): 193, 196–98.

27. ChaeRan Y. Freeze, "The Mariinsko Sergievskii Shelter for Converted Jewish Children in St. Petersburg," in *Jews in the East European Borderlands: Essays in Honor of John D. Klier*, ed. Eugene M. Avrutin and Harriet Murav (Boston: Academic Studies Press, 2012), 27–49.

28. "Chastnyi priiut," *Strannik* 189: 198; Alekseev, *O religioznom dvizhenii evreev*, 32.

29. Freeze, "Mariinsko Sergievskii Shelter," 32–33.

30. DAmK f. 253, op. 1, d. 2, l. 630b., Clarification of conversion of minor-aged Jews and adults, 1875–1878. In another report, the orphanage committee stated that it spent between 2,000 and 3,500 rubles annually on assisting Jewish converts. See TsGIA-SPb f. 542, op. 3, d. 6, "Kniga dlia zapisi raskhoda summ ot sbora ezhegodnykh i edinovremennykh pozhertvovanie v pol'zu ishchushchikh prisoedineniia k pravoslavniiu i vnov prisoedinennykh k nemu evreev (1869–1872)."

31. Alekseev, *O religioznom dvizhenii evreev*, 34.

32. "Po povodu perekhoda evreev v pravoslavie," *Novorossiiskii telegraf* 4200 (September 26, 1888).

33. "Chastnyi priiut," *Strannik* 189: 190.

34. There is evidence of several students at the state rabbinical seminaries converting or attempting to convert. N. P. Gur'ev, a teacher at the Vilna Rabbinical Seminary, con-

verted to Orthodoxy in 1868. *Vilenskie gubernskie vedomosti* (1868 no. 70) reported that the Vilna Orthodox Cathedral was besieged by rabbinical students who attended Gur'ev's baptism. Many students expressed interest in converting, and one even wrote to the St. Petersburg orphanage asking for admission. See "Chastnyi priiut," *Strannik* 54: 68n1. In addition, a graduate of the Vilna Rabbinical Seminary, Moisei Volkovyskii, converted in 1870 (YIVO RG 46, Box III:64, Conversion of Jewish merchant's son Moisei Volkovyskii, 1870), and there is evidence of at least four other students starting the conversion process between 1871 and 1872 but not completing it. See YIVO RG 46, Box III:51, Conversion of the Jew Kadesh Moiseevich Lev, 1871; and LVIA f. 577, op. 1, d. 46, Students of the Vilna Rabbinical Academy who converted to Orthodoxy, 1872 [CAHJP HM2 9924.6].

35. "Rukopolozhenie vo sviashchenniki iz evreev," *Strannik* 1 (1876): 184–85.

36. O. Brin, "Vospominaniia novokreshchennago evreia," *Strannik* 7 (1877): 76–77. Brin was born to a traditional Jewish family, rose to the level of *ilui* ("best," or "prod-igy") in yeshiva, married at a young age, and became a Chabad Hasid. In the 1850s, he moved to the Russian interior, where he often engaged Orthodox priests in theological debates. Following a bout with typhus, Brin converted and moved to Kishinev to mis-sionize local Jews. To finance this, Brin worked at a local cemetery.

37. DAmK f. 253, op. 1, d. 2, l. 61.

38. Ibid., 63ob.

39. Lindenmeyr, *Poverty Is Not a Vice*, 145.

40. On the rise of Jewish philanthropy in the nineteenth century as a response to missionary work, see Derek J. Penslar, *Shylock's Children: Economics and Jewish Identity in Modern Europe* (Berkeley: University of California Press, 2001), 103–4. On this phe-nomenon in early twentieth-century America, where missionaries preyed on poor East European immigrants, see Jonathan D. Sarna, "The Impact of Nineteenth-Century Christian Missions on American Jews," in *Jewish Apostasy in the Modern World*, ed. Todd M. Endelman (New York: Holmes and Meier, 1987), 232–54.

41. ChaeRan Y. Freeze, "Lilith's Midwives: Jewish Newborn Child Murder in Nineteenth-Century Vilna," *Jewish Social Studies* 16, no. 2 (Winter 2010): 1–27.

42. In Kiev in the early twentieth century there were municipal and private phil-anthropic projects that did serve Jews or created special Jewish divisions, due to Jewish philanthropic giving or organizing. These included a Jewish division of the Russian So-ciety for Protection of Women and a Day Shelter for Working Class Children. Jewish women, however, were not always willing to use the services of non-Jewish organiza-tions. See Meir, *Kiev*, 197–201, 239.

43. Brian Horowitz, *Jewish Philanthropy and Enlightenment in Late-Tsarist Rus-sia* (Seattle: University of Washington Press, 2009), 138–39. On Jewish philanthropy in imperial Russia, see also Natan Meir, "From Communal Charity to National Welfare: Jewish Orphanages in Eastern Europe before and after World War I," *East European Jewish Affairs* 39, no. 1 (April 2009): 19–34.

44. Meir, *Kiev*, 213.

45. "Missionerskaia deiatel'nost' sredi evreev," *Golos* 75 (Wednesday, March 16, 1877); Iv. Pavlovskii, "O neobkhodimosti priiutov dlia evreev, ishchushchikh kreshcheniia," *Sovremennost'* 137 (December 9, 1876).

46. On Catholic missionary work among Jews in the empire through the Mariae Vitae Congregation and its sixteen convents in the northwest region, see Elena Keidosiute, "Missionary Activity of Mariae Vitae Congregation," *Pardes: Zeitschrift der Vereinigung für Jüdische Studien* (2010): 57–72.

47. W. T. Gidney, *The Jews and Their Evangelization* (London, 1899), 104.

48. For a full list of missions, missionaries, institutions, and their convert yields, see ibid., appendix A.

49. GARF f. 109, III eksp., 1871 g., d. 40, Permission for Professor Pavl Kassel' to live in Russia for religious study related to missionizing among Jews, 1871 [CAHJP HM3 268.7].

50. Gidney, *The Jews*, 96, 101.

51. Ibid., 91.

52. W. T. Gidney, *At Home and Abroad: A Description of the English and Continental Missions of the London Society for Promoting Christianity amongst the Jews* (London: Operative Jewish Converts' Institution, 1900), x.

53. Ibid., 101–3.

54. Ibid., 104; Raphael Mahler, "Hamediniyut klapei hamisyonerim bePolin hakongresa'it bi-tekufat haberit hakedoshah," in *Sefer Shiloh: Kovets ma'amarim lezikhro*, ed. Michael Hendel (Tel Aviv, 1960), 169–81, esp. 175.

55. Gidney, *At Home and Abroad*, 104–7. Raphael Mahler surmised that Nicholas I allowed foreign evangelicals to operate in Congress Poland because they could undermine the rebellious Catholic element there. See Mahler, "Hamediniyut klapei hamisyonerim," 170.

56. Gidney, *At Home and Abroad*, 108, 110. According to Mahler's data, 361 Jews converted from 1821 to 1854 under the auspices of the London mission. See Mahler, "Hamediniyut klapei hamisyonerim," 181n39.

57. Gidney, *At Home and Abroad*, 111. For two cases of Berdichev Jews baptized by the London Society in Warsaw in 1892, see DAKO f. 1, op. 128, d. 638, Conversion to Lutheranism of Jews Roiter and Zalibauskaia, 1892.

58. Gidney, *At Home and Abroad*, 116; "Otchet Londonskago obshchestva dlia rasprostr. khristianstva mezhdu evreiami," *Golos* 181 (August 11, 1877). According to the London Society's 1877 report, it operated missions in two Russian cities—Warsaw and Kishinev—and hoped to spread to more cities. Gidney cynically regarded Rabinovich's New Testament Israelites sect as an "endeavour to graft the Gospel upon Judaism" (Gidney, *At Home and Abroad*, 116). Though he worked with the London Society, Rabinovich was chiefly affiliated with the Mildmay Mission. See Kai Kjaer-Hansen, *The*

Herzl of Jewish Christianity: Joseph Rabinowitz and the Messianic Movement (Edinburgh: Handel Press, 1995), 75–80, 162–73. For more on Rabinovich, see Chapter 6.

59. "Angliiskii missioner sredi evreev," *Volynskie eparkhial'nye vedomosti* 33 (1886).

60. Raymond Lillevik, *Apostates, Hybrids, or True Jews? Jewish Christians and Jewish Identity in Eastern Europe, 1860–1914* (Eugene, OR: Pickwick, 2014), 43–58, 63–89. Reports of Gurland's conversion were picked up in the British evangelical journal *The Scattered Nation* 3 (1868), "How Rabbi Gurland Became a Christian," 213–15. On Gurland, also see Arnol'd Semenovich Khodorovskii (A. S. Ardov), *Evrei-Evangelisty* (Moscow, 1914), 47–49.

61. Korresp. iz Vilny, "O rasprostranenii khristianstva mezhdu evreiami," *Sankt-Peterburgskie vedomosti* 197 (1888).

62. "Rukopolozhenie vo sviashchenniki iz evreev," 185.

63. According to Hans Brandenburg, son of German evangelicals in Russia, Bible distribution and cheap printing were the key to the evangelical movement in imperial Russia. Hans Brandenburg, *The Meek and the Mighty: The Emergence of the Evangelical Movement in Russia* (London: Mowbrays, 1976), 55.

64. *Nastavlenie sviashchennikam voennykh zavedenii* (St. Petersburg, 1843), 3–7. Ironically, many Orthodox clerics and evangelical missionaries complained that most Jews did not know the basic tenets of their faith or the Hebrew Bible. See TsDIAK f. 182, op. 1, d. 26, ll. 10–18, Synod ukase regarding basis for allowing converted Jew Temkin to missionize in Kiev, Podolia, and Volynia dioceses in order to convert the local Jews, 1838 [CAHJP HM2 9884.29]; Gidney, *At Home and Abroad*, 66–68.

65. *SZ* (1832 ed.), vol. XIV, part 1, chap. 3, section II:1, no. 43.

66. There were even fears of a Russian translation of the Hebrew Bible; the Society for the Spread of Enlightenment among the Jews of Russia and a Jewish school in St. Petersburg were both denied translation permission in the reform period. See RGIA f. 821, op. 8, d. 270 (1866); RGIA f. 797, op. 3, d. 369 (1866). For a study of early modern German Protestant scholarly interest in missionizing Jews in Yiddish—a language easily comprehensible and familiar—in the German lands and beyond, see Aya Elyada, "Yiddish—Language of Conversion? Linguistic Adaptation and Its Limits in Early Modern *Judenmission*," *Leo Baeck Institute Yearbook* 53, no. 1 (2008): 3–27.

67. On the politics of Bible translation in the Russian Orthodox Church, see Stephen K. Batalden, "The Politics of Modern Russian Biblical Translation," in *Bible Translation and the Spread of the Church: The Last 200 Years*, ed. Philip C. Stine (Leiden: Brill, 1990), 68–80; Stephen K. Batalden, "The BFBS Petersburg Agency and Russian Biblical Translation, 1856–1875," in *Sowing the Word: The Cultural Impact of the British and Foreign Bible Society, 1804–2004*, ed. Stephen Batalden, Kathleen Cann, and John Dean (Sheffield: Sheffield Phoenix Press, 2004), 169–96.

68. As a sidebar to these translation politics, a Kurland Jew in 1797 presented a birthday gift to Paul I (r. 1796–1801) of the Pentateuch translated into Russian and Ger-

man with introductory poems in Hebrew with a German translation, for placement in the imperial library. See RGADA f. 1239, op. 3, ed. khr. 58387, Request of Simon Isaac, 1797 [CAHJP HM2 9558.5].

69. Shmuel Leib Tsitron, *Avek fun folk: tipn un silueten funm noenten over*, vol. II (Warsaw: Ahiasaf, 1920), chap. 8.

70. It apparently caught enough attention that it warranted a Jewish rejoinder. In 1836 a maskil from Pinsk, Reuven Holdhor, wrote *Divrei shalom ve'emet/Slova mira i pravdy*, in parallel Hebrew and Russian, to counter Temkin's anti-Jewish tract. It emphasized biblical and Talmudic laws prescribing Jewish patriotism, civility, and the obligation to obey the law of the land. See Eli Lederhendler, *The Road to Modern Jewish Politics: Political Tradition and Political Reconstruction in the Jewish Community of Tsarist Russia* (New York: Oxford University Press, 1989), 104–5.

71. Tsitron anecdotally notes that Temkin's conversion was a cause célèbre in ecclesiastic and administrative circles because he was thought to be a rabbi (Tsitron, *Avek fun folk*, chap. 8).

72. Louis Greenberg, *The Jews in Russia: The Struggle for Emancipation* (New Haven, CT: Yale University Press, 1944), 55. Orshanskii also cites the "Temkin affair" as an example of an imperial conversionist policy toward Jews. See I. G. Orshanskii, *Russkoe zakonodatel'stvo o evreiakh: Ocherki i issledovaniia* (St. Petersburg, 1877), 26–59.

73. "Belorussia" was the term used by the Synod. See, for example, RGIA f. 796, op. 120, d. 628, l. 42–420b., Converted Jews Temkin and Levison, 1839 [CAHJP RU 586].

74. According to another source, Temkin also received 2,000 rubles annually for missionary-related expenses. See TsGIA-SPb f. 19, op. 42, d. 12, "Po ukazu sv. prav. sinoda ob ispytanii Aleksandra Antovil'skogo v iskrennosti poznaniiakh i sposobnosti k obrashcheniiu evreev v x-vo (1850–1851)."

75. RGIA f. 796, op. 120, d. 628, ll. 42–430b. [CAHJP RU 586].

76. See, for example, ibid., ll. 44, 45; TsDIAK f. 182, op. 1, d. 26, l. 1 (1838) [CAHJP HM2 9884.29].

77. Presumably, Temkin and his accomplice profited from offering the converts as Jewish recruits, in that the kahal paid *khappers*, or catchers, (in this case Temkin and his friend) for procuring recruits. In this instance, since the two recruits, as apostates, were not wanted by the Jewish community, the kahal would have been spared from having to recruit two Jewish boys. On *khappers* and the 1827 Jewish Conscription Law that put the onus of filling conscription quotas on the kahal, see Michael Stanislawski, *Tsar Nicholas I and the Jews: The Transformation of Jewish Society in Russia, 1825–1855* (Philadelphia: Jewish Publication Society of America, 1983), 25–31.

78. TsDIAK f. 182, op. 1, d. 26, ll. 50–510b. (1838) [CAHJP HM2 9884.29]. Upon conversion, Temkin left his Jewish wife, who refused to convert, and married a Christian widow.

79. Ibid., ll. 160b.–170b.

80. TsGIA-SPb f. 19, op. 42, d. 12 (1850–1851).

81. For an in-depth biography of Levison, see M. S. Agurskij, "Die Judenchristen in der Russisch-Orthodoxen Kirche," *Ostkirchliche Studien* 23, no. 2/3 (September 1974): 142.

82. Vasilii Levison, "Ierusalimskiia pis'ma," *Dukhovnaia beseda* 31 (July 30, 1866): 65–78, 100–103, 112–28, 153–66, 225–32, 269–78, esp. 115–17, 121.

83. RGIA f. 796, op. 120, d. 628, ll. 3–50b. [CAHJP RU 586].

84. Ibid.

85. Ibid., ll. 16–180b., 320b.–330b.

86. Ibid., ll. 16–180b. Michael Meyer has documented the conversion trajectory of many of Mendelssohn's disciples and family members, but Levison's claim that thousands converted as a result of Mendelssohn's writings is more polemics than fact. Michael A. Meyer, *The Origins of the Modern Jew: Jewish Identity and European Culture in Germany, 1749–1824* (Detroit: Wayne State University Press, 1967).

87. Saul M. Ginsburg, *Historische Werk* (New York: S.M. Ginsburg Testimonial Committee, 1937), II:239–43. Mendelssohn's *Bi'ur* was used in maskilic schools in the Russian Empire, for example in the school opened in Odessa in 1826 by Bezalel Stern. See Stanislawski, *Tsar Nicholas I*, 58.

88. Greenberg, *The Jews in Russia*, 33–40. Under Nicholas I, the state led by Minister of Public Enlightenment Uvarov devised a series of Jewish educational reform policies. To bolster the 1844 opening of Jewish state schools and the mandating of Russian language training for all Jewish teachers and students, the state hired the enlightened German Jew Max Lilienthal to rally Russian Jewry behind the government's reforms. Jews at the time suspected the schools were intended to convert Jewish children.

89. RGIA f. 797, op. 120, d. 628, ll. 16–180b., esp. l. 17.

90. GARF f. 109, IV eksp., 1831 g., d. 88, Jew Goldman who has declared a desire to convert to Christianity, 1831 [CAHJP HM2 9561.20].

91. RGIA f. 796, op. 120, d. 628, ll. 41–44 [CAHJP RU 586]. The MVD granted Levison Russian subjecthood in December 1839 (ll. 47–48).

92. Ibid., ll. 42–46.

93. Agurskij, "Die Judenchristen," 149, 153. Agursky argued that racism was at the heart of imperial disinterest in Jewish conversion throughout the nineteenth century. Most scholars argue that racialization did not develop and underlie conversion discourses until the late imperial period. See Eugene M. Avrutin, "Racial Categories and the Politics of (Jewish) Difference in Late Imperial Russia," *Kritika* 8, no. 1 (Winter 2007): 13–40.

94. RGIA f. 796, op. 120, d. 628, ll. 32–37, 49–54, qt. from l. 530b.

95. Agurskij, "Die Judenchristen," 147.

96. TsGIA-SPb f. 19, op. 44, d. 28, l. 1, "Po prosheniiu sester evreek Zary Dore i Elle Marianny Markuze, o prosveshchenii ikh sv. kreshcheniem (1852)."

97. S. A. Vengerov, *Kritiko-biograficheskii slovar' ruskikh pisatelei i uchenykh*

(St. Petersburg, 1889), 375–76 ("Alekseev, Aleksandr"), 939 ("Alekseev-Nakhlas"); Agurskij, "Die Judenchristen," 168–75. In all likelihood, Alekseev's own exposure to Hasidism was through the Chernobyl or Twersky dynasty, which predominated at this time in Ukraine and was the subject of much anti-Hasidic criticism, including for its tsadikcentrism. The author thanks Gadi Sagiv for discussing the possible spaces of Alekseev's Hasidic youth.

98. According to Alekseev's autobiography, published in *Novgorodskie gubernskie vedomosti* (1868, nos. 7–24), Father Peter, an Orthodox priest in Saratov, effected Alekseev's conversion by serving as a father figure when the cantonist was in an emotionally and physically vulnerable state. See John Klier, "State Policies and the Conversion of Jews in Imperial Russia," in *Of Religion and Empire: Missions, Conversion, and Tolerance in Tsarist Russia*, ed. Robert P. Geraci and Michael Khodarkovsky (Ithaca, NY: Cornell University Press, 2001), 104.

99. A. Alekseev, *Besedy pravoslavnago khristianina iz evreev s novoobrashchennymi iz svoikh sobratii ob istinakh sviatoi very i zabluzhdeniiakh talmudicheskikh, s prisovokupleniem stat'i o talmude* (St. Petersburg, 1872), 5; Alekseev, *O religioznom dvizhenii evreev*, chap. 28.

100. Alekseev, *O religioznom dvizhenii evreev*, 196–97.

101. Ibid., 196–98.

102. For a bibliography, see Agurskij, "Die Judenchristen," 175–76; Vengerov, *Kritiko-biograficheskii slovar'*, 376, 939.

103. Alekseev, *Bogosluzhenie*, 61–62.

104. *Evreiskaia entsiklopediia: Svod znanii o evreistve i ego kul'ture v proshlom i nastoiashchem* (St. Petersburg: Brokgauz-Efron, 1906–1913), I:839–40. Iulii Gessen, author of the encyclopedia entry, credits Alekseev with helping to refute the Saratov blood libel. Gessen's claim is uncorroborated by historian Simon Dubnov, who only lauds the converted Jew Daniel Khvolson as the one to scientifically disprove the blood libel. See Simon M. Dubnow, *History of the Jews in Russia and Poland: From the Earliest Times until the Present Day* (Philadelphia: Jewish Publication Society of America, 1916), II:150–53.

105. Unpublished letter, dated June 20, 1873, and found inside Alekseev, *Besedy pravoslavnago khristianina*. The book was accessed at Columbia University.

106. Alekseev, *Besedy pravoslavnago khristianina*, 67, 72–73.

107. Ibid., 127n1.

108. Ibid., 112–17.

109. Ibid., 89–90. Alekseev refers to this custom as "blinde nacht," but it is more commonly referred to as "nittel nacht."

110. Alekseev, *Bogosluzhenie*, 1–2.

111. Elisheva Carlebach, *Divided Souls: Converts from Judaism in Germany, 1500–1750* (New Haven, CT: Yale University Press, 2001), 170–99. On the early modern genre of Christian ethnographies of Jews—most written by converts from Judaism—which turned anti-Jewish polemics from a theological discussion of Judaism to a discourse

on Jewish ethnicity and culture, see Yaakov Deutsch, *Judaism in Christian Eyes: Ethnographic Descriptions of Jews and Judaism in Early Modern Europe* (Oxford: Oxford University Press, 2012).

112. A. A. Alekseev, *Ocherki domashnei i obshchestvennoi zhizni evreev: Ikh verovaniia, prazdniki, obriady, talmud, kagal* (Novgorod, 1882); Alekseev, *Bogosluzhenie.*

113. Carlebach, *Divided Souls,* 183, 187–88.

114. Agursky, "Conversions of Jews," 82–83.

115. Alekseev, *Ocherki,* 7–8.

116. Alekseev, *Bogosluzhenie,* 3.

117. Ibid., 18.

118. Ibid., 40. Throughout, I transliterate Alekseev's Yiddish terms from the Russian in which he wrote. His transliterated Yiddish is characterized by the Litvak switching of *sh* for *s,* referred to as *sabisdike-losn* (*Tisri* for the Hebrew month of *Tishrei*), but his general vowel pronunciations seem to reflect his origins from the southern part of the Pale of Settlement. The author thanks Miriam Udel for helping to unpack Alekseev's Yiddish.

119. Ibid., 94.

120. Ibid., 67, 107.

121. Ibid., 137–40, qt. on 140.

122. Ibid., 43.

123. Ibid., 115.

124. Ibid., 128.

125. Ibid., 3.

126. Ibid., 21.

127. Ibid., 34, 40, 43, 52–53.

128. Ibid., 85.

129. In all likelihood, this source refers to Hayim Vital's canonical kabbalistic work from the late sixteenth century.

130. Alekseev, *Bogosluzhenie,* 2, 37–38, 160–63. Alekseev also quotes Tertullian (from an 1849 Russian translation) and the Book of Maccabees.

131. Ibid., 10–11.

132. Ibid., 163–66.

133. Ibid., 170–73.

134. Ibid., 174.

135. Ibid., 174–75.

136. Alekseev, *O religioznom dvizhenii evreev,* 177, 192–93; Alekseev, *Besedy pravoslavnago khristianina,* 7.

137. A short biography of Kuznetskii, under the name Nefanail, appears in I. F. Pavlovskii, *Kratkii biograficheskii slovar' uchenykh i pisatelei Poltavskoi gubernii s poloviny XVIII veka* (Poltava, 1912), 136.

138. Most scholars believe that *The Epistle of Rabbi Samuel* is not the work of an

eleventh-century Jewish convert, but of a fourteenth-century Dominican friar to whom
the epistle opens with a dedication. The earliest manuscript appeared in the mid-
fourteenth century in Latin, and claimed to be a "translation" from the "original" Arabic.
See Ora Limor, "The Epistle of Rabbi Samuel of Morocco: A Best-Seller in the World
of Polemics," in *Contra Iudaeos: Ancient and Medieval Polemics between Christians and
Jews*, ed. Ora Limor and Guy G. Stroumsa (Tübingen: Mohr Siebeck, 1996), 179, 183–85.

139. Kuznetskii read the 1788 Russian edition, *Zlatoe sochinenie ravvina Samuila*. On
the *Epistle*'s translation and use in Muscovy, see Judith Kalik, "The Orthodox Church
and the Jews in the Polish-Lithuanian Commonwealth," *Jewish History* 17 (2003): 229.

140. Agurskij, "Die Judenchristen," 158–60.

141. Ibid., 161. It was unclear to Agursky if this was a Synod directive or a local
diocesan initiative. He surmises that Kuznetskii was appointed by local initiative since
there was no mention of him in the papers of Metropolitan Filaret, who was a member
of the Synod.

142. Nikolai Kuznetskii, "Zamechatel'noe obrashchenie odnogo evreia v khristianstvo," *Strannik* 7 (1862): 339.

143. Ibid., 341, 344–45.

144. Nikolai Kuznetskii, "Zamechatel'noe obrashchenie odnogo evreia, umiravshago
ot kholery," *Strannik* 7 (1862): 349–59; Red., "K evreiskomu voprosu. Evrei-missioner,"
Volynskie gubernskie vedomosti 14 (February 1, 1868); "Rukopolozhenie vo sviashchenniki
iz evreev"; Brin, "Vospominaniia novokreshchennago evreia."

145. Agurskij, "Die Judenchristen," 161–63, qt. on 163.

146. For a list of legislation against Jews, including Christian converts of Jewish
birth, in the late imperial period, see Hans Rogger, *Jewish Policies and Right-Wing Politics in Imperial Russia* (Berkeley: University of California Press, 1986), 35–36.

147. Cited in John D. Klier, *Imperial Russia's Jewish Question, 1855–1881* (Cambridge:
Cambridge University Press, 1995), 263–64; Saul M. Ginsburg, *Meshumodim in tsarishn
Russland* (New York: "CYCO" Bicher Farlag, 1946), 66–67.

148. Klier, *Imperial Russia's Jewish Question*, 264; *Evreiskaia entsiklopediia*, IV:917.

149. RGIA f. 821, op. 8, d. 184, ll. 10b.–2, "Po vse poddanneishei pros'by kreshchen-
ago iz evreev Iakova Brafmana: Ob uchrezhdenie missionernago obshchestva dlia obrashcheniia byvshikh ego edinovertsev v khristianstvo (1858)."

150. Ibid., l. 30b.

151. Klier, *Imperial Russia's Jewish Question*, 281. See also Yohanan Petrovsky-
Shtern's entry on Brafman in the *YIVO Encyclopedia of Jews in Eastern Europe*, ed. Gershon David Hundert (New Haven, CT: Yale University Press) I:222–23.

152. Ginsburg, *Meshumodim*, 71; *Evreiskaia entsiklopediia*, IV:918. Ginsburg notes
that the Ministry of Public Enlightenment took funds from the Jewish candle tax and
received 2,500 rubles from the Vilna Educational District.

153. On the anti-Semitic convert type among East European Jewish apostates,

see Todd M. Endelman, "Memories of Jewishness: Jewish Converts and Their Jewish Pasts," in *Jewish History and Jewish Memory: Essays in Honor of Yosef Hayim Yerushalmi*, ed. Elisheva Carlebach, John M. Efron, and David N. Myers (Hanover, NH: University Press of New England, 1998), 311–29. Endelman suggests that this type was more common in Eastern Europe where Jews were more traditional and hence apostasy necessitated a more radical break from their past.

154. According to Dreizin, his wife, Braindl, age thirty-two, twice expressed her desire to convert to Orthodoxy, but both times fellow Jews convinced her to retract her statement. Since Braindl refused a divorce, the couple legally stayed married.

155. The Foreign Bible Society, active in Russia under Alexander I, translated and published the New Testament and the Bible into Hebrew but not Yiddish. See Zacek, "The Russian Bible Society."

156. YIVO RG 46, Box III:68, ll. 12–130b.

157. Ibid.

158. John Klier, "State Policies," 92; Dubnow, *History of the Jews*, III:10.

159. YIVO RG 46, Box III:68, ll. 14–18.

160. At this point, Dreizin was also a teacher of Jewish languages at the Lithuanian Theological Seminary (ibid., l. 38–380b.).

161. For example, see YIVO RG 46, Box III:68, ll. 40–400b., 41–410b., 42.

162. Ibid. l. 51–510b.

163. Ibid., l. 41–410b.

164. Dreizin calls Dr. Altgauzen the head of the "Department of Biblical Books" in Vilna. In July 1893 Dreizin reported to the Vilna archbishop on his progress, and noted that the Kiev governor had given him permission to keep a storehouse in Berdichev of the copies of the New Testament donated to him by the British Foreign Bible Society (via Dr. Altgauzen) and to distribute copies to Jews in Kiev Province (ibid., l. 50).

Chapter 3

1. Glenn Dynner, *Yankel's Tavern: Jews, Liquor, and Life in the Kingdom of Poland* (New York: Oxford University Press, 2013), 17–18.

2. Julia Brauch, Anna Liphardt, and Alexandra Nocke, "Exploring Jewish Space," in *Jewish Topographies: Visions of Space, Traditions of Place*, ed. Julia Brauch, Anna Liphardt, and Alexandra Nocke (Hampshire, Eng.: Ashgate, 2008), 2.

3. S. P—ii, "Iz Bresta Litovskogo," *Pravoslavnoe obozrenie* 5 (May 1866): 10.

4. For a recent cultural studies approach to the marketplace of one shtetl to rehabilitate the shared space of Jews and Christians in small-town Eastern Europe, see Yohanan Petrovsky-Shtern, "The Marketplace in Balta: Aspects of Economic and Cultural Life," *East European Jewish Affairs* 37, no. 3 (December 2007): 277–98. For another model of studying interethnic contact in a diverse imperial metropolis, see Natan M. Meir, *Kiev, Jewish Metropolis: A History, 1859–1914* (Bloomington: Indiana University

Press, 2010), 190–210. Meir argues that Jewish-Christian relations in late imperial Kiev extended beyond the commercial to include cooperation in voluntary societies, charities, and educational institutions.

5. Benjamin Nathans, *Beyond the Pale: The Jewish Encounter with Late Imperial Russia* (Berkeley: University of California Press, 2002), 100.

6. Dynner, *Yankel's Tavern*, 6–7.

7. Hirsz Abramowicz, *Profiles of a Lost World: Memoirs of East European Jewish Life before World War II*, ed. Dina Abramowicz and Jeffrey Shandler (Detroit: Wayne State University Press, [1958] 1999), 65.

8. Glenn Dynner, "Hasidism and Habitat: Managing the Jewish-Christian Encounter in the Kingdom of Poland," in *Holy Dissent: Jewish and Christian Mystics in Eastern Europe*, ed. Glenn Dynner (Detroit: Wayne State University Press, 2011), 106–8. Dynner notes that the Hasidic fear of village apostasy was in part grounded in reality as increasingly onerous concession fees for Jewish tavernkeepers in the Kingdom of Poland over the course of the nineteenth century drove some Jews to convert (108).

9. Abramowicz, *Profiles of a Lost World*, 65.

10. Dynner, *Yankel's Tavern*, 10.

11. Ibid., 1–2.

12. Yohanan Petrovsky-Shtern, *Golden Age Shtetl: A New History of Jewish Life in East Europe* (Princeton, NJ: Princeton University Press, 2014), 20, 26.

13. Salo W. Baron and Arcadius Kahan, *Economic History of the Jews*, ed. Nachum Gross (New York: Schocken Books, 1975), 136; John D. Klier, *Imperial Russia's Jewish Question, 1855–1881* (Cambridge: Cambridge University Press, 1995), 311–12. Under Nicholas I, the state centralized its tax-collection system, thus opening up opportunities to buy the right to collect state liquor taxes, a lucrative opportunity that enriched prominent families such as the Gintsburgs and Varshavskiis. See Nathans, *Beyond the Pale*, 40.

14. Marni Davis, "Despised Merchandise: American Jewish Liquor Entrepreneurs and Their Critics," in *Chosen Capital: The Jewish Encounter with American Capitalism*, ed. Rebecca Kobrin (New Brunswick, NJ: Rutgers University Press, 2012), 115–17.

15. Klier, *Imperial Russia's Jewish Question*, 312.

16. Ibid., 318. Klier notes that a *gradus* was a measure of alcoholic strength (486n46). This statistic is also cited in Hans Rogger, *Jewish Policies and Right-Wing Politics in Imperial Russia* (Berkeley: University of California Press, 1986), 127.

17. Glenn Dynner, "Legal Fictions: The Survival of Rural Jewish Tavernkeeping in the Kingdom of Poland," *Jewish Social Studies* n.s. 16, no. 2 (Winter 2010): 28–66.

18. Petrovsky-Shtern, *Golden Age Shtetl*, 3, 16, 343–47.

19. Rosa Lehmann, *Symbiosis and Ambivalence: Poles and Jews in a Small Galician Town* (New York: Berghahn Books, 2001), 47–48, 60–62.

20. According to the 1897 imperial Russian census, 51 percent of Jews still lived in shtetls and villages (with less than 10,000 inhabitants). See Eugene M. Avrutin, *Jews*

and the Imperial State: Identification Politics in Tsarist Russia (Ithaca, NY: Cornell University Press, 2010), 97n45. In 1881, of the 2.9 million Jews living in the Pale of Settlement (out of about 4 million Jews in the empire as a whole), 1.13 million lived in small towns and 580,000 in villages (1.19 million lived in cities). See Rogger, *Jewish Policies*, 145.

21. On the survival of some shtetls through the Soviet period and World War II, see Jeffrey Veidlinger, *In the Shadow of the Shtetl: Small-Town Jewish Life in Soviet Ukraine* (Bloomington: Indiana University Press, 2013).

22. On Polish fiction and the popular theme of the Jewish tavernkeeper, see Magdalena Opalski, *The Jewish Tavern Keeper and His Tavern in Nineteenth-Century Polish Literature* (Jerusalem: Zalman Shazar Center, 1986).

23. Steven M. Lowenstein, *The Berlin Jewish Community: Enlightenment, Family, and Crisis, 1770–1830* (Oxford: Oxford University Press, 1994), 120–33; Michael A. Meyer, *The Origins of the Modern Jew: Jewish Identity and European Culture in Germany, 1749–1824* (Detroit: Wayne State University Press, 1967), 85–114.

24. Scott Ury, *Banners and Barricades: The Revolution of 1905 and the Transformation of Warsaw Jewry* (Stanford, CA: Stanford University Press, 2012). Clerics in the southwest region viewed the city as the only place amenable to conversion—due to the interfaith friendships it fostered and its distance from the kahal. See TsDIAK f. 182, op. 1, d. 26, ll. 10–160b.

25. Dynner, *Yankel's Tavern*, 5.

26. On the Berlin salons as sites of Jewish female conversion in the late eighteenth century, see Deborah Hertz, *Jewish High Society in Old Regime Berlin* (New Haven, CT: Yale University Press, 1988). On coffeehouses and late nineteenth-century literary modernism, see Shahar Pinsker, *Literary Passports: The Making of Modernist Hebrew Fiction in Europe* (Stanford, CA: Stanford University Press, 2010).

27. YIVO RG 46, Box II:27, l. 4, Conversion of Jewess Malka Mendeliovna Lin (1871).

28. Ibid., ll. 9–12. On the imperial Russian legal precedent of granting a new legal social status to subjects in search of social mobility, see Alison K. Smith, "'The Freedom to Choose a Way of Life': Fugitives, Borders, and Imperial Amnesties in Russia," *Journal of Modern History* 83, no. 2 (June 2011): 243–71.

29. D. Z. Feldman and O. Iu. Minkina, "K voprosu o priniatii evreiskimi zhenshchinami khristianstva v Rossii v kontse XVIII–nachale XIX vekov," in *"Prekrasnaia Evreika" v Rossii XVII–XIX vekov: Obrazy i real'nost*, ed. D. Z. Feldman, O. Iu. Minkina, and A. Iu. Kononova (Moscow: Drevlekhranilishche, 2007), 72–74.

30. Nathans, *Beyond the Pale*, 4.

31. Annmaria Orla-Bukowska, "Maintaining Borders, Crossing Borders: Social Relationships in the Shtetl," *Polin* 17 (2004): 177.

32. John D. Klier, "What Exactly Was a Shtetl?," in *The Shtetl: Image and Reality*, ed. Gennady Estraikh and Mikhail Krutikov (Oxford: Legenda, 2000), 25.

33. Ibid., 27–28.

34. Ibid., 26.

35. YIVO RG 46, Box I:10, ll. 3–40b., Conversion of Jewess Sheina Leibovna Dlugolenskaia, 1872.

36. *PSZ* II, vol. XXXVI, no. 37,709 (January 22, 1862).

37. YIVO RG 46, Box I:10, l. 8.

38. Joseph Roth, *The Radetzky March*, trans. Joachim Neugroschel (Woodstock, NY: Overlook Press, [1932] 1995), 77–78.

39. S. Ansky, *The Dybbuk and Other Writings*, ed. David G. Roskies, trans. Golda Werman (New York: Schocken, 1992), 53–70, esp. 53.

40. Gabriella Safran, *Wandering Soul: The Dybbuk's Creator, S. An-sky* (Cambridge, MA: Harvard University Press, 2010), 9–13. Safran notes that Ansky's later sketch about a tavern was undoubtedly drawn from his own experiences growing up in a tavern. In an autobiographical mode, Ansky depicts a young Jewish female tavernkeeper named Chanka (his own mother was Chana) who, along with her grandmother Malka, runs the tavern. Contrary to Russian stereotypes of exploitative Jewish tavernkeepers, Ansky depicts Chanka as caring for her drunken clients and even offering local Slavic folk songs as antidotes to their socioeconomic despair.

41. Quoted in Safran, *Wandering Soul*, 12.

42. Jewish families often invoked gender stereotypes to cast their daughters' conversions as insincere, fickle, and whimsical. See ChaeRan Freeze, "When Chava Left Home: Gender, Conversion, and the Jewish Family in Tsarist Russia," *Polin* 18 (2005): 153–88.

43. YIVO RG 46, Box II:40, l. 6–60b., Conversion of Jewess Yevka Mordkheleva Blokh, 1874.

44. Ibid., l. 10–100b. In a similar case in 1863, the older sister and guardian of Sorka Niseliovna refused to allow her underage sister to convert, arguing that Sorka's plan to convert was insincere and only the result of local soldiers who promised her money if she converted. See YIVO RG 46, Box IV:100, l. 7–70b., Conversion of Jewess Sorka Niseliovna, 1863.

45. YIVO RG 46, Box II:40, ll. 12–130b.

46. Ibid., ll. 14–150b.

47. Ibid., ll. 12–130b.

48. LVIA f. 377, op. 1, d. 812, Complaint of female Jewish convert from Merech, Anna Kviatkovskaia, about her forced return by Jews to Judaism, robbery and marriage to a Jew; and about her father's and the Merech rabbi's participation in her abduction, 1825–1830 [CAHJP HM2 9728.2].

49. Nathans, *Beyond the Pale*, 210.

50. On reading the shtetl as a site of religious contact, see Michał Galas, "Interreligious Contacts in the Shtetl: Proposals for Future Research," *Polin* 17 (2004): 41–50.

51. Aside from Stanislawski's statistics on the predominance of female converts in the late imperial period, based on 244 Jewish conversion petitions in YIVO RG 46, archive of the Vilna Ecclesiastic Consistory, from the years 1819–1911, similar statistics are in archival inventories of Jewish conversions in various locales both within and without the Pale of Jewish Settlement. According to the Roman Catholic Religious College (RGIA f. 822), in conversions to Catholicism the number of Jewish women started to equal and then surpass that of Jewish men from 1862 and on. The number of converts was, in 1862, eighteen men and seventeen women; in 1875, sixteen men and thirty-nine women; in 1880, fifteen men and sixty-five women. According to statistics from the archival inventory lists of the Kiev Ecclesiastic Consistory (TsDIAK f. 127), 746 Jews (384 men, 362 women) converted to Orthodoxy under their auspices between 1893 and 1903. In specific years, though, the rates of female conversion surpassed that of men—e.g. in 1894, 1895, 1900. In contrast, statistics of Jewish conversion in Kiev from the first half of the nineteenth century show a higher ratio of men to women. According to the records of the Vilna Ecclesiastic Consistory (LVIA f. 605, op. 4), 136 Jews, of whom 74 were female, converted to Orthodoxy between the years 1863 and 1871. Of the 136 neophytes discussed in sixty-two case files, approximately 127 were considered "adults," or above the age of fourteen. Of these 127, there were 69 women, or 54 percent of the cohort. According to Synod statistics from 1910 on heterodox conversions to Orthodoxy, Jewish men tended to outpace female converts in large cities, but in the western provinces as a whole, women converts slightly outnumbered men. In St. Petersburg, 68 Jewish men converted and 60 Jewish women; in Kharkov, 56 men converted as compared to 48 women (ll. 90, 235). In Kiev Province, though, as a whole, 30 Jewish men converted versus 33 women (l. 93). See RGIA f. 821, op. 10, d. 278, "Statisticheskie svedeniia o kolichestve lits, pereshedshikh v pravoslaviiu iz drugikh ispovedanii (1910)." The author thanks Natan Meir for generously sharing this source.

52. Notable exceptions in East European Jewish history include Rachel Manekin, "The Lost Generation: Education and Female Conversion in *Fin-de-Siècle* Kraków," *Polin* 18 (2005): 189–219; Freeze, "When Chava Left Home"; Avrutin, *Jews and the Imperial State.*

53. Paula Hyman, *Gender and Assimilation in Modern Jewish History: The Roles and Representations of Women* (Seattle: University of Washington Press, 1995), 19. Also see Marion A. Kaplan, *The Making of the Jewish Middle Class: Women, Family, and Identity in Imperial Germany* (New York: Oxford University Press, 1991).

54. On female revolutionaries who converted in imperial Russia, see Naomi Shepherd, *A Price below Rubies: Jewish Women as Rebels and Radicals* (London: Weidenfeld & Nicolson, 1993), 3n2.

55. Hyman, *Gender and Assimilation,* 21.

56. Todd M. Endelman, "Gender and Assimilation in Modern Jewish History," in *Gendering the Jewish Past,* ed. Marc Lee Raphael (Williamsburg, VA: College of William and Mary, 2002), 37.

57. Based on post-Soviet ethnographies of Ukrainian shtetls that survived World War II, one scholar has noted the permeability of ethno-religious boundaries in small towns, with a range of intercommunal interactions—from generosity to libel. For example, around the holiday of Passover, Jews would often offer matzo to non-Jews. See Aleksandr L'vov, "Mezhetnicheskie otnosheniia: Ugoshchenie matsoi i 'krovavyi navet,'" in *Shtetl, XXI vek: Polevye issledovaniia*, ed. V. A. Dymshits, A. L. L'vov, and A. V. Sokolova (St. Petersburg: Izd-vo Evropeiskago Universiteta, 2008), 65–82.

58. Sv. [Priest] Viktor Il'iashevich, "Iz Umanskago uezda," *Kievskie eparkhial'nye vedomosti* 6 (March 30, 1882).

59. NIAB f. 1781, op. 3, ed. khr. 51, ll. 145–620b., esp. 1570b.–59, Jewish conversions to Catholicism, 1801–1833.

60. As discussed in Chapter 4, in 1827 the Third Section of the tsar's Chancellery indicted more than nine Jews for the crime of seducing two Catholic domestic servants to Judaism. The courts found that the two Catholic maidens were working in Jewish homes where they were enticed to convert. See DAVO f. 361, op. 1, d. 79, Ukase of Volynian provincial administration regarding the Third Section's indictment of over nine Jews for seduction, 1827 [CAHJP HM2 9637.5]; LVIA f. 377, op. 1, d. 126, Rosenberg from Vidzy asks about bringing justice to the Jew Liun who is in prison for seducing two women to Judaism from Catholicism, 1823 [CAHJP HM2 9724.6]. Also, the Maria Drich murder trial, discussed in the next chapter, which involved the murder of a Christian domestic servant in a Jewish home who fell in love with the family's son. See "Ubiistvo evreiami khristianki," *Sankt-Peterburgskie vedomosti* 103 (1885); "Ubiistvo evreiami khristianki," *Sankt-Peterburgskie vedomosti* 107 (1885); "Po liutsinskomu delu," *Nedel'naia khronika voskhoda* 23 (1885).

61. YIVO RG 46, Box III:76, ll. 13–140b., Conversion of Vilna Jewish townswoman Pera Girsenovich, 1874.

62. Lee Shai Weissbach, trans. and ed., *A Jewish Life on Three Continents: The Memoir of Menachem Mendel Frieden* (Stanford, CA: Stanford University Press, 2013), 190.

63. Pauline Wengeroff, *Rememberings: The World of a Russian-Jewish Woman in the Nineteenth Century*, ed. Bernard D. Cooperman, trans. Henny Wenkart (College Park: University of Maryland Press, 2000). Paula Hyman's work on rural acculturation in Alsace is also helpful for thinking about non-urban cultural encounters and exchanges. See Paula E. Hyman, "Social Contexts of Assimilation: Village Jews and City Jews in Alsace," in *Assimilation and Community: The Jews in Nineteenth-Century Europe*, ed. Jonathan Frankel and Steven J. Zipperstein (Cambridge: Cambridge University Press, 1992), 110–29.

64. Eugene M. Avrutin, "Ritual Murder in a Russian Border Town," *Jewish History* 26 (2012): 309–26; Hillel J. Kieval, "Neighbors, Strangers, Readers: The Village and the City in Jewish-Gentile Conflict at the Turn of the Nineteenth Century," *Jewish Studies Quarterly* 12, no. 1 (2005): 61–79.

65. Frequent and often intense ordinary Jewish/Christian relationships could lead

to apostasy. See Jeremy Cohen, "The Mentality of the Medieval Jewish Apostate: Peter Alfonsi, Hermann of Cologne, and Pablo Christiani," in *Jewish Apostasy in the Modern World*, ed. Todd M. Endelman (New York: Holmes and Meier, 1987), 20–47.

66. YIVO RG 46, Box II:25, l. 2–20b., Conversion of Jew Faiba Nakhim Bendstovich Bodanes, 1853–1855.

67. Ibid., Box I:12, Conversion of Jewess Malka Leibovna Vulfovichovna Kuks, 1864–1865.

68. Ibid., Box II:34, l. 2, Conversion of Jewess Roshka Shmulovna Slovatitskaia, 1870.

69. Ibid., Box I:21, l. 2, Conversion of Avram Pinkhusovich, 1896.

70. Ibid., Box III:50, Conversion of Jewess Lia Leizerovich, 1899.

71. Ibid., Box III:56, l. 3, Conversion of Jewess Masha Teitelbaum, 1899.

72. Ibid., Box III:62, l. 3, Conversion of Jewess of Lida Uezd Khaika Volskaia, 1900.

73. Ibid., Box III:63, l. 2, Conversion of townsman Vinnik, that is Yablonskii, 1901.

74. Ibid., Box IV:99, l. 1, Conversion of Jew Mendel' Mirkin, 1910–1911.

75. Aleksandr Alekseev, *Bogosluzhenie, prazdniki, i religioznye obriady nyneshnikh evreev* (Novgorod, [1861] 1865), 44.

76. Ibid., 47.

77. Ibid., 52.

78. Ibid., 72.

79. Ibid., 98–105, 116, 126.

80. Freeze, "When Chava Left Home," 167–68.

81. I have found evidence of abduction claims from as early as 1802: LVIA f. 378 B/S, 1802 g., d. 115, Complaint of Matush Movshovich, kahal leader in Sveichana, about the abduction of the young daughter of Girsh Abramovich and her being hidden under the watch of those preparing her for conversion, 1802 [CAHJP HM2 9730.7]. For early nineteenth-century claims, also see ibid., 1824 g., d. 381, Complaint that a twelve-year-old girl was forcibly taken to a convent and converted, 1824 [CAHJP HM2 9771.8]; ibid., 1824 g., d. 609, Petition of a Jew that his seven-year-old brother was taken by the Tel'shi police to be converted, 1824 [CAHJP HM2 9771.11].

82. Gershon Hundert, *Jews in Poland-Lithuania in the Eighteenth Century: A Genealogy of Modernity* (Berkeley: University of California Press, 2004); Moshe Rosman, "A Minority Views the Majority: Jewish Attitudes towards the Polish Lithuanian Commonwealth and Interaction with Poles," *Polin* 4 (1989): 31–41.

83. LVIA f. 378 B/S, 1815 g., d. 184, ll. 2–4, Communication of police to military governor of Vilna Province [CAHJP HM2 9733.20].

84. For another reported case of abduction in which the conversion influence was a Catholic caretaker in a Jewish home, see the case of Feygele in Chapter 1.

85. LVIA f. 378 B/S, 1858 g., d. 231, ll. 1–20b., 7–8, Request of Jewess Yoseliova, 1858 [CAHJP HM3 231.7].

86. Ibid., ll. 3–6, Letter from the Kovno Provincial Administration to the Vilna/Grodno/Kovno Governor-General Nazimov.

87. YIVO RG 46, Box I:12, Conversion of Jewess Malka Leibovna Vulfovichovna Kuks, 1864–1865.

88. Ibid., Box II:26, l. 2, Conversion of Jewess Rutka Abramovna Movshik, 1866.

89. Ibid., Box III:88, l. 2–20b., Conversion of Jewess Sora Shenderovna Arliukova, 1866. The gendarmerie was a military police force, separate from the civil police.

90. Ibid., Box II:34, ll. 2, 5, Conversion of Jewess Roshka Shmulovna Slovatitskaia, 1870.

91. Ibid., l. 9. The Grodno convent's mother superior argued that the negative report on Slovatitskaia's behavior was fabricated by local Jews to thwart her conversion. The police then publicized the information in an attempt to curry favor with local Jews. Interestingly, there were two Jews who came to the neophyte's defense from the beginning of her conversion journey—the Bialystok crown rabbi Markus and first-guild merchant Volkovisskii, who testified that Slovatitskaia voluntarily and willfully desired baptism and was not coaxed by wily Christians (ll. 1–3, 4–6).

92. Ibid., III:76, ll. 12–15, 26–26ob., 28.

93. Ibid., Box III:86, Conversion of Jewesses Dverka Movshovna and Yustina Kulbinskaia, 1864–1865.

94. Ibid., Box II:24, Conversion of Jewish maiden Sora Lea Taich from Slonim, 1874–1875.

95. DAmK f. 286, op. 1, d. 101, Petition of the landowner, Mogilev Province, Gorets District, Kotov F. S. to convert the Jewess Meri Zalmanova Yofo to Orthodoxy, 1883. The title on the outside of the document is misworded.

96. YIVO RG 46, Box III:81, l. 2, Petition of Vilna townswoman Mira Beker to convert, 1892.

97. "Povestvovanie Marii Leshchinskoi o svoei zhizni i ob obrashchenii iz iudeistva v khristianstvo," *Kievskie eparkhial'nye vedomosti* 25 (June 20, 1879), 6–11. The discussion of Leshchinskaia that follows is based on this article.

98. The narrative locates Mezerich near the town of Kanev in Kiev Province, but the town of Mezerich was located in the province of Volynia to the northwest of Kiev Province. From the rest of the story, it seems that Kanev, a town to the southeast of Kiev, anchors the geography of her married life.

99. For more examples, see DAKO f. 2, op. 1, d. 27758, Seduction to Judaism of the convert from Judaism Ita Nakhmanova who married the peasant Voitkovskii, 1848 [CAHJP HM3 572.2]. As early as 1800 there is a record of a Jewish father seeking legal action against a certain Kapello for "abducting" his daughter, who then converted and married Kapello. The abduction claim here seems to belie a Jewish daughter's elopement. See RGADA f. 1239, op. 3, d. 37932 [CAHJP HM2 9412.7].

100. Michael Stanislawski, "Jewish Apostasy in Russia: A Tentative Typology," in

Jewish Apostasy in the Modern World, ed. Todd M. Endelman (New York: Holmes and Meier, 1987), 200. Another file indirectly references a romantic conversion as the boy's mother Daria, a convert from Judaism, was now married to a noncommissioned army officer and petitioned the Vilna archbishop to grant her custody of her son so that he too could convert to Russian Orthodoxy. See YIVO RG 46, Box III:47, Conversion of Jewish boy Berko Leibovich, 1847.

101. YIVO RG 46, Box I:8, Conversion of Jewess Rozali Neiman, Brest-Litovsk, 1864–1868.

102. Ibid., Box III:75, Report of Priest of Foundling Hospital Iusus Mladenets about the conversion of the Jewess Tsina Gorodishch, 1896–1897.

103. In 1891 Konstantin Uranovskii converted to Orthodoxy in the hope of marrying a Christian girl; when the marriage did not take place, Uranovskii unhappily remained Orthodox until 1908, when he petitioned to legally return to his ancestral faith (ibid., 89). Grodno townsman David Khlavnovich Yuzpe's 1910 petition for conversion stated he was attracted to Orthodoxy and an Orthodox girl whom he intended to marry after his conversion (ibid., 54).

104. Eugene M. Avrutin, "Returning to Judaism after the 1905 Law on Religious Freedom in Tsarist Russia," *Slavic Review* 65, no. 1 (Spring 2006): 102.

105. DAKO f. 1, op. 114, d. 220, ll. 82–87, Reversions from Orthodoxy to Judaism, 1906–1908.

106. Ibid., ll. 171–89.

107. Manekin, "The Lost Generation"; Isaac Remba, *Banim akhlu boser* (Tel Aviv: Ha-Vaad ha-Tsiburi le-Hotsa'at Kitve Aizik Rembah, 1973).

108. TsGIA-SPb, f. 2219, op. 1, d. 31, ll. 133–360b., as translated and annotated in Nadieszda Kizenko, "Written Confessions to Father John of Kronstadt, 1898–1908," in *Orthodox Christianity in Imperial Russia: A Source Book on Lived Religion*, ed. Heather J. Coleman (Bloomington: Indiana University Press, 2014), 166–68. On the history of written confessions in Russia, see Nadieszda Kizenko, "Written Confessions and the Construction of Sacred Narrative," in *Sacred Stories: Religion and Spirituality in Modern Russia*, ed. Mark D. Steinberg and Heather J. Coleman (Bloomington: Indiana University Press, 2007), 93–118.

109. On using narratives in archival records as historical sources, see Natalie Zemon Davis, *Fiction in the Archives: Pardon Tales and Their Tellers in Sixteenth-Century France* (Stanford, CA: Stanford University Press, 1987).

110. Remba, *Banim akhlu boser*.

111. Brian Horowitz, *Empire Jews: Jewish Nationalism and Acculturation in Nineteenth- and Early Twentieth-Century Russia* (Bloomington, IN: Slavica, 2009), 219.

112. On conversion rules, see GARF f. 109, V/D, kn. 3, d. 22, ll. 154–590b. Also see ibid., I eksp., 1829 g., d. 449, "Vsepoddanneishii doklad shefa zhandarmov Benkendorfa: Ob obshchestve zhidov, delaiushchikh znachitel'nyi podryv po otkupam" [CAHJP RU

649 and 1285]; ibid., V/D, kn. 3, d. 22, l. 185, Letter from Benckendorff to State Secretary Bludov on taking measures against Jewish tricks to convert to Christianity; ibid., I eksp., 1830 g., d. 303, ll. 29–30, Regarding Jewish converts living in St. Petersburg, October 1830 [CAHJP RU 350]. On post-baptism surveillance, see *SZ* (1832 ed.), vol. XIV, part 1, chap. 3, section II:1, no. 43.

113. Elena Keidosiute, "Missionary Activity of Mariae Vitae Congregation," *Pardes: Zeitschrift der Vereinigung für Jüdische Studien* (2010): 4.

114. YIVO RG 46, Box III:80, l. 8, Conversion of Iurberg Jewish townsman David Bressel, 1870–1871.

115. RGIA f. 822, op. 1, d. 6685, Communication of chief of police regarding the question whether Jews who desire to convert can stay in St. Petersburg for more than six weeks, 1837 [CAHJP HM2 7920.17]. In the early twentieth century the Holy Synod adopted several measures to counter instrumental Jewish baptisms, including a 1903 edict prohibiting baptized Jews from relocating out of the Pale unless they earned the right to residency before baptism. See Avrutin, *Jews and the Imperial State*, 117, 120n13.

116. "Missionerskaia deiatel'nost' sredi evreev," *Golos* 75 (March 16, 1877).

117. DAKO f. 1, op. 140, d. 858, Petition of Jews to allow them temporary residence in Kiev in order to convert to Orthodoxy (1904), especially l.12–120b., regarding the petition of Roza Gross and her three children to convert in Kiev.

118. Agnieszka Jagodzińska, "Christian Missionaries and Jewish Spaces: British Missions in the Kingdom of Poland in the First Half of the Nineteenth Century," in *Space and Conversion in Global Perspective*, ed. Giuseppe Marcocci, Wietse de Boer, Aliocha Maldavsky, and Ilaria Pavan (Leiden: Brill, 2015), 107, 113.

119. *Nedel'naia khronika voskhoda* 46 (1882). For the original report of the St. Vladimir Brotherhood, see "Spisok lits krestivshikhsia iz evreev i prisoedinivshikhsia iz katolikov k pravoslaviiu, v Kievo-sofiiskom sobore, c 9-go avgusta 1881 goda po 1-e avgusta 1882 goda pri posredstve Kievskago sv. vladimirskago bratstva," *Kievskie eparkhial'nye vedomosti* 20 (October 30, 1882).

120. Shmuel Werses, *'Hakizah ami': Sifrut hahaskalah ba'idan hamodernizaziyah* (Jerusalem: Magnes Press, 2000), 339–40.

121. Statistics cited in Mikhail Agursky, "Conversions of Jews to Christianity in Russia," *Soviet Jewish Affairs* 20, no. 2–3 (1990): 80.

122. Ibid.

123. "Kreshchennye iz evreev," *Kievskie eparkhial'nye vedomosti* 1 (January 7, 1881); "Novokreshchennye iz evreev," *Kievskie eparkhial'nye vedomosti* 7 (February 18, 1881); "Novokreshchennye iz evreev," *Kievskie eparkhial'nye vedomosti* 20 (May 20, 1881).

124. "Prosveshchenie sv. kreshcheniem i prisoedinenie k pravoslavnoi tserkvi," *Kievskie eparkhial'nye vedomosti* 35 (September 2, 1881).

125. On the St. Petersburg shelter's multilayered educational program, see ChaeRan

Y. Freeze, "The Mariinsko Sergievskii Shelter for Converted Jewish Children in St. Petersburg," in *Jews in the East European Borderlands: Essays in Honor of John D. Klier*, ed. Eugene M. Avrutin and Harriet Murav (Boston: Academic Studies Press, 2012), 27–49.

126. "Spisok lits ... ," *Kievskie eparkhial'nye vedomosti* 20 (October 30, 1882).

127. DAmK f. 14, op. 1, d. 35, l. 2, Report of Brotherhood, July 15, 1872–July 15, 1873.

128. TsDIAK f. 442, op. 152, d. 745, Most humble petition of the Jewess Rivka Varnovitskaia, about returning her son to her ... who has converted to Orthodoxy, and is left without care, 1843.

129. Ibid., f. 127, op. 1047, d. 328, Conversion of Jewess Rukhel Volkova Liublinskaia, now Maria, 1894 [CAHJP HM2 9683.3].

130. YIVO RG 46, Box IV:98, l. 2, Conversion of townswoman Rakhil Miller, 1909.

131. DAmK f. 316, op. 1, d. 210, l. 47, List of Jewish cantonists in the Kiev Battalion who have expressed a desire to convert to Orthodoxy, 1854. The commander again issued a call for godparents in the fall of 1854.

132. Ibid., f. 253, op. 1, d. 2., l. 5, Clarification of conversion of Jewish minors and adults, 1875–1878.

133. Iv. Pavlovskii, "O neobkhodimosti priiutov dlia evreev, ishchushchikh kreshcheniia," *Sovremennost'* 137 (December 9, 1876).

134. "Zatrudneniia Kievskago vladimirskago bratstva otnositel'no evreev, prinimaiushchikh khristianstvo," *Kievlianin* 225 (October 19, 1883). Converts from Judaism were singled out as prime candidates to financially support the Brotherhood's cause and assist converts in finding jobs and a productive life post-baptism.

Chapter 4

1. On violence between Jews and their neighbors, with Jews as both victims and resisters, see Adam Teller, "The Shtetl as an Arena of Polish-Jewish Integration," *Polin* 17 (2004): 26; Judith Kalik, "The Orthodox Church and the Jews in the Poland-Lithuanian Commonwealth," *Jewish History* 17, no. 2 (2003): 229–37; Jan T. Gross, *Neighbors: The Destruction of the Jewish Community in Jedwabne, Poland* (Princeton, NJ: Princeton University Press, 2001).

2. On the spectrum of interfaith relationships, see Rosa Lehmann, *Symbiosis and Ambivalence: Poles and Jews in a Small Galician Town* (New York: Berghahn Books, 2001), 128–29.

3. On reading religious violence not as undermining social stability but as legitimating the working out of kinks in confessional coexistence, see David Nirenberg, *Communities of Violence: Persecution of Minorities in the Middle Ages* (Princeton, NJ: Princeton University Press, 1996). Anxieties over interfaith intimacies and porous boundaries animated a range of discourses on Jewish-Christian relations, including tales of host desecration and genealogical thinking in medieval Iberia. See Jonathan Boyarin, "Jews, Indians, and the Identity of Christian Europe," *AJS Perspectives* (Fall 2005), 12–13.

4. Benjamin Nathans, *Beyond the Pale: The Jewish Encounter with Late Imperial Russia* (Berkeley: University of California Press, 2002), 285–86. The original title of the play was *Syny Israilia* (Sons of Israel); Nathans cites the 1899 published script by Krylov and Litvin.

5. Hillel Kazovsky, "Jewish Artists in Russia at the Turn of the Century: Issues of National Self-Identification in Art," *Jewish Art* 21–22 (1995–1996): 38.

6. On empire and the Jewish exercise of power through both mimicry and contestation, see David Biale, *Power and Powerlessness in Jewish History* (New York: Schocken, 1986); Riv-Ellen Prell, ed., "Empire in Jewish Studies," Special issue, *AJS Perspectives* (Fall 2005), esp. the articles by Ra'anan Boustan (8–10) and Sarah Stein (14–16).

7. The term "figuring ground" is from Kenneth Mills and Anthony Grafton, eds., *Conversion: Old Worlds and New* (Rochester, NY: University of Rochester Press, 2003), xv.

8. A. Ansky, "In the Tavern," in *Dybbuk and Other Writings*, ed. David G. Roskies, trans. Golda Werman (New York: Schocken, 1992), 53–70, esp. 68.

9. Sholem Asch, *Salvation* [*Der tehilim yid*, 1934], trans. Willa and Edwin Muir (New York: Schocken, 1968), 180–87.

10. For complaints against various *kehilot*, see TsDIAK f. 442, op. 149, d. 6289 (Boguslav kahal); op. 142, d. 94 (Radom kahal, 1835); op. 158, d. 1000 and op. 159, d. 586 (Belotserkov kahal, 1847–1849); op. 84, d. 420 (Lipian kahal, 1853). For examples of complaints against family members pursuing converts, see DAKO f. 1, op. 140, d. 517, l. 5–50b., "O razreshenii vremennago prebyvaniia Revveke Srebnik v Kieve dlia priniatiia pravoslaviia (1904)." One female convert said that her parents kept her under surveillance for an entire year after her wish to convert became known. See YIVO RG 46, Box III:52, Conversion of townswoman from the Miadelskii Jewish community Sheina Khodos, 1901.

11. Iv. Pavlovskii, "O neobkhodimosti priiutov dlia evreev ishchushchikh krescheniia," *Sovremennost'* 137 (December 9, 1876); RGIA f. 821, op. 8, d. 191, "Po otnosheniiu glavnago nachal'nika IIIgo otd. cob. e. i. v. kantseliarii: Kasatel'no evreiskago mal'chika Iankelia Basevicha (1864)." In the latter case, an Orthodox priest in Congress Poland refused to grant a Jewish father converting to Orthodoxy permission to take his children from the Jewish mother out of fear of rousing the ire of the Jewish community.

12. The St. Petersburg shelter even paid the transportation cost of Jews from the western provinces who sought its protection for conversion. See TsGIA-SPb f. 542, op. 3, d. 6, "Kniga dlia zapisi raskhoda summ ot sbora ezhegodnykh i edinovremennykh pozhertvovanie v pol'zu ishchushchikh prisoedineniia k pravoslavnuiu i vnov prisoedinennykh k nemu evreev (1869–1872)"; A. Alekseev, *O religioznom dvizhenii evreev i rasprostranenii khristianstva mezhdu nimi, s prilozheniem obiasneniia vazhneishikh mest sv. pisaniia, svidetel'stvuiushchikh ob Iususe Khriste, kak litse messii i nastavleniia, kak vesti delo missionerstva sredi evreev* (Novgorod, 1895), 34. In her study of the St. Petersburg shelter, Freeze notes the phenomenon of Jewish families responding to conversions with

attempted kidnappings. See ChaeRan Freeze, "The Mariinsko Sergievskii Shelter for Converted Jewish Children in St. Petersburg," in *Jews in the East European Borderlands: Essays in Honor of John D. Klier*, ed. Eugene M. Avrutin and Harriet Murav (Boston: Academic Studies Press, 2012), 45.

13. Red., "K evreiskomu voprosu. Evrei-missioner," *Volynskie gubernskie vedomosti* 14 (February 1, 1868).

14. O. Brin, "Vospominaniia novokreshchennago evreia," *Strannik* 7 (1877).

15. S. P—ii, "Iz Bresta Litovskago," *Pravoslavnoe obozrenie* 5 (May 1866): 9–16.

16. "Zatrudneniia Kievskago vladimirskago bratstva otnositel'no evreev, prinimaiushchikh khristianstvo," *Kievlianin* 225 (1883).

17. "How Rabbi Gurland Became a Christian," *Scattered Nation* 3 (1868): 213–15, esp. 214.

18. Of nine such cases I found, six involved the alleged abduction of daughters: RGADA f. 1239, op. 3, d. 37932 (1800) [CAHJP HM2 9412.7]; LVIA f. 378 BS,1802, d. 115 [HM2 9730.7]; ibid., 1824, d. 381 [HM2 9771.8]; ibid., d. 485 [HM2 9771.9]; ibid., d. 609 [HM2 9771.11]; TsDIAK f. 422, op. 35, d. 966 (1858); ibid., op. 41, d. 290; ibid., op. 44, dd. 428, 477 (1865).

19. ChaeRan Freeze, "When Chava Left Home: Gender, Conversion, and the Jewish Family in Tsarist Russia," *Polin* 18 (2005): 165–67.

20. YIVO RG 46, Box IV:105, Conversion of the Jew Il'ia Abramovich Eliovich, 1862.

21. Ibid., Box I:10, Conversion of Jewess Sheina Leibovna Dlugolenskaia, 1872.

22. LVIA f. 377, op. 1, d. 812, Complaint of female Jewish convert from Merech, Anna Kviatkovskaia, about her forced return by Jews to Judaism, robbery and marriage to a Jew; and about her father's and the Merech rabbi's participation in her abduction, 1825–1830 [CAHJP HM2 9728.2].

23. Ibid., ll. 110b., 16–17.

24. Ibid, ll. 3–5, Petition of the Converted Jewess Anna Kviatkovskaia; l. 12–120b.

25. "Iz Berdicheva," *Kievskie eparkhial'nye vedomosti* 50 (1879).

26. "Po delu Shmulia i Khavy Mintses, Aizenberga i drug. 17 Maia 1888 goda," *Sudebnaia gazeta* 11 (1889): 11–13; "Iz Varshavy," *Sankt-Peterburgskie vedomosti* 296 (1886).

27. "Evreiskie protsessy," *Novorossiiskii telegraf* 3292 (1886).

28. "Sudebnyi otdel: sovrashchenie v iudeistvo," *Odesskii vestnik* 45 (1886).

29. "Sovrashchenie v iudeistvo (okonchanie)," *Odesskii vestnik* 46 (1886).

30. Freeze, "When Chava Left Home."

31. YIVO RG 46, Box III:85, Desire of recruit Aizikovich to convert to Orthodoxy, 1842.

32. Before 1855, the Orthodox Church had few periodicals; it had repeatedly rejected the idea of establishing a provincial ecclesiastic press, thus denying rank-and-file clergymen an outlet for publishing. See Gregory Freeze, "The Orthodox Church and Serfdom in Prereform Russia," *Slavic Review* 48, no. 3 (Autumn 1989): 371n36.

33. For further analysis of fanaticism as a language to discredit minority faiths and critique imperial toleration, see Ellie R. Schainker, "On Faith and Fanaticism: Converts from Judaism and the Limits of Toleration in Late Imperial Russia," *Kritika* (forthcoming, 2016).

34. "A Martyr's Death," *Strannik* 2 (1876), cited in Michael Agursky, "Conversions of Jews to Christianity in Russia," *Soviet Jewish Affairs* 20, no. 2–3 (1990): 75.

35. "The case against the Jew Prizant," *Kievlianin* 283 (1885); "Sudebnaia gazeta," *Nedel'naia khronika voskhoda* 1 (1886): 25–26. Cited in Agursky, "Conversions of Jews," 75. See also *Elisavetgradskii vestnik* 1 (1886).

36. "Fanatizm evreev," *Volynskie eparkhial'nye vedomosti* 30 (1886). The reporter added that Jewish violence to avenge conversion had been going on in the western region for about a century, but that 90 percent of the cases went unprosecuted.

37. "Na zakonnom osnovanii," *Kievlianin* 286 (1884).

38. "Ubiistvo evreiami khristianki," *Sankt-Peterburgskie vedomosti* 103 (1885).

39. "Ubiistvo evreiami khristianki," *Sankt-Peterburgskie vedomosti* 107 (1885).

40. "Po liutsinskomu delu," *Nedel'naia khronika voskhoda* 23 (1885).

41. Bribery is an interesting nonviolent politics of group resistance to conversion. For a provocative case of a lieutenant and priest accused of accepting a bribe from a Jewish community in exchange for returning a convert to his Jewish kin, see DAZhO f. 1, op. 1, d. 227, "O poluchenii podporuchikom Panteleimonom Goritsynym vziatki ot Liubarskogo evreiskogo kagala za vozvrashchenie emu zhelaiushchego priniat' pravoslavie evreia i ob uchastii v etom sviashchennika Samulevicha (1796)."

42. "Sudebnaia khronika: Ubiistvo (evreiskago malchika, priniavshago pravoslavie) iz religioznago fanatizma," *Kievlianin* 215 (1881); "Sudebnaia khronika: Ubiistvo iz religioznago fanatizma (prodolzhenie)," *Kievlianin* 221 (1881); A. E. Koniuchenko, "K voprosu o perekhode iudeev v pravoslavie v dorevoliutsionnoi rossii," *Vestnik cheliabinskogo gosudarstvennogo universiteta* 2012 no. 16 (270) *Istoriia. vyp.* 51: 96–97nn27–32. The author details six cases of alleged intimidation, abduction, or murder of apostates that were investigated by the governor-general's office of the southwest region (Kiev, Volynia, Podolia) between 1870 and 1892. One of the cases is the Garun murder; the other five involve female converts; of the three women who were allegedly abducted or murdered, all had converted to marry Christians, two of whom were described as peasants. According to Koniuchenko (97n31), the archival file of the Garun case from the governor-general's office of the southwest is TsDIAK f. 442, op. 521, d. 53 (1879).

43. "Sudebnaia khronika: zhertva evreiskago fanatizma," *Kievlianin* 6 (1889).

44. Eugene M. Avrutin, *Jews and the Imperial State: Identification Politics in Tsarist Russia* (Ithaca, NY: Cornell University Press, 2010).

45. YIVO RG 46, Box II:42, l. 1–10b., Conversion of Jewess Sora Efraimova Goldshteinova, Grodno 1862.

46. Ibid., Box I:12, Conversion of Jewess Malka Leibovna Vulfovichovna Kuks, May 7, 1864–February 24, 1865.

47. Ibid., Box III:88, ll. 1, 2–20b., Conversion of Jewess Sora Senderovna Arliukova, 1866.

48. Ibid., Box III:58, Conversion of Jewess Kheina Etka Ioselevna Zhimanskaia, 1870; ibid., Box II:27, l. 4, Conversion of Jewess Malka Mendeliovna Lin, 1871.

49. Ibid., Box III:81, l. 2, Mira Beker's conversion petition to Archbishop Donat, October 21, 1892. On the abusive stepparent trope in female conversion narratives, see Freeze, "When Chava Left Home."

50. YIVO RG 46, Box III:56, Conversion of Jewess Masha Teitelbaum, 1899. In her conversion petition, Masha asked for a quick baptism—"the sooner the better since they [my family] are looking for me" (l. 3, Conversion petition, December 4, 1898).

51. Ibid., Box III:76, ll. 7–70b., 10.

52. Ibid., l. 22, Petition of Vilna townswoman Chaia-Basia Samsonova Gershenovicheva to Tsar Alexander II. Mira Beker, a seventeen-year-old girl who was training for conversion in Vilna's Mariinskii Convent, left the convent at the behest of her mother who had asked her to return home (ibid., Box III:81, l. 4, Petition of Vilna townswoman Mira Beker to convert, 1892).

53. Ibid., ll. 26–260b., 28.

54. TsDIAK f. 127, op. 1047, ed. khr. 324, l. 6, Conversion of the Jewish widow of Pavel Fried, following the conversion of her three children after their father's death, 1894 [CAHJP HM2 9683.2].

55. For an example of an interfaith gathering at a police station as a local Jew affirmed her desire to convert and both Jewish and Christian clerics notarized her statement, see YIVO RG 46, Box I:10, l. 8. For a case of Jewish communal authorities confirming a neophyte's registration and residential permit, see ibid., Box I:16, l. 4, Reply of Botskov Kahal to Bel'sk zemstvo court.

56. For example, the Bialystok crown rabbi Markus was documented as having affirmed the Jewess Roshka Shmulovna Slovatitskaia's voluntary desire to convert to Russian Orthodoxy in 1870. See ibid., Box II:34, ll. 1–6. Likewise, in 1875 the Vilna Jewish community provided the requisite evidence of Ester Anglin's registration in the community and handed over her passport so that she and her baby son could be baptized in St. Petersburg with the help of the Mariinsko-Sergievskii Shelter (DAmK f. 253, op. 1, d. 3, Conversion of Jewess Ester Anglin with her son, 1875–1877).

57. DAKO f. 1, op. 140, d. 858, ll. 25–270b., esp. 27–270b., Petition of Jews to allow them temporary residence in Kiev in order to convert to Orthodoxy, 1904 [CAHJP HM2 9424.3].

58. LVIA f. 381, op. 1, d. 1978, Communication of the St. Petersburg Provincial Administration regarding the Jew Benedikt Rybakovskii, a convert to Orthodoxy, 1823 [CAHJP HM3 447.13].

59. "Rukopolozhenie vo sviashchenniki iz evreev," *Strannik* 1 (1876): 184–85.

60. YIVO RG 46, Box I:11, esp. l. 80b., Regarding the conversion of the Jewish prisoner Zakharia Stein to Orthodoxy, November–December 1871.

61. *PSZ* II, vol. 36:37,709, no. 6 (December 4, 1861), Ukase on the order of preparation for non-Christians converting to Orthodoxy.

62. GARF f. 1165, op. 1, ed. xr. 338, ll. 1–20b., Third Section of the Tsar's Special Chancellery in Communication with the St. Petersburg Chief of Police and Synod Chief Procurator about satisfying the request of the Jew Moisei Simkin, expert dyer, to allow him to convert to Orthodoxy, December 4–9, 1816 [CAHJP HM2 9443.10].

63. YIVO RG 46, Box I:12, esp. l. 9, Conversion of Jewess Malka Leibovna Vulfovichovna Kuks, May 7, 1864–February 24, 1865.

64. Ibid., Box I:10, ll. 9, 14–15, Conversion of Jewess Sheina Leibovna Dlugolenskaia, 1872.

65. According to the 1862 law raising the legal age of independent conversion to fourteen, neophytes under the age of twenty required a six-month course of conversion study before baptism. For an adult, conversion training could be as short as forty days.

66. For a comparative example among natives in the American West on reservations, see Thomas Biolsi, "The Birth of the Reservation: Making the Modern Individual among the Lakota," *American Ethnologist* 22, no. 1 (February 1995): 28–53.

67. YIVO RG 46, Box III:76, l. 10 (1874).

68. DAKO f. 1, op. 128, d. 638, esp. ll. 5, 7, Conversion to Lutheranism of Jews Roiter and Zalibauskaia, 1892.

69. RGIA f. 822, op. 1, d. 4561, Report of Bishop Lipskii about permission to convert the Jew Yosel Abramovich Brukman, 1830 [CAHJP HM2 7919.11]. For a similar case of a Jewish community trying to enlist a Jew undergoing conversion training, see YIVO RG 46, Box II:33, Conversion of Jew Ovseeia Yankelovich Aizenshtein, 1851–1852. In this case, Aizenshtein was not the convert's legal name. To avoid conscription and because conversion proceedings in the Catholic church were protracted, the neophyte changed his name and petitioned for baptism in an Orthodox church. As a result, when Grodno authorities asked the Jewish communal leadership for confirmation of Aizenshtein's identity and proof of estate registration, four kahal members swore that no such man was registered in their community (l. 7).

70. YIVO RG 46, Box III:47 (Berko Leibovich, 1847); Box III:85 (Aizikovich, 1842); Box II:36 (Movsha Yankel, 1854). In 1852 the Boguslav Jewish community unsuccessfully tried to forestall the conversion of Itsko Pshenichnikov by arguing that he was on a communal recruit list. See GAKO f. 2, op. 1, d. 37501 (1852) [CAHJP HM3 637.13].

71. TsDIAK f. 442, op. 78, d. 266, Petition of Zhitomir Jewess townswoman Ester Rosenbergova about the wrongful recruitment of her husband and brother who had expressed their desire to convert, 1845–1851.

72. "Na zakonnom osnovanii," *Kievlianin* 286 (1884). For a similar case, see

"Zatrudneniia Kievskago vladimirskago bratstva otnositel'no evreev, prinimaiushchikh khristianstvo," *Kievlianin* 225 (1883).

73. Paul W. Werth, "Empire, Religious Freedom, and the Legal Regulation of 'Mixed' Marriages in Russia," *Journal of Modern History* 80, no. 2 (June 2008): 296–331.

74. On the Rabbinic Commission, see ChaeRan Freeze, *Jewish Marriage and Divorce in Imperial Russia* (Hanover, NH: University Press of New England, 2002).

75. RGIA f. 821, op. 8, d. 196 [CAHJP HM2 7774.4].

76. In the case of the conversion of Shmuil Girshovich Reikhstat in 1835, the Belits Jewish community (Grodno Province) was asked to confirm the neophyte's registration and affirm his good behavior. The kahal attested to the eighteen-year-old's clean criminal record and good behavior, which was important documentary evidence that he would pursue his stated desire of enrolling in gymnasium. Reikhstat was literate in many languages and had a strong educational record. See YIVO RG 46, Box II:37, l. 14, Belits kahal letter to provincial and ecclesiastic authorities, June 18, 1835. In the case of the adolescent convert Beniamin Leskes from the Snipiskii Jewish community, a letter cosigned by six Jewish merchants in Vilna confirmed his excellent behavior and ability to serve as a role model. See ibid., Box III:48, l. 5. In addition to that letter, there were two other Jewish testimonies in Leskes's record—confirmation by the Snipiskii kahal of his registration as of the ninth revision, and testimony from the kahal as to his exemption from conscription (ll. 3–4).

77. Ibid., Box II:34, l. 9.

78. Ibid., Box III:65, l. 5–50b., Conversion of Vilna Jewish townsman Solomon Isaakov Vankopp, 1870–1871.

79. *Ulozhenie o nakazaniiakh ugolovnykh i ispravitel'nykh* (St. Petersburg, 1866), articles 184, 185.

80. LVIA f. 605, op. 4. This inventory list includes 62 conversion files on Jews, encompassing 136 neophytes who started conversion training.

81. YIVO RG 46, Box II:38, Conversion of Jewess Sora Abramova Leibova Ovsee-vichova, Grodno, 1845–1849.

82. LVIA f. 822, op. 1, d. 4689, Report from Minsk Consistory, Prelate Rava, permitting the conversion of the Jewess Sheina Freida Meier, daughter of Gordon and wife of Kevel, August 1830 [CAHJP HM2 7920.4].

83. YIVO RG 46, Box I:13, Return to Judaism of veteran Nikolai Tiskevich, 1840.

84. Nicholas B. Breyfogle, "The Religious World of Russian Sabbatarians (*Subbotniks*)," in *Holy Dissent: Jewish and Christian Mystics in Eastern Europe*, ed. Glenn Dynner (Detroit: Wayne State University Press, 2011), 359–92; John Doyle Klier, *Russia Gathers Her Jews: The Origins of the "Jewish Question" in Russia, 1772–1825* (Dekalb: Northern Illinois University Press, 1986), 25.

85. DAVO f. 361, op. 1, d. 79, Ukase of the Volynian provincial administration regarding the Third Section's indictment of over nine Jews for seducing two Roman Catholic girls to Judaism who had been servants in Jewish homes, 1827 [CAHJP HM2

9637.5]. On this case, also see LVIA f. 377, op. 1, d. 126, Jew from Vidzy asks for justice for the Jew Liun who is in prison for seducing two women to Judaism from Catholicism, 1823 [CAHJP HM2 9724.6].

86. GARF f. 1165, op. 1, ed. xr. 338, Third Section's communication with Petersburg Chief of Police and Synod Head Procurator about satisfying the request of the Jew Moisei Simkin, expert dyer, to allow him to convert to Orthodoxy, December 4–9, 1816 [CAHJP HM2 9443.10].

87. LVIA f. 380, op. 83, d. 311, l. 3–30b., Request of Jewess Mera Rubinovna Zandmanova regarding her husband's intention to convert to Christianity, 1843 [CAHJP HM3 429.13].

88. GARF f. 109, I eksp., 1845 g., d. 131, l. 7 [CAHJP RU 607]. For Blank's conversion record, see DAZhO f. 1, op. 10, d. 1794 [CAHJP RU 607].

89. Agursky, "Conversions of Jews," 70. Agursky cites the acclaimed Yiddish writer Mendele Mokher Seforim's treatment of this in his novel *Dos vintschfingerl* (The Wishing Ring).

90. Escaping an arranged marriage was one of the factors underlying Deborah Lewkowicz's conversion during a spate of Jewish female adolescent conversions in late nineteenth-century Austrian Galicia. See Rachel Manekin, "The Lost Generation: Education and Female Conversion in *Fin-de-Siècle* Kraków," *Polin* 18 (2005): 189–219.

91. YIVO RG 46, Box IV:92, l. 16–160b., "Ob okreshchenii evreia Leiby Mordukhovicha Gol'dberga (1870)."

92. On the Synod's attitude toward Jewish divorce and *agunot*, see Freeze, *Jewish Marriage and Divorce*, 188, 237–38, 267. On the problem of the Synod's involvement in dissolving mixed marriage and the Jewish spouse's need for a rabbinic divorce, see M. Sh., "K voprosu o razvode mezhdu suprugami-evreiami pri perekhoda odnogo iz nikh v pravoslavie," *Voskhod* 4 (1892): 1–11. In contrast to the Russian state's casual and inconsistent attention to the problem of *agunot* as it related to male conversion, the Austrian empire only allowed a convert to remarry once his previous marriage was dissolved according to Jewish law. See Nancy Sinkoff, "The Maskil, the Convert, and the *Agunah*: Joseph Perl as a Historian of Jewish Divorce Law," *AJS Review* 27, no. 2 (2003): 292. The Catholic Church's recognition of Jewish marriage according to Old Testament criteria and sensitivity to the problem of *agunot* can also be seen in prerevolutionary France and early modern Germany. See Elisheva Carlebach, *Divided Souls: Converts from Judaism in Germany, 1500–1750* (New Haven, CT: Yale University Press, 2001), 138–40.

93. If Jews wanted to hold runaway wives accountable, they turned to the criminal courts. For example, in 1811 a Jewish male petitioned the Volynian Consistory to start a legal case against a female relative, Lea Abramovicha, who ran away from her Jewish husband, stole some of his personal items, and converted to Orthodoxy (DAZhO f. 1, op. 3, d. 1012).

94. Freeze, "When Chava Left Home," 162.

95. RGIA f. 821, op. 8, d. 196, l. 1–10b. [CAHJP HM2 7774.4].

96. Ibid., l. 3–30b., Mogilev Roman Catholic Archdiocese Bishop Stanevskii to the MVD, Department of Foreign Confessions, August 17, 1869.

97. Ibid., ll. 11–12.

98. *SZ* (1857 ed.), vol. XI, p. 80. For evidence of these laws in practice, see YIVO RG 46, Box I:2 (1840–1842), which involves a Jewish wife who declared her wish to stay married to her converted husband and claimed she was interested in converting in the future. See ibid., Box III:76 (1874) for a case where a young wife converted and the religious consistory asked civil authorities to track down the Jewish husband and inquire whether he wanted to stay married to his converted wife or divorce her and whether he would promise not to threaten her or her children if they wished to live with the mother (ll. 31–32). In this case, the husband declared he did not want to stay married to his converted wife (l. 37).

99. RGIA f. 821, op. 8, d. 196, l. 7–70b. [CAHJP HM2 7774.4].

100. In a second round of communication between Bishop Stanevskii and the MVD, Stanevskii reiterated that Mary did not petition for permission to remarry but rather only for permission to obtain an exit visa and stay abroad (l. 7).

101. RGIA f. 821, op. 8, d. 350, ll. 1–2, Regarding the children of the bugler Beniaminovich, who were left without a mother due to marital dissolution [CAHJP HM2 7999.5].

102. Ibid., l. 6.

103. Ibid., l. 7–70b.

104. DAKO f. 1, op. 295, d. 29182, l. 2, Senate decree regarding rules for Jews converting to Christianity, 1842; DAOO f. 1, op. 2, d. 80, ll. 3–4, Permission for Jewish family Gershkovich, agriculturists, to convert to Orthodoxy, 1841 [CAHJP HM2 9025.2]. A case that came before the Vilna provincial administration in 1830 suggests that legal practice varied before the 1842 Senate decree. After the convert from Judaism to Catholicism Konstantin Lovitskii relapsed to Judaism, the local court in Braslav (Kovno Province) was instructed to find his son and daughters and take them out of the Jewish mother's custody and into the state's charge. See LVIA f. 604, op. 1, d. 2704, ll. 3–6, Conversion from one faith to another, 1830. Five years later, the son still had not been found and there was no information about the whereabouts of the daughters (ll. 10, 12–130b.).

105. DAVO f. 361, op. 1, d. 66, l. 505–5050b., State Council Decree regarding Laws for mixed marriages between Evangelicals and Jews or Muslims, 1826 [CAHJP HM2 9637.4].

106. *PSZ* II, vol. XXXVI, no. 37,709 (January 22, 1862), as quoted in V. O. Levanda, *Polnyi khronologicheskii sbornik zakonov i polozhenii, kasaiushchikhsia evreev, ot ulozheniia Tsaria Alekseia Mikhailovicha do nastoiashchago vremeni, ot 1649–1873* (St. Petersburg, 1874), 973n893.

107. For example LVIA f. 378, 1827 g., d. 203, l. 12–120b [CAHJP HM2 9772.20].

108. YIVO RG 46, Box III:47, l. 1.

109. Ibid., ll. 5, 6–70b.

110. DAmK f. 253, op. 1, d. 2.

111. Nirenberg, *Communities of Violence*, 127.

Chapter 5

1. YIVO RG 46, Box I:18, l. 4–40b., Seduction of retired private Ivan Bondarev from Orthodoxy to Judaism, Bialystok, October 8, 1872–March 31, 1878.

2. Ibid., ll. 5–50b., 8–90b.

3. *Ulozhenie o nakazaniiakh ugolovnykh i ispravitel'nykh* (St. Petersburg, 1866), articles 184, 185.

4. Eugene M. Avrutin, "Returning to Judaism after the 1905 Law on Religious Freedom in Tsarist Russia" *Slavic Review* 65, no. 1 (Spring 2006): 102. To put these numbers in perspective, in 1904, 874 Jews converted to Orthodoxy; in 1913, 1,198 converted, and 35 converts from Judaism legally "deviated" from Orthodoxy. See *Vsepoddanneishii otchet ober-prokurora Sv. Sinoda za . . . god* (St. Petersburg) for the years 1904 and 1913, published, respectively, in 1909 and 1915.

5. On the history of freedom of conscience debates, see Paul W. Werth, "The Emergence of 'Freedom of Conscience' in Imperial Russia," *Kritika* 13, no. 3 (2012): 585–610; Paul W. Werth, *The Tsar's Foreign Faiths: Toleration and the Fate of Religious Freedom in Imperial Russia* (Oxford: Oxford University Press, 2014), 188–201. Werth analyzes a variety of historical actors, aside from apostates, who started to talk about freedom of conscience in the 1860s.

6. GARF f. 109, op. 3, d. 2317, Conversion of the Jews for the benefit of the empire by gradually attracting them to the Christian faith and then through merging and finally completely mixing them with other subjects [CAHJP HMF 815]. Archivists roughly date this memorandum to the 1820s–1830s.

7. Historian D. Z. Feldman found the Catholic Church's Inquisition tribunals an appropriate analogy when analyzing early modern Russia's treatment of Judaizers. In Feldman's analysis of the 1738–1740 case of the Orthodox apostate to Judaism Alexander Voznitsyn (retired naval lieutenant-captain) and his Jewish seducer, Borukh Leibov (tax farmer from Smolensk), which he calls Russia's last "inquisition" trial, the Senate sentenced the two to burning at the stake and ordered the burning of some of the Jewish religious articles (*talit, tefilin*) recovered in the case. Following the trial, the state decided to take measures to protect the borderlands from Jewish penetration, especially from Judaizing, and it exiled its Jewish population abroad. See D. Z. Feldman, "Poslednii inkvizitsionnyi koster v Rossii: Moskovskoe sledstvie po delu Aleksandra Voznitsyna i Borukha Leibova 1738–1740 gg." *Paralleli* no. 6–7 (2005): 23–24, 31.

8. Olga Litvak, *Conscription and the Search for Modern Russian Jewry* (Bloomington: Indiana University Press, 2006), 63–72, 191.

9. On the history and setting of Maimon's painting, see Musya Glants, "Poteriana i naidena v Amerike: Kartina Moiseia Maimona 'Marrany i inkvizitsiia v Ispanii,'" *Paralleli* no. 8–9 (2003): 131–42. On Maimon's own explanation of his work, see M. Maimon, "Istoriia odnoi kartiny," *Evreiskaia letopis'* (1923).

10. Litvak, *Conscription*, 195. On early twentieth-century Russian Jewish historiography and the paradigm of Iberian expulsion, see 187–98.

11. Yirmiyahu Yovel, *The Other Within: The Marranos: Split Identity and Emerging Modernity* (Princeton, NJ: Princeton University Press, 2009).

12. For the argument that marranos constituted Europe's "first modern Jews," see Yosef Hayim Yerushalmi, *From Spanish Court to Italian Ghetto: Isaac Cardoso, a Study in Seventeenth-Century Marranism and Jewish Apologetics* (Seattle: University of Washington Press, 1981), 44. On marranos as anticipating the challenge of split identities to modern nation-states or centralizing states, see Yovel, *The Other Within*.

13. *SZ* (1832 ed.), vol. XIV, part 1, chap. 3, section 2, I:43.

14. For example, in the seduction case against on-leave private Rozenfrukt, the Ministry of War furnished evidence that the convert took communion at the Nikolaev Military Cathedral in 1865 and 1867. See RGIA f. 821, op. 8, d. 201, l. 2 [CAHJP HM2 8000.16].

15. *PSZ* II, vol. XXV, no. 23,905 (February 28, 1850).

16. John Klier, "State Policies and the Conversion of Jews in Imperial Russia," in *Of Religion and Empire: Missions, Conversion, and Tolerance in Tsarist Russia*, ed. Robert P. Geraci and Michael Khodarkovsky (Ithaca, NY: Cornell University Press, 2001), 92–112. On legal discrimination as a response to revolutionary politics, see Eli Weinerman, "Racism, Racial Prejudice, and Jews in Late Imperial Russia," *Ethnic and Racial Studies* 17 (1994): 455–56. On discriminatory legislation in the imperial army against Jews after the 1905 revolution, see Joshua A. Sanborn, *Drafting the Russian Nation: Military Conscription, Total War, and Mass Politics, 1905–1925* (Dekalb: Northern Illinois University Press, 2003), chap. 3.

17. Eugene M. Avrutin, "Racial Categories and the Politics of (Jewish) Difference in Late Imperial Russia," *Kritika* 8, no. 1 (Winter 2007): 13–40; Weinerman, "Racism"; Marina Mogil'ner, "Evreiskaia antropologiia v kontekste evropeiskikh rasovykh issledovanii," in *Istoriia i kultura rossiiskogo i vostochnoevropeiskogo evreistva*, ed. Oleg Budnitskii (Moscow: Dom evreiskoi knigi, 2004), 116–37. Avrutin argues that racial categories and ideologies influenced the creation and maintenance of social boundaries and hierarchies, even if exclusionary racism did not rear its head politically.

18. Weinerman, "Racism," 456, 463.

19. Avrutin, "Racial Categories."

20. Robert Crews, "Empire and the Confessional State: Islam and Religious Politics in Nineteenth-Century Russia," *American Historical Review* 108, no. 1 (February 2003): 50–83. Crews notes that especially in the wake of the French Revolution, the

Russian state protected and supported imperial confessions to protect its subjects from Jacobinism.

21. See Israel Halpern, "The Jews of Eastern Europe: From Ancient Times until the Partitions of Poland," in *The Jews*, ed. Louis Finkelstein (New York: Schocken, 1970), 297.

22. For a sample of such cases of Christian converts to Judaism and the discovery of "Judaizing" in the empire, see DAVO f. 361, op. 1, d. 79 (1827) [CAHJP HM2 9637.5]; LVIA f. 377, op. 1, d. 126 (1823) [CAHJP HM2 9724.6]; TsDIAK f. 442, op. 152, d. 194a (1843–54) [CAHJP HM2 9484.5]: Lipovets Jews, led by a rabbi, supposedly seduced a Christian to convert, circumcised him, and gave him the name and identity papers of a deceased Jew; RGIA f. 797, op. 2, dd. 5492, 8876, 8886, 8926, 8982, 9032; RGIA f. 822, op. 1, d. 2198 (1818); TsGIA-SPb f. 19, op. 81, d. 4 (1889–1890). For a case of Judaizing that did not involve actual Jews, see RGIA f. 821, op. 8, d. 209, ll. 31–45, 117–190b., 129–1290b., 136–39. In this case, the Orthodox couple Georgii and Akulina Durov from Omsk were found to have Judaized in 1898 due to their own "misunderstanding" of the Bible, imputing sole authority to the Old Testament. For their deviation and causing the apostasy of their children, the couple were sentenced to exile and deprivation of all rights and property. With the liberalization of the statute governing religious crimes in 1905, the wife, who was still alive, was permitted to relocate to her hometown and rejoin her former legal estate.

23. John Doyle Klier, *Russia Gathers Her Jews: The Origins of the "Jewish Question" in Russia, 1772–1825* (Dekalb: Northern Illinois University Press, 1986), 25.

24. *SZ* (1832 ed.), vol. XIV, part 1, chap. 3, section 2, I:43. On imperial laws regulating Jewish-Christian relations, see Avrutin, "Returning to Judaism."

25. Meyer Posnanskii, a twenty-two-year-old Jew from Congress Poland who entered the imperial army in 1854, expressed his desire to convert in 1862 but avoided conversion training. He was subsequently transferred from a unit stationed in Grodno to one in Mogilev, where, far from the Grodno Jews who probably influenced him and "seduced him from salvific conversion," he would be better positioned, so the ecclesiastic authorities thought, to act on his wish to convert. YIVO RG 46, Box II:31, l. 3, Letter from the Grodno Religious Superintendant to the Vilna Ecclesiastic Consistory, February 15, 1864.

26. The other legal term for apostasy often employed was *otpadenie* (falling away, or defection). Nonlegal terms used to connote intentions to apostatize or attempts by Jews to seduce converts included *otvlech'* (to distract, divert) and *vozvrashchenie* (return). In 1830 the Vilna provincial administration fired two kahal leaders and a rabbi in Kovno Province after a former community member relapsed to Judaism from Catholicism, ostensibly in collusion with local Jews. The provincial administration resolved to inform other provincial administrators to prevent these men from ever holding communal office again. See LVIA f. 604, op. 1, d. 2704, Conversion from one faith to another, 1830 [CAHJP HM3 285.14].

27. Communion in Russia from the sixteenth century was commonly taken only yearly, since strict laws forbade Orthodox believers from taking communion "unworthily." Fear of punishment combined with church architecture that kept the liturgy and symbols of the Eucharist away from the congregation prevented worshipers from connecting with the rite and freely observing it. See Nadieszda Kizenko, *A Prodigal Saint: Father John of Kronstadt and the Russian People* (University Park: Pennsylvania State University Press, 2000), 10.

28. YIVO RG 46, Box I:13, Return to Judaism of retired soldier Nikolai Tiskevich, 1840.

29. Yohanan Petrovsky-Shtern, *Jews in the Russian Army, 1827–1917: Drafted into Modernity* (Cambridge: Cambridge University Press, 2009), 113–20.

30. On religious protections for adult Jewish soldiers, see ibid., 65–72. For two cases of active soldiers relapsing in the 1860s not discussed in this chapter, see TsGIA-SPb f. 19, op. 51, d. 14; RGIA f. 821, op. 8, d. 192 (1866) [CAHJP HM2 8000.19].

31. RGAVMF f. 33, op. 1, d. 1042, l. 100, Jewish cantonists renouncing Orthodoxy, December 12, 1855–June 3, 1856 [CAHJP HM2 8281.4].

32. Ibid., ll. 147ob.–48.

33. Ibid., l. 148–148ob.

34. Ibid., ll. 147–48ob.

35. Ibid., l. 157.

36. Ibid., l. 554–554ob.

37. RGAVMF f. 283, op. 3, d. 3456, ll. 1–7ob., Cantonists who have left Orthodoxy, 1855–1859 [CAHJP HM2 8282.35].

38. RGIA f. 821, op. 8, d. 197, l. 10ob., Relapsed former cantonists from Vologda [CAHJP HM2 7774.3].

39. Ibid., l. 130ob.

40. RGAVMF f. 283, op. 3, d. 4141, Relapse of convert from Judaism, seaman Mikhael Beilin, 1876–1877 [CAHJP HM2 8282.41]. For more on Beilin, see TsGIA-SPb f. 487, op. 1, d. 1191, Guilt of retired seaman Beilin for joining Judaism from Christianity. For a similar case, that of Moisei Volondarskii, see RGIA f. 821, op. 8, d. 209, l. 2–20ob., Volondarskii letter to the tsar, October 1896 [CAHJP HM2 7777.5]; Petrovsky-Shtern, *Jews in the Russian Army*, 122.

41. Petrovsky-Shtern, *Jews in the Russian Army*, 120–23.

42. Sanborn, *Drafting the Russian Nation.* The traditional belief in conversion to the state religion as a sign of political loyalty held sway among imperial officials until after the 1905 revolution, when nationality became a determining factor in political loyalty (69).

43. RGIA f. 821, op. 8, d. 198 [CAHJP HM2 7774.1].

44. The Department of Military Settlements informed the Kiev military governor in November 1827 of the tsar's interest in cantonist converts and that successes in cantonist conversions should be reported monthly. See TsDIAK f. 533, op. 5, d. 172, ll. 1–3,

Jewish cantonist recruits, 1827 [CAHJP HM2 9450.15]. In May 1828 the commander of the Kiev Cantonist Battalion reported that of his 287 Jewish cantonists, 8 had converted to Orthodoxy (l. 5).

45. RGIA f. 821, op. 8, d. 198, l. 1.

46. Ibid., l. 20b.

47. Without documentary evidence on the Jewish side of the reception of relapsed converts by Jews, it is hard to know whether there were significant consequences for baptized Jews returning to Jewish society. Literature on medieval and early modern conversions and repentant apostates shows that relapsed converts had to undergo re-Judaizing (alternatively dubbed "de-Christianizing") folk rituals as an act of public penitence in order to regain acceptance in the Jewish community. See Edward Fram, "Perception and Reception of Repentant Apostates in Medieval Ashkenaz and Pre-modern Poland," *AJS Review* 21, no. 2 (1996). 311, 316; Elisheva Carlebach, "'Ich will dich nach Holland schicken . . .': Amsterdam and the Reversion to Judaism of German-Jewish Converts," in *Secret Conversions to Judaism in Early Modern Europe*, ed. Martin Mulsow and Richard H. Popkin (Leiden: Brill, 2004), 51–70; Yosef Hayim Yerushalmi, "The Inquisition and the Jews of France in the Time of Bernard Gui," *Harvard Theological Review* 63 (1970): 318–19, 363–64.

48. YIVO RG 46, Box I:18, ll. 5–60b., 8–90b., 12.

49. DAOO f. 37, op. 1, d. 2709, Convert from Orthodoxy to Judaism retired officer Nikolai Alekseev, from Kherson Province [CAHJP HM2 9026.12].

50. RGIA f. 821, op. 8, d. 209, ll. 4–170b., 28–280b.

51. For the cases of Ivan Spiegal, Shmuil Rozenfrukt, and Meier Golshtein, see ibid., d. 200 [CAHJP HM2 8000.18], d. 201 [CAHJP HM2 8000.16], and d. 202 [CAHJP HM2 8000.17]; Petrovsky-Shtern, *Jews in the Russian Army*, 121–22.

52. "Delo o vozvrashchenii kreshchennago evreia v iudeistvo (iz sudebnoi khroniki)," *Kievlianin* 131 (1877), which published the court record of the "Kievskaia palata ugolovnago i grazhdanskago suda, VII."

53. For other cases of Jews who served in the Polish army and desired to convert to Catholicism, see RGIA f. 797, op. 4, d. 17835, "O evreev sluzhivshikh v pol'skoi armii i zhelaiushikh priniat' rimskokatolichesky ispovedanii (1833)."

54. Ibid., f. 822, op. 1, d. 902, ll. 1–3, Complaint of Vilna Jews, 1803–1804 [CAHJP HM2 7919.8].

55. Ibid., l. 1570b.

56. It appears that the mother also converted to Catholicism, even though the father initially absconded with the boys to convert them despite her protests.

57. RGIA f. 822, op. 1, d. 902, ll. 1570b–580b.

58. Ibid., l. 160–1600b.

59. Ibid., d. 589, Ukase about not attracting Jews to Catholicism, 1801.

60. LVIA f. 604, op. 1, d. 2703, Female relapse, 1830 [CAHJP HM3 285.13].

61. Ibid., d. 2704, Conversion from one faith to another, 1830 [CAHJP HM3 285.14].

62. Ibid. f. 378 B/S, 1859 g., d. 727, ll. 20b–3, Grodno Provincial Administration to governor-general of Vilna, Grodno, and Kovno, May 12, 1859 [CAHJP HM3 234.18].

63. Ibid., ll. 30b–5.

64. For example, see RGIA f. 797, op. 55, d. 260, Regarding a female petitioner.

65. For Kiev, see TsDIAK f. 127, op. 10, 28, 41, 68, 71, 73, 75, 84, 94, 110, 113, 126, 200, 204, 212, 214, 216, 219, 221, 222, 223, 231, 240, 244, 262, 290, 339, 382, 413, 450, 635, 636, 638, 641. For Volynia, see DAZhO f. 1, op. 1–3.

66. RGIA f. 797, op. 19, dd. 43380, 43386 (1849).

67. TsDIAK f. 127, op. 1047, dd. 234, 401, 446, 492, 502, 547, 605, 690a, 900, 918, 921, 1045, 1280. Delo 68 records the seduction of a peasant, Anton Tselomudry, to Judaism in 1893; delo 764, the petition of a Jewish father requesting that his converted daughter be returned to his custody; delo 864, the 1896 complaint of a convert from Judaism, Olga Shender, that her male relative Yosi Shender was attempting to seduce her back to Judaism.

68. RGIA f. 797, op. 55, d. 260, "Po vsepoddanneishemu prosheniiu meshchanki Eleny Kirichenko o dozvolenii ei priniavshei sv. kreshchenie vozvratitsia v iudeistvo (1885–1886)"; DAOO f. 37, op. 1, d. 3228, Jewish relapsed convert from Orthodoxy, Serafima Lev, formerly Khaia, 1881 [CAHJP HM2 9026.16].

69. RGIA f. 821, op. 8, d. 209 [CAHJP HM2 7777.5]: Zhidkov (l. 70–700b), Korabel'nikov (ll. 61–650b.), Kolesnikova (ll. 77–770b., 86), Ignat'ev (l. 79–790b.), Olovenkova (ll. 81–810b., 88).

70. Ibid., l. 70–700b.

71. Ibid., ll. 81–810b., 88.

72. Ibid., ll. 77–770b., 86. According to the MVD, the woman in question, Koles-nikova, was a Karaite.

73. PSZ III, vol. XXV, no. 26,126 (April 17, 1905).

74. Paul W. Werth, "The Limits of Religious Ascription: Baptized Tatars and the Revision of 'Apostasy,' 1840s–1905," Russian Review 59, no. 4 (October 2000): 507. Imperial toleration rested on the belief that religion was a component of ethnic or national identity.

75. RGIA f. 821, op. 8, d. 209, l. 150–1500b. [CAHJP HM2 7777.5].

76. Avrutin, "Returning to Judaism."

77. DAKO f. 1, op. 114, d. 220, Conversions from Orthodoxy to Judaism, 1906–1908. For the case of the Orthodox man's desire to convert to Judaism, see ll. 32–40.

78. Ibid., ll. 106–1060b. (Sergei Il'ich Titinger), 122–1220b. (Aleksei Antonov Aizen-berg, né Movsha Shlimovich Kron).

79. Ibid., l. 82–820b.

80. The MVD instituted official notation of the Jewish origins of converts in discussions between 1900 and 1902. The rule was repealed in 1906. For a fuller discussion

of the terms *evrei-khristian* (Jewish-Christian) and *iz evreev* (of the Jews), see Avrutin, "Returning to Judaism," 100, 109.

81. DAKO f. 1, op. 114, d. 220, ll. 102–15. Interestingly, all of the Jewish witnesses in the file wrote their names in Russian, except for one, who signed his name in Yiddish as well.

82. Ibid., ll. 14–19.

83. RGIA f. 821, op. 8, d. 209, l. 106–1060b.

84. DAKO f. 1, op. 114, d. 220, ll. 41–70.

85. YIVO RG 46, Box III:89, l. 3–30b., Communication of the Vilna governor regarding the desire of the townsman Konstantin Uranovskii to return to Judaism, 1908.

86. Klier, *Imperial Russia's Jewish Question*, 417–49, esp. 436–38.

87. For more on the theory and practice of race in imperial Russia, see Chia Yin Hse, "A Tale of Two Railroads: 'Yellow Labor,' Agrarian Colonization, and the Making of Russianness at the Far Eastern Frontier, 1890s–1910s," *Ab Imperio* 3 (2006): 217–53.

88. Statistical estimates of conversion coverage are drawn from the index of periodical and published literature on the Jews in the Russian-language press during this period: *Sistematicheskii ukazatel' literatury o evreiakh na russkom iazyke* (St. Petersburg, 1892).

89. On this new accusation of ritual murder, see Ellie R. Schainker, "On Faith and Fanaticism: Converts from Judaism and the Limits of Toleration in Late Imperial Russia," *Kritika* (forthcoming, 2016).

90. Theodore R. Weeks, *Nation and State in Late Imperial Russia: Nationalism and Russification on the Western Frontier, 1863–1914* (Dekalb: Northern Illinois University Press, 1996); Mikhail Dolbilov, "Russification and the Bureaucratic Mind in the Russian Empire's Northwestern Region in the 1860s," *Kritika* 5, no. 2 (Spring 2004): 245–71; Darius Staliunas, "Did the Government Seek to Russify Lithuanians and Poles in the Northwest Region after the Uprising of 1863–64?" *Kritika* 5, no. 2 (Spring 2004): 273–89; Andreas Kappeler, "The Ambiguities of Russification," *Kritika* 5, no. 2 (Spring 2004): 291–97; Darius Staliunas, *Making Russians: Meaning and Practice of Russification in Lithuania and Belarus after 1863* (Amsterdam: Rodopi, 2007), 3–18.

91. Eugene M. Avrutin, *Jews and the Imperial State: Identification Politics in Tsarist Russia* (Ithaca, NY: Cornell University Press, 2010), 126–27.

92. Avrutin, "Racial Categories," 33.

93. Ibid., 34.

94. Ibid., 16.

95. GARF f. 102, op. 76a, d. 1987, Changing surnames of Jews who have been baptized, 1901 [CAHJP HM3 264.3]. According to this file, from 1897 to 1901 eleven to fourteen converts from Judaism petitioned for a surname change.

96. Avrutin, *Jews and the Imperial State*, 117, 120n13.

97. Sanborn, *Drafting the Russian Nation*, chap. 3. Sanborn highlights the army's

fear of Jewish subversive politics, lack of patriotism, and perceived sympathy for Germans.

98. Avrutin, "Racial Categories."

99. Charles Steinwedel, "To Make a Difference: The Category of Ethnicity in Late Imperial Russian Politics, 1861–1917," in *Russian Modernity: Politics, Knowledge, Practices*, ed. David L. Hoffmann and Yanni Kotsonis (New York: St. Martin's Press, 2000), 67–86; Charles Steinwedel, "Making Social Groups, One Person at a Time: The Identification of Individuals by Estate, Religious Confession, and Ethnicity in Late Imperial Russia," in *Documenting Individual Identity: The Development of State Practices in the Modern World*, ed. Jane Caplan and John Torpey, 67–82 (Princeton, NJ: Princeton University Press, 2001), 67–82.

100. Avrutin, "Racial Categories," 35.

101. This is part of Hans Rogger's argument why there was no state mission to Jews in the post-reform period; the state lacked a coherent nation-building plan that rested on Russian Orthodoxy as the unifying thread of imperial belonging, and Jewishness was increasingly seen as something that transcended religion. See Hans Rogger, *Jewish Policies and Right-Wing Politics in Imperial Russia* (Berkeley: University of California Press, 1986), 36–39.

102. For positive coverage of "sincere" converts, see Nikolai Kuznetskii, "Zamechatel'noe obrashchenie odnogo evreia v khristianstvo," *Strannik* 7 (1862): 339–48; Nikolai Kuznetskii, "Zamechatel'noe obrashchenie odnogo evreia, umiravshago ot kholery," *Strannik* 7 (1862): 349–59; "Rukopolozhenie vo sviashchenniki iz evreev," *Strannik* 1 (1876): 184–85; O. Brin, "Vospominaniia novokreshchennago evreia," *Strannik* 7 (1877): 73–79; Priest Viktor Il'iashevich, "Iz Umanskago uezda," *Kievskie eparkhial'nye vedomosti* 6 (March 30, 1882); "Kreshchenie evreiskago semeistva," *Khersonskie eparkhial'nye vedomosti* 14 (1887).

103. "Po evreiskomu voprosu," *Novoe vremia* 4498 (1888); "Po povodu perekhoda evreev v pravoslavie," *Novorossiiskii telegraf* 4184 (September 10, 1888).

104. "Evrei stali eksploatirovat' khristianskuiu religiiu," *Novorossiiskii telegraf* 4157 (August 12, 1888); "Po povodu perekhoda evreev v pravoslavie," *Novorossiiskii telegraf* 4200 (September 26, 1888); "O perekhode evreev v pravoslavie," *Novorossiiskii telegraf* 4588 (November 7, 1888).

105. The governor-general of New Russia, A. G. Stroganov, for example, threatened to shut down *Razsvet* in 1860 after the editor, Osip Rabinovich, carried reports and editorials on the case of a young Jewish girl, Tsipa Mendak, nine, who was abducted in Lithuania and converted to Catholicism without her parents' consent. To keep his paper, Rabinovich could only reprint news on the Mendak case published in the non-Jewish press, and, in general, had to avoid coverage of the church. See Alexander Orbach, *New Voices of Russian Jewry: A Study of the Russian-Jewish Press of Odessa in the Era of the Great Reforms, 1860–1871* (Leiden: Brill, 1980), 41–42.

106. "Delo Aizenberga," *Evreiskaia biblioteka* 8 (1880): 62.

107. "Delo otstavnogo riadovogo Terenteva o sovrashchenii v iudeistvo," *Voskhod* 4 (1881): 46.

108. "Delo otstavnogo riadovogo Terenteva o sovrashchenii v iudeistvo," 45.

109. "Otpadenie ot pravoslaviia," *Sudebnaia gazeta* 17 (1885): 5–8.

110. Ibid., 6.

111. Ibid., 7.

112. Ibid., 6.

113. Ibid., 7.

114. Ibid.

115. Ibid., 8.

116. Ibid., 6.

117. Ibid., 7.

118. "Delo Aizenberga," 61.

119. Ibid., 62–63.

120. Ibid.

121. "Sudebnaia Khronika," *Nedel'naia khronika voskhoda* 7 (1883); "Obrashchenie v iudeistvo," *Russkii evrei* 7 (1883): 17–18.

122. "Sudebnaia Khronika."

123. The *Razsvet* article is quoted in *Zemshchina* 1053 (July 24, 1912), as cited in Eugene M. Avrutin, "A Legible People: Identification Politics and Jewish Accommodation in Tsarist Russia" (PhD diss., University of Michigan, 2004), 203–4.

124. For a discussion of this school of thought, typified by the nineteenth-century Russian Jewish legal scholar I. G. Orshanskii, see Avrutin, "A Legible People," chap. 6.

Chapter 6

1. A. Alekseev, *Besedy pravoslavnago Khristianina iz Evreev s novoobrashchennymi iz svoikh sobratii ob istinakh sviatoi very i zabluzhdeniiakh talmudicheskikh, s prisovokupleniem stat'i o talmude* (St. Petersburg, 1872), iii, 9.

2. Ibid.

3. On this "qualia" model of confessional boundaries and their crossing, see David Nirenberg, "The Judaism of Christian Art," in *Judaism and Christian Art: Aesthetic Anxieties from the Catacombs to Colonialism*, ed. Herbert L. Kessler and David Nirenberg (Philadelphia: University of Pennsylvania Press, 2011), 387–427.

4. Nicholas B. Breyfogle, "The Religious World of Russian Sabbatarians (*Subbotniks*)," in *Holy Dissent: Jewish and Christian Mystics in Eastern Europe*, ed. Glenn Dynner (Detroit: Wayne State University Press, 2011): 361.

5. Paweł Maciejko, *The Mixed Multitude: Jacob Frank and the Frankist Movement, 1755–1816* (Philadelphia: University of Pennsylvania Press, 2011), esp. 260. It was the lingering indeterminate status of the Frankists and the belief that they should be accorded

more of a Christian than Jewish status that partially animated Alexander I's Israelite-Christian manifesto in 1817.

6. Paul W. Werth, *The Tsar's Foreign Faiths: Toleration and the Fate of Religious Freedom in Imperial Russia* (Oxford: Oxford University Press, 2014), 103.

7. Breyfogle, "Religious World," 373.

8. Philip E. Miller, *Karaite Separatism in Nineteenth-Century Russia: Joseph Solomon Lutski's Epistle of Israel's Deliverance* (Cincinnati: Hebrew Union College Press, 1993).

9. See, for example, YIVO RG 46, Box I:14, Conversion of the Jew Khonon Dolitskii (1838) for a Mitnagid; and Box I:1, Conversion of the Jew Sheptel Moshkovich (1847–1849) for a Jew who said he did not belong to any sect. See also, LVIA f. 605, op. 2, d. 64, l. 2, The Jew Zelman Nurok who wants to convert to Orthodoxy, 1840 [CAHJP HM3 286.2].

10. Paul Werth notes that this imperial support for Jewish sects was exceptional given the state's overall reticence to arbitrate schisms within the tolerated confessions. See Werth, *The Tsar's Foreign Faiths*, 91–103, esp. 93–94. The state's acceptance of a non-orthodox sect was mainly contingent on its having a large number of adherents, which would make it difficult to suppress it, and on whether the sect supported the goals of a well-ordered state (102–3).

11. V. V. Grigorev, *Evreiskiia religioznyia sekty v Rossii* (St. Petersburg, 1847), 5.

12. For scholarship on this new Russian Jewish frontier, see Steven J. Zipperstein, *The Jews of Odessa: A Cultural History, 1794–1881* (Stanford, CA: Stanford University Press, 1985).

13. "Povestvovanie Marii Leshchinskoi o svoei zhizni i ob obrashchenii iz iudeistva v kh-vo," *Kievskie eparkhial'nye vedomosti* 25 (1879).

14. Steven J. Zipperstein, "Heresy, Apostasy and the Transformation of Joseph Rabinovich," in *Jewish Apostasy in the Modern World*, ed. Todd M. Endelman (New York: Holmes and Meier, 1987), 206.

15. Simon Dubnov analyzed all three men and their respective movements as "religious reforms," comparable to reforms in West/Central Europe that had evolved earlier in the century but never made significant inroads in Eastern Europe. See Simon R. Dubnow, *History of the Jews in Russia and Poland: From the Earliest Times until the Present Day* (Philadelphia: Jewish Publication Society of America, 1916), II:333–35.

16. Sergei I. Zhuk, *Russia's Lost Reformation: Peasants, Millennialism, and Radical Sects in Southern Russia and Ukraine, 1830–1917* (Baltimore: Johns Hopkins University Press, 2004).

17. Laura Engelstein, *Castration and the Heavenly Kingdom: A Russian Folktale* (Ithaca, NY: Cornell University Press, 1999).

18. Nicholas B. Breyfogle, *Heretics and Colonizers: Forging Russia's Empire in the South Caucasus* (Ithaca, NY: Cornell University Press, 2005).

19. Zhuk, *Russia's Lost Reformation*.

20. Heather J. Coleman, *Russian Baptists and Spiritual Revolution, 1905–1929* (Bloomington: Indiana University Press, 2005).

21. Arnol'd Semenovich Khodorovskii (A. S. Ardov), *Evrei-Evangelisty* (Moscow, 1914); Hans Brandenburg, *The Meek and the Mighty: The Emergence of the Evangelical Movement in Russia* (London: Mowbrays, 1976), 135–55.

22. Brandenburg, *Meek and the Mighty*, 64–65, 122.

23. According to Vilkovir, Gordin's Brotherhood initially attracted sixty families. See Iosif Vilkovir, *Iudaizm i ego opponenty ili golos' izrail'tianina po povodu knigi "Evrei-reformatory"* (Kherson, 1884), 1.

24. V. Portugalov, *Znamenatel'naia dvizheniia v evreistve* (St. Petersburg, 1884), 42.

25. For Gordin's biography, see Zalman Reizen, *Leksikon fun der yiddisher literatur, prese, un filologye* (Vilna: Kletskin Verlag, 1928), I:519–30.

26. Dubnow, *History of the Jews*, II:334–35.

27. Zipperstein, "Heresy, Apostasy," 218–19.

28. Kai Kjaer-Hansen, *The Herzl of Jewish Christianity: Joseph Rabinowitz and the Messianic Movement* (Edinburgh: Handel Press, 1995), 3.

29. RGIA f. 821, op. 8, d. 345, ll. 14–15, 24–24ob., The Sect of New Israelites in New Russia and Gordin's Holy Biblical Brotherhood [CAHJP HM2 7777.3]. The MVD's decision to permit this sect was based on *SZ* (1857 ed.), vol. XI, part 1, p. 1063.

30. "Dvizhenie v srede evreev k khristianstvu," *Khersonskie eparkhial'nye vedomosti* 2 (January 15, 1885).

31. RGIA f. 821, op. 8, d. 345, ll. 8–90ob.

32. Ibid., l. 9 (emphasis in the original).

33. Zipperstein, "Heresy, Apostasy," 219.

34. Ibid., l. 16–16ob.

35. Ibid., l. 17–17ob.

36. Ibid., l. 24–24ob. On religious tolerance for the empire's non-Orthodox subjects, see *SZ* (1832 ed.), vol. I, part 1, article 7, no. 44–46.

37. Zhuk, *Russia's Lost Reformation*, 359–60. The Orthodox Church's fear of Stundism was both religious and cultural. According to some vocal Orthodox clerics and laymen, Stundism threatened to destroy the Russian peasant identity by replacing Orthodox values with German (evangelical) ones and mixing Slavic ethnic culture (dress, hairstyles, church architecture) with German, Dutch, and even Jewish culture. Implicit in this religious and cultural opposition to Stundism was a religious-ethnic definition of Orthodoxy as Russian (326–28).

38. RGIA f. 821, op. 8, d. 345, l. 38–380ob.

39. Breyfogle, *Heretics and Colonizers*, 12. Many imperial officials believed Jews themselves were responsible for the Subbotnik movement.

40. Stundists also conducted readings and interpretations of the Bible in private homes, like many evangelicals, and it is possible that the ministry's ban on Russian con-

versations aimed to ensure that evangelical meetings could not include Russian peasants since virtually all were illiterate in German.

41. RGIA f. 821, op. 8, d. 345, l. 97.

42. Ibid., ll. 109–10.

43. Zhuk, *Russia's Lost Reformation*, 356. Zhuk cites RGIA f. 1405, op. 89, d. 2269, ll. 1–10b., 3–30b.

44. RGIA f. 821, op. 8, d. 345, ll. 112–112ob., 118–190b.

45. Zhuk, *Russia's Lost Reformation*, 356.

46. Based on the press entries in the *Sistematicheskii ukazatel'* and articles from four Russian Jewish newspapers the 1880s (*Voskhod, Nedel'naia khronika voskhoda, Razsvet, Russkii evrei*), about 63 percent of press coverage of "conversion" focused on the Christianizing Jewish sects.

47. RGIA f. 821, op. 8, d. 199, "O raziasnenii poltavskomu gubernatoru voprosa o sushchestvovanii dvukh religioznykh napravlenii / ortodoksal'nogo i reformatskogo / sredi evropeiskikh evreev (1870)" [CAHJP HM2 7774.2].

48. In response to the anti-Hasidic backlash in the late eighteenth and early nineteenth centuries and members of both camps involving the Russian government in the schism, the 1804 Statute on the Jews acknowledged two Jewish communities in Russia—Hasidic and Mitnagdic. For gentile depictions of Russian Jews as religious fanatics, who were usually equated with Hasidim, see the writings of Alexander Alekseev, who describes imperial Russian Jewry as Polish Jews who are primarily Hasidim, "the strictest Jewish sect, who adhere to the letter of the law" (Alekseev, *Besedy*, 10).

49. On progressive synagogues in the Russian Empire in Warsaw, Odessa, Riga, Vilna, and St. Petersburg, see Michael A. Meyer, "The German Model of Religious Reform and Russian Jewry," in *Between East and West: Aspects of Modern Jewish History*, ed. Isadore Twersky (Cambridge, MA: Harvard University Press, 1985), 69–75; Zipperstein, *Jews of Odessa*; Benjamin Nathans, *Beyond the Pale: The Jewish Encounter with Late Imperial Russia* (Berkeley: University of California Press, 2002), 136–49; Alexander Guterman, "The Congregation of the Great Synagogue in Warsaw: Its Changing Social Composition and Ideological Affiliations," *Polin* 11 (1998): 112–26.

50. RGIA f. 821, op. 8, d. 199.

51. Alekseev, *Besedy*, iii. For the translation of Jost's work into Russian, see I. M. Jost, *Religioznye sekty evreev* (Moscow, 1864).

52. Alekseev, *Besedy*, 12n2.

53. Ibid., 10–11.

54. "Chastnyi priiut v S. Peterburge dlia prisoediniaemykh v pravoslavnoi tserkvi evreev," *Strannik* 54 (1870): 67.

55. There are different views in *Voskhod* about the identity of the author. Lev Osipovich Gordin averred that Ben-Sion was a pseudonym of a Jew who supported, but was not involved in, the sects (N.N., "Popytki religioznoi reformy u evreev [po povodu knigi

'Evrei-Reformatory' Em. Ben-Siona. Spb., 1882 g.]," *Voskhod* 7–8 [1882]: 1); Simon Dubnov, under the pen name Kritikus, suggested that Ben-Sion was a pseudonym of Jacob Priluker himself (Kritikus, "Sredi krainostei," *Voskhod* 12 [1885]: 23).

56. Emmanuel Ben-Sion, *Evrei-reformatory: "Novyi Israil" i "Dukhovno-Bibleiskoe Bratstvo": Opyt sotsialno-religioznoi reformy i novoi postanovki evreiskago voprosa v Rossii* (St. Petersburg, 1882), part II, esp. 20, 41–42.

57. Michael A. Meyer, *Response to Modernity: A History of the Reform Movement in Judaism* (New York: Oxford University Press, 1988); Meyer, "The German Model."

58. Zipperstein, "Heresy, Apostasy."

59. Ben-Sion, *Evrei-reformatory*, 20, 22. For example, *Russkii evrei* in July 1881 (no. 29) published an article on Gordin's Biblical Brotherhood by an Elisavetgrad correspondent. The article responded to the great "noise" (*shum*) created by the sect's appearance. The correspondent included a short biography of Gordin and tried to list the sect's code of ethics and laws. But he admitted that he could not contain his laughter while listening in on one of the sect's biweekly religious meetings. A Bible stood on a table near the lecturer, yet the preacher read from some textbook on physics or chemistry. "It was impossible to refrain from laughter at the sight of women diligently yawning and falling asleep, lulled by the lectures." The writer chided the sect for promoting the economic reorientation of Jews toward agriculture yet doing nothing practical to reach that goal. He listed the sects' members and their typically Jewish professions—tailor, notary, bookseller, medical assistant, apprentice, and store manager. A few issues later, *Russkii evrei* published a letter in response from a reader G., a Brotherhood sympathizer, who lambasted the correspondent for spreading disinformation about the sect (1881, no. 36, "Dva slova pravdy v pol'zu 'bratev-bibleitsev'").

60. Ben-Sion, *Evrei-reformatory*, 32.

61. Ibid., 32.

62. Ibid., 16.

63. Ibid., 54.

64. Ibid., 59.

65. Ibid. He notes that he started learning Talmud at age six.

66. Ibid., 59–60, footnote.

67. Ben-Sion noted that a Jew illiterate in the Talmud in Russia circa 1882 was *not* considered an *am ha'arez* (ignoramus). He cited as evidence changing Jewish elementary school curricula and a cadre of Jewish intellectuals who were not Talmudic scholars (Ben-Sion, *Evrei-reformatory*, 63).

68. N.N., "Popytki religioznoi reformy," 1.

69. On Gordon's evolving program for Jewish religious reform in imperial Russia, which persisted even after the devastating pogroms of 1881–1882, see Michael Stanislawski, *For Whom Do I Toil? Judah Leib Gordon and the Crisis of Russian Jewry* (Oxford: Oxford University Press, 1988). On Stanislawski's discussion of Gordon's

response to the Christianizing Jewish sects in the 1880s and Gordon's article in *Voskhod*, see 191–93.

70. N.N., "Popytki religioznoi reformy," 16.

71. S.B., "Sdelat'sia-li evreiam khristianami?," *Voskhod* 4 (1884): 33–35. This article was written in response to Isidore Singer's *Sollen die Juden Christen werden? Ein offenes Wort an Freund und Feind* (Vienna, 1884). Singer argued that to solve the problem of Judaism as a separate and contentious religion in the modern era, Jews needed to compromise and convert to Christianity, thus becoming Jewish Christians, akin to German Christians or French Christians, who were a national community within Christianity. Singer called this a "compromise" since the core of Judaism was similar to the fundamentals of Christianity—monotheism and the Golden Rule "do unto others as you would have others do unto you."

72. For another response to Ben-Sion's book questioning the premise that religious reforms could solve the Jewish question, see "Chego dobivaiutsia evrei reformatory," *Russkii evrei* 43 (October 28, 1882).

73. N.N., "Popytki religioznoi reformy," 17.

74. Mariia Saker, "Korrespondentsiia. Odessa, 10-go Fevralia 1882 g.," *Nedel'naia khronika voskhoda* 8 (February 19, 1882): 184–85. For Saker's biography, see Carole B. Balin, *To Reveal Our Hearts: Jewish Women Writers in Tsarist Russia* (Cincinnati: Hebrew Union College Press, 2000), 3.

75. Shael, "Nastoiashchii smysl 'sekt,' poiavliaiushchikhsia v lone evreistva v poslednee vremia," *Russkii evrei* 7 (February 12, 1882).

76. N.N., "Popytki religioznoi reformy," 24–25.

77. Ibid., 15.

78. Ibid., 18–19.

79. Ibid., 20.

80. Ibid., 26.

81. Portugalov, *Znamenatel'naia dvizheniia*, 47.

82. Ibid., 48.

83. Ibid., 41.

84. Vilkovir, *Iudaizm i ego opponenty*.

85. A. Verbov, "'Novomu Izrailiu,'" *Nedel'naia khronika voskhoda* 51 (December 21, 1882): 1405–6.

86. F.Ia.K., "Korrespondentsii. Odessa, 15 Fevralia," *Nedel'naia khronika voskhoda* 8 (February 24, 1885): 218–21.

87. "Dvizhenie v srede evreev k khristianstvu," *Khersonskie eparkhial'nye vedomosti* 2 (January 15, 1885).

88. S.M., "Bibliografiia," *Voskhod* 8 (1888): 45–46.

89. S. Zaks, "Korrespondentsii. Zlatopol', 29 Ianvaria," *Nedel'naia khronika voskhoda* 7 (February 14, 1888): 158–59.

90. "Slovo, proiznesennoe I. Rabinovichem na evr-oi iazyke v khrame izrail'tian novago zaveta v g. Kishineve 5 Iiulia 1886 g.," *Khersonskie eparkhial'nye vedomosti* 21 (November 1, 1886).

91. "Borba s kagalom i talmudom v srede evreistva," *Sankt-Peterburgskie vedomosti* 8 (1885).

92. "Ob antitalmudich. dvizhenii v srede Bessarab. evreev," *Sankt-Peterburgskie vedomosti* 16 (1885).

93. "Evreiskie quasi-bibleitsy," *Kievlianin* 250 (November 11, 1884).

94. "Obrashchenie sekty novago izrailia v protestantstvo," *Volynskie eparkhial'nye vedomosti* 25 (1886).

95. "Simvol very 'Novago Izrailia,'" *Khersonskie eparkhial'nye vedomosti* 5 (March 1, 1886).

96. "Dvizhenie v srede evreev k khristianstvu," *Khersonskie eparkhial'nye vedomosti* 2 (January 15, 1885). John Klier noted that even after the rumor of Rabinovich's murder was disproved in 1885, newspapers still reprinted it two years later as evidence of Jewish fanaticism. See John D. Klier, *Imperial Russia's Jewish Question, 1855–1881* (Cambridge: Cambridge University Press, 1995), 437.

97. A. Alekseev, *O religioznom dvizhenii evreev i rasprostranenii khristianstva mezhdu nimi, s prilozheniem obiasneniia vazhneishikh mest sv. pisaniia, svidetel'stvuiushchikh ob Iususe Khriste, kak litse messii i nastavleniia, kak vesti delo missionerstva sredi evreev* (Novgorod, 1895), 7.

98. Ibid., 6.

Epilogue

1. Todd M. Endelman, *Leaving the Jewish Fold: Conversion and Radical Assimilation in Modern Jewish History* (Princeton, NJ: Princeton University Press, 2015), 11.

2. Ibid., 90.

3. Ibid., 108–9.

4. Ibid., 91.

5. Ibid., 98.

6. Ibid., 274.

7. Ibid., 315–16, 333.

8. Ibid., 317.

9. Ibid., 318–19.

10. Mendel Goldshtein, *Kreshcheniia pered sudom evreiskago intelligenta (publitsisticheskii etiud)* (Kiev, 1912).

11. Quoted in ChaeRan Freeze, "When Chava Left Home: Gender, Conversion, and the Jewish Family in Tsarist Russia," *Polin* 18 (2005): 153.

12. CAHJP RU 1592.

13. David Ellenson and Daniel Gordis, *Pledges of Jewish Allegiance: Conversion,*

Law, and Policymaking in Nineteenth- and Twentieth-Century Orthodox Responsa (Stanford, CA: Stanford University Press, 2012), 56–57, 162.

14. For further discussion, see Ellie R. Schainker, "When Life Imitates Art: Shtetl Sociability and Conversion in Imperial Russia," in *Bastards and Believers: Converts and Conversion between Judaism and Christianity*, ed. Paweł Maciejko and Theodor Dunkelgrün (Philadelphia: University of Pennsylvania Press, forthcoming).

15. Chaim Zhitlovskii, *Zikhroynes fun mayn Leben*, 2 vols. (New York, 1935), I:40. For the full story, see I:39–42. The author thanks Gabriella Safran for this reference.

16. For other mentions of converts from Judaism and their integration into Jewish life, see ibid., I:269–73.

17. Vladimir Medem, *The Life and Soul of a Legendary Jewish Socialist*, trans. Samuel A. Portnoy, original pub. 1923 (New York: Ktav, 1979), 179.

18. Gabriella Safran, *Rewriting the Jew: Assimilation Narratives in the Russian Empire* (Stanford, CA: Stanford University Press, 2000), 4.

19. Alyssa Pia Quint, "The Rise of the Modern Yiddish Theater," unpublished manuscript, chap. 4.

20. Sholem Asch, *Salvation* (New York: Schocken, 1968), originally published as *Der tehilim yid* (Warsaw: Kultur-Lige, 1934).

21. Saul M. Ginsburg, *Meshumodim in tsarishn Russland* (New York: "CYCO" Bicher Farlag, 1946); Shmuel Leib Tsitron, *Meshumodim: tipn un silueten funm noenten over*, 4 vols. (Warsaw: Farlag Tsentral, 1923–1928); Ezriel Nathan Frenk, *Meshumodim in Poyln in 19-tn yor-hundert* (Warsaw: M.Y. Fried, 1923).

22. Shulamit S. Magnus, "Good Bad Jews: Converts, Conversion, and Boundary Redrawing in Modern Russian Jewry, Notes toward a New Category," in *Boundaries of Jewish Identity*, ed. Susan A. Glenn and Naomi B. Sokoloff (Seattle: University of Washington Press, 2010), 132–60. Aside from Yiddish publications, Russian scholarship was also interested in converts from Judaism. An example is a 1907 study of Jewish converts to Catholicism in Poland and Lithuania from the late medieval to modern periods. See I. K. Antoshevskii, *Evrei khristiane: Istoriko-genealogicheskiia zametki* (St. Petersburg, 1907).

23. "S.-Peterburg, 16 Oktiabria 1888 g.," *Nedel'naia khronika voskhoda* 42 (1888): 1001–4.

24. Brian Horowitz, *Empire Jews: Jewish Nationalism and Acculturation in Nineteenth- and Early Twentieth-Century Russia* (Bloomington, IN: Slavica, 2009), 31–33.

25. Jeremy Dauber, *The Worlds of Sholem Aleichem: The Remarkable Life and Afterlife of the Man Who Created Tevye* (New York: Schocken, 2013), 406n174.

26. Sholem Aleichem, "The Lottery Ticket," in Sholem Aleichem, *The Old Country*, trans. Julius and Frances Butwin (New York: Crown Publishers, 1946), 347–70.

27. Isaac Babel, "Old Shloyme," in *Isaac Babel's Selected Writings*, ed. Gregory Freidin, trans. Peter Constantine (New York: Norton, 2010), 3–5.

28. In 1903, 836 Jews converted to Russian Orthodoxy, and in 1904, 874 converted. Compare this to 1,198 converts from Judaism in 1913, and 1,387 in 1914. See the synodal *Vsepoddanneishii otchet* for the years 1903–1904 (publ. 1909), 1913 (publ. 1915), and 1914 (publ. 1916).

29. Mordechai Altshuler, *Soviet Jewry on the Eve of the Holocaust: A Social and Demographic Profile* (Jerusalem: Ahva Press, 1998), 69–76.

30. Safran, *Rewriting the Jew*, 8; Steven J. Zipperstein, "Heresy, Apostasy and the Transformation of Joseph Rabinovich," in *Jewish Apostasy in the Modern World*, ed. Todd M. Endelman (New York: Holmes and Meier, 1987), 206–31.

31. David E. Fishman, *The Rise of Modern Yiddish Culture* (Pittsburgh: University of Pittsburgh Press, 2005), 165–66n14.

32. Ibid., 64, 68–70.

33. Ibid., 101–2. On Zhitlovskii and his racial/linguistic conception of Jewishness that even encompassed converts, see Matthew Hoffman, "From *Pintele Yid* to *Racenjude*: Chaim Zhitlovsky and Racial Conceptions of Jewishness," *Jewish History* 19, no. 1 (2005): 65–78.

34. Nurit Govrin, *"Me'ora Brener": ha-ma'avak al hofesh ha-bitui* (Jerusalem: Yad Yizhak ben Zevi, 1985), 133–39.

35. Judith Deutsch Kornblatt, *Doubly Chosen: Jewish Identity, the Soviet Intelligentsia, and the Russian Orthodox Church* (Madison: University of Wisconsin Press, 2004), 66–69.

36. Ibid., 79.

37. M. S. Agurskij, "Die Judenchristen in der Russisch-Orthodoxen Kirche," *Ostkirchliche Studien* 23, no. 2–3 (September 1974): 137–76; Mikhail Agursky, "Unrequited Love: The Cultural Affinities of Jews and Russians," *Midstream* 33, no. 9 (1987): 39–43; Mikhail Agursky, "Conversions of Jews to Christianity in Russia," *Soviet Jewish Affairs* 20, no. 2–3 (1990): 69–84; Mikhail Agursky and Dmitry Segal, "Jews and the Russian Orthodox Church: A Common Legacy—A Common Hope," *St. Vladimir's Theological Quarterly* 35, no. 1 (1991): 21–31.

38. On Agursky, see Kornblatt, *Doubly Chosen*, 76–78. For his unedited memoirs, published in four installments, see "Epizody vospominanii," *Ierusalimskii zhurnal* 2–5 (1999–2000).

39. On Brother Daniel, see Nechama Tec, *In the Lion's Den: The Life of Oswald Rufeisen* (Oxford: Oxford University Press, 1990); Kornblatt, *Doubly Chosen*, 113–22. On the Rufeisen court case, see Asher Felix Landau, *Select Judgments of the Supreme Court of Israel* (Jerusalem: Transaction Press, 1971), *Oswald Rufeisen v. Ministry of the Interior*.

40. Kornblatt, *Doubly Chosen*, 9.

41. Anna Shternshis, "Kaddish in a Church: Perceptions of Orthodox Christianity among Moscow Elderly Jews in the Early Twenty-First Century," *Russian Review* 66 (April 2007): 273–94.

42. Kornblatt, *Doubly Chosen*, 9.

BIBLIOGRAPHY

Archival Sources

CAHJP   Central Archives for the History of the Jewish People. Jerusalem.

DAKO   Derzhavnyi arkhiv Kyivs'koi oblasti. Kiev.
Fond 1   Kievskoe gubernskoe pravlenie
Fond 2   Kantseliariia Kievskogo grazhdanskogo gubernatora

DAmK   Derzhavnyi arkhiv m. Kyieva. Kiev.
Fond 14   Kievskoe Sv. Vladimirskoe Bratstvo
Fond 253   Priiut dlia kreshchennykh v pravoslavnuiu veru evreiskikh detei
Fond 286   Kievskii komitet pravoslavnogo missionerskogo obshchestva
Fond 316   Blagochinnyi Kievo-Pecherskikh i Staro-Kievskikh tserkvei

DAOO   Derzhavnyi arkhiv Odes'koi oblasti. Odessa.
Fond 1   Kantseliariia Novorossiiskogo i Bessarabskogo general-gubernatora
Fond 37   Khersonskoi dukhovnoi konsistorii

DAVO   Derzhavnyi arkhiv Volyns'koi oblasti. Lutsk.
Fond 361   Lutskii povitovii sud

DAZhO   Derzhavnyi arkhiv Zhytomyrs'koi oblasti. Zhitomir.
Fond 1   Volynskaia dukhovnaia konsistoriia

GARF   Gosudarstvennyi arkhiv Rossiiskoi Federatsii. Moscow.
Fond 102   Departament politsii, MVD
Fond 109   Tret'e otdelenie sobstvennoi ego imperatorskogo velichestva
              kantseliarii
Fond 1165   Osobennaia kantseliariia MVD

LVIA   Lietuvos valstybės istorijos archyvas. Vilnius.
Fond 377   Kantseliariia ego imperatorskogo vysochestva Tsesarevicha
              Konstantina Pavlovicha
Fond 378   Kantseliariia Vilenskogo, Kovenskogo, i Grodnenskogo general-
              gubernatora g. Vil'na (B/S=*bendrasis skyrius* [General Section])
Fond 380   Kantseliariia Vilenskogo gubernatora
Fond 577   Vilenskoe ravvinskoe uchilishche
Fond 604   Litovskaia rimsko-katolicheskaia dukhovnaia konsistoriia
Fond 605   Litovskaia pravoslavnaia dukhovnaia konsistoriia Vil'na

NIAB   Natsional'nyi istoricheskii arkhiv Belarusi. Minsk.
Fond 1781   Mogilevskaia rimsko-katolicheskaia konsistoriia sinoda

RGADA   Rossiiskii gosudarstvennyi arkhiv drevnikh aktov. Moscow.
Fond 1239   Moskovskoe otdelenie obshchego arkhiva ministerstva
              imperatorskogo dvora—Moskovskii dvortsovyi arkhiv

RGAVMF   Rossiiskii gosudarstvennyi arkhiv voenno-morskogo flota. Moscow.
Fond 33   Morskoi general-auditoriat i upravlenie flota general-auditora
Fond 205   Kantseliariia nachalnika glavnogo morskogo shtaba
Fond 283   Inspektorskii departament morskogo ministerstva

RGIA   Rossiiskii gosudarstvennyi istoricheskii arkhiv. St. Petersburg.
Fond 383   Pervyi departament ministerstva gosudarstvennykh imushchestv
Fond 796   Kantseliariia sviateishego sinoda
Fond 797   Kantseliariia ober-prokurora sviateishego sinoda
Fond 821   Departament dukhovnykh del inostrannykh ispovedanii, MVD
Fond 822   Rimsko-katolicheskaia dukhovnaia kollegiia
Fond 1409   Sobstvennaia ego imperatorskogo velichestva kantseliariia

RGVIA   Rossiiskii gosudarstvennyi voenno-istoricheskii arkhiv. Moscow.
Fond 405   Departament voennykh poselenii

TsDIAK   Tsentral'nyi derzhavnyi istorychnyi arkhiv Ukrainy, Kyiv. Kiev.
Fond 127   Kievskaia dukhovnaia konsistoriia
Fond 182   Kantseliariia Kievskogo mitropolita
Fond 442   Kantseliariia Kievskogo, Podol'skogo i Volynskogo
             general-gubernatora
Fond 533   Kantseliariia Kievskogo voennogo gubernatora

TsGIA-SPb   Tsentral'nyi gosudarstvennyi istoricheskii arkhiv Sankt-Peterburga.
             St. Petersburg.
Fond 19   Peterburgskaia dukhovnaia konsistoriia
Fond 422   Petrogradskaia khoral'naia sinagoga
Fond 487   Prokurorskii nadzor Petrogradskogo okruzhnogo suda
Fond 542   Mariinsko-Sergievskii priiut dlia kreshchaemykh i kreshchennykh v
             pravoslavnuiu veru evreiskikh detei

YIVO   Institute for Jewish Research. New York.
RG 46   Lithuanian Ecclesiastic Consistory of the Russian Orthodox Church

Contemporary Periodicals

Dukhovnaia beseda (Petersburg, 1858–1876)

Elisavetgradskii vestnik (Elisavetgrad, 1876–1894; 1912)

Evreiskaia biblioteka (Petersburg, 1871–1880)

Evreiskii mir (Petersburg, 1909–1911)

Golos (Petersburg, 1863–1884)

Grazhdanin (Petersburg, 1872–1877; 1882–1914)

Khersonskie eparkhial'nye vedomosti (Kherson, 1860–1918)

Kievlianin (Kiev, 1864–1918)

Kievskie eparkhial'nye vedomosti (Kiev, 1861–1917)

Nedel'naia khronika voskhoda (Petersburg, 1882–1906)

Novgorodskie gubernskie vedomosti (Novgorod, 1838–1917)

Novoe vremia (Petersburg, 1868–1917)

Novorossiiskii telegraf (Odessa, 1869–1900)

Odesskii vestnik (Odessa, 1827–1894)

Pravoslavnoe obozrenie (Moscow, 1860–1891)

Russkii evrei (Petersburg, 1879–1884)

Sankt-Peterburgskie vedomosti (Petersburg, 1728–1917)

Scattered Nation (London, 1866–1871)

Sovremennost' (Petersburg, 1871–1881)

Strannik (Petersburg, 1860–1917)

Sudebnaia gazeta (Petersburg, 1882–1905)

Vilenskie gubernskie vedomosti (Vilna, 1838–1917)

Volyn (Zhitomir, 1882–1917)

Volynskie eparkhial'nye vedomosti (Zhitomir, 1867–1917)

Volynskie gubernskie vedomosti (Zhitomir, 1838–1917)

Voskhod (Petersburg, 1881–1906)

Others

Abramowicz, Hirsz. *Profiles of a Lost World: Memoirs of East European Jewish Life before World War II.* Edited by Dina Abramowicz and Jeffrey Shandler. Detroit: Wayne State University Press, [1958] 1999.

Agurskij, M. S. "Die Judenchristen in der Russisch-Orthodoxen Kirche." *Ostkirchliche Studien* 23, no. 2–3 (September 1974): 137–76.

Agursky, Mikhail. "Conversions of Jews to Christianity in Russia." *Soviet Jewish Affairs* 20, no. 2–3 (1990): 69–84.

———. "Unrequited Love: The Cultural Affinities of Jews and Russians." *Midstream* 33, no. 9 (1987): 39–43.

Agursky, Mikhail, and Dmitry Segal. "Jews and the Russian Orthodox Church: A Common Legacy—A Common Hope." *St. Vladimir's Theological Quarterly* 35, no. 1 (1991): 21–31.

Aleichem, Sholem. *The Bloody Hoax.* Translated by Aliza Shevrin. Bloomington: Indiana University Press, 1991. Originally published as *Der blutiger shpas* (Warsaw: Kultur-Lige, 1923).

———. *The Old Country.* Translated by Julius and Frances Butwin. New York: Crown Publishers, 1946.

Alekseev, A. *Besedy pravoslavnago khristianina iz evreev s novoobrashchennymi iz svoikh sobratii ob istinakh sviatoi very i zabluzhdeniiakh talmudicheskikh, s prisovokupleniem stat'i o talmude.* St. Petersburg, 1872.

———. *O religioznom dvizhenii evreev i rasprostranenii khristianstva mezhdu nimi, s prilozheniem obiasneniia vazhneishikh mest sv. pisaniia, svidetel'stvuiushchikh ob Iususe Khriste, kak litse messii i nastavleniia, kak vesti delo missionerstva sredi evreev.* Novgorod, 1895.

Alekseev, A. A. *Ocherki domashnei i obshchestvennoi zhizni evreev: Ikh verovaniia, prazdniki, obriady, talmud, kagal.* Novgorod, 1882.

Alekseev, Aleksandr. *Bogosluzhenie, prazdniki, i religioznye obriady nyneshnikh evreev.* Novgorod, [1861] 1865.

Altshuler, Mordechai. *Soviet Jewry on the Eve of the Holocaust: A Social and Demographic Profile.* Jerusalem: Ahva Press, 1998.

Amburger, Eric. *Geschichte der Behördenorganisation Russlands von Peter dem Grossen bis 1917.* Leiden: Brill, 1966.

Ansky, S. *The Dybbuk and Other Writings*. Edited by David G. Roskies, translated by Golda Werman. New York: Schocken, 1992.

Antoshevskii, I. K. *Evrei khristiane: Istoriko-genealogicheskiia zametki*. St. Petersburg, 1907.

Asch, Sholem. *Salvation*. Translated by Willa and Edwin Muir. New York: Schocken, 1968. Originally published as *Der tehilim yid* (Warsaw: Kultur-Lige, 1934).

Assaf, David. *Untold Tales of the Hasidim: Crisis and Discontent in the History of Hasidism*. Translated by Dena Ordan. Waltham, MA: Brandeis University Press, 2010.

Avrutin, Eugene M. *Jews and the Imperial State: Identification Politics in Tsarist Russia*. Ithaca, NY: Cornell University Press, 2010.

———. "A Legible People: Identification Politics and Jewish Accommodation in Tsarist Russia." PhD diss., University of Michigan, 2004.

———. "The Politics of Jewish Legibility: Documentation Practices and Reform during the Reign of Nicholas I." *Jewish Social Studies* 11, no. 2 (2005): 136–69.

———. "Racial Categories and the Politics of (Jewish) Difference in Late Imperial Russia." *Kritika* 8, no. 1 (Winter 2007): 13–40.

———. "Returning to Judaism after the 1905 Law on Religious Freedom in Tsarist Russia." *Slavic Review* 65, no. 1 (Spring 2006): 90–110.

———. "Ritual Murder in a Russian Border Town." *Jewish History* 26 (2012): 309–26.

Babel, Isaac. *Isaac Babel's Selected Writings*. Edited by Gregory Freidin, translated by Peter Constantine. New York: Norton, 2010.

Balin, Carole B. *To Reveal Our Hearts: Jewish Women Writers in Tsarist Russia*. Cincinnati: Hebrew Union College Press, 2000.

Baron, Salo W., and Arcadius Kahan. *Economic History of the Jews*. Edited by Nachum Gross. New York: Schocken, 1975.

Basil, John D. *Church and State in Late Imperial Russia: Critics of the Synodal System of Church Government (1861–1914)*. Minneapolis: University of Minnesota, 2005.

Batalden, Stephen K. "The BFBS Petersburg Agency and Russian Biblical Translation, 1856–1875." In *Sowing the Word: The Cultural Impact of the British and Foreign Bible Society, 1804–2004*. Edited by Stephen Batalden, Kathleen Cann, and John Dean, 169–96. Sheffield: Sheffield Phoenix Press, 2004.

———. "The Politics of Modern Russian Biblical Translation." In *Bible Translation and the Spread of the Church: The Last 200 Years*. Edited by Philip C. Stine, 68–80. Leiden: Brill, 1990.

Beizer, Mikhail. *The Jews of St. Petersburg: Excursions through a Noble Past*. Translated by Michael Sherbourne. Philadelphia: Jewish Publication Society, 1989.

Ben-Sion, Emmanuel. *Evrei-reformatory: "Novyi Israil" i "Dukhovno-Bibleiskoe Bratstvo": Opyt sotsialno-religioznoi reformy i novoi postanovki evreiskago voprosa v Rossii*. St. Petersburg, 1882.

Biale, David. *Power and Powerlessness in Jewish History*. New York: Schocken, 1986.

Biolsi, Thomas. "The Birth of the Reservation: Making the Modern Individual among the Lakota." *American Ethnologist* 22, no. 1 (February 1995): 28–53.

Boyarin, Jonathan. "Jews, Indians, and the Identity of Christian Europe." *AJS Perspectives* (Fall 2005): 12–13.

Brandenburg, Hans. *The Meek and the Mighty: The Emergence of the Evangelical Movement in Russia.* London: Mowbrays, 1976.

Brauch, Julia, Anna Liphardt, and Alexandra Nocke, eds. *Jewish Topographies: Visions of Space, Traditions of Place.* Hampshire, Eng.: Ashgate, 2008.

Breyfogle, Nicholas B. *Heretics and Colonizers: Forging Russia's Empire in the South Caucasus.* Ithaca, NY: Cornell University Press, 2005.

———. "The Religious World of Russian Sabbatarians (*Subbotniks*)." In *Holy Dissent: Jewish and Christian Mystics in Eastern Europe.* Edited by Glenn Dynner, 359–92. Detroit: Wayne State University Press, 2011.

Carlebach, Elisheva. *Divided Souls: Converts from Judaism in Germany, 1500–1750.* New Haven, CT: Yale University Press, 2001.

———. "'Ich will dich nach Holland schicken . . .': Amsterdam and the Reversion to Judaism of German-Jewish Converts." In *Secret Conversions to Judaism in Early Modern Europe.* Edited by Martin Mulsow and Richard H. Popkin, 51–70. Leiden: Brill, 2004.

Clark, Christopher. *The Politics of Conversion: Missionary Protestantism and the Jews in Prussia, 1728–1941.* Oxford: Clarendon Press, 1995.

Cohen, Jeremy. "The Mentality of the Medieval Jewish Apostate: Peter Alfonsi, Hermann of Cologne, and Pablo Christiani." In *Jewish Apostasy in the Modern World.* Edited by Todd M. Endelman, 20–47. New York: Holmes and Meier, 1987.

Coleman, Heather J. *Russian Baptists and Spiritual Revolution, 1905–1929.* Bloomington: Indiana University Press, 2005.

Corpis, Duane J. *Crossing the Boundaries of Belief: Geographies of Religious Conversion in Southern Germany, 1646–1800.* Charlottesville: University of Virginia Press, 2014.

Crews, Robert. "Empire and the Confessional State: Islam and Religious Politics in Nineteenth-Century Russia." *American Historical Review* 108, no. 1 (February 2003): 50–83.

Crews, Robert D. *For Prophet and Tsar: Islam and Empire in Russia and Central Asia.* Cambridge, MA: Harvard University Press, 2006.

Dauber, Jeremy. *The Worlds of Sholem Aleichem: The Remarkable Life and Afterlife of the Man Who Created Tevye.* New York: Schocken, 2013.

Davis, Marni. "Despised Merchandise: American Jewish Liquor Entrepreneurs and Their Critics." In *Chosen Capital: The Jewish Encounter with American Capitalism.* Edited by Rebecca Kobrin, 113–40. New Brunswick, NJ: Rutgers University Press, 2012.

Davis, Natalie Zemon. *Fiction in the Archives: Pardon Tales and Their Tellers in Sixteenth-Century France.* Stanford, CA: Stanford University Press, 1987.

———. *Trickster Travels: A Sixteenth-Century Muslim between Worlds.* New York: Hill and Wang, 2007.

de le Roi, J. F. A. *Judentaufen im 19. Jahrhundert.* Leipzig, 1899.

Deutsch, Yaakov. *Judaism in Christian Eyes: Ethnographic Descriptions of Jews and Judaism in Early Modern Europe.* Oxford: Oxford University Press, 2012.

Deych, Genrich M. *Putevoditel': Arkhivnye dokumenty po istorii evreev v Rossii v XIX–nachale XX vv.* Edited by Benjamin Nathans. Moscow: Blagovest, 1994.

Dolbilov, Mikhail. "Russification and the Bureaucratic Mind in the Russian Empire's Northwestern Region in the 1860s." *Kritika* 5, no. 2 (Spring 2004): 245–71.

———. *Russkii krai, chuzhaia vera: Etnokonfessional'naia politika imperii v Litve i Belorussii pri Aleksandre II.* Moscow. Novoe literaturnoe obozrenie, 2010.

Dubnov, Simon. *The Book of Life: Memoirs and Reflections.* Translated by Dianne Sattinger, edited by Benjamin Nathans and Viktor Kel'ner. Madison: University of Wisconsin Press, forthcoming.

Dubnow, Simon M. *History of the Jews in Russia and Poland: From the Earliest Times Until the Present Day.* 3 volumes. Translated by I. Friedlaender. Philadelphia: Jewish Publication Society of America, 1916.

Dynner, Glenn. "Hasidism and Habitat: Managing the Jewish-Christian Encounter in the Kingdom of Poland." In *Holy Dissent: Jewish and Christian Mystics in Eastern Europe.* Edited by Glenn Dynner, 104–30. Detroit: Wayne State University Press, 2011.

———, ed. *Holy Dissent: Jewish and Christian Mystics in Eastern Europe.* Detroit: Wayne State University Press, 2011.

———. "Legal Fictions: The Survival of Rural Jewish Tavernkeeping in the Kingdom of Poland." *Jewish Social Studies* n.s. 16, no. 2 (Winter 2010): 28–66.

———. *Yankel's Tavern: Jews, Liquor, and Life in the Kingdom of Poland.* New York: Oxford University Press, 2013.

Eliashevich, D. A. *Pravitelstvennaia politika: Evreiskaia pechat' v Rossii, 1797–1917.* St. Petersburg: Mosty kul'tury, 1999.

Ellenson, David, and Daniel Gordis. *Pledges of Jewish Allegiance: Conversion, Law, and Policymaking in Nineteenth- and Twentieth-Century Orthodox Responsa.* Stanford, CA: Stanford University Press, 2012.

Elyada, Aya. "Yiddish—Language of Conversion? Linguistic Adaptation and Its Limits in Early Modern *Judenmission.*" *Leo Baeck Institute Yearbook* 53, no. 1 (2008): 3–27.

Endelman, Todd M. "Gender and Assimilation in Modern Jewish History." In *Gendering the Jewish Past.* Edited by Marc Lee Raphael. Williamsburg, VA: College of William and Mary, 2002.

——, ed. *Jewish Apostasy in the Modern World*. New York: Holmes and Meier, 1987.

——. "Jewish Converts in Nineteenth-Century Warsaw: A Quantitative Analysis." *Jewish Social Studies* 4, no. 1 (Fall 1997): 28–59.

——. *Leaving the Jewish Fold: Conversion and Radical Assimilation in Modern Jewish History*. Princeton, NJ: Princeton University Press, 2015.

——. "Memories of Jewishness: Jewish Converts and Their Jewish Pasts." In *Jewish History and Jewish Memory: Essays in Honor of Yosef Hayim Yerushalmi*. Edited by Elisheva Carlebach, John M. Efron, and David N. Myers, 311–29. Hanover, NH: University Press of New England, 1998.

Engelstein, Laura. *Castration and the Heavenly Kingdom: A Russian Folktale*. Ithaca, NY: Cornell University Press, 1999.

——. "Holy Russia in Modern Times: An Essay on Orthodoxy and Cultural Change." *Past and Present*, no. 173 (November 2001): 129–56.

Estraikh, Gennady, and Mikhail Krutikov, eds. *The Shtetl: Image and Reality*. Oxford: Legenda, 2000.

Evreiskaia entsiklopediia: Svod znanii o evreistve i ego kul'ture v proshlom i nastoiashchem. 16 vols. St. Petersburg: Brokgauz-Efron, 1906–1913.

Feldman, D. Z. "Poslednii inkvizitsionnyi koster v Rossii: Moskovskoe sledstvie po delu Aleksandra Voznitsyna i Borukha Leibova 1738–1740 gg." *Paralleli*, no. 6–7 (2005): 3–82.

Feldman, D. Z., and O. Iu. Minkina. "K voprosu o priniatii evreiskimi zhenshchinami khristianstva v Rossii v kontse XVIII–nachale XIX vekov." In *"Prekrasnaia Evreika" v Rossii XVII–XIX vekov: Obrazy i real'nost'*. Edited by D. Z. Feldman, O. Iu. Minkina, and A. Iu. Kononova, 55–104. Moscow: Drevlekhranilishche, 2007.

Fishman, David E. *The Rise of Modern Yiddish Culture*. Pittsburgh: University of Pittsburgh Press, 2005.

Fram, Edward. "Perception and Reception of Repentant Apostates in Medieval Ashkenaz and Premodern Poland." *AJS Review* 21, no. 2 (1996): 299–339.

Freeze, ChaeRan. "When Chava Left Home: Gender, Conversion, and the Jewish Family in Tsarist Russia." *Polin* 18 (2005): 153–88.

Freeze, ChaeRan Y. *Jewish Marriage and Divorce in Imperial Russia*. Hanover, NH: University Press of New England, 2002.

——. "Lilith's Midwives: Jewish Newborn Child Murder in Nineteenth-Century Vilna." *Jewish Social Studies* 16, no. 2 (Winter 2010): 1–27.

——. "The Mariinsko Sergievskii Shelter for Converted Jewish Children in St. Petersburg." In *Jews in the East European Borderlands: Essays in Honor of John D. Klier*. Edited by Eugene M. Avrutin and Harriet Murav, 27–49. Boston: Academic Studies Press, 2012.

Freeze, Gregory. "The Orthodox Church and Serfdom in Prereform Russia." *Slavic Review* 48, no. 3 (Autumn 1989): 361–87.

Freeze, Gregory L. "The Rechristianization of Russia: The Church and Popular Religion, 1750–1850." *Studia Slavica Findlandensia* 7 (1990): 101–36.

Frenk, Ezriel Nathan. *Meshumodim in Poyln in 19-tn yor-hundert.* Warsaw: M.Y. Fried, 1923.

Galas, Michał. "Inter-religious Contacts in the Shtetl: Proposals for Future Research." *Polin* 17 (2004): 41–50.

Geraci, Robert P. *Window on the East: National and Imperial Identities in Late Tsarist Russia.* Ithaca, NY: Cornell University Press, 2001.

Geraci, Robert P., and Michael Khodarkovsky, eds. *Of Religion and Empire: Missions, Conversion, and Tolerance in Tsarist Russia.* Ithaca, NY: Cornell University Press, 2001.

Gerasimova, Viktoria Aleksandrovna. "Kreshchenye evrei v Rossii v XVIII v.: Osobennosti sotsiokul'turnoi adaptatsii." PhD diss., Russian State University for Humanities, Moscow, 2013.

Gidney, W. T. *At Home and Abroad: A Description of the English and Continental Missions of the London Society for Promoting Christianity amongst the Jews.* London: Operative Jewish Converts' Institution, 1900.

———. *The Jews and Their Evangelization.* London, 1899.

Ginsburg, Saul M. *Historische Werk.* 3 vols. New York: S.M. Ginsburg Testimonial Committee, 1937.

———. *Meshumodim in tsarishn Russland.* New York: "CYCO" Bicher Farlag, 1946.

Glants, Musya. "Poteriana i naidena v Amerike: Kartina Moiseia Maimona 'Marrany i inkvizitsiia v Ispanii.'" *Paralleli*, no. 8–9 (2003): 131–42.

Goldshtein, Mendel. *Kreshcheniia pered sudom evreiskago intelligenta (publitsisticheskii etiud).* Kiev, 1912.

Govrin, Nurit. "'Me'ora Brener'": ha-ma'avak al hofesh ha-bitui.* Jerusalem: Yad Yizhak ben Zevi, 1985.

Greenberg, Louis. *The Jews in Russia: The Struggle for Emancipation.* New Haven, CT: Yale University Press, 1944.

Grigorev, V. V. *Evreiskiia religioznyia sekty v Rossii.* St. Petersburg, 1847.

Gross, Jan T. *Neighbors: The Destruction of the Jewish Community in Jedwabne, Poland.* Princeton, NJ: Princeton University Press, 2001.

Grossman, Avraham. *Hasidot u-mordot: Nashim Yehudiyot be-Eropah be-yeme-ha-benayim.* Jerusalem: Merkaz Zalman Shazar, 2001.

Guterman, Alexander. "The Congregation of the Great Synagogue in Warsaw: Its Changing Social Composition and Ideological Affiliations." *Polin* 11 (1998): 112–26.

Halpern, Israel. "The Jews of Eastern Europe: From Ancient Times until the Partitions of Poland." In *The Jews.* Edited by Louis Finkelstein, 305–42. New York: Schocken, 1970.

Hamburg, G. M. "Religious Toleration in Russian Thought, 1520–1825." *Kritika* 13, no. 3 (Summer 2012): 515–59.

Hartley, Janet M. *Alexander I*. London: Longman, 1994.

Hertz, Deborah. *Jewish High Society in Old Regime Berlin*. New Haven, CT: Yale University Press, 1988.

Hoffman, Matthew. "From *Pintele Yid* to *Racenjude*: Chaim Zhitlovsky and Racial Conceptions of Jewishness." *Jewish History* 19, no. 1 (2005): 65–78.

Horowitz, Brian. *Empire Jews: Jewish Nationalism and Acculturation in Nineteenth- and Early Twentieth-Century Russia*. Bloomington, IN: Slavica, 2009.

———. *Jewish Philanthropy and Enlightenment in Late-Tsarist Russia*. Seattle: University of Washington Press, 2009.

Hse, Chia Yin. "A Tale of Two Railroads: 'Yellow Labor,' Agrarian Colonization, and the Making of Russianness at the Far Eastern Frontier, 1890s–1910s." *Ab Imperio* 3 (2006): 217–53.

Hundert, Gershon. *Jews in Poland-Lithuania in the Eighteenth Century: A Genealogy of Modernity*. Berkeley: University of California Press, 2004.

Hyman, Paula. *Gender and Assimilation in Modern Jewish History: The Roles and Representations of Women*. Seattle: University of Washington Press, 1995.

Hyman, Paula E. "Social Contexts of Assimilation: Village Jews and City Jews in Alsace." In *Assimilation and Community: The Jews in Nineteenth-Century Europe*. Edited by Jonathan Frankel and Steven J. Zipperstein, 110–29. Cambridge: Cambridge University Press, 1992.

Jagodzińska, Agnieszka. "Christian Missionaries and Jewish Spaces: British Missions in the Kingdom of Poland in the First Half of the Nineteenth Century." In *Space and Conversion in Global Perspective*. Edited by Giuseppe Marcocci, Wietse de Boer, Aliocha Maldavsky, and Ilaria Pavan, 103–26. Leiden: Brill, 2015.

James, William. *The Varieties of Religious Experience*. New York: Longmans, Green, 1902.

Kalik, Judith. "The Orthodox Church and the Jews in the Poland-Lithuanian Commonwealth." *Jewish History* 17, no. 2 (2003): 229–37.

Kanarfogel, Ephraim. "Changing Attitudes toward Apostates in Tosafist Literature, Late Twelfth–Early Thirteenth Centuries." In *New Perspectives on Jewish-Christian Relations*. Edited by Elisheva Carlebach and Jacob J. Shachter, 297–328. Leiden: Brill, 2012.

Kaplan, Marion A. *The Making of the Jewish Middle Class: Women, Family, and Identity in Imperial Germany*. New York: Oxford University Press, 1991.

Kappeler, Andreas. "The Ambiguities of Russification." *Kritika* 5, no. 2 (Spring 2004): 291–97.

———. *The Russian Empire: A Multiethnic History*. Harlow, Eng.: Pearson Education, 2001.

Katz, Jacob. *Exclusiveness and Tolerance*. Oxford: Oxford University Press, 1961.

———. *Halakhah ve-Kabalah*. Jerusalem: Magnes Press, 1984.

Katz, Steven T. *The Shtetl: New Evaluations*. New York: New York University Press, 2007.

Kaźmierczyk, Adam. *Rodziłem się Żydem . . . Konwersje Żydów w Rzeczypospolitej XVII–XVIII wieku*. Kraków: Księgarnia Akademicka, 2015.

Kazovsky, Hillel. "Jewish Artists in Russia at the Turn of the Century: Issues of National Self-Identification in Art." *Jewish Art* 21–22 (1995–1996): 20–39.

Keidosiute, Elena. "Missionary Activity of Mariae Vitae Congregation." *Pardes: Zeitschrift der Vereinigung für Jüdische Studien* (2010): 57–72.

Khodorovskii, Arnol'd Semenovich (A. S. Ardov). *Evrei-Evangelisty*. Moscow, 1914.

Kieval, Hillel J. "Neighbors, Strangers, Readers: The Village and the City in Jewish-Gentile Conflict at the Turn of the Nineteenth Century." *Jewish Studies Quarterly* 12, no. 1 (2005): 61–79.

Kivelson, Valerie A., and Ronald H. Greene, eds. *Orthodox Russia: Belief and Practice under the Tsars*. University Park: Pennsylvania State University Press, 2003.

Kizenko, Nadieszda. *A Prodigal Saint: Father John of Kronstadt and the Russian People*. University Park: Pennsylvania State University Press, 2000.

———. "Written Confessions and the Construction of Sacred Narrative." In *Sacred Stories: Religion and Spirituality in Modern Russia*. Edited by Mark D. Steinberg and Heather J. Coleman, 93–118. Bloomington: University of Indiana Press, 2007.

———. "Written Confessions to Father John of Kronstadt, 1898–1908." In *Orthodox Christianity in Imperial Russia: A Source Book on Lived Religion*. Edited by Heather J. Coleman, 152–71. Bloomington: Indiana University Press, 2014.

Kjaer-Hansen, Kai. *The Herzl of Jewish Christianity: Joseph Rabinowitz and the Messianic Movement*. Edinburgh: Handel Press, 1995.

Klier, John. "State Policies and the Conversion of Jews in Imperial Russia." In *Of Religion and Empire: Missions, Conversion, and Tolerance in Tsarist Russia*. Edited by Robert P. Geraci and Michael Khodarkovsky, 92–112. Ithaca, NY: Cornell University Press, 2001.

Klier, John D. *Imperial Russia's Jewish Question, 1855–1881*. Cambridge: Cambridge University Press, 1995.

———. "What Exactly Was a Shtetl?" In *The Shtetl: Image and Reality*. Edited by Gennady Estraikh and Mikhail Krutikov, 23–35. Oxford: Legenda, 2000.

Klier, John Doyle. *Russia Gathers Her Jews: The Origins of the "Jewish Question" in Russia, 1772–1825*. Dekalb: Northern Illinois University Press, 1986.

Knight, Nathaniel. "Ethnicity, Nationality and the Masses: *Narodnost'* and Modernity in Imperial Russia." In *Russian Modernity: Politics, Knowledge, Practices*. Edited by David L. Hoffman and Yanni Kotsonis, 41–64. New York: St. Martin's Press, 2000.

Kohler, Max J. *Jewish Rights at the Congresses of Vienna (1814–15) and Aix-la-Chapelle (1818)*. New York: American Jewish Committee, 1918.

Koniuchenko, A. E. "K voprosu o perekhode iudeev v pravoslavie v dorevoliutsionnoi rossii." *Vestnik cheliabinskogo gosudarstvennogo universiteta* 2012 no. 16 (270) *Istoriia. vyp.* 51: 93–98.

Kornblatt, Judith Deutsch. *Doubly Chosen: Jewish Identity, the Soviet Intelligentsia, and the Russian Orthodox Church*. Madison: University of Wisconsin Press, 2004.

Landau, Asher Felix. *Select Judgments of the Supreme Court of Israel*. Jerusalem: Transaction Publishers, 1971.

Lederhendler, Eli. *The Road to Modern Jewish Politics: Political Tradition and Political Reconstruction in the Jewish Community of Tsarist Russia*. New York: Oxford University Press, 1989.

Lehmann, Rosa. *Symbiosis and Ambivalence: Poles and Jews in a Small Galician Town*. New York: Berghahn Books, 2001.

Levanda, V. O. *Polnyi khronologicheskii sbornik zakonov i polozhenii, kasaiushchikhsia evreev, ot ulozheniia Tsaria Alekseia Mikhailovicha do nastoiashchago vremeni, ot 1649–1873*. St. Petersburg, 1874.

Levenvald, V. *Veroispovedanie izrail'skago khristianina*. St. Petersburg, 1832.

Lillevik, Raymond. *Apostates, Hybrids, or True Jews? Jewish Christians and Jewish Identity in Eastern Europe, 1860–1914*. Eugene, OR: Pickwick, 2014.

Limor, Ora. "The Epistle of Rabbi Samuel of Morocco: A Best-Seller in the World of Polemics." In *Contra Iudaeos: Ancient and Medieval Polemics between Christians and Jews*. Edited by Ora Limor and Guy G. Stroumsa, 177–94. Tübingen: Mohr Siebeck, 1996.

Lindenmeyr, Adele. *Poverty Is Not a Vice: Charity, Society, and the State in Imperial Russia*. Princeton, NJ: Princeton University Press, 1996.

Litvak, Olga. *Conscription and the Search for Modern Russian Jewry*. Bloomington: Indiana University Press, 2006.

Lowenstein, Steven M. *The Berlin Jewish Community: Enlightenment, Family, and Crisis, 1770–1830*. Oxford: Oxford University Press, 1994.

Luria, Keith P. "The Politics of Protestant Conversion to Catholicism." In *Conversion to Modernities*. Edited by Peter van der Veer, 23–46. New York: Routledge, 1996.

L'vov, Aleksandr. "Mezhetnicheskie otnosheniia: Ugoshchenie matsoi i 'krovavyi navet.'" In *Shtetl, XXI vek: Polevye issledovaniia*. Edited by V. A. Dymshits, A. L. L'vov, and A. V. Sokolova, 65–82. St. Petersburg: Izd-vo Evropeiskago Universiteta, 2008.

Maciejko, Paweł. *The Mixed Multitude: Jacob Frank and the Frankist Movement, 1755–1816*. Philadelphia: University of Pennsylvania Press, 2011.

MacMullen, Ramsay. *Christianizing the Roman Empire, A.D. 100–400*. New Haven, CT: Yale University Press, 1984.

Magnus, Shulamit S. "Good Bad Jews: Converts, Conversion, and Boundary Redrawing in Modern Russian Jewry: Notes toward a New Category." In *Boundaries of Jewish Identity*. Edited by Susan A. Glenn and Naomi B. Sokoloff, 132–60. Seattle: University of Washington Press, 2010.

Mahler, Raphael. "Hamediniyut klapei hamisyonerim bePolin hakongresa'it bi-tekufat haberit hakedoshah." In *Sefer Shiloh: Kovets ma'amarim lezikhro*. Edited by Michael Hendel, 169–81. Tel Aviv: Ḥug yedidim beshituf im hameḥlakah leḥinukh uletarbut shel iri'at Tel-Aviv-Yafo, 1960.

Manekin, Rachel. "The Lost Generation: Education and Female Conversion in *Fin-de-Siècle* Kraków." *Polin* 18 (2005): 189–219.

Martin, Alexander M. *Romantics, Reformers, Reactionaries: Russian Conservative Thought and Politics in the Reign of Alexander I*. Dekalb: Northern Illinois University Press, 1997.

Medem, Vladimir. *The Life and Soul of a Legendary Jewish Socialist*. Translated by Samuel A. Portnoy. New York: Ktav Publishing House, [1923] 1979.

Meir, Natan. "From Communal Charity to National Welfare: Jewish Orphanages in Eastern Europe before and after World War I." *East European Jewish Affairs* 39, no. 1 (April 2009): 19–34.

Meir, Natan M. *Kiev, Jewish Metropolis: A History, 1859–1914*. Bloomington: Indiana University Press, 2010.

Meyer, Michael A. "The German Model of Religious Reform and Russian Jewry." In *Between East and West: Aspects of Modern Jewish History*. Edited by Isadore Twersky, 65–91. Cambridge, MA: Harvard University Press, 1985.

———. *The Origins of the Modern Jew: Jewish Identity and European Culture in Germany, 1749–1824*. Detroit: Wayne State University Press, 1967.

———. *Response to Modernity: A History of the Reform Movement in Judaism*. New York: Oxford University Press, 1988.

Miller, Philip E. *Karaite Separatism in Nineteenth-Century Russia: Joseph Solomon Lutski's Epistle of Israel's Deliverance*. Cincinnati: Hebrew Union College Press, 1993.

Mills, Kenneth, and Anthony Grafton, eds. *Conversion: Old Worlds and New*. Rochester, NY: University of Rochester Press, 2003.

Minkina, Ol'ga. "The Election of Jewish Deputies in Vilna in 1818: Government Projects and Jewish Claims." *East European Jewish Affairs* 43, no. 2 (2013): 206–16.

———. *"Syny Rakhili": Evreiskie deputaty v Rossiiskoi imperii, 1772–1825*. Moscow: Novoe literaturnoe obozrenie, 2011.

Miron, Dan. *The Image of the Shtetl and Other Studies of Modern Jewish Literary Imagination*. Syracuse, NY: Syracuse University Press, 2000.

Mogil'ner, Marina. "Evreiskaia antropologiia v kontekste evropeiskikh rasovykh issledovanii." In *Istoriia i kultura rossiiskogo i vostochnoevropeiskogo evreistva*. Edited by Oleg Budnitskii, 116–37. Moscow: Dom Evreiskoi knigi, 2004.

———. *Homo imperii: istoriia fizicheskoi antropologii v Rossii.* Moscow: Novoe literaturnoe obozrenie, 2008.

Moseley, Marcus. *Being for Myself Alone: the Origins of Jewish Autobiography.* Stanford, CA: Stanford University Press, 2005.

Moss, Kenneth B. "At Home in Late Imperial Russian Modernity—Except When They Weren't: New Histories of Russian and East European Jews, 1881–1914." *Journal of Modern History* 84 (June 2012): 401–52.

Nastavlenie sviashchennikam voennykh zavedenii, kasatel'no obrashcheniia vospitannikov iudeiskogo ispovedaniia v khristianskuiu veru. St. Petersburg, 1843.

Nathans, Benjamin. *Beyond the Pale: The Jewish Encounter with Late Imperial Russia.* Berkeley: University of California Press, 2002.

Nirenberg, David. *Communities of Violence: Persecution of Minorities in the Middle Ages.* Princeton, NJ: Princeton University Press, 1996.

———. "The Judaism of Christian Art." In *Judaism and Christian Art: Aesthetic Anxieties from the Catacombs to Colonialism.* Edited by Herbert L. Kessler and David Nirenberg, 387–427. Philadelphia: University of Pennsylvania Press, 2011.

Nock, A. D. *Conversion: The Old and New in Religion from Alexander the Great to Augustine of Hippo.* Oxford: Oxford University Press, 1933.

Opalski, Magdalena. *The Jewish Tavern Keeper and His Tavern in Nineteenth-Century Polish Literature.* Jerusalem: Zalman Shazar Center, 1986.

Orbach, Alexander. *New Voices of Russian Jewry: A Study of the Russian-Jewish Press of Odessa in the Era of the Great Reforms, 1860–1871.* Leiden: Brill, 1980.

Orla-Bukowska, Annmaria. "Maintaining Borders, Crossing Borders: Social Relationships in the Shtetl." *Polin* 17 (2004): 171–95.

Orshanskii, I. G. *Russkoe zakonodatel'stvo o evreiakh: Ocherki i issledovaniia.* St. Petersburg, 1877.

Pavlovskii, I. F. *Kratkii biograficheskii slovar' uchenykh i pisatelei Poltavskoi gubernii s poloviny XVIII veka.* Poltava, 1912.

Penslar, Derek J. *Shylock's Children: Economics and Jewish Identity in Modern Europe.* Berkeley: University of California Press, 2001.

Petrovsky-Shtern, Yohanan. *Golden Age Shtetl: A New History of Jewish Life in East Europe.* Princeton, NJ: Princeton University Press, 2014.

———. *Jews in the Russian Army, 1827–1917: Drafted into Modernity.* Cambridge: Cambridge University Press, 2009.

———. *Lenin's Jewish Question.* New Haven, CT: Yale University Press, 2010.

———. "The Marketplace in Balta: Aspects of Economic and Cultural Life." *East European Jewish Affairs* 37, no. 3 (December 2007): 277–98.

Philipson, David. *Max Lilienthal, American Rabbi: Life and Writings.* New York: Bloch Publishing Company, 1915.

Pinsker, Shahar. *Literary Passports: The Making of Modernist Hebrew Fiction in Europe.* Stanford, CA: Stanford University Press, 2010.

Polnoe sobranie zakonov Rossiiskoi Imperii. 3 series. St. Petersburg: 1830–1913.

Polonsky, Antony, ed. "The Shtetl: Myth and Reality." Special issue, *Polin* 17 (2004).

Poole, Randall A. "Religious Toleration, Freedom of Conscience, and Russian Liberalism." *Kritika* 13, no. 3 (Summer 2012): 611–34.

Portugalov, V. *Znamenatel'naia dvizheniia v evreistve.* St. Petersburg, 1884.

Prell, Riv-Ellen, ed. "Empire in Jewish Studies." Special issue, *AJS Perspectives* (Fall 2005).

Preobrazhenskii, Ivan. *Otechestvennaia tserkov' po statisticheskim dannym s 1840–41 po 1890–91 gg.* St. Petersburg, [1897] 1901.

Rakovsky, Puah. *My Life as a Radical Jewish Woman: Memoirs of a Zionist Feminist in Poland.* Edited and introduced by Paula E. Hyman. Bloomington: Indiana University Press, 2002.

Rambo, Lewis. *Understanding Religious Conversion.* New Haven, CT: Yale University Press, 1993.

Reizen, Zalman. *Leksikon fun der yiddisher literatur, prese, un filologye.* 4 vols. Vilna: Kletskin Verlag, 1927–1929.

Remba, Isaac. *Banim akhlu boser.* Tel Aviv: Ha-Vaad ha-Tsiburi le-Hotsa'at Kitve Aizik Rembah, 1973.

Rogger, Hans. *Jewish Policies and Right-Wing Politics in Imperial Russia.* Berkeley: University of California Press, 1986.

Rosenzweig, Franz. "Renaissance of Jewish Learning and Living." In *Franz Rosenzweig: His Life and Thought.* Edited by Nahum N. Glatzer, 214–34. New York: Schocken, 1961.

Rosman, Moshe. "A Minority Views the Majority: Jewish Attitudes towards the Polish Lithuanian Commonwealth and Interaction with Poles." *Polin* 4 (1989): 31–41.

Roth, Joseph. *The Radetzky March.* Translated by Joachim Neugroschel. Woodstock, NY: Overlook Press, [1932] 1995.

Safran, Gabriella. *Rewriting the Jew: Assimilation Narratives in the Russian Empire.* Stanford, CA: Stanford University Press, 2000.

———. *Wandering Soul: The Dybbuk's Creator, S. An-sky.* Cambridge, MA: Harvard University Press, 2010.

Sanborn, Joshua A. *Drafting the Russian Nation: Military Conscription, Total War, and Mass Politics, 1905–1925.* Dekalb: Northern Illinois University Press, 2003.

Sarna, Jonathan D. "The Impact of Nineteenth-Century Christian Missions on American Jews." In *Jewish Apostasy in the Modern World.* Edited by Todd M. Endelman, 232–54. New York: Holmes and Meier, 1987.

Schainker, Ellie R. "Jewish Conversion in an Imperial Context: Confessional Choice and Multiple Baptisms in Nineteenth-Century Russia." *Jewish Social Studies* n.s. 20, no. 1 (Fall 2013): 1–31.

———. "On Faith and Fanaticism: Converts from Judaism and the Limits of Toleration in Late Imperial Russia." *Kritika* (forthcoming, 2016).

———. "When Life Imitates Art: Shtetl Sociability and Conversion in Imperial Russia." In *Bastards and Believers: Converts and Conversion between Judaism and Christianity*. Edited by Paweł Maciejko and Theodor Dunkelgrün. Philadelphia: University of Pennsylvania Press, forthcoming.

Schrader, Abby. *Languages of the Lash: Corporal Punishment and Identity in Imperial Russia*. Dekalb: Northern Illinois University Press, 2002.

Seeman, Don. "Apostasy, Grief, and Literary Practice in Habad Hasidism." *Prooftexts* 29, no. 3 (Fall 2009): 398–432.

Shandler, Jeffrey. *Shtetl: A Vernacular Intellectual History*. New Brunswick, NJ: Rutgers University Press, 2014.

Shchedrin, Vasily. "Jewish Bureaucracy in Late Imperial Russia: The Phenomenon of Expert Jews, 1850–1917." PhD diss., Brandeis University, 2010.

Shepherd, Naomi. *A Price below Rubies: Jewish Women as Rebels and Radicals*. London: Weidenfeld & Nicolson, 1993.

Shevzov, Vera. *Russian Orthodoxy on the Eve of Revolution*. New York: Oxford University Press, 2004.

Shmeruk, Chone. "*Mayufes*: A Window on Polish-Jewish Relations." *Polin* 10 (1997): 273–86.

Shochat, Azriel. *Mosad 'Ha-Rabanut mi-Ta'am' be-Rusyah*. Haifa: University of Haifa, 1975.

Shternshis, Anna. "Kaddish in a Church: Perceptions of Orthodox Christianity among Moscow Elderly Jews in the Early Twenty-First Century." *Russian Review* 66 (April 2007): 273–94.

Sinkoff, Nancy. "The Maskil, the Convert, and the *Agunah*: Joseph Perl as a Historian of Jewish Divorce Law." *AJS Review* 27, no. 2 (2003): 281–99.

Sistematicheskii ukazatel' literatury o evreiakh na russkom iazyke so vremeni vvedeniia grazhdanskago shrifta (1708 g.) po dekabr' 1889 g. St. Petersburg, 1892.

Slezkine, Yuri. "Savage Christians or Unorthodox Russians? The Missionary Dilemma in Siberia." In *Between Heaven and Hell: The Myth of Siberia in Russian Culture*. Edited by Galya Diment and Yuri Slezkine, 15–31. New York: St. Martin's Press, 1993.

Smirnoff, Eugene. *A Short Account of the Historical Development and Present Position of Russian Orthodox Missions*. London: Rivingtons, 1903.

Smith, Alison K. "'The Freedom to Choose a Way of Life': Fugitives, Borders, and Imperial Amnesties in Russia." *Journal of Modern History* 83, no. 2 (June 2011): 243–71.

Stacey, Robert C. "The Conversion of the Jews to Christianity in Thirteenth-Century England." *Speculum* 67 (1992): 263–83.

Staliunas, Darius. "Did the Government Seek to Russify Lithuanians and Poles in the Northwest Region after the Uprising of 1863–64?" *Kritika* 5, no. 2 (Spring 2004): 273–89.

———. *Making Russians: Meaning and Practice of Russification in Lithuania and Belarus after 1863.* Amsterdam: Rodopi, 2007.

Stanislawski, Michael. *For Whom Do I Toil? Judah Leib Gordon and the Crisis of Russian Jewry.* Oxford: Oxford University Press, 1988.

———. "Jewish Apostasy in Russia: A Tentative Typology." In *Jewish Apostasy in the Modern World.* Edited by Todd M. Endelman, 189–205. New York: Holmes and Meier, 1987.

———. *Tsar Nicholas I and the Jews: The Transformation of Jewish Society in Russia, 1825–1855.* Philadelphia: Jewish Publication Society of America, 1983.

Steinwedel, Charles. "To Make a Difference: The Category of Ethnicity in Late Imperial Russian Politics, 1861–1917." In *Russian Modernity: Politics, Knowledge, Practices.* Edited by David L. Hoffmann and Yanni Kotsonis, 67–86. New York: St. Martin's Press, 2000.

———. "Making Social Groups, One Person at a Time: The Identification of Individuals by Estate, Religious Confession, and Ethnicity in Late Imperial Russia." In *Documenting Individual Identity: The Development of State Practices in the Modern World.* Edited by Jane Caplan and John Torpey, 67–82. Princeton, NJ: Princeton University Press, 2001.

Svod zakonov Rossiiskoi Imperii. St. Petersburg, 1832, 1842, 1857.

Taylor, Philip S. *Anton Rubenstein: A Life in Music.* Bloomington: Indiana University Press, 2007.

Tec, Nechama. *In the Lion's Den: The Life of Oswald Rufeisen.* Oxford: Oxford University Press, 1990.

Teller, Adam. "The Shtetl as an Arena of Polish-Jewish Integration." *Polin* 17 (2004): 25–40.

Tsitron, Shmuel Leib. *Avek fun folk: tipn un silueten funm noenten over.* 2 vols. Warsaw: Ahiasaf, 1920.

———. *Meshumodim: tipn un silueten funm noenten over.* 4 vols. Warsaw: Farlag Tsentral, 1923–1928.

Ulozhenie o nakazaniiakh ugolovnykh i ispravitel'nykh. St. Petersburg, 1866.

Ury, Scott. *Banners and Barricades: The Revolution of 1905 and the Transformation of Warsaw Jewry.* Stanford, CA: Stanford University Press, 2012.

van der Veer, Peter, ed. *Conversion to Modernities: The Globalization of Christianity.* New York: Routledge, 1996.

Veidlinger, Jeffrey. "From Shtetl to Society: Jews in 19th-Century Russia." *Kritika* 2, no. 4 (Fall 2001): 823–34.

———. *In the Shadow of the Shtetl: Small-Town Jewish Life in Soviet Ukraine*. Bloomington: Indiana University Press, 2013.

Vengerov, S. A. *Kritiko-biograficheskii slovar' russkikh pisatelei i uchenykh*. St. Petersburg, 1889.

Vilkovir, Iosif. *Iudaizm i ego opponenty ili golos' izrail'tianina po povodu knigi "Evrei-reformatory."* Kherson, 1884.

Vishlenkova, Elena. *Zabotias' o dushakh poddannykh: Religioznaia politika v Rossii pervoi chetverti XIX veka*. Saratov: Izdatel'stvo Saratovskogo Universiteta, 2002.

Viswanathan, Gauri. *Outside the Fold: Conversion, Modernity, and Belief*. Princeton, NJ: Princeton University Press, 1998.

Vsepoddanneishii otchet ober-prokurora Sv. Sinoda za . . . god. St. Petersburg, 1909, 1915, 1916.

Waldron, Peter. "Religious Toleration in Late Imperial Russia." In *Civil Rights in Imperial Russia*. Edited by Linda Edmondson, 103–20. Oxford: Oxford University Press, 1989.

Weeks, Theodore R. *Nation and State in Late Imperial Russia: Nationalism and Russification on the Western Frontier, 1863–1914*. Dekalb: Northern Illinois University Press, 1996.

Weinerman, Eli. "Racism, Racial Prejudice, and Jews in Late Imperial Russia." *Ethnic and Racial Studies* 17 (1994): 442–95.

Weissbach, Lee Shai, trans. and ed. *A Jewish Life on Three Continents: The Memoir of Menachem Mendel Frieden*. Stanford, CA: Stanford University Press, 2013.

Wengeroff, Pauline. *Rememberings: The World of a Russian-Jewish Woman in the Nineteenth Century*. Edited by Bernard D. Cooperman, translated by Henny Wenkart. College Park: University of Maryland Press, 2000.

Werses, Shmuel. *'Hakizah ami': Sifrut hahaskalah ba'idan hamodernizaziyah*. Jerusalem: Magnes Press, 2000.

Werth, Paul W. *At the Margins of Orthodoxy: Mission, Governance, and Confessional Politics in Russia's Volga-Kama Region, 1827–1905*. Ithaca, NY: Cornell University Press, 2002.

———. "The Emergence of 'Freedom of Conscience' in Imperial Russia." *Kritika* 13, no. 3 (2012): 585–610.

———. "Empire, Religious Freedom, and the Legal Regulation of 'Mixed Marriages' in Russia." *Journal of Modern History* 80 (June 2008): 296–331.

———. "In the State's Embrace? Civil Acts in an Imperial Order." *Kritika* 7, no. 3 (Summer 2006): 433–58.

———. "The Limits of Religious Ascription: Baptized Tatars and the Revision of 'Apostasy,' 1840s–1905." *Russian Review* 59, no. 4 (October 2000): 493–511.

———. "Lived Orthodoxy and Confessional Diversity: The Last Decade on Religion in Modern Russia." *Kritika* 12, no. 4 (Fall 2011): 849–65.

———. *The Tsar's Foreign Faiths: Toleration and the Fate of Religious Freedom in Imperial Russia*. Oxford: Oxford University Press, 2014.

Wessel, Martin Schulze. "Confessional Politics and Religious Loyalties in the Russian-Polish Borderlands." *Kritika* 15, no. 1 (Winter 2014): 184–96.

Yerushalmi, Yosef Hayim. *From Spanish Court to Italian Ghetto: Isaac Cardoso, a Study in Seventeenth-Century Marranism and Jewish Apologetics*. Seattle: University of Washington Press, 1981.

———. "The Inquisition and the Jews of France in the Time of Bernard Gui." *Harvard Theological Review* 63 (1970): 317–76.

Yovel, Yirmiyahu. *The Other Within: The Marranos: Split Identity and Emerging Modernity*. Princeton, NJ: Princeton University Press, 2009.

Zacek, Judith Cohen. "The Russian Bible Society, 1812–1826." PhD diss., Columbia University, 1964.

Zhitlovskii, Chaim. *Zikhroynes fun mayn leben*. 2 vols. New York: Dr. Chaim Zhitlowsky Jubilee Committee, 1935.

Zhuk, Sergei I. *Russia's Lost Reformation: Peasants, Millennialism, and Radical Sects in Southern Russia and Ukraine, 1830–1917*. Baltimore: Johns Hopkins University Press, 2004.

Zipperstein, Steven J. "Heresy, Apostasy and the Transformation of Joseph Rabinovich." In *Jewish Apostasy in the Modern World*. Edited by Todd M. Endelman, 206–31. New York: Holmes and Meier, 1987.

———. *The Jews of Odessa: A Cultural History, 1794–1881*. Stanford, CA: Stanford University Press, 1985.

Zorin, Andrei. "Ideologiia 'pravoslaviia-samoderzhaviia-narodnosti': Opyt rekonstruktsii." *Novoe literaturnoe obozrenie* 26 (1997): 71–104.

INDEX

Note: Page numbers followed by *f*, *m*, or *t* indicate figures, maps, and tables, respectively. Endnotes are indicated by an *n* following the page number and preceding the note number.

STANFORD STUDIES IN JEWISH HISTORY AND CULTURE
Edited by David Biale and Sarah Abrevaya Stein

This series features novel approaches to examining the Jewish past in the form of innovative work that brings the field into productive dialogue with the newest scholarly concepts and methods. Open to a range of disiplinary and interdisciplinary approaches from history to cultural studies, this series publishes exceptional scholarship balanced by an accessible tone that illustrates histories of difference and addresses issues of current urgency. Books in this list push the boundaries of Jewish Studies and speak compellingly to a wide audience of scholars and students.

Devin E. Naar, *Jewish Salonica: Between the Ottoman Empire and Modern Greece*
2016

Naomi Seidman, *The Marriage Plot: Or, How Jews Fell in Love with Love, and with Literature*
2016

Ivan Jablonka, *A History of the Grandparents I Never Had*
2016

For a complete listing of titles in this series, visit the Stanford University Press website, www.sup.org.